RELIGIONS OF ASIA

Second Edition

JOHN Y. FENTON
Emory University

NORVIN HEIN
Yale University

FRANK E. REYNOLDS
The University of Chicago

ALAN L. MILLER
Miami University, Ohio

NIELS C. NIELSEN, Jr.
Rice University

RELIGIONS OF ASIA

SECOND EDITION

ST. MARTIN'S PRESS/NEW YORK

Acquiring Editor: Don Reisman
Development Editor: Jeannine Ciliotta
Project Editor: Emily Berleth
Production Supervisor: Julie Toth
Text Design: Betty Binns Graphics
Cover Design: Darby Downey
Cover Photo: Elisa Daggs
Graphics: G&H/Soho
Photo Researcher: Robert Sietsema; Julie Lundborg Whitworth

Library of Congress Catalog Card Number: 88-60069

Manufactured in the United States of America.
21098
fedcba

For information, write St. Martin's Press, Inc.
175 Fifth Avenue, New York, NY 10010

ISBN: 0-312-01327-2

ACKNOWLEDGMENTS

Verses from the *Bhagavad Gita,* trans. Franklin Edgerton. Copyright 1955. Reprinted by permission of George Allen & Unwin.
Verses from *A History of Sanskrit Literature.* Arthur Anthony McDonals, 1965. Reprinted by permission of Motilal Banarsidass.
Excerpts from *The Principal Upanishads* by S. Radhakrishnan 1953. Reprinted by permission of Unwin Hyman Ltd., London, England.
From *The Buddhist Experience: Sources and Interpretations* by Stephen Beyer. © 1974 by Dickenson Publishing Co., Inc. Reprinted by permission of Wadsworth Publishing Company.
Reprinted with permission of Macmillan Publishing Company and Unwin Hyman Ltd., from *Entering the Path of Enlightenment: The Bodhicaryavatara of Santideva,* translated by Marion L. Matics. Copyright © 1970 by Marion L. Matics.
Verses from the Dao De Jing from *Sources of Chinese Tradition,* comp. William Theodore De Bary, Wing-tsit Chan, and Burton Watson; vol. 1 of 2 vols. Reprinted by permission of Columbia University Press.
Excerpts from *A Sourcebook on Chinese Philosophy,* trans. and comp. Wing-tsit Chan. Copyright © 1963 by Princeton University Press. Reprinted by permission.
From *The Great Asian Religions,* eds. Wing-tsit Chan, Isma'il Ragi al Faruqi, Joseph M. Kitagawa and P. T. Raju. © Copyright 1969 by Macmillan Publishing Co., Inc. Reprinted by permission.

Preface

We were very pleased with the reception given by students and faculty to the first edition of *Religions of Asia*. Their encouragement, along with their criticism, has been the primary guide for our work on this second edition.

Like its predecessor, the second edition of *Religions of Asia* is adapted from a broader text, *Religions of the World,* which was prepared under the general editorship of Niels C. Nielsen, Jr, and which is now also in its second edition with St. Martin's Press. To make our volume stand independently, changes have been made within several chapters, and information has been added on the symbol systems of Asian religions. Additionally, as was done with the new edition of *Religions of the World,* the content on each religion has been extensively updated by a scholar who specializes in its study.

We believe that the study of religion is an inherently fascinating endeavor. However, in order to make the contents of our book even more accessible to students, this new edition has been streamlined, and its text has been given more unity in style and approach. The major change in the organization of the book is in the introductory chapter, which combines the first two chapters of the first edition. This chapter focuses on the problem of how to define religion and the functions it performs. In contrast to *Religions of the World,* however, this discussion is developed within the context of Asian religions and their symbol systems.

Since much can be learned about religions from their manifestations in everyday life and in the works of art they have inspired, we have provided an abundance of photographs and other illustrations. Time lines and maps will help students keep their chronological and geographical bearings. We have also included a number of special features—descriptions of special rites and ceremonies, extracts from original writings or scriptures, and other materials that could not easily be woven into our exposition but greatly enhance it. (A list of time lines, maps, and special features appears in the table of contents.)

The text comprises an introduction and four parts. Each part examines the historical, geographical, social, and political settings in which the religion under study arose and developed—and which, in turn, it profoundly affected—and explains the basic teachings and rites, the rise of schisms and splinter groups, and the contributions of individuals. The introduction examines the concerns shared by all religions, then illustrates the general characteristics and underlying unity of

Asian religious symbol systems. Parts I through IV explore Asia's major religions: Hinduism, Buddhism, the religions of China and Japan, and Jainism and Sikhism.

Perhaps it is useful to call attention to a few features that may not be evident at first glance. An annotated bibliography appears at the end of the text. It suggests both primary and secondary sources for students who wish to do additional reading and research. We have used the Pinyin system of romanizing Chinese characters that was adopted by the People's Republic in the 1950s. But since many readers will be more familiar with the traditional Wade–Giles system, a conversion table for the two systems is presented in Part III. Important terms are often given in both forms (the Wade–Giles form in parentheses) at the points in the text where they appear.

Our readers and critics will want to know how responsibility for the work was divided. John Y. Fenton served as general editor and also wrote chapter one. Part I is by Norvin Hein; Part II is by Frank E. Reynolds; the first four chapters of Part III are by Alan L. Miller and the last chapter is by Niels C. Nielsen, Jr.

We are deeply indebted to reviewers and users of the first edition, whose criticisms, suggestions, and encouragement were indispensable. They include Raymond Adams, Fordham University; Wendell C. Beane, University of Wisconsin—Oshkosh; Howard Burkle, Grinnell College; Fred W. Clothey, University of Pittsburgh; John Evden, Williams College; Nancy Falk, Western Michigan University; Anne Feldhaus, Arizona State University; Amos N. Farquharson, Broward Community College; Richard D. Hecht, University of California—Santa Barbara; John C. Holt, Bowdoin College; C. Warren Hoving, Oregon State University; Howard McManus, Mercer University; Harry B. Partin, Duke University; Sonya A. Quitslund, George Washington University; Lynda Sexson, Montana State University; Robert C. Williams, Vanderbilt University; Glenn E. Yocum, Whittier College; and Grover A. Zinn, Oberlin College.

Finally, we wish to thank the people at St. Martin's Press. We are especially grateful to Jeannine Ciliotta, our development editor, who, with rare skill, organized and edited the second edition; to Emily Berleth, who guided the book through development and production; and to June Lundborg, who researched the photos for the second edition.

Contents

Special Features, Maps, and Time Lines

Key to Pronunciation of Asian Words

Sanskrit and Pali

Vowels

- **a** as *o* in *done*
- **ā** as in *father*
- **i** as in *pit*
- **ī** as in *machine*
- **u** as *oo* in *book*
- **ū** as in *super*
- **e** as *ay* in *say* (except when followed by a double consonant, when as in *pet*)
- **o** as in *go*
- **ṛ** as *ri* in *merrily*
- **ai** as in *gait*
- **au** or **ou** as in *house*

Consonants as in English except

- **c** as *ch* in *church*
- **ñ** as *ny* as Spanish *señor* (except in combination *jñ*, which is pronounced *jy* as in *Jack*)
- **bh** as *bh* in *clubhouse*
- **ph** as *ph* in *uphill*
- **kh** as *kh* in *lakehouse*
- **gh** as *gh* in *doghouse*
- **ṭh** as *th* in *anthill*
- **ḍh** as *dh* in *madhouse*
- **ś** or **ṣ** as *sh* in *shine*
- **ṃ** or **ṅ** as *ng* in *sing*

Chinese (Pinyin System)

Vowels

- **a** as in *father*
- **i** as in *machine*
- **u** as in *super*
- **ü** as German *ü* (position lips for *u*, but tongue for *i*)
- **e** as *o* in *done*
- **o** as in *go* (except in *-ong* as *oo* in *book*)
- **ai** as in *aisle*
- **au** as in *how*
- **ei** as in *eight*
- **ou** as in *low*
- **ui** as in *weigh*

Consonants as in English except

- **c** as *ts* in *its*
- **h** as German *ch*, far back in throat
- **q** as English *ch*
- **r** (position tongue for English *ch*, but say *r*)
- **x** as English *sh*, but further back and softer
- **z** as *ds* in *birds*
- **zh** as *z* in *azure*

Japanese

Short vowels

- **a** as in *father*
- **i** as in *machine*
- **u** as in *super*
- **e** as *ay* in *say*, except when final, when as in *pet*
- **o** as in *go*

Long vowels

- **a**, **ū**, **ō** — same sound as corresponding short vowel, but held half again as long

Diphthongs are extended in time like long vowels

- **ae** as *i* in *bite*
- **ai** as *i* in *bite*
- **ui** as *uoy* in *buoy*
- **oi** as *oy* in *boy*
- **ei** as in *eight*

Consonants as in English except

- **r** (made far forward and briefly trilled)
- **g** as in *gone*, except in the body of a word when as *ng* in *song*
- **kk** as *k-c* in *black-cap*
- **tt** as in *white-tie*
- **tch** as in *white-church*
- **pp** as in *shrimp-paste*
- **ss**, **nn**, **mm** — as in English, but held half again as long

RELIGIONS OF ASIA

Second Edition

1 The Concept of Religion and the Religions of Asia

Some years ago at a discussion in America conducted by a guru, a Hindu religious leader, an American professor of religion was asked the following question: "How do *you* define religion?" Before the American could frame his reply, the guru declared that religion throughout the world and for all peoples was simply and clearly "devotion to God." The professor pointed out certain complexities inherent in any definition of religion, but the guru immediately went on to affirm that the God he and his followers worshiped was really the same one worshiped by religious people everywhere. For him there was no conflict or competition between the Hindu spiritual message and the beliefs of Christians, Jews, Buddhists or members of other faiths.

The Problem of Cross-Cultural Definition

As we study human history, we discover that religion, or something very like it, appears to have been a part of every human society. But the religions of humankind have always been extremely diverse. While it is true that the guru's "devotion to God" does describe certain forms of religion broadly, if we examine the phrase more closely we discover that "devotion" and "God" have different meanings from one religious tradition to another.

Clearly, "devotion to God" is not a broad enough definition even to include all forms of Hindu religion. For example, some Hindus regard devotion to a personal deity as an inferior type of religion suited primarily for people who are spiritually less mature. Some Buddhists consider any kind of dependence on a divine being a means to avoid the real problems of life. A satisfactory characterization of religion must include all the realities to which the different religious traditions intend to relate, as well as the full range of actual religious relationships to these realities. "Devotion" is only one of these relationships.

A good characterization of religion should also give more information. It should suggest answers to such questions as: What does religion entail? What is at stake? Is it simply a private matter? Or does it include a tradition or traditions developed in community and passed on from generation to generation? How does being religious differ from not being religious?

The more we think about religion, the more we see that religious interests seem to overlap with other interests and activities. There appears to be no uniquely religious emotion or no uniquely religious state of consciousness. The rituals, forms of social organization, and concepts found within religious traditions are also found outside them. What makes an action or idea religious in one case, but not in another? It seems almost obvious that devotion is religious only when it is directed toward some divine being or beings, as is true of other human activities and institutions. To answer the question "What is religion?" in more general

A Sikh pilgrim bathes in the Holy Lake surrounding the Golden Temple at Amritsar, India. *Raghu Rai/Magnum.*

terms, then, we must first specify the nonhuman realms of reality toward which religions are directed and with which they are involved.

Divine beings of various sorts figure in many and perhaps all religious traditions,[1] though they sometimes have no close relationship with the dominant concerns of the traditions in which they appear. For example, the gods and goddesses of Theravāda Buddhism have little to do with a person's ultimate fate; in fact, these deities are themselves thought to be in need of liberation or salvation. Nonetheless, they may legitimate a believer's possession of a piece of land; they may control the weather; or they may enable the healing of diseases. Conversely, Theravādin Buddhist monks teach that the goal of all religious striving is impersonal, without form or shape or movement, and that it can be attained only by self-effort, by following a path leading to individual liberation from the limitations of human life.

Thus if we wish to describe the object or intent of religion in general, we must find a description that does not merely point to characteristics shared by all or most religions, but one that also shows religion's common central concern.

To distinguish what is religious from what is not, we need a definition that is exclusive as well as inclusive. If relationship to an extrahuman object is what differentiates religion from nonreligion, then that object has to be unique to religion. It must be something—some being or some power—that is intrinsic to religion and found only in religion.

Some persons have identified this ascribed object as transcendence or the Transcendent, that is, a real being or power that resides in another world beyond the limits of the human and natural worlds. While identification of the object of religion as transcendent is certainly not incorrect, it would be one-sided if we did not also recognize that religious people also want to be related to the immanent realities, that is, those in this world, and to give significance to human life and human concerns.

To describe an object of worship—for example, Śiva, the Lord of life and death in Hinduism—as transcendent or supernatural would be only partly true, and it would misleadingly suggest that Śiva is not involved with human affairs. While not wrong, the concept of the supernatural is a rather parochial, or limited, notion that depends on our Western concept of nature. But other cultures and religions understand nature (and hence what lies beyond it) in very different terms.

We know that people of other cultures perceive the world and nature differently from the way we do because of how they describe them. The *emic* (inside) *meaning* of a religious tradition is a description of that tradition by its adherents using their own language and their own categories and systems of organization. Because the categories for interpreting other cultures created within Western scholarly disciplines sometimes do not describe these cultures very well, some scholars sidestep the problem of general cross-cultural characterization of religion in favor of the meaning it has for each religion's adherents.

Religion means whatever the people of a given culture mean by it. However, few cultures are so homogeneous that everyone within them is in complete agreement about what religion means. The meaning of religion varies among subgroups and even among individuals within a given culture. The concept of religion is often quite ambiguous, meaning different things to different people and possibly different things to the same people at different times.

If investigators of religion used only emic approaches to the study of religion, they would not be able to make cross-cultural interpretations, and they might even find it difficult to interpret a single religious tradition. In practice, most investigators use *etic* (outside) *interpretive categories* devised within their scholarly disciplines in addition to emic categories. Historians of religion use categories like the sacred, deity, worship, ritual, myth, priest, and symbol as organizing principles to describe phenomena that are similar in many different religions.

Some of the categories for understanding non-Western religious traditions developed by Europeans and Americans in the last two centuries have in fact served colonialist and racist interests. The suggestions, for example, that other religious traditions are primitive, magical, natural, pagan, or superstitious do not increase our understanding, but cloud it, and tend either to provide justification for European expansion or to depict the religions of other peoples as romantic or exotic. The political and economic independence of former European colonies and the indigenous scholarship in the field of religion that has developed in these centuries since World War II make it obvious that this type of interpretation will no longer be tolerated.

Emic and etic approaches can and should be complementary and mutually corrective. Emic categories narrow the investigation to fit a particular context, whereas the cross-cultural categories developed within various scholarly disciplines broaden the base of the interpretation. The use of etic categories enables investigators to generalize the significance of a local study and to use what is discovered about one religious tradition to clarify something in another. Our understanding of religion must be formulated so that its cross-cultural etic description and its emic meaning for its adherents are complementary. Taken together, both categories make possible an adequate interpretation of religion.

The systemic nature of religious traditions can be conveniently illustrated by the Indian Jain tradition. The routine daily worship patterns of both householders and monastics in the Jain religious traditions include the composition of a design composed of uncooked rice particles in front of the worshiper as he or she meditates. This design represents the cosmos. The bottom figure in the design is a right-handed *swastika* (from Sanskrit *swa*, self, and *asti*, existing) surmounted by three dots in a horizontal row. Above the dots is a crescent opened upward. (See chapter 14.) The rotating wheel of the swastika represents the world of birth, change, and death, and rebirth into the same or even another life form. At the top of the design the upturned crescent represents release from all suffering and from the continual round of death and rebirth. Between the *swastika* and the symbol of release, the three dots denote right faith, right knowledge, and right conduct, the means by which human beings may pass from this world to the realm of eternal peace (*kaivala*).

The Jain path to liberation requires a life of absolute nonviolence (*ahimsa*) toward *all* living things that is conceived more radically than in any other religious tradition; absolute truthfulness; absence of greed; chastity; and renunciation of all attachments.

While the realm above the crescent in the Jain cosmos corresponds with "heaven" in Christian tradition, it is emically different from the "heaven" that is a realm in the Christian system. Furthermore, no personal god plays any role in securing the release of human beings from the round of rebirth. The whole responsibility falls upon the individual. The sacred reality in the Jain system is

Indian pilgrims praying on Chandragiri Hill in Śravanabeḷgolā during Jain festival. *Alex Webb/ Magnum.*

emically unique, as is the means of salvation or transformation.

Over the past hundred years many scholars have tried to define religion because of the need for cross-cultural categories of understanding. Emic meanings of religion have not solved the problem, although they have helped correct etic categories. Some of the earlier scholarly approaches have been too vague to be of value, and others have been only partially helpful, since they have focused on certain aspects of religion and have not offered a picture of religion as a whole. In addition, many theories of religion fit the needs of only one academic discipline, especially the characterizations of religion made by social scientists and humanists, which tend to be quite different from each other.

By utilizing and combining the constructive contributions of earlier scholars, we hope to meet at least some of the concerns of both social scientists and humanists in this book. We will describe religion in a threefold way:

1. A religion is a *relationship* between human beings and sacred realities.
2. The dynamics of religious relationships are mediated through *processes* of symbolic transformation.
3. Each religion is expressed in and transmitted by its own *cultural tradition,* which constitutes a *system* of symbols.

Now we shall explain this characterization.

Religious Relationships with Sacred Realities

Religion consists of relationships between the basic needs of human beings and sacred satisfaction of these needs. Both nonreligious and religious people share these needs, but they acquire a special quality in religious contexts. These needs can be described as desires for sanction, vitality, significance, and value. Nonreligious people, and often religious people, seek to satisfy these needs in nonreligious ways. But religious people also seek such satisfaction from dimensions of reality they find outside the human realm.

The question of whether these needs are shared by all human beings is debatable and does not have to be settled here. The need for sanction is met nonreligiously in a variety of ways, ranging from the overriding importance of gaining the acceptance and approval of parents and peers in childhood to the certification procedures by which schools and universities "prove" that we are legitimately trained and capable people. The need for vitality or life power is seen perhaps most obviously in our culture in the enormous sums of money we spend to maintain or improve our health. Our need for significance or truth shows in our appeals to rules and standards. It is also shown in our use of precedents in law and our conscious or unconscious emulation of prominent people as role models. Finally, our need for what we think is valuable, pleasurable, or good is so fundamental that it comes close to the root of all our motivations.

The sources of religious sanction, vitality, significance, and value usually differ from these because of the special character of the realities with which religion is concerned. Religious people seek extrahuman satisfactions of their needs because they perceive human life to be not entirely self-sufficient. From a religious point of view, human reality achieves its fullest development only if it is lived in a community of relationships with other realms of being. Human life has to be brought into proper relationship with a wider symbolic context within which life acquires its significance. In some religious traditions, for example, newborn children are not regarded as complete until a spiritual dimension is added to their biological nature. Through symbolic acts such as the giving of the sacred cotton threads (*upanāyana*) in Hindu tradition to upper-class boys or young men as a symbolic second birth (*dvija*) or the recitation of sacred words in other traditions, infants are inducted into human culture and receive an identity, an acknowledged place in society, and a sanctioned status in a religious community.

From the religious viewpoint, the evolution from child to adult is not merely a natural process of physical maturation, but also a symbolic change that relates children positively to extrahuman sources of continued vitality. These symbolic processes also transform children into adults, persons with a new significance and value who are recognized and treated as such by their community. The transition is a symbolic rebirth that changes the children's social status and legitimizes that new status by reference to a sacred model of male or female adulthood. Properly related to this symbolic order, human cultural events, such as confirmation among Christians or bar mitzvah among Jews, are aligned with extrahuman reality from which meaning, value, and sanction are believed to derive. Relating human life to these patterns puts human beings in touch simultaneously with the power of life and with what is real, truly significant, and most valuable.

Religious needs are also expressed in the context of an assumed prior relationship with the sources by which they are satisfied. Myths, or sacred stories, typically recount how human beings and these sources became involved with each other. Myths depict an ideal relationship, account for the breakdown of that relationship, and provide ways to restore it. Such myths also provide models for individuals to emulate so that they may form interlocking relationships with sacred realities and with the rest of the world.

Most of the early Hindu creation myths revolve around biological and agricultural imagery. They involve two basic creation processes. In the first, the original world egg (or seed or womb) divides and continues to subdivide until all parts of the world have evolved. The two elements initially produced by the process are usually heat or energy and attraction of desire. In some variants, the two elements are male and female. These elements interact to produce additional divisions, structures, and relations until the world is complete.

In the second process of creation, the original being or Self *(Puruṣa)*, in the shape of a human being (who might be androgynous or bisexual), is cut into parts as a sacrificial ritual; these body parts then become various aspects of the universe and different types of human beings. In the *Puruṣa Sūkta* or *Hymn of Man* (see following box), the primal Person is all beings as well as their transcendent source.

The story of the creation process is richly ambiguous. The Puruṣa gives birth to a second being (Virāj), possibly female; this being then gives birth reciprocally to the Puruṣa. How the Puruṣa can be "all that yet hath been and all that is to be" and also be the child of Virāj is not explained. The next stage is also ambiguous and possibly reciprocal like the first stage. Gods and seer-priests (for whose existence the myth does not give an account) use the Puruṣa as a sacrificial victim. From the burning of the victim, all animals and hymns used in the sacrificial ritual were produced. Finally, the Puruṣa's body was divided into parts to create the four social classes, sun and moon, *gods*, earth, atmosphere, and sky.

Who performed the sacrifice or caused it to occur is not explained by the myth. Perhaps the sacrifice was a spontaneous or free act of the Primal Person. Maybe the Puruṣa first divided into two beings so that one could sacrifice the other or each could give birth to the other. Or perhaps the gods and seers performed the original sacrifice. But how could this be when gods, seers, and the universe came into being as a result of a sacrifice? Does the Puruṣa come into being eternally as a self-contained process simultaneous with the performance of the sacrifice by human priests? Although the myth does not answer these questions, it is suggestive of several possibilities. Perhaps there is no answer. In any case, a statement at the end of the myth is clear: The process of sacrifice described in the myth is the "earliest holy ordinance"—that is, sacrifice is the basic principle of the universe, that process upon which all else depends. Note that the two processes of creation discussed share the same underlying structure: the division of the One into the Many.

These creation myths, especially the myth of the Puruṣa, give expression to the fundamental religious relation and the fundamental symbolic process of transformation in the Hindu religious tradition. According to Hindus, the many beings of our world and our experience come from the One. There is no radical separation between human beings and their world, and the One from which they derived. They share in some way the being of the One, perhaps as fragments or parts, perhaps in some more encompassing way.

The creation story in the *Puruṣa Sukta* is only one of the many creation stories in Vedic literature. Later Hindu theologies do not always refer explicitly to this hymn. But since the boundaries within which the human relation to sacred realities is to be understood in Hindu tradition are basically similar, the *Puruṣa Sukta* can be used as a representative myth: Human beings and the manifold beings in the world relate to the Primal Person as part to whole within a sacrificial framework. The questions left unanswered by the myth are asked and answered by later Hindu theologians, thereby giving human-sacred relations a more specific concrete form.

Religious need and religious satisfaction are in a relationship specific to each religious tradition. The notion of sin, for example, is specifically Christian. Sin presupposes a broken relationship with

Śiva as Ardhanārīsvara, the Half-Woman Lord. As this statue reveals, Śiva possessed a dual nature, for both masculine and feminine forces are active in the cosmos. *Borromeo/EPA.*

The *Puruṣa Sūkta* (Hymn of Man)

The *Puruṣa Sūkta* is a late hymn of the Ṛigveda (10:90) that gives a representative Vedic account of the ultimate origin of the world from the preexistent Primal Person. The parts of the created world derive from the dismemberment of the Primal Person in a sacrificial ritual. The world as we know it is thus part of the body of God.

A thousand heads hath Puruṣa, a thousand eyes, a thousand feet.
On every side pervading earth he fills a space ten fingers wide.

This Puruṣa is all that yet hath been and all that is to be,
The lord of immortality which waxes greater still by food.

So mighty is his greatness; yea, greater than this is Puruṣa.
All creatures are one-fourth of him, three-fourths eternal life in heaven.

With three-fourths Puruṣa went up; one-fourth of him again was here.
Thence he strode out to every side over what eats not and what eats.

From him Virāj[1] was born; again Puruṣa from Virāj was born.
As soon as he was born he spread eastward and westward o'er the earth.

[1]Female counterpart of the male principle, Purusa.

When gods prepared the Sacrifice with Puruṣa as their offering,
Its oil was spring; the holy gift was autumn; summer was the wood.

They balmed as victim on the grass Puruṣa born in earliest time.
With him the deities and all Sādhyas and Ṛṣis[2] sacrificed.

From that great general Sacrifice the dripping fat was gathered up.
He formed the creatures of the air, and animals both wild and tame.

From that great general Sacrifice Ṛcs[3] and Sāma-hymns[4] were born;
Therefrom were spells and charms produced; the Yajus[5] had their birth from it.

From it were horses born, from it all cattle with two rows of teeth:
From it were gathered kine, from it the goats and sheep were born.

[2]Saints and prophets of old.
[3]Stanzas of the Ṛigveda.
[4]Stanzas of the Sāmaveda.
[5]Ritual formulas of the Yajurveda.

When they divided Puruṣa, how many portions did they make?
What do they call his mouth, his arms? What do they call his thighs and feet?

The Brâhman[6] was his mouth, of both his arms was the Rājanya made.
His thighs became Vaiśya, from his feet the Śūdra was produced.

The moon was gendered from his mind, and from his eye the sun had birth;
Indra and Agni from his mouth were born, and Vāyu from his breath.

Forth from his navel came mid-air; the sky was fashioned from his head;
Earth from his feet, and from his ear the regions. Thus they formed the worlds.

Seven fencing-sticks had he, thrice seven layers of fuel were prepared,
When the gods, offering sacrifice, bound, as their victim, Puruṣa.

Gods, sacrificing, sacrificed the victim: these were the earliest holy ordinance.
The mighty ones attained the height of heaven, there where the Sādhyas, gods of old, are dwelling.

[6]The four social classes.

God whose restoration through salvation in Jesus Christ expresses symbolically a Christian cosmos. The assumption that sin means the same thing in Judaism as it does in Christianity is a continual source of misunderstanding between Christians and Jews.

The Christian "saving from sin" also does not translate into the Buddhist "enlightenment that overcomes ignorance." These concepts are different relationships between need and satisfaction that belong to different systems of symbols.

Human need is qualified as religious need through the relationship of that need to the object intended by a particular religious tradition. Human need then becomes part of a particular religious system of meaning which also gives to that need a new significance. Need and satisfaction are binary oppositions: Just as hot and cold, inside and outside, up and down, wet and dry define each other in their opposition, religious need and religious satisfaction also give each other their meanings.

Pollution, for example, has its meaning in its being at the polar extreme from purification, and purification has its meaning in its polar tension with pollution. What constitutes pollution varies among cultures. Generally, in the Hindu and Shintō religious tradition, the prime sources of pollution are bodily secretions and human and animal corpses. For Hindus, animal foods such as beef and pig are also polluting. Dietary pollution can be avoided by not eating proscribed foods. But the forms of pollution deriving from physiological processes such as urination, defecation, sexual intercourse, childbirth, and death are periodically unavoidable. *Ordinary purity* is a temporary state achieved by cleansing, by changing to clean clothes, and sometimes by penance or seclusion. To engage in religious rituals, *extraordinary purity* is required; this is achieved by such methods as fasting, abstaining from sexual intercourse, new clothing, elaborate cleansing, and reciting words of power from the sacred tradition.

As the chapter concerned with Japanese Shintō myths explains in greater detail, pollution enters the world in the process of creation when the original father attempts to rescue his wife from the land of the dead and is pursued by desire, death, and decay. But the Shintō myth not only explains the origin of pollution; it also provides the means of restoring purity with rituals instituted by the gods *(kami)* during the period when the earth was still being created.

Human needs for sanction, vitality, significance, and value may well be universal. Religious qualifications of these needs are *not* universal. The characterization of a religious need such as Christian salvation is *acquired* by individuals in particular cultures and religious traditions. For this reason, for example, Christian evangelism spends much of its initial effort toward "the conviction of sin"—that is, establishing the need for Christian salva-

Shintō shrine in the Mie prefecture. The gate through which visitors enter, the torii, is found only at shrines, not at temples. *Sekai Bunka Photo.*

tion and getting individuals to assimilate or adopt this characterization as a true account of what their need "really" is. Buddhist "evangelism" convicts people of ignorance. Their lives are rediagnosed so that they come to re-understand the pervasiveness of pain in their lives and to recognize their ignorance about its causes. When this diagnosis has been internalized, the need for enlightenment and Nirvāṇa has been acquired.

Most people acquire a specific religious diagnosis of their need in the process of growing up in their family and culture. This sense of specific religious need is reinforced by the practice of the religious tradition. Persons without such culturalization would have to acquire it through proselytization and conversion.

Even when the same words are used, the fundamental religious need is sometimes understood differently in different religious systems. Ignorance *(avidya)* in Hindu tradition, for example, concerns the loss of one's true identity as part of or unity with the perfect nonduality of eternal reality. Religious need is marked by fragmentation, isolation, and separation from the organic whole of the universe in Hindu tradition. In the Buddhist tradition, the fundamental ignorance *(avidya)* is our belief that any reality can be eternal, perfect, or unchanging. Thus, although ignorance and enlightenment are comparable in the two traditions, they do not have the same meaning for practitioners.

Just as the character of religious need differs among the religious traditions, so does its opposite, religious satisfaction. In one part of the Hindu tradition, the religious satisfaction that comes as liberation involves merging one's individuality into the featureless ocean of the nondual reality called the *Brahman*. The Brahman is the True Self of the self. But according to Buddhist tradition there is no self, and there is no ultimate reality like the *brahman*. Since suffering is caused by the craving for eternal realities, Buddhists believe that liberation occurs when the craving for such putative realities ceases. Craving ceases of itself when our ignorance about the true character of experience is dispelled. Both Hinduism and Buddhism originated in India and share a great deal from Indian culture; but although the goals of religious aspiration in the two traditions are structurally comparable, they are systemically or emically disparate.

Sacred Realities

We have chosen the term *sacred* to characterize religious concern because sacred realities can be described concretely. In addition, sacredness is the most inclusive category, and it is unique to religion.

Our first task is to show that the term *sacred* can be inclusive without being too vague. The difficulty is that for religious people, sacred reality is ultimately indefinable. Religious people receive their own meaning and definition from the sacred realm. But although the sacred realm is the source of this definition, it cannot itself be defined. This is the central impasse in the interpretation of any religious tradition. The heart of religion, sacred reality, is a mystery.

Sacred reality cannot be defined, either by scholars who interpret religions or by religious people themselves. But religious people do characterize the sacred realms of their particular traditions. The involvement with sacred sanction takes particular traditional forms that are expressed in various kinds of communication. The possibility of satisfying religious needs is based on some kind of ascribed prior relationship with sacred spheres. Because of that relationship, there is trust that the sacred sources of meaning have a reliable character, that they are disposed to give their sanction, and that there are concrete ways in which human beings can invoke or evoke the sacred realms and thereby participate in their presence.

Religious traditions express and communicate these relationships and processes through oral and written words, actions, institutional structures, and symbols. These traditions also express such relationships through the arrangement, segmentation, and direction of time and space as well as through the organization of cultures.

The task of religion scholars is to describe and interpret the expressed character of sacred-human relationships in the various religious traditions. Religion scholars do not have to solve the mystery of sacred realms; rather, their task is to describe and interpret the way religious people have already solved that mystery.

The tension between the mystery and the characterization of sacred realms often makes it extremely difficult to interpret a religious tradition. The opening lines of the Chinese classic attributed to Lao-zi, the *Dao De Jing* (Classic of the Way and Its Power), articulate this tension:

The (Tao [or Dao, *Way*] *that can be told of is not the eternal Tao . . .*
Nameless, it is the origin of Heaven and earth;
Nameable, it is the mother of all things. . . .
That they are the same is the mystery.[2]

Sacred reality in itself (in this case the Dao itself) cannot be described directly, and what can be described is not sacred reality in and of itself. But this reality does satisfy religious needs. That the unnamable is also namable, that the transcendent is also immanent, is the mystery intrinsic to sacred reality. Somehow the nameless origin becomes the recognizable mother of all things.

Religion in general does not exist except in its variations; religion in general is an etic category. There may or may not be realities outside the human realm that correspond to some religious systems of symbols, but at our level of analysis the sacred in general does not exist. Sacredness, like religion, is found only in its variations. Our description of sacredness in general as the unique religious object is an etic generalization about emic characterizations.

The characterizations about sacred realities that religious people have already made fall within a range of variations. There is polytheism—the religious vision, for example in traditional Japanese Shintō, that apprehends sacred realities as plural. These sacred realities are sometimes viewed as personal beings to whom devotion is due and sometimes as nonpersonal forces to which relationship is possible through processes such as ritual. The many sacred realities or deities are understood by some Hindus to be facets or faces of the one great God or impersonal, eternal reality. Other Hindus emphasize monotheism, the belief in one God, while still others maintain that personal gods are just symbols for the nondual transpersonal nature of the eternally real.

The sacred reality of the Buddhist tradition is much more difficult to describe briefly. On the one hand, one could say that sacred reality is for Buddhists neither one nor many, and on the other hand, one could say that it is the One in the midst of the Many. All eternal realities are denied, and belief in them is thought to be the prime cause of human suffering. Yet there is, for the Buddhist, something about ordinary experience that truly satisfies religious needs if we can ever be transformed in such a way that we no longer live asleep, unaware, self-defensive, angry, selfish, and afraid. Sacred reality is before us in an ordinariness that is awesome, but which we, in our ignorance, cannot see.

In ordinary English we sometimes refer to books, buildings, images, places, or even time periods as "sacred." This usage is appropriate, but employs sacred in the secondary sense of "something associated with sacred realities." No one worships books, images, or buildings. A sacred text, for example, is regarded as such because it leads to or makes possible a relation to sacred reality, not because the text is itself expected to satisfy religious needs.

Across cultures, religious characterizations of sacred realities share general ascribed traits that are unique to religion and that can be described etically. In *The Idea of the Holy,* the German philosopher and theologian Rudolf Otto (1869–1947) focused on the individual psychology of elite religious experience.[3] With some changes, his description can be broadened into a general characterization of sacredness. Following Otto's pattern, we divide the sacred realms of reality into five categories. Ascribed sacred realities will have all five traits.

1. *Sacred Ultimacy.* The sacred realms of reality are sources of satisfaction of religious needs for sanction, vitality, significance, and value at the ultimate or most fundamental level. Nothing supersedes or encompasses the sacred, which has a primordial quality: it accounts for and is the basis for other things but accounts for itself and is the basis for itself without depending on anything else.

Sacred ultimacy must be further specified lest it be misunderstood. As the satisfaction of religious needs, sacred ultimacy is characterized in the monotheistic (single God) theology of the medieval Christian Thomists as *esse, verum,* and *bonum* (being, truth, and goodness). In the Vedānta theology of Hinduism, sacred ultimacy is described as *sat, cit,* and *ananda* (being, consciousness, and bliss). Both traditions intend the sacred as the single, universal foundation of all other truth, reality, and goodness. But in religious traditions that worship many gods, sacred ultimacy is frequently visualized as gods and goddesses in local, limited, and plural forms. In a cross-cultural generalization, sacred ultimacy must be described in such a way as to include the whole range of variations.

It is difficult for people reared in Western traditions to grasp the possibility of plural, limited ultimates. "Limited ultimates" may even sound contradictory, rather like the impossible notion of two or more monotheistic gods. The theological idea that ultimacy should be universal is present in many religious traditions, but is only one variation of the more general religious awareness of what is fundamental or ultimate. More generally, the ultimacy of sacred realms is their capacity to provide all that is needed to satisfy religious need. Religious need may be universal in some religious contexts, though not in others. Sacred sources of limited ultimacy still provide all that is needed in limited situations, and the religious supplicant need search no further for satisfaction.

What is of ultimate concern for religious people is not always the most important thing in the world for them. For example, an individual might petition a deity for success in a risky business venture, which would be a religious request for power. When the venture was finished, the business and the petition might be of no further concern to that individual unless the need arose again. In another example, some of the local village deities of folk Hinduism are worshiped in hope of relief in times of affliction, yet may be ignored outside the epidemic season or when no one is sick.

Religion is the ultimate concern of human beings insofar as it involves the ultimate capacity of sacredness to meet the needs of religious people.

2. *Sacred Mystery.* Sacred reality transcends human reality and remains a mystery that human beings can never fully penetrate. Sacredness belongs to realms that remain "other," even as they penetrate the human realm. What is revealed is also concealed, but enough is revealed to be tantalizing. This inkling of sacred realms provides at least part of the materials out of which particular traditions build characterizations of sacredness. Religious language referring to the sacred conveys more than can be said, and in some cases the negative is used to prevent comparing sacred reality to anything else.

As an example, the ancient Hindu sage Yajnavalkya describes (in the *Brihad Aranyaka Upanishad*) our inability to grasp ultimate reality because of its nonduality:

> For where there is a duality, as it were, there one sees another; there one smells another; there one tastes another; there one speaks to another; there one hears another; there one thinks of another; there one touches another; there one understands another. But where everything has become just one's own self, then whereby and whom would one see? then whereby and whom would one smell? then whereby and whom would one taste? then whereby and to whom would one speak? then whereby and whom would one hear? then whereby and of whom would one think? then whereby and whom would one touch? then whereby and whom would one understand? whereby would one understand him by means of whom one understands this All?
>
> That Soul *(Atman)* is not this, it is not that *(neti, neti)*. It is unseizable, for it cannot be seized; indestructible, for it cannot be destroyed; unattached, for it does not attach itself; is unbound, does not tremble, is not injured.
>
> Lo, whereby would one understand the understander?[4]

Brahman (that is, ultimate reality) is said to be *nirguṇa*, or absolutely without qualities. About Brahman, one can only say *neti, neti* (not this, not this). How can such a concept be conveyed to a religious community? As the ninth-century Hindu theologian Śaṅkara explained, language can refer to the Brahman first as a symbol that serves to focus religious aspiration. But ultimately language can reveal the Brahman only as symbols lose their individual content. Language must be used negatively to indicate what language cannot state directly. For the Brahman is nondual, prior to all linguistic distinctions. Properly used, religious language points beyond itself, revealing and concealing sacred reality at the same time.

3. *Sacred Awe.* Human religious need becomes apparent whenever people approach this utterly different reality on which they depend. Religious people react to sacred realms with awe, fear, reverence, homage, and submission. Sacred realities are not under human control, and religious needs may or may not be satisfied. Sacred power can bring punishment and destruction. Failure to satisfy religious needs may sometimes be understood as being due to human faults, but at other times may be unfathomable. Crossing the threshold of a sacred space requires a transformation that makes it possible to move safely from ordinary to extraordinary reality. Sacred power is typically treated with meticulous care and is sometimes surrounded by detailed rules of required or forbidden behavior *(taboo)*.*

4. *Sacred Fascination.* Sacred realities attract religious persons as the ultimate source of their satisfaction. The revelation of sacred reality is intrinsically interesting, fascinating, and marvelous in its depth and profundity. For example, the dramatic climax of the Bhagavadgītā is the self-revelation of Lord Kṛṣṇa in his true form to the human hero Arjuna, who responds to the wonder of this revelation as follows:

Thou art the Imperishable, the supreme Object of Knowledge;
Thou art the ultimate resting-place of this universe;
Thou art the immortal guardian of the eternal right,
Thou art the everlasting Spirit, I hold.

Without beginning, middle, or end, of infinite power,
Of infinite arms, whose eyes are the moon and sun,
I see Thee, whose face is flaming fire,
Burning this whole universe with Thy radiance.

For this region between heaven and earth
Is pervaded by Thee alone, and all the directions;
Seeing this Thy wondrous form,
The triple world trembles, O exalted one![5]

As this Hindu scripture makes clear, despite Lord Kṛṣṇa's ultimacy, mystery, and awe, a wonderful and fascinating relationship between him and his devotee is possible. Something is shared between worshipers and the sacred realms that makes interaction with sacred realities possible. The polar opposition between the sacred and the human realms also constitutes a positive relation. Sacred stories describe the nature of this relation, how it is broken, and how it may be restored.

5. *The Ability to Satisfy Religious Needs.* The expectation of human religious involvement with sacred realms is that the broken relationship between the human and the sacred spheres can be restored. In this way religious people believe that their needs will be satisfied.

In the Bhagavadgītā, Lord Kṛṣṇa promises Arjuna:

Having become *brahman*, serene of spirit, he does not grieve, he does not crave: equable to all creatures, he achieves the ultimate *bhakti* (devotion) of me. Through this *bhakti* he recognizes me for who I am and understands how great I really am, and by virtue of his true knowledge he enters me at once. Even though performing all acts, he has his shelter in me and by my grace attains that supreme abode that is everlasting.

Relinquish all your acts to me with your mind, be absorbed in me, embrace the yoga of the spirit, and always have your mind on me. With your mind on me you will by my grace overcome all hazards; but when you are too self-centered to listen, you will perish (Bhagavadgītā 18:54–58, 65–66).

Keep your mind on me, honor me with your devotion and sacrifice, and you shall come to me. Abandon all the Laws and instead seek shelter with me alone. Be unconcerned, I shall set you free from all evils (Bhagavadgītā 18:65–68).[6]

The faith and assurance that sacred satisfaction is available through human interaction with the sacred realms is the foundation of the existence and

Taboo or *tabu*, a Melanesian word, refers to the prohibitions and special ritual precautions that many religious traditions prescribe for those occasions when human beings come into close contact with sacred powers. This considered behavior safeguards sacred objects from pollution and protects people from the dangerous power sometimes associated with them.

Prayer takes many forms. A Japanese woman prays after placing a red slip of paper with a petition to the deities on a statue in the Tokaku-ji temple grounds near Tokyo. To bring good luck, an Indian girl draws rice patterns on the earth outside her Madras hut. *Religious News Service; Arthur Tress/Photo Researchers.*

continuation of religious traditions. Religious people expect that sacred reality will renew human vitality and power, justify human existence and identity in the context of the cosmos, and provide value structures, significance, and vitality for both individual lives and entire cultures. Sacred sanctions spill over into the total structure of human society and regenerate the human world into a symbolic cosmos that human beings can understand and feel they belong to. The relationship to sacred realities draws people together into religious community.

We need to keep in mind, however, that certain ambivalences are associated with sacred satisfaction. Adherents to a religious tradition cannot be sure that following religious procedures will necessarily restore the ideal relationship with the sacred realms. Sacred realities are independent variables, and requests may be denied or forgiveness withheld.

The satisfaction of religious needs is always partial and temporary. The spiritual gift of a prophet or religious leader may be withdrawn; institutions may become corrupt; and all forms of sacred sanction lose their power and require periodic renewal. Yet people's religious needs continue. Being religious is a continuing way of life.

These ambivalences reveal a universal condition: Human beings need sacred sanctions and values, and the satisfaction of these needs comes only from the sacred realm, which is other than human and not under human control. How the gap between human need and sacred power can be bridged is the essential problem of religion. Different traditions resolve this problem in different ways, which are what separates one tradition from another. Nonetheless, all traditions affirm that they indeed have bridged the gap between the human and the sacred spheres. Not only has sacred satisfaction been received, but it can be received again in the future. The process by which the religious problem is resolved is called symbolic transformation.

Symbolic Transformation

We can view the process by which human religious need is transformed into sacred satisfaction as a series of four successive phases.

1. *Diagnosis of Disorder.* First, people must recognize and acknowledge that a religious need requires sacred satisfaction. The frequency with which such a need is diagnosed varies. Worship, for example, may follow a regular liturgical or ritual schedule or be primarily a response to crises. Some people attempt to engage in worship constantly (as in the admonition "Remember God always"). The need for sacred satisfaction may also be expressed in some form of confession of specific human faults or in the general humbleness of the human condition. Its acknowledgment may also contain an account of how sacred sanction has been disrupted or lost.

2. *Symbolic Distancing.* People who need sacred satisfaction must be symbolically distanced or removed from their normal state. Distancing gives dramatic expression to religious need and puts supplicants in a clear-cut category of humanness at a polar extreme opposite sacred realms. Here religious need for sacred satisfaction reaches its greatest intensity, which in turn facilitates transformation into the next phase. People can achieve symbolic distancing by removing themselves from normal social intercourse, by fasting, and by giving away or destroying material goods. Even the cosmos can be symbolically separated from its normal sanction: Community borders may be closed; the inhabitants may be told to maintain vigils; holidays may be decreed; and the usual forms of social behavior may be reversed. At such times the primary sacred symbols of the society may be hidden or concealed. For example, the cross and other religious images in Catholic churches once were covered by dark cloths during the last two weeks of Lent as a sign of mourning for Christ's suffering.

3. *Liminality.* In the liminal phase (the term comes from the latin *limen*, meaning "threshold" or "boundary"), the intensity of symbolic distancing is increased until the people are separated not only from normal cultural categories, but also from all possible cultural categories, and symbolically the whole world disappears. The symbolic boundary is reached when one has moved as far from normal as possible. The liminal state is one without any structure, though the specific character of the liminality varies from one religious tradition to another. The transition to the liminal phase is frequently pervaded by death symbols and punctuated by regression to a helpless condition in which all cultural capacities are lost. This situation is fraught with danger, and demons may appear and destroy the worshipers' most secret forms of self-reliance.

In one of many Christian examples, the liminal phase corresponds to the mourning period between Jesus' death on Good Friday and his resurrection on Easter Sunday. Several mystical traditions describe this state as a darkness so complete that both the way back to normal life and the way forward to sacred satisfaction are totally obscured. One can only wait, hoping and trusting that sacred satisfaction will come.

4. *Restoration or Rebirth.* The emergence of sacred satisfaction restores people as symbolically new, reborn beings who are sanctioned, empowered, significant, and valuable. Restoration is often accompanied by actions symbolizing rebirth, transfiguration, release from bondage, or healing. People who have been confined in a cave, secluded in a forest or desert, or left on a mountain come forth to new life in society. They may receive new names, new clothes, and gifts. Changes in language and behavior as well as intimacy with new peers ratify and express a new form of being. Feasting often puts the seal on the transformation.

Although some persons may have intense encounters with sacred realms directly and without external ritual supports, others partake of symbolic transformation by participating in dramatic ritual scenarios. Still others may undergo symbolic equivalents through reduced or subdued ceremonies in which human religious leaders transmit sacred satisfaction to worshipers through ascribed symbols of sacred power.

THE HINDU SACRED THREAD CEREMONY

The Hindu *upanayana* (investiture with the sacred thread) ritually transforms upper-class, primarily brāhmaṇ, young boys into students. Brāhmaṇ boys may be initiated between eight and sixteen years of age, but in contemporary times sometimes have the ceremony performed just before marriage.

Just before the sacred thread ritual begins, the boy takes his last meal from his mother as a child. Symbolic distancing from childhood was traditionally marked by shaving the boy's head and giving him a bath. Special clothes (a girdle, deerskin, staff, and the sacred thread) then demarcate the liminal state. The rebirth to student status is ushered in by the teacher's taking the boy's "heart" into his will as symbolic father and mother. The transition from one life stage to the other is thought of as a gestation process in which the teacher becomes pregnant with the boy and by virtue of sacred sounds *(mantra)* gives him a second birth *(dvija)*.

The student stage of life is a provisional, in-between period when the boy is no longer a child, but not yet fully an adult. After periods of training that vary considerably (in contemporary times often less than one hour), the transition from student status is ended with another bath which introduces the boy to adult life, when he is ready for marriage. Marriage is the normal, whole state in Hindu tradition. A man is sufficiently complete to perform the central religious acts of worship and procreation only when he is married. Local marriage customs vary considerably, but all weddings transform the two individuals into a couple by a process of re-creation or rebirth. The groom takes the bride's "heart" into his in a way that is reminiscent of the teacher's participation in the rebirth of the Hindu upper-class boy. The constituting act of the new couple is walking together three times around a sacred fire with their garments tied together. This is followed by their first meal together as a new family.

THE FOUR NOBLE TRUTHS IN BUDDHISM

The four stages in processes of symbolic transformation which are so clear in rites of passage from one stage of life to the next are also manifest in processes by which the fundamental quality of life is changed, such as the progress from suffering and ignorance to peace and wisdom in the Buddhist tradition. The famous Four Noble Truths provide a summary statement of what Theravada Buddhists understood the thrust of the Buddha's message to be, and they exhibit the four phases in the process of symbolic transformation in a most straightforward way.

The first and second of the Four Noble Truths set forth a diagnosis of the unsatisfactory character of the human condition (see the following box). The first Truth states that life is suffering. This means that everything we do and can experience is, without exception, characterized by being less than perfect, only temporary, and not solid or substantial enough to sustain us. While Hindus might initially agree with this description, they would, in most cases, affirm the Puruṣa as an enduring, perfect, eternal Being, both for the universe at large and in the innermost depths of each being. Buddhists deny that there is a permanent self within either individuals or the universe at large. Any deities there may be are also imperfect, transitory, and without permanent substance.

The first Truth is meant to be a sober, entirely realistic statement of what life is really like. Life is suffering because people try to get something from experience that it cannot provide. The unrealistic approach causes constant frustration. Because the frustration is so unpleasant, people habitually misrepresent their experience so that life will at least seem to be pleasant. The perpetuation of unrealistic devices, such as repressing what is unpleasant and selectively perceiving and remembering only that which feeds the ego, is like a disease that the second Noble Truth proceeds to diagnose. The root of the sickness that infects all experience is the very

The Four Noble Truths

The Four Noble Truths are presented in southern Buddhist scriptures as part of the Buddha's first sermon near Banāras after his achievement of enlightenment. Like a great physician, the Buddha diagnoses the causes of all human dis-ease or frustration and prescribes the remedy that leads to a noble or satisfactory life.

Thus I have heard. Once the Lord was at Vārānasī, at the deer park called Iwipatana. There he addressed the five monks:

There are two ends not to be served by a wanderer. What are these two? The pursuit of desires and of the pleasure which springs from desire, which is base, common, leading to rebirth, ignoble, and unprofitable; and the pursuit of pain and hardship, which is grievous, ignoble, and unprofitable. The Middle Way of the Tathāgata[1] avoids both these ends. It is enlightened, it brings clear vision, it makes for wisdom, and leads to peace, insight, enlightenment, and Nirvāna. What is the Middle Way? . . . It is the Noble Eightfold Path—Right Views, Right Resolve, Right Speech, Right Conduct, Right Livelihood, Right Effort, Right Mindfulness,[2] and Right Concentration. This is the Middle Way . . . .

And this is the Noble Truth of Sorrow. Birth is sorrow, age is sorrow, disease is sorrow, death is sorrow; contact with the unpleasant is sorrow, separation from the pleasant is sorrow, every wish unfulfilled is sorrow—in short all the five components of individuality[3] are sorrow.

And this is the Noble Truth of the Arising of Sorrow. It arises from craving, which leads to rebirth, which brings delight and passion, and seeks pleasure now here, now there—the craving for sensual pleasure, the craving for continued life, the craving for power.

And this is the Noble Truth of the Stopping of Sorrow. It is the complete stopping of that craving, so that no passion remains, leaving it, being emancipated from it, being released from it, giving no place to it.

And this is the Noble Truth of the Way which Leads to the Stopping of Sorrow. It is the Noble Eightfold Path—Right Views, Right Resolve, Right Speech, Right Conduct, Right Livelihood, Right Effort, Right Mindfulness, and Right Concentration.[4]

[1]"He who has thus attained," one of the titles of the Buddha.
[2]*Sati*, literally "memory." At all times the monk should as far as possible be fully conscious of his actions, words, and thoughts, and be aware that the agent is not an enduring individual, but a composite and transitory collection of material and psychic factors.
[3]Forms, sensations, perceptions, psychic dispositions, and consciousness.

[4]From *Saṃyutta Nikāya,* 5.421ff. In all quotations from the Pali scriptures, except where specified, reference is made to the Pali Text Society's edition of the text.

thing that, from the Hindu point of view, makes a person religious. And that is the desire for being. Craving of all kinds, including craving for union with Being, is unrealistic because it cannot be satisfied. Craving for being is perpetuated by our ignorance of the realistic appraisal of experience given in the first Noble Truth. Life need not be suffering, however. According to the third Noble Truth, if the desire to get something out of life that it cannot provide can be rooted out, suffering will cease. If people could live within the dimensions of what experience can actually provide, life would no longer frustrate.

There is no creation myth in the Buddhist tradition which, like the Hindu Puruṣa myth, describes the ultimate origins of the universe. Both the world and unrealistic living in the world are generally believed to be without beginning. Nevertheless, the change from unrealistic to realistic living requires a complete transformation, a rebirth into reality. The fourth Noble Truth states that there is a way in which this transformation can be brought about. This way is the Eightfold Path.

The meditation path to enlightenment is in some respects sequential with the completion of later stages of the path presupposing the successful completion of earlier stages. But the steps of the Eightfold Path must be worked on at the same time. The three sections of the Eightfold Path concern changing how one sees experience, modifying one's behavior to conform to this new vision, and raising consciousness to a much higher level of efficiency so that reality can be experienced as it really is. This change from ordinary ways of understanding, behaving, and consciousness is a symbolic movement that distances one from normality. Although the ultimate aim is a new way of being in the world, it is approached initially by a process of divesting oneself of ignorant, selfish, and unaware ways of being.

The goal of the path is realistic insight into the nature of things; this is stated in the first two steps of the path in the first section, called *wisdom*. The first step, *right understanding*, means initially that one must intellectually understand that experience is really just the way the Four Noble Truths say it is. Eventually, this understanding must be deepened into a direct intuition of reality. It is significant that the second step of the path, *right thought*, emphasizes the moral character of knowing. *Right thought* refers not to ideas, but to human consciousness working without hatred, ill will, or aversion, and operating instead out of love. A mind operating out of hatred or anxiety will always skew understanding in its own self-interest.

The second section of the path concerns modification of behavior to conform to reality. It does no good simply to hypothesize about Buddhist philosophy without any change in the way a person lives. In the third step, language must be changed so that it does not continue to falsify or cover up experience. Only the truth should be spoken. In the fourth step, all acts that flow out of craving and ignorance must be avoided because they perpetuate the very source of suffering. Obviously, this includes all acts of aggression and self-indulgence. Fifth, the way a person earns a living must not be based on aggression, taking advantage of or misleading others, or catering to the self-indulgent desires of others. A vocation should be conducive to rooting out all desire and ignorance. Ideally, in the Theravada tradition, this vocation is that of monk or nun. In practice, this way of living is also possible for lay persons. The moral requirements of the second section of the Eightfold Path are incumbent upon everyone who wishes to live realistically. The Buddhist ethic is universal and thus in sharp contrast to the pluralistic norms of Hindu duty. Hindu tradition sanctions life in society in its various forms as duty, whereas Buddhist tradition tends to exalt the monastic vocation.

The third section of the Eightfold Path is concerned with raising the power and penetration of consciousness to the supernormal capacity required if insight into reality is to be achieved. *Right effort,* the sixth step, involves a mental purification process in which a person strives to maintain increasingly wholesome states of mind, such as being at peace, being attractive, and being accepting, and to avoid unwholesome states of mind, such as anxiety, pride, and fear. The seventh and eighth steps of the Eightfold Path deal with processes of meditation, which consist of paying attention selectively. People with unwholesome states of mind cannot pay attention very well. People who have not strengthened their attention through meditation cannot pay attention well enough to penetrate through the veils of ordinary perception into the nature of reality.

Initial training in meditation in the Theravada tradition is usually in right concentration or tranquility meditation *(samādhi)* (the eighth step). The techniques are broadly similar to those of Hindu yoga, the aim being to reach a state of consciousness that is empty of all content. This is accomplished in much the same way as in the yoga tradition. However, human craving and ignorance are difficult to root out, and therefore samādhi has subsidiary techniques to deal with these problems.

Traditionally, there are forty different topics of meditation designed to overcome particular kinds of ignorance and craving. If reality is to be understood, nothing can be left out of one's awareness. Repression merely feeds ignorance. Death is a fact, as are birth, disease, and old age; all must be faced realistically. People who will not face death are hiding from reality.

A mind that cannot concentrate sharply, exclusively, and durably upon a chosen object is like a television set that cannot pick up broadcast signals because its tuning equipment is out of alignment. Samādhi tunes the consciousness so that perception becomes a penetrating, reliable research instrument. Theravada Buddhists use yoga techniques not for yoga ends, but for the Buddhist goal of insight into reality. In fact, the highest samādhi state must be examined carefully until the meditator comes to realize that this state is also transitory, imperfect, and without real substance. Trances are merely altered states of consciousness, not union with ultimate reality or with God. Real freedom from craving and ignorance is possible only by means of the uniquely Buddhist practice of insight meditation *(vipassana)* or mindfulness *(sati)* (the seventh step).

In modern times, insight meditation is sometimes taken up without previous samādhi training, and concentration is learned along with insight meditation. A traditional form of insight meditation examines the meditator's own present experience, organized according to four categories or objects of attention that are believed to include all aspects of possible subjective experience. The first object is material form and sensation which are experienced together. If one is paying attention to air entering the nostrils, for example, the air and the physical sensation of the air are felt simultaneously. One simply pays attention to observe whether this experience is characterized by transitoriness, imperfection, and lack of substantiality. If one's attention wanders, for example, to awareness of whether the sensation is pleasant or unpleasant, or neither, this awareness can be taken up as a second object of attention, and it can be noted whether feelings about sensations are dependent upon changes in sensation, or whether they vary independently.

In this way, one should eventually discover simply by observation that notions of pleasantness and unpleasantness are not part of sensation, but something that ego adds, partly out of habitual association, partly because of false conceptions, and partly in self-defense. Both attachment and aversion then begin to break up of their own accord. The third object of mindfulness is what might be called general emotional and personality dispositions, such as whether one is at peace or anxious.

The fourth object is mental contents or ideas. These are observed in the same way as the first two objects with much the same kind of results: Habitual associations break down, true causal relations in personal experience begin to become evident, fixed ideas become reconstructed in accordance with the new realistic experience, and insight into reality gradually begins to dawn.

The Eightfold Path is thus a series of processes through which people gradually untie all the knots with which they have encumbered their lives. The process is one of undoing and discarding false understanding, unrealistic behavior, and unaware and unwholesome kinds of consciousness. The movement away from ordinary understanding, behavior, and awareness is here a matter of degree that results eventually in a total divorce from the old way of living, but does not yet translate into the new birth or transformation promised as the Buddhist enlightenment. The "between" period of the Buddhist meditator may last for a very long time, even years (even several lifetimes, according to Buddhist belief).

Meditation cannot produce transformation; it only provides the occasion by negating all of the ways of thinking and acting that impede awakening. Total nonreliance on all the old defense mechanisms of self-protection opens up the possibility of fundamental change—which, if it occurs, does so mysteriously, evoked but not produced by the Eightfold Path. For the Eightfold Path is not intended to produce or to project reality. The path is a process of symbolic transformation into a reality that overcomes the human condition of craving and ignorance. This reality is *sacred*. It is ultimate, mysterious, awe-ful, and fascinating, and it satisfies the religious need to overcome ignorance, craving, and suffering.

SYMBOLIC TRANSFORMATION IN MAHĀYĀNA BUDDHISM

The Mahāyāna schools of Buddhism may initially appear to be much more difficult to understand than the southern Theravada tradition. The Theravada Eightfold Path is a clearly demarcated step-by-step method for symbolic transformation. Mahāyāna Buddhists often emphasize that they do not follow a method. However, if we use the four phases of symbolic transformation as a way to understand the "non method," the process of transformation in Mahāyāna Buddhism will be much easier to comprehend.

No-method arises out of paradoxes inherent in the Buddhist processes of symbolic transformation. Two questions summarize the problem: (1) How can ego de-construct or get rid of ego? (2) If the self or ego is not a substantial reality, who is it who is trying to de-construct ego to discover reality? Dealing with the first question leads in the Mahāyāna to the use of negative methods that presumably are less ego-tainted. But as we have seen, the Eightfold Path is also a negative method, untying knots to uncover reality. The final transition is mysterious, not a product of the method. Dealing with the second question leads to emphasis in the Mahāyāna on what comes to be called "the Buddha nature" already present in every being. Since beings have never been separated from reality (Buddha nature), enlightenment is not the work of ego, but the uncovering of what we already are. As we have seen, Theravada Buddhism also presupposes a prior relation to reality that becomes actual when ignorance and craving are eliminated.

Mahāyāna Buddhist tradition continues to have problems with these two questions, just as Theravada Buddhism does. In fact, these problems are one of the central reasons why the True Pure Land *(Jodo Shinshu)* Buddhist tradition in Japan developed a radical doctrine of salvation by reliance on the power of another rather than upon one's own efforts. In this view, ego, and therefore craving and ignorance, can be overcome only by relying on a power outside oneself (the Bodhisattva Amida*). Ego will never be able to overcome itself on its own resources.

Some Mahāyāna schools champion sudden enlightenment rather than the obviously gradual method of the Eightfold Path. *Sudden* enlightenment sounds easier, faster, and more dramatic—but in fact, the difference seems to be largely verbal. Even so-called sudden methods of enlightenment are typically preceded by long periods of preparation.

The greatest difference between Mahāyāna and Theravada Buddhism lies in the methods of symbolic transformation that are employed. While the Eightfold Path is not very often used explicitly in the Mahāyāna tradition, in most cases the three sections of the Eightfold Path (wisdom, morality, meditation) usually appear in the Mahāyāna method in altered form. Mahāyāna meditation methods also proceed in the same sequence as do those of Theravada Buddhism: first to tranquility *(samādhi)*, or the empty mind, and then to insight. Three of these methods of symbolic transformation will be illustrated briefly in the following sections.

The Middle Way (Mādhyamika) School Buddhism is the "middle way" because it avoids a variety of extremes, such as the extremes of overindulgence and asceticism. The Middle Way school derives its name from the Buddha's opposition to extreme views about the nature of reality (e.g., that reality exists or does not exist, is eternal or not

**Amida* (Japanese) or *Amitābha* (Sanskrit) is a bodhisattva who vowed to bring all who call on his name to rebirth in the Pure Land (a realm without suffering).

eternal) as its fundamental stance. The Middle Way School *diagnosis* is as follows: The school denies the capacity of words to convey the nature of reality adequately. While concepts have a certain limited practical value, they also perpetuate ignorance (and therefore craving) by fomenting differences, separations, and relations among things that have no more than conventional usefulness. Concepts always express unjustifiably extreme views—for example, that the self does or does not exist, or that it is or is not a thing. Since concepts condition perception, the reality of the self can be grasped only when all such conceptual alternatives are discarded. Insight into reality and therefore freedom from suffering and ignorance are possible only when the mind ceases to function conceptually.

Symbolic distancing, in the Middle Way school, is carried out by turning conceptuality against itself. This is accomplished by reducing all ideas about reality to absurdity by showing that they are self-contradictory, that they do not fit experience, and/or that they depend upon assumptions that depend upon other assumptions that depend upon other assumptions in an infinite regression. Rigorous logic is used to demonstrate the universal illogic of all concepts. The process of symbolic transformation is gradual as first one and then another cherished idea is shown to be demonstrably false. Alternative ideas also prove to be false. Eventually, the mind is emptied of all views and concepts. This is the *liminal* point. Finally, and presumably in an irrational transition, insight dawns as all of the concepts that hide reality disappear, and experience is totally *transformed.*

The Yogācāra School Yogācāra (way of yoga) is, as its name indicates, influenced by Hindu yoga meditation practices. But the borrowed techniques are used in the Yogācāra for Buddhist purposes. The analogue for the relation of ordinary experience to reality for the Yogācāra school is the relationship of the individual consciousness to the universal, collective consciousness that the individual consciousness embodies, expresses, and springs from. All experience is empty of substance in the sense that it is no more than (and no less than) the mental activity of the universal mind.

The movement away from ordinary experience is *symbolic distancing.* Ordinary experience is really like dreaming experience, which seems completely real while we are dreaming. Upon awakening, its lack of substantial reality becomes manifest. In the same way, from the vantage point of alternate levels of experience made possible through yoga, ordinary experience can also be shown to be lacking in substantial reality.

Symbolic transformation, or realization that this is the case, is accomplished in two primary ways. One is the practice of meditation until tranquility (samādhi) is experienced. Individual consciousness then merges with the source of all consciousness. From this vantage point, ordinary consciousness appears as unreal as dream consciousness seems to one who is awake. Total loss of individual consciousness is for Yogācāra Buddhists the *liminal* state. It is not transformation; transformation is insight into the emptiness of *all* experience, including the experience of tranquility.

The other way employed in Yogācāra is the practice of projecting imaginary alternative worlds that eventually become so realistic in appearance, durability, and detail that the world of experience that is projected seems as real or perhaps even more so than ordinary experience. This also is *symbolic distancing,* since we move away from normality to a state that is its polar opposite. Once we are caught between the supposedly "real" world and the projected world, we have reached the threshold or *liminal* state from which transformation is possible. However, since the practitioner knows the alternative world is a deliberate projection, insight occurs into the projected, unsubstantial character of ordinary experience. The point of these two methods is neither to retreat into tranquility nor to escape into fantasy, but to discover reality within the phenomena of experience.

The Chan/Zen School The Chan/Zen (Chinese/Japanese) school of Mahāyāna Buddhism distrusts the use of trances, visions, and logic to achieve insight, considering such methods more likely to prolong attachment to escape, to ego, or to concepts than to evoke insight. Nevertheless, the views of the Yogācāra school are more or less presupposed by Chan/Zen as the proper analogue of the relation of ordinary experience to reality.

***Left,* Ryoanji temple, Kyoto, Japan, founded in 1473; *right,* garden at Ryoanji temple. Rocks resting on water (raked gravel) symbolize the insubstantiality, imperfection, and impermanence, of all things.** *Editorial Photocolor Archives.*

Like the Middle Way school and Yogācāra, the intent is to empty the mind completely so that reality can be experienced directly. The human mind that is full of concepts that organize the world in the ordinary way is the source of craving and therefore of ignorance and suffering. Emptying the mind of concepts is a process of *symbolic distancing*. In one of the Chan/Zen traditions (Lin-ji/Rinzai), symbolic transformation is carried out with the aid of conceptually unsolvable puzzles that masters assign to students. One of the puzzles that is used frequently follows: A monk once asked Master Joshu, "Has a dog the Buddha-nature or not?" Joshu said, *Mu*![1] *Mu* is Japanese for "nothing," that is, for emptiness. All the questions concerning reality we have been discussing are contained in this riddle. They are:

1. Is all of reality without exception characterized by transitoriness, lack of substantiality, and imperfection?
2. What kind of reality does reality have? Does it exist, or does it not exist?
3. Does reality exclude phenomena such as dogs, or does reality include them?
4. How?
5. Are dogs real?
6. Is the Buddha nature real?

To all these questions, the answer is *emptiness*—not the concept "emptiness," but the state of being absolutely empty. An empty person allows all phenomena without discrimination to enter his or her experience and is totally unattached to anything in that experience.

The riddle is conceptually unsolvable. To solve the riddle requires insight into reality. The master prods the student to empty his or her mind by forcing the student to solve the unsolvable. Answers proffered by the student, whether objective-conceptual or subjective-experiential, uniformly receive a negative response from the master. In time, the student not only becomes so disoriented from ordinary experience that return is no longer possible, but he or she also begins to run out of possible answers.

When there are no answers left, the student has reached the liminal stage, where insight may occur. A chance stimulus or perhaps some drastic, dramatic action from the master may catalyze the breakthrough to insight. The method does not produce insight. As with all successful processes of symbolic transformation, the transition to sacred reality is itself mysterious.

CALENDAR RITUALS

Calendar rites may celebrate birthdays of religious founders, special days of gods or goddesses or holy men and women, the new year, seasonal changes, and central events in the religious history of a community, such as the exodus of the ancient Hebrews from bondage in Egypt or the revelation of the Qur'ān to Muḥammad. People also engage in personal and communal worship, prayer, and meditation at regular intervals, ranging from several times each day to weekly observances.

Jains celebrate the birth of Mahavira, the 6th century B.C. founder of the tradition, with a ritual bathing of his image in late summer or early fall that in part reenacts major events in the process of Mahavira's becoming a Jina or conqueror of life's problems. Sikhs commemorate the birthdays and martyrdoms of several of their founding teachers *(gurus)*, while many Hindus give offerings to Lord Kṛṣṇa as part of his birthday observance in August of each year.

The traditional Chinese Confucian ritual tradition was based upon a prior relationship among human beings, earth, and heaven, rather than directly upon myths of creation. The Chinese emperor, for example, occupied a pivotal point in the balance among these three spheres. Through his moral and ritual conduct, he was able to maintain harmony and thus to ensure the support of heaven and earth for human endeavors. Part of the emperor's role was his conduct of the sacrifice on the Altar of Heaven at the turning points of the seasons each year.

RITUALS PERFORMED WHEN NEEDED

The sacrifice *(yajña)* system of the early Vedic period in India is close in time and mentality to the myth of the Puruṣa discussed above. The forms of

The emperor played an important role in Chinese religious activities. At the Altar of Heaven, he paid homage to Heaven at the time of the winter solstice. *Eastfoto.*

sacrifice vary from fairly simple rituals to those that are complicated, elaborate, and expensive. Sacrifice is a process of symbolic transformation in which worshipers return something to sacred realities, something that can be given because it derived from sacred realities. The bond between the Vedic worshiper and the deities precedes the sacrifice and is expressed in myths. Food and animal life, together with speech and hymns of praise, can be offered to the deities because these gifts derive from the cosmic sacrifice.

When the deities accept these gifts, the worshipers expect the deities to give gifts such as protection, sanction of the social order, economic benefits, support in warfare, health, long life, and when needed, rain. The bond of continuing exchange between sacrificers and deities constitutes *religio*, the binding together of human beings and sacred realities in a process of mutual exchange (*religio* is the Latin for "religion"). While giving up something and returning it to its source is not the only element in the ritual, it is the key process—the symbolic means by which human needs are satisfied. Meeting religious needs by sacrificing something in order to gain satisfactions is a fundamental motif in Hindu tradition.

Carrying out the sacrificial ritual by acting out the sacrificial principle that underlies the created world symbolically reconstructs the world, or a part of it. The ritual becomes a model for proper order in human and nonhuman worlds. The yajña ritual is essentially a model of the universe, a prism through which the world is seen to be orderly, and by means of which the world comes to be understood as a universe, a single world with an underlying structure.

After many centuries, key elements in the Hindu symbolic view of the world are derived by extending meanings implicit or explicit in the yajña. For example, the relationship between the acts *(karma)* done in the ritual and the effects they are intended to produce becomes the model for cause-effect relationships in general. Every action produces a fruit that is commensurate with the action. Applied to the moral sphere, each good act has as its fruit a good result, and each bad act brings forth a bad result. The universe thus has a moral structure as well as a causal one.

The idea of moral structure derived from ritual is reinforced by the early Vedic notion that the reliable movements of the stars were evidence of a general world order *(ṛta)*. Eventually, the theory developed into the belief that all things fit within an all-encompassing cause-and-effect structure *(dharma)*. For the universe as a whole, this order is eternal and uniform. But just as the world in the myth of the Puruṣa was made from different parts of the Puruṣa's body, with different functions and qualities, so also dharma has different functions and qualities according to the locale in the universe in which it is operating.

Applied to human culture, dharma becomes duty—a person's social and religious obligations in his or her particular status and function in society. Duty varies according to social class and the individual's personal situation. The uniformity of dharma in its plurality of expressions thus provides a strong sense of the unity of the Hindu tradition. The structure of reality is One; it appears differently to different people.

Sacred Places

Dedication rites may transform an ordinary place into a holy site. The dedication of a temple puts that territory more or less permanently in a liminal position between ordinary human culture and sacred realms. To enter a sacred place means to leave the world behind and to enter a border area from which concourse with the sacred becomes easier. Frequent worship in such a place renews its power of access.

In much of the Hindu devotional tradition, it is believed that the formless God condescends to take on form for the benefit of devotees. God, who is everywhere, appears in particular places and particular forms, being really present in images and in the houses of God, the temples. While some Hindus worship God in only one form others adore the one God who is manifest in the form of a variety of deities. For them, God is simultaneously one and many.

All these ways of devotion are accommodated within the structure and symbolism of the larger Hindu temples. Traditional temples are con-

Top, temples of Kandariya Mahādeo and Devi Jogadanta, Khajurāho, India; _bottom left,_ steps of Khajurāho temple; _bottom right,_ detail of relief, temple of Kandariya Mahādeo.
Borromeo/EPA; Magnum; Editorial Photocolor Archives.

structed according to precise plans so that access to God might be especially possible. The place of access is symbolically made equivalent to the original creation by ritual processes. Just as the myth of creation's themes are biological and sacrificial, so is the consecration of a Hindu temple and of the space in which it is to be built.

The location for a Hindu temple is symbolically distanced from its normal state when the ground upon which the temple is to be built is taken out of ordinary use, and the deities that inhabit the space are asked to leave. The surface of the ground is plowed and reworked until it is shapeless. The space is then purified using forces that are naturally creative, such as the breath (the vital force of creation) and *mantras* (scripture passages that are the force of creation represented in sound). The forces are transferred to water and to other substances that are sprinkled and scattered over the ground until the purification is complete.

The ground has now been brought into the liminal phase from which its rebirth or re-creation is possible. The Puruṣa is invoked and placed firmly in the middle of the site in order to provide the ground with a firm foundation in the creation process itself. Finally, a *maṇḍala* (a symbolic diagram often in the shape of a circle or square) is traced on the site, and seeds are planted and allowed to germinate.

The maṇḍala, which represents the universe, is begun by moving outward from the center until it is complete. The maṇḍala symbolizes the manifest many who derive from the original Puruṣa. At the same time, it represents the human body, both of the Puruṣa and of human beings. The lower and higher parts of the diagram represent the lower self and the higher self; the deities placed in the diagram are also within the human body; and the maṇḍala represents, in microscopic form, the macroscopic universe. It also represents separation, the maṇḍala being on earth while God is on high, until the deity descends to occupy its image.

The ground having been sanctified,the temple is built following the creative symbolism and structural form of the maṇḍala. The building is structured around two contrasting movements: expansion and contraction. Over the site of the divine image, a tower thrusts toward the sky. Beneath the tower, space is compressed into a small rectangular room that is both the seat of the divine image and the womb or egg from which the world was created. The temple structure represents a series of contrasting movements or tensions between the One and the many.

The god is present in this small space, but also expands like the tower to the whole universe. The god is present within all beings, including the being of worshipers, but is also present in the image. These tensions are duplicated in a variety of ways within the temple. For example, the temple is usually dedicated to one god, but sometimes it contains the image of other deities as well. Again, God is present in the image and the temple, but God is not identical to any temple or image and is not confined by any space. Finally, tension exists between worship in a temple building and the temple within the human body: The Ātman which is the Brahman.

Thus, the worshiper who contains God, or the Brahman, within his own being comes to worship God, or the Brahman, in a temple, even though God and the Brahman are everywhere. What is together is separated so that it may be brought together again. After circling the temple site on foot, the worshiper makes the transition from the outside to the inside and comes face to face *(darśana)* with the presence of deity.

Seeing the image and paying homage to it may constitute the rite of worship for an individual, but the individual sometimes sponsors a more elabo rate form of worship, called *pūjā*, performed by a priest of the temple. Pūjā continues on a lesser scale the sacrificial exchange of gifts in the Vedic yajña. Praise, various kinds of libations, flowers, and food are offered to the deity in hope of continued creative gifts. The food offered to the deity is then shared as a blessing *(prasād)* by all present.

Just as a religious site may become permanently betwixt-and-between the human and sacred realms, some religious roles that mediate between people and the sacred also become permanent. Initiation rites transform such persons to a liminal status often expressed in a life style that is quite different from the rest of the culture.

Permanent Religious Roles

Buddhist monks and nuns do not marry. They do not belong to ordinary social groups, they possess no property, they are isolated from the rest of society except for the restricted, role-determined relationships of those whose careers are dedicated to overcoming human ignorance and craving with lay Buddhists who support their careers and who are inspired by their example. The saffron, red, or black robes of monks clearly indicate their special role on the edge—between those who are enmeshed in social cares and the ideal goal of *nirvāṇa* (liberation).

Monastic communities and lay communities each support the other. Lay communities provide (in Theravāda Buddhism) for the material needs of the monastic orders. Monastic communities provide the spiritual model for the true religious life and services for the lay communities. These services include not only education, but various forms of worship attended by lay persons, training in meditation, and the performance of rituals connected with transitions through the stages of life, as well as with the annual agricultural cycle. Finally, Buddhist monks also help lay people meet the crises of life, such as illness, possession by spirits, or other misfortunes. If an extraordinary sickness, for example, does not yield to ordinary medical treatment or to the ministrations of exorcisers, monks may read special passages from the Buddhist scriptures to invoke the power of the Buddha's words against the spirit that is causing the sickness.

Clearly, Buddhist monastic communities exist both to facilitate the monastic life and to serve lay people. Monastic compounds often contain Buddha images and relics. In Theravada Buddhism, images represent the continuing presence of the power and influence of the Buddha, and proper respect and gratitude are directed toward them. In Mahāyāna Buddhism, images of Buddhas and especially of bodhisattvas frequently become objects of devotion, particularly for the laity.

The division of status between monasteries and lay persons can easily be overstressed. Even in the Theravada tradition, lay persons have often been depicted as being of equal spirituality with monks and nuns. Lay persons often take leading roles in temple rituals. Furthermore, governments in most Buddhist countries have functioned not only to support monastic communities, but also at times to regulate, to reform, and to integrate monastic orders. In Mahāyāna Buddhism, especially in East Asia, the monastic life is an aid to an ideal that is, in fact, open to all.

Priests who are not monks or nuns may temporarily observe similar restrictions in preparation for mediation as proxies for the people they represent. The Shintō priests of Japan are not monastics, but to ensure that they are sufficiently purified to offer worship to the deities, they take special cleansing precautions and observe temporary restrictions in preparation for mediation.

The founders of some of the Asian religious traditions such as the Buddha for the Buddhist tradition, Mahavira for the Jain tradition, Krṣṇa for some of the Hindu devotional traditions, or Nanak for the Sikh tradition are generally interpreted by followers as in-between figures who in one way or another mediate between human beings and sacred reality. While for Theravada Buddhism the Buddha's authority is based upon what he discovered in his own experience, the northern (Mahāyāna) branch tends to view the Buddha much as many Hindus see Krṣṇa, namely as an immediate manifestation of sacred reality under the limitations of humanity. The *guru* or teacher in Hindu tradition has often been understood as a mediator who serves as a channel of liberating truth and/or of contact with sacred realities or reality. The first *guru* of the Sikh tradition, Nanak, as well as the nine *gurus* succeeding Nanak are understood to have been revealers of the Truth in ways that are parallel to that of many Hindu *gurus*. But in the Sikh tradition the succession of living human teachers is believed to have ended with the tenth *guru*. The Truth revealed by the first ten *gurus* and recorded in a text called the *Granth Sahib* now serves as the instrument which both embodies and mediates the Truth for contemporary devotees of the True Name (*Sat Nam*, sacred reality in the Sikh tradition).

Prophets and *shamans* (religious healers) often do not undergo formal installation rituals, but ac-

Top, **Afternoon prayer, Mandalay, Burma; *bottom,* Chinese Buddhist nuns.** *Hiroji Kubota; Boris Erwitt.*

counts of their "calls" to a spiritual role contain initiation stories that follow the four-phase structure of symbolic transformation. Since the gift of prophets and shamans is personal rather than institutional, they may eventually lose their power of mediation.

Shamanic contacts with spirits and deities to obtain guidance and power were prominent features of ancient Chinese and Japanese imperial government. Even now in Japan, blind women (called *miko*) sometimes are called as spokespersons for the *kami* (deities), and many of the New Religions of Japan in the nineteenth and twentieth centuries have been founded by women with such contacts with the *kami*. As noted in the section on modern Chinese religion, a mid-nineteenth-century rebellion in which some 20 million people were killed was inspired by shamanic revelations.

Treatment of Physical Illness

Symbolic transformations may also be concerned with such crises as physical illness. Cultures employing traditional religious forms of healing often distinguish between ordinary illnesses that can be diagnosed and treated at home or by medical doctors and extraordinary illnesses that resist normal types of diagnosis and treatment and exhibit symptoms traditionally associated with religious problems.

Examination of extraordinary symptoms by a religious diagnostician may show the cause to be a broken relationship with sacred forces. Diagnosis and treatment may include physical ministrations, and religious treatment often has psychosomatic effects. But the treatment is based mainly on restructuring the patient's social and sacred relationships.

Popular religious Taoism, an ancient Chinese movement discussed subsequently in this book, based a great deal of its appeal upon diagnosis and prescription for human physical as well as spiritual and moral ills. Buddhist monks also help people meet crises of life such as illness, possession by spirits, or other misfortunes. If an extraordinary sickness does not yield to ordinary medical treatment or to the ministrations of exorcisers, monks may read special passages from the Buddhist scriptures to invoke the power of the Buddha's words against the spirit that is causing the sickness.

Some human physical problems, such as chronic sickness, old age, and death, are never cured. But even problems that resist solution are subject to religious transformation. Grief and tragedy can be turned into hope, and human suffering can be given meaning, sanction, and if not a known purpose, at least an acknowledged cause. But resolution is sometimes possible only by relying on the mystery of sacred power.

Life after Death

The interplay between religious need and sacred satisfaction entails the repetition of the processes of symbolic transformation. This is necessary because sacred satisfaction is only partial and temporary. From a religious point of view, this polarity is part of the human condition. There are, however, forms of religious transformation whose intent is to overcome the human condition. These transformations lead to conditions of existence beyond death that are no longer subject to human contingency and to sacred satisfaction that is no longer partial and temporary. The human condition is left behind, and the need for repeated symbolic transformations is ended.

Probably all religious traditions perform funeral ceremonies to transform the dead into their new status as well as to strengthen and sustain survivors. In many cultures, however, interest in post-death existence is confined to the interaction of ancestors and other spirits with the survivors. Ancestors sometimes bring aid, but more often they bring misfortune if their living descendants fail to meet moral, ritual, or social obligations to the deceased.

The belief in some form of life after death is widespread. In one type of belief in life after death, the *soul* is thought to be reborn. (The term *soul* here refers to the spirit or spirits that animate an individual. In many religious traditions the soul is thought to survive death.) In some traditions the souls of the dead become part of the enlivening spirits of their descendants, but in other traditions (for example, Hinduism and Buddhism), the dead may be reborn into any form of life, including nonhuman forms. Rebirth does not transcend the polarity between religious need and sacred satisfaction. The new life form remains in this world. It is subject to need and will inevitably end in another death.

The broader Buddhist religious symbol system borrowed from the Hindu religious tradition. It was influenced by, and in turn influenced, the Hindu tradition in India. In some respects, the two traditions share a common fund of symbols. These include parallel (not identical) conceptions of moral causality (or karma) and of rebirth after death according to the disposition of a person's karma. And the devas or deities of the Hindu tradition play important roles in Buddhist tradition *not* as salvation mediators, but as the overseers of various powers of nature and of territories that form their domains.

The Buddhist concept of the six realms *(lokas)* or spheres that constitute the universe is also modified Hindu symbolic tradition. In addition to the realms of human beings and animals, there are four other realms into which it is possible to be reborn at death. These four are the realm of deities or devas, the realm of the titans or ogres who continually fight with each other, the realm of the hungry ghosts, and the realm of the various hells or "purgatories" in which bad karma is punished.

Life in any of these realms of birth, like life in the human realm, is always temporary. Thus, all six realms, as part of reality, exhibit the universal characteristics of insubstantiality, imperfection, and transitoriness. Being reborn as a deity would certainly be pleasurable, but deities are not above the round of rebirth, and the pleasure they enjoy is most likely to blind them to the need for insight into the nature of reality. Deities also must eventually face death and rebirth. Without insight, even the life of a deity is really a form of suffering.

Insight into reality makes it possible to overcome craving or attachment, thus ending all suffering. Life then becomes realistic and in a higher sense pleasurable because of the joy derived from enjoying things as they ought to be enjoyed. With the end of craving karma is no longer produced, so that at death a fully enlightened person will no longer face rebirth.

In Theravada Buddhism, the fully enlightened being is believed to attain *nirvāṇa*, an indescribable kind of reality achieved through detachment from the false notion of self. Whether it exists and whether it relates to the six realms of transitoriness, imperfection, and insubstantiality are matters about which both Buddhist and Western interpreters have argued at great length. Belief in nirvāṇa after death receives less emphasis in Mahāyāna tradition because the mission of the bodhisattva is to postpone nirvāṇa until all beings in the six realms are saved.

Some religious traditions, such as Christianity and Islam and the Śrī Vaiṣṇava tradition in Hinduism, believe in a permanent heaven that excludes another death. The dead are transformed into spiritual beings who reside forever in the sacred realm. Passage to this realm often depends on the quality of the life the persons lived on earth. Eternal heavens are sometimes complemented by eternal hells that are also beyond the polarity between religious need and sacred satisfaction. Those in hell continue to have needs but are forever separated from the sacred realm and sacred satisfaction. Similarly, within the Hindu and Buddhist traditions, the highest aim is permanent liberation from the round of birth and death and rebirth. Within the Hindu and Buddhist traditions, however, there are several hells, none eternal, in which the dead reside until the effect of their evil deeds have reached fruition.

The Focus or Goal of a Religion

The expectation of judgment is a powerful sanction for the behavior of the living, and for some people the central focus of religion is its otherworldly promise. Religious need is, nevertheless, immanent as well as transcendent, and religion is, in general, as much this-worldly as it is otherworldly. Although in some cases concern about heaven leads

Many religious traditions encompass the idea of hell. This Japanese painting entitled *Jigoku Zōshi (Hell Scroll)* dates from the end of the twelfth century. *The National Museum, Tokyo.*

to largely otherworldly attitudes, the freedom and assurance that come from otherworldly ideals often give significance to life in this world and to active involvement in it.

Although the goal of the Hindu religious tradition is ultimate liberation from the round of rebirth, it also provides for meeting a wide range of other religious needs. The Bhagavadgītā, in addition to teaching how liberation is possible, is very much concerned with life as duty or vocation within society. The law of karma provides a powerful sanction for moral behavior. It promises not only that one may become a better person by doing good deeds, but it also offers assurance of a good birth in the next life. The ritual forms of Hindu tradition give symbolic form to the major transitions in the lives of individuals, to the cycles of agriculture, to the annual patterns of the lunar calendar, to the days of the week, and even to the periods within a single day. In addition, Hindus seek material benefits from religious practice. At the beginning of a new year, for example, businesspeople perform pūjā for the goddess Lakṣmī to insure good income in the coming year. People seek help for crises as well, whether the problem be childlessness, sickness, or disaster.

Traditionally, the basic aims of life have been classified in Hindu tradition in a hierarchy of four. These aims are arranged hierarchically because they range from the more constricted to more expansive versions of the same basic drive. This drive, common to all human beings, is the thirst for being. In its most restricted form, it is expressed in an individual's desire for self-gratification, especially for sensual gratification. The thirst for being is here a selfish attempt to attract beings to oneself.

Only when a person realizes that this kind of behavior brings frustration does the thirst for being expand to broader kinds of fulfillment in the aim for social and material success. Eventually, this kind of purpose also becomes dissatisfying because it is still aimed primarily at the fulfillment of the ego. In Hindu tradition, the next highest stage is the performance of one's role in society and one's religious practice out of sense of duty. At this stage, the practice of religion may become selfless. The Bhagavadgītā shows how life in this world and the performance of duty as one's part in the cosmic sacrifice can be completely satisfying.

The fourth, and officially the highest, aim of life in Hindu tradition is liberation, the desire for the eternal peace of God, or for union with the Being of Brahman. This desire is for a permanent resolution of all worldly problems and human conflicts in a status that overcomes the human and the created conditions. Some Hindus abandon social life in order to devote all their time and energy to realizing this goal. Many Hindus follow this path in modified forms in old age after they have retired from active work. But Hindu society is not made up primarily of those who have withdrawn from society to pursue liberation. Particularly among urban, professional people, the predominant role model for the religious life is that of karma-yogin—an individual actively involved in a business or profession, with a sense of doing so as part of a larger creative process.

Some religious people, the *mystics*, try to merge with the sacred realm as continuously as possible. To do so, they diminish the human side of the polarity between the human and sacred realms to such an extent that, for them, the sacred becomes all. Mystics move into the liminal state by removing themselves symbolically from their culture and their own selfhood. They then dwell in an unstructured, pathless state while awaiting the final enlightenment that will dissolve all barriers between the human and sacred realms. Some mystics withdraw from the world, but others achieve a kind of selflessness that frees them for even more practical involvement.

The permanent transformation beyond the interplay between religious need and sacred satisfaction is not always individual. The Western religions—Judaism, Zoroastrianism, Christianity, and Islam—teach that all creation will be fulfilled in a final transformation at the end of time. The purpose of history will be achieved with the inauguration of a new heaven and a new earth. Then either the human realm will ascend to the sacred realm, or heaven will descend to earth. In the Hindu and Buddhist traditions, however, history moves in long cycles, in which the end of time in one cycle is followed, after a totally dormant period, by the beginning of a whole new cycle.

Cultural Traditions as Systems of Symbols

Religions form cultural traditions to express and transmit symbolic systems. Religious traditions thus express religious needs at the cultural level and participate in the religious polarity of need and satisfaction. Yet the realization of sacred satisfaction is always partial and temporary. Religion is therefore distinguishable from culture, but not separable from it.

Religion is social by nature. The transformation of the human-sacred relationship typically includes a transformation of human relationships that reconstitutes society as a religious community. The patterns of religious tradition are passed from one generation to another and are learned by most people much as language is learned, simply as part of growing up in a particular culture.

Tradition is also transmitted by special communication devices. Words and sounds convey conceptual content in sacred narratives, in systematized statements of beliefs, in statements of behavioral norms that are sometimes codified into law, and in systematic explanations and defenses (theologies). The practice of all religious traditions takes place in communal settings and usually in oral form, but many have also compiled written collections of their central stories and teachings, such as the Bible and the Qur'an, the Buddhist *Tripitaka* and Mahāyāna *Sūtras*, the Hindu *Vedas*, and the Shintō *Kojiki* and *Nihon Shoki*.

Symbolic transformation is conveyed most directly in acts of worship and ritual and in the interchange among members of a religious community who act out and thus reinforce the symbolic structure of the community. Behavioral norms and patterns of community relation are taught as much by their practice as by formal instruction. The symbolic layout of space and time accepted by community members defines individual boundaries and exemplifies the boundaries of the community's symbolic structure.

Religious institutions can be almost any form of cultural association. Some are based on nonvoluntary kinship and family groups, neighborhood and occupational groups, or social classes. Others take the form of voluntary groups, such as association with a church, mosque, monastery, or temple. Often religion is transmitted in ways that are so close to the surface that their effect may go largely unnoticed. This is especially true of symbolic cues hidden in social interaction and of symbols that reverberate throughout a religious tradition. For example, the customary Hindu *namaste* greeting (with palms together in front of the face or forehead) is on one level a greeting ("I salute you"). At the same time, *namaste* maintains distance by avoiding touching. In addition, it expresses respect and hierarchy; it conveys the idea that the feet of the one being addressed are worth more than the head of the one making the gesture. When greeting holy men, gurus, or images of deities, Hindus sometimes extend the gesture to include touching their feet.

Religious tradition, like language, tends to retain its existing structures and vocabulary to make communication possible within a continuous frame of reference. There can be major innovations, however, and new religious structures can be formed out of the old. Few societies are completely homogeneous, and diverse subgroups within a society often have their own sense of religious legitimacy that may conflict with the sense of authorization of the other subgroups or the "official" tradition of the culture as a whole. Variant religious patterns within a culture reflect in part special interests—for example, those of occupational groups or of particular localities. These variations are like the dialects of a language or a person's own speech idiosyncrasies.

Individual differences occur within the overall structure of possibilities offered by a religious system and cannot be understood without reference to that system, even when they represent a reaction to it.

Religious traditions are systems of symbols that are emically disparate. Meaning within such systems is a matter of internal interaction, as the various parts of a system acquire meaning in relation to each other. The parts of a system are usually not transferable to other systems, and many religious systems are mutually incompatible. Both a Jewish bar mitzvah and a Roman Catholic confirmation can be understood as rites of passage, but the rites are not interchangeable, nor do they carry the same meaning in their respective communities.

Overview

We have characterized religion in a way that we hope will prove useful in a cross-cultural perspective. We believe that religious traditions are sufficiently comparable to enable us to make generalizations about common structures. But our characterization is not intended to represent the essence of all traditions. Specific religious traditions are not just accidental variations of a common religious core.

We have characterized religion as a relationship, a process, and a system. You will learn from your study of Asian religions that religious people seek to bring human life into relationship with a wider, other-than-human, symbolic context, in which life is thought to acquire its fundamental sanction, value, significance, and vitality. Although different Asian religions characterize the sacred realms in different ways, they all ascribe to sacred reality or realities the qualities of ultimacy, mystery, awe, fascination, and the ability to satisfy religious needs.

These religious needs are satisfied by a process we have called symbolic transformation, which usually has four phases: (1) recognition of specific religious needs, (2) intensification of religious need by symbolic distancing, (3) a liminal phase, and (4) satisfaction through symbolic restoration, renewal, realignment, and/or rebirth. Repeated symbolic transformations are typical of the rhythms of religious life, and these processes reflect the continuous polarity between religious need and sacred satisfaction.

Religion is a communal involvement of people who express their relationship with sacred realities and one another through systems of symbols, which, in turn, are transmitted through cultural traditions from one generation to another. Cultural traditions persist, develop, and change through time. Like languages, religious traditions tend to retain their structure and vocabulary. The persistence of ritual structures and symbols over time makes communication possible within a framework of symbols. Even when there are religious innovations, the continuity with previous traditions generally is clear.

Major religious innovations are caused partly by a tradition's internal dynamics and by the interaction of the religious tradition with cultural forces and other religious traditions. Religious traditions are clearly historical in nature, but the ultimacy and mystery of sacred realms reflect timelessness and constancy. Despite changes in religious traditions, sacred realities are able to persist because they are not identified with the institutional forms they sanctify. Ultimate realities are referred to as ancient, eternal, or from the beginning and are not subject to the vicissitudes of history. But religious characterizations of sacredness are subject to change because the mystery of sacred realities is never fully grasped. This difference between inherited religious forms and their source in sacred realities makes possible the development of new understandings, and thus religious traditions have a capacity for self-criticism and for new formulations of the process of symbolic transformation.

Notes

1 Melford E. Spiro, "Religion: Problems of Definition and Explanation," in *Anthropological Approaches to the Study of Religion*, ed. R. Banton, A.S.A. Monographs no. 3 (London: Tavistock, 1963), pp. 85–126.

2 "Selections from the Lao Tzu (or Tao-te Ching)," in *Sources of Chinese Tradition*, comp. William Theodore de Bary, Wing-tsit Chan, and Burton Watson, vol. 1 of 2 vols. (New York: Columbia University Press, 1960), p. 51. According to the Pinyin system of romanization, Lao Tzu is written as Laozi and the work ascribed to him as the *Dao De Jing*.

3 Rudolph Otto, *The Idea of the Holy*, trans. John W. Harvey, rev. ed. (London and New York: Oxford University Press, 1950 and 1958). First published in Germany in 1917; first English-language version, 1923.

4 From the Brihad Aranyaka Upanishad 4:5:15 from Robert Ernest Hume, trans., *The Thirteen Principal Upanishads Translated From the Sanskrit*, 2nd edition. London: Oxford University Press, 1931, p. 147.

5 *The Bhagavad Gita*, trans. Franklin Edgerton (New York: Harper & Row, Pub., 1955), chap. 11, vs. 18–20, p. 57.

6 J. A. B. Van Buitenen, trans. and ed., *The Bhagavadgītā in the Mahābhārata: A Bilingual Edition* (Chicago: The University of Chicago Press, 1981), pp. 143–145.

PART ONE

HINDUISM

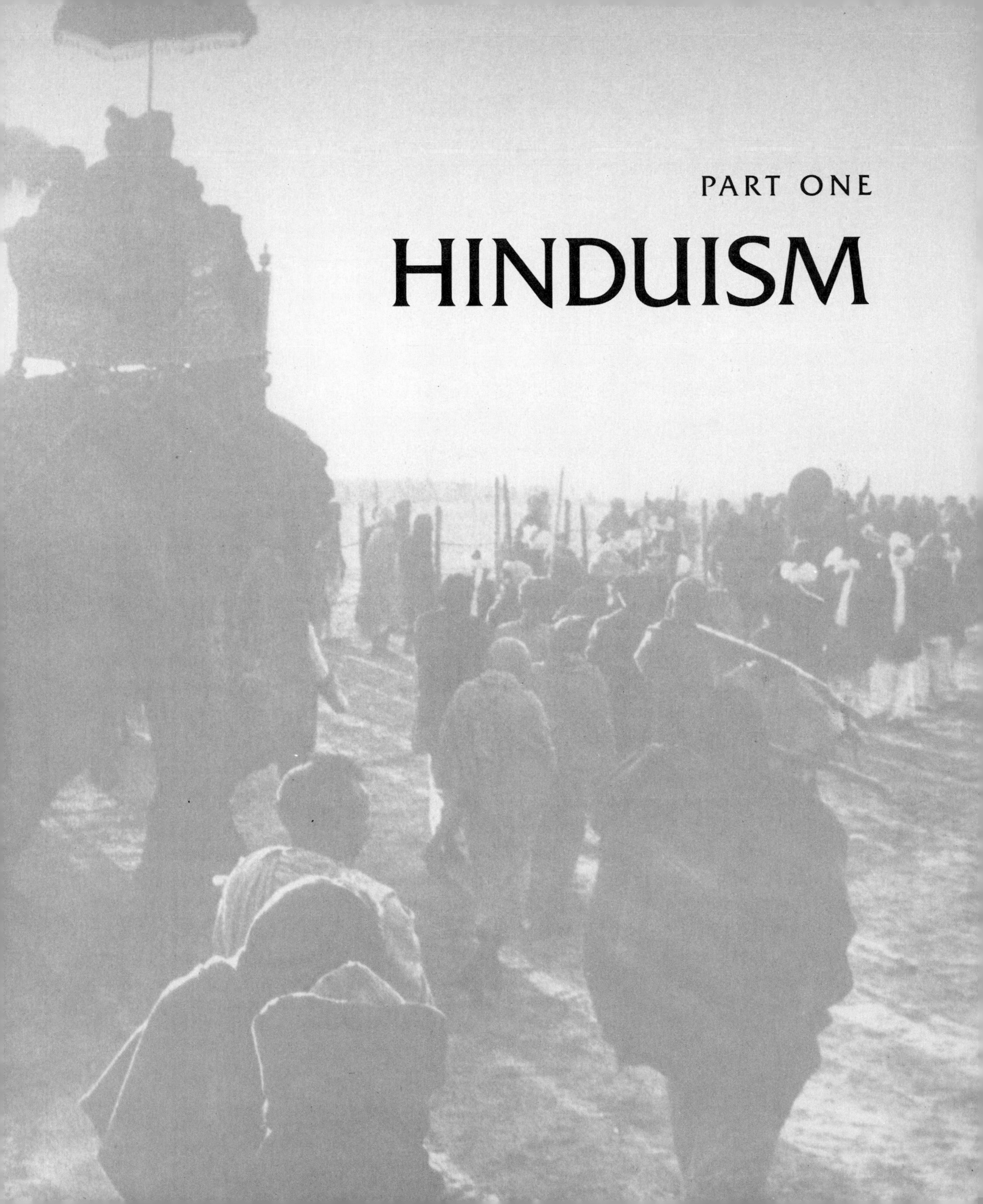

PHOTOGRAPH BY MARILYN SILVERSTONE/MAGNUM

We first consider Hinduism, India's principal religion, in relation to its geographical setting. Chapter two outlines the Indus Valley civilization that disintegrated about 1500 B.C. as Aryan invaders entered India from the northwest, and discusses the religion of the Vedas, Hinduism's oldest scriptures, which reflect the outlook of the early Aryans.

In chapter three we look at the rise of classical Hinduism and its rites, the Way of Action, as well as the new literary forms that were created at this time. We also examine the caste system that divided Indian society into distinct social classes. By describing a typical Indian community, Kṛishṇapur, we see how the caste system works and what the concepts of karma and rebirth mean.

Chapter four considers the Way of Knowledge, an outlook that originated in the new teachings of the Upanishads. We are introduced to the Vedānta tradition and the philosophy of its great teacher Śaṅkara. Chapter five presents the Way of Devotion, an approach to religion that places hope for liberation in the power of a personal God. This chapter also examines two great theistic movements, one centered on Śiva and his feminine powers and the other based on Viṣṇu. We conclude in chapter six with a sketch of modern Hinduism.

2 The Earliest Forms of Hinduism

Hindu is a fairly new term, of Persian origin. After their conquest of northern India in the twelfth century A.D., Muslims used it to describe persons belonging to the original population of Hind, or India. As used here, India means the whole Indian subcontinent. But the subcontinent is also the birthplace of Jainism, Buddhism, and Sikhism, and to distinguish Hinduism from these faiths, we sometimes call it Brahmanism, that is, the religion taught by the ancient priestly class of *brāhmaṇs*. Although the brāhmaṇs did not create all of Hinduism, their leadership has been so dominant that the name is appropriate. Their authority is one of the factors that sets Hinduism apart from all other beliefs. The geographical connotation of the term Hinduism is significant, however, because the Hindu religion derives much of its nature from the special characteristics of its homeland.

Hinduism, literally "the belief of the people of India," is the predominant faith of India and of no other nation. About 85 percent of all Indians declare themselves to be Hindu, along with a substantial minority of the population of Bangladesh (formerly East Pakistan). In addition, conversions and migrations in ancient and modern times have created small groups of Hindus in Sri Lanka (Ceylon), Indonesia, Fiji, Africa, Great Britain, and the Americas. But like Confucianism in China and Shinto in Japan, Hinduism belongs primarily to the people of one country.

Hinduism arose among a people who had no significant contact with the biblical religions. Hindu teaching does not consist of alternative answers to the questions asked by Western faiths. For instance, Hinduism does not insist on any particular belief about God or gods. Those reared in religions holding firmly to definite beliefs regarding God are often baffled by Hinduism's relaxed attitude in theology. We need to realize that the beliefs on which Hindus insist relate to problems that are especially acute in the Indian environment and that the hopes of Hindus are shaped by what seems desirable and possible under the special conditions of Indian life. Hindus, like others, seek superhuman resources to help preserve life and achieve its highest conceivable blessedness, but they perceive life's threats and promises as those posed by the Indian land and climate.

The Geographical Setting

Two geographical factors have determined many of the themes and emphases of Hindu religious thought: (1) India is an agricultural land; and (2) India is an isolated land.

INDIA AS A LAND OF FARMERS

We sometimes forget the ancient fame of India as a vast and fertile land of fabulous richness. Throughout history, the rich alluvial soil of India's northern river valleys, which extend for about two thousand miles from east to west, has always supported a very large population. Indians have depended more exclusively on farming than have the people of most other major cultures. And despite the recent growth of industrial cities, India still remains overwhelmingly a land of farming villages.

The Hindu cosmology (view of the universe) is the creation of minds constantly aware of the germination of plants and the reproduction of domestic animals. Nature itself is seen as feminine, and female deities have a prominent place in classical Hindu mythology.

The persistent anxieties of India's farmers have had a dramatic impact on Hindu religion. India has always been both blessed and cursed by natural conditions, the most frightening of which is the matter of adequate water. The average rainfall is plentiful, but several times a century the monsoon clouds fail to roll in from the sea, the rain does not fall, and the crops do not grow. This possibility may have something to do with the great attention paid to water in Hinduism's rituals. Scarcely any ritual is performed without preliminary bathings, sprinklings, sippings, libations to a deity, or other ceremonial uses of water. In Hindu mythology the formal position of king of the gods is held by Indra, the god of rain, and in the conceptions of many of the goddesses there are manifestations of the ever present concern with water.

Most of the goddesses have a clear connection with the fertility of the earth, and Hindu theologians have built into their personalities something of the character of the forces controlling the agricultural world. In their worship of these deities, Hindus attempt to establish better relations with a generative force conceived as a usually generous mother who can sometimes be moody and is capable of violent tantrums. The ambivalence of this power is recognized in the beliefs that the goddess appears in different forms and moods and that the divine mother is not only the affectionate Sītā or Pārvatī, but also the dangerous Kālī, an irritable parent who sometimes destroys her children in inexplicable rages. The dual focus of worship symbolizes the alternating pattern of abundant harvests and catastrophic droughts. And the persistent anxiety about the food supply explains Hinduism's great tolerance for the pursuit of practical goals in worship. Those who study Hindu rituals or read popular literature often perceive them as materialistic in spirit. It is understandable that prescientific peoples living with such natural threats to survival should be preoccupied with physical well-being.

INDIA'S ISOLATION AND STABILITY

A second important geographical factor in the formation of Indian religion is the barrier of mountains and seas that separates India from the rest of the world and shields its way of life from disruption by outsiders. On India's southern flanks the seas are wide, and heavily populated lands are distant. Hostile armadas of seagoing peoples have never landed invading forces that were able to overwhelm India by the power of foreign armies alone. India's long northern border is protected by the Himalayas, mountains so high that no army coming from China, Burma, or Tibet has ever conquered India. Although passes on the northwest border through the Afghan mountains have been used as gateways by many bands of invaders, they have had to cross wide barren regions that have limited the size of their armies. Only an almost prehistoric Aryan incursion has ever penetrated India in such force as to permeate and transform Indian civilization.

In historical times, Persians, Greeks, Scythians, Huns, Mongols, and others have invaded India in modest numbers and set up kingdoms on the northern plains. But they were always few in relation to the population of the rest of the country, and they were able to rule successfully only by using Indian assistants, Indian administrative institutions, and Indian languages. The invaders soon married In-

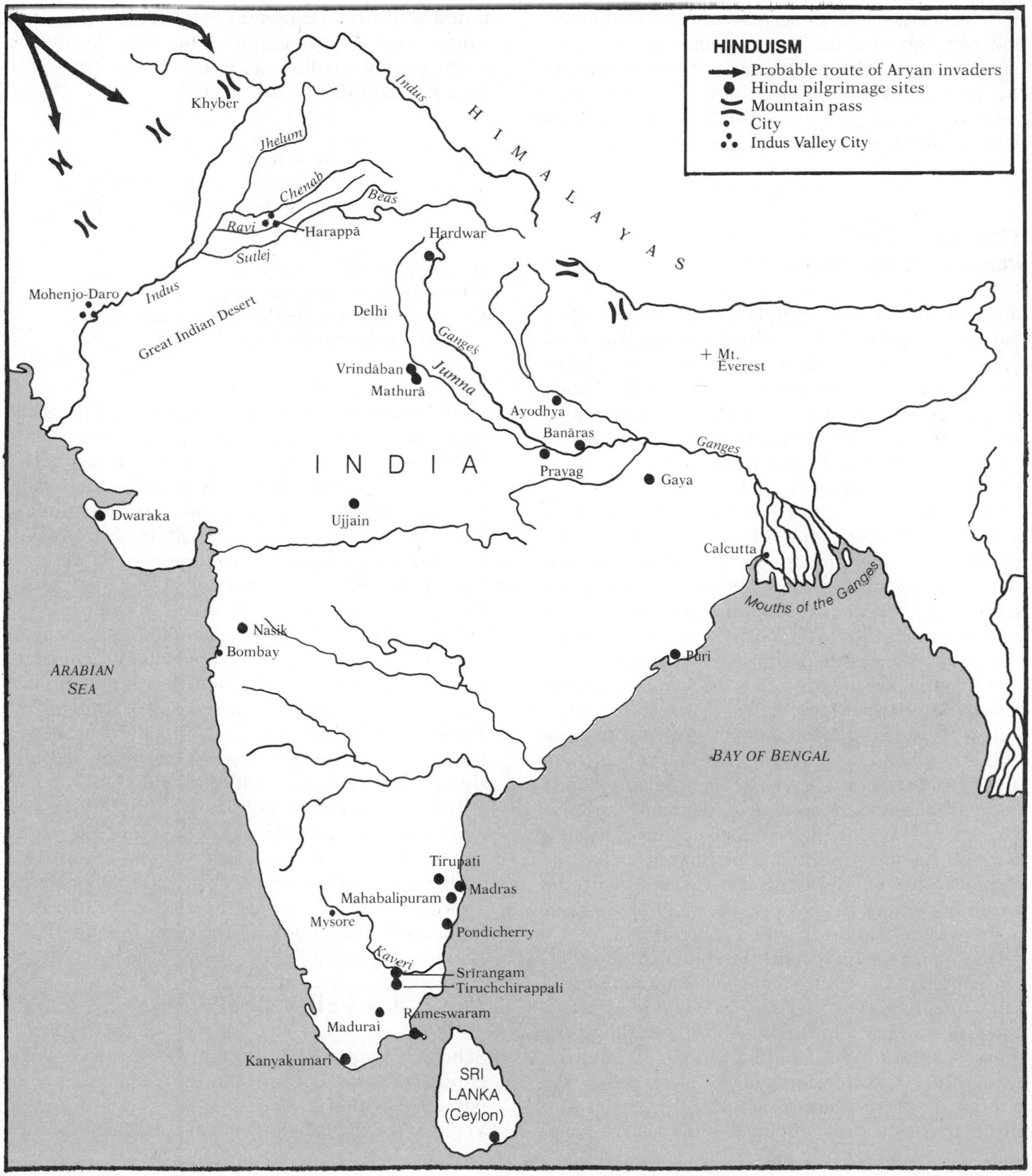
HINDUISM
Probable route of Aryan invaders
Hindu pilgrimage sites
Mountain pass
City
Indus Valley City
Khyber
Indus
HIMALAYAS
Jhelum
Chenab
Beas
Ravi
Harappā
Sutlej
Hardwar
Mohenjo-Daro
Indus
Great Indian Desert
Delhi
Ganges
Jumna
Vrindāban
Mathurā
Mt. Everest
Ayodhya
Banāras
Ganges
INDIA
Prayag
Gaya
Dwaraka
Ujjain
Calcutta
Mouths of the Ganges
Nasik
Bombay
ARABIAN SEA
Puri
BAY OF BENGAL
Tirupati
Madras
Mahabalipuram
Mysore
Pondicherry
Kaveri
Srīrangam
Tiruchchirappali
Rameswaram
Madurai
Kanyakumari
SRI LANKA (Ceylon)

dian women, came to terms with the brāhmaṇs, and were given a traditional Indian status in society. Even the Muslim and British dominations of the past millennium—each powerful in its own way—did not cause any radical displacement of the age-old Hindu social order.

The Quest for Inner Peace and Harmony

India's cultural security also has helped determine the concerns that are prominent in the Hindu religion. Anxiety regarding the survival of a loved tradition is not a significant worry in the Hindu scriptures. India's natural defensive advantages made the established order of Hinduism easy to maintain, and they imposed on Hindus the opposite problem: a confining stability.

India's more traditional villages preserve even today a pattern of social relations that has not essentially changed for more than two thousand years. For centuries most Hindus have accepted the tasks of an inherited occupation and died in the rank in which they were born. Hindu society's demands on its members are extremely heavy, and its restraints are deeply felt even when they are not resisted or even resented. The frustration of individual Hindus is experienced as a general sense of living in a bondage involving no external object of blame. It is not characteristic of Hindus to blame their problems on society or to demand that their discontents be remedied by social changes in their favor. It has been an axiom of Hinduism that the responsibility for resolving one's tensions with the world lies squarely with oneself: inner adjustment is the way to tranquillity and contentment.

One distinguishing mark of Hinduism is its intense interest in techniques of self-examination and self-control that can enable individuals to attain peace of mind and harmony with the world. At the most ordinary level, these methods of inducing tranquillity take the form of moral teaching. The Hindu literature presents as ideal the person who through mastery of impulse preserves his emotional stability and mental balance. In the second canto of the Bhagavadgītā (Song of the Lord), one of the classic writings of Hinduism, the truly holy man is described in these terms:

When he sets aside desires,
All that have entered his mind, O Pārtha,
And is contented in himself and through himself,
He is called a man of steady wisdom.

He whose mind stirs not in sorrows,
Who in joys longs not for joys,
He whose passion, fear and wrath are gone,
That steady-minded man is called a sage.[1]

Hinduism has other methods for calming the troubled mind. In disciplines called *yoga,* Hindu teachers of meditation offer guidance in subjective processes through which it is possible to dissolve desires, still one's passions, enter into equanimity, and relieve the tedium of life with inner feelings of joy that are believed to be a foretaste of an everlasting freedom and immortality. As a final resort, the seeker of tranquillity is urged to enter into the separated life of the world-abandoning *sannyāsī.*

If a religion can be defined by what it believes to be the most blessed condition that humanity can know, then Hinduism is the religion of tranquillity. Tranquillity of mind is understood to be also a tranquillity of being, a reward for which a Hindu should be willing to sacrifice all else.

The salient characteristics we have mentioned will be discussed further as we explore more fully the Hindu way of life. We have pointed out that such prominent features of the Hindu religion have a cause. Behind them lies the distinctive nature of India itself as a physical setting for human life.

The Indus Valley Civilization

Scholars long believed that the history of the Hindu tradition began when the Vedas were composed. The oldest of the Hindu scriptures, the Vedas were the religious poems of a people called

Aryans, who migrated to India in about the middle of the second millennium B.C. But in the twentieth century, archaeologists have been able to show, in publications beginning with Sir John Marshall's *Mohenjo-Daro and the Indus Civilization*,[2] that the Aryans were neither India's first civilized people nor the creators of all that is old in Hinduism. At least a thousand years before the Aryans arrived, earlier inhabitants had already created a literate culture in northwestern India. We do not know the name of these earlier civilizers because their system of writing has not been deciphered, but since their home was in the basin of the Indus River and its borderlands, they are commonly referred to as "the Indus Valley civilization." It is now known that the great stream of Hinduism came from two sources. The younger source was the religious tradition of the Aryan invaders. The older was the religious heritage of the civilization of the Indus Valley.

THE RUINS AT MOHENJO-DARO AND HARAPPĀ

The people who created the early culture of the Indus Valley were of a racial mixture not very different from that of India's modern population. They grew a variety of food grains and kept cattle, sheep, goats, pigs, and chickens as domestic animals. They manufactured rather crude tools and weapons of copper and bronze. Their bullock carts were built in a style still used today by the farmers of that region. To write their language they used over 250 characters that have little relation to any alphabet now known. By 2400 B.C. their civilization was at its height and was engaged in trade by sea with Mesopotamia. The sites of sixty of their towns have been found, and two of them, Mohenjo-Daro and Harappā, appear to be the ruins of cities that were political capitals.

This culture of the Indus was contemporary with those of the Euphrates and the Nile. At the Indus sites archaeologists have found the first planned cities known to history. The residential portion of each Indus city was laid out upon a grid of major thoroughfares crossing each other at right angles. The houses were supplied with water from wells carefully lined and curbed with masonry. Each house had a paved bathroom with a hand-flushed toilet draining out into covered sewers that were buried under the street. The administrative center was a somewhat elevated walled citadel next to the residential city. The major cities had public granaries located in or directly below the citadels.

Clay toy from the Indus Valley civilization (third millennium B.C.). The toy oxen pull a cart built in a style still used by Indus Valley farmers. *Museum of Fine Arts, Boston.*

Throughout a region a thousand miles long from north to south and almost as wide, this single style of urban living prevailed. The same units of length were used everywhere, and weights were of such a strict uniformity that an inspection system can be assumed. It is likely that the authorities controlled the people in a characteristic Indian way, by supervision of the food supply rather than by extensive use of arms. Some kind of difference between rulers and ruled was strongly felt, as evidenced by the separateness of the citadels and by the strength of their walls in comparison with the weak defenses of the cities themselves.

INDUS RELIGIOUS BELIEFS

Discerning the religious ideas and practices of the Indus people is difficult because their writings cannot yet be read. A few beliefs can be inferred from the large-scale physical arrangements of the cities. Most of our clues to their religious ideas come from a few clay and stone images and from the hundreds of personal seals found on the Indus sites. The short inscriptions on these seals might tell us much if we could read them, but at present we can glean information only from the beautiful pictorial designs cut in intaglio on the seals' faces.

First we shall look for the meaning of one of the most striking characteristics of the remains of this civilization: the centuries-old uniformity of its artifacts, seen in every visible pattern of its life throughout all periods of this culture's sure existence of at least five hundred years. The Indus potters never altered the shape of their wares, and the complex alphabet already used by writers in the twenty-fifth century B.C. never was modified. The design of the culture's flat copper ax heads did not change. The outer boundaries of the Indus cities did not expand or contract, the thoroughfares were never relocated, and the house sites and the house outlines did not vary. What does this lack of change mean and what may we suppose about the thoughts of those who lived in this way?

In this highly organized society, such a complete avoidance of innovation must have been deliberate and enforced by social authority. Underlying this commitment to an unchanging life there must have been an exceptional reverence for the ways of the ancestors. Despite our almost total ignorance of their thought, we contemplate the historical sweep of their technical development and conclude that the Indus people regarded the heritage of their past as sacred and inviolable.

Another aspect of the physical culture that appears to be full of meaning is the scrupulous care with which it handled water. In the citadel of Mohenjo-Daro, a seat of government, archaeologists have found not only an assembly hall and a granary but also a large bathing pool. The pool is flanked by many dressing rooms and imposing arcades and has broad steps for the safe descent of bathers into the water. Formal and solemn bathing must have been regarded as somehow essential to effective government.

Something of this vanished society's feelings about water is communicated to us by its superb hydraulic masonry. Quite obviously, the Indus people believed that water either contained a power or liberated and preserved a power of such importance to human life that it had to be handled with great care. We propose that the ancient Indus people already entertained some of the standard Hindu notions of the metaphysical functions and purifying powers of water that were to prevail throughout later ages of Indian life. In later Hindu philosophical speculation, water is often the figure for the formless primary substance of original creation. In historical times, wells, pools, and streams have been believed to be the residences of divine beings, and waterside places have been the sacred destinations of religious pilgrimages. Bathing has been the principal means for removing contamination caused by contact with unclean substances and persons, and the great pool at the citadel of Mohenjo-Daro may have been the means by which rulers attained the purity deemed necessary for the performance of their high civic functions. Or, equally likely, bathing may have been a means by which the relatively unclean members of the general populace prepared themselves for contact with their aloof rulers who, as supervisors of the ancient heritage, shared something of the holiness of the heritage itself.

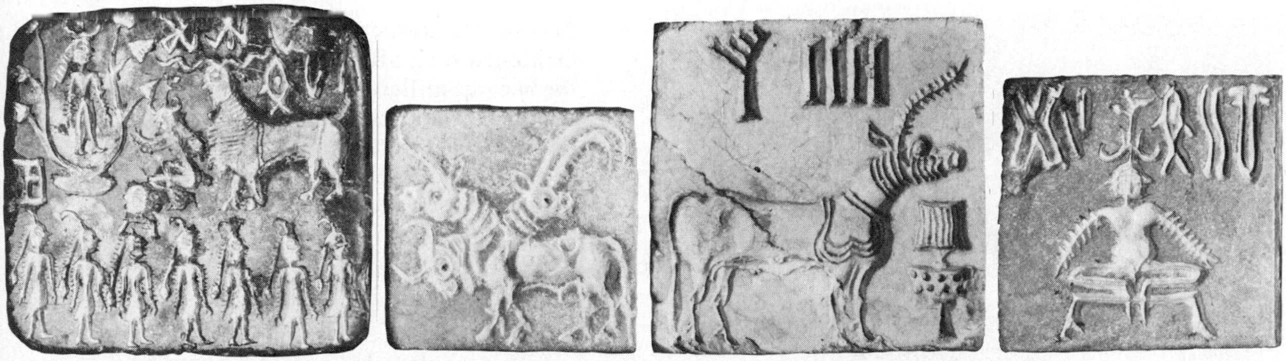

Steatite seals from Mohenjo-Daro often depict powerful and sometimes fantastical animals. Although the writing of the Indus Valley dwellers has not been deciphered, some of their religious sentiments are revealed by the hundreds of personal seals found at excavation sites throughout the valley.
Borromeo/EPA.

The study of the engravings on the Indus seals enables us to recover, again from nonverbal materials, an aspect of religious feeling. The design of these seals is dominated by magnificent representations of animals. On many seals, figures of powerful bulls are seen; on others, a mysterious bovine unicorn, or tigers, rhinoceroses, antelopes, and elephants. The animals are always male, and free. Though the culture used bulls as draft animals, the beasts on the seals are never shown in harness or hitched to carts. All the animals have been carved with special attention to their mighty horns and flanks and with obvious awareness of their extraordinary strength. Before the impressive unicorn is always seen an unusual two-tiered stand believed to be an incense burner. The people whose minds dwelt on these creatures apparently perceived in them a superhuman power that they admired and wished to activate on their own behalf.

There also is evidence in the seals of a comparable power existing in plants. One seal shows a solitary tree amid whose branches a three-horned goddess or god is seen. A suppliant approaches on bended knee, attended by a goatlike animal and assisted by seven persons in a formal row, wearing identical dress and coiffure. The tree can be identified by its leaf. It is India's sacred fig tree, the kind of tree under which the Buddha sat on the night of his enlightenment. It is still sacred in northern India as the holy *pīpal* tree, which is never cut down by Hindu villagers.

The divine force seen in the tree was sometimes conceived in other forms. Among the clay figurines found in almost every house, the most common is a feminine figure whose large breasts and hips are indicators of fertility. So many of these figures lack lower extremities that it seems they were intended to appear to be partly submerged in the earth.[3] Attached to the head of one such image is a cup in which oil or incense has been burned. Thus it appears that an earth-dwelling fertility figure, feminine in nature, was an object of worship.

The fertile earth is the center of attention again in a seal that seems to refer to the planting and germination of grain crops. On one side of the seal is an inverted nude figure from whose genital region a stalk of grain with a bearded head—or perhaps a tree—grows upright. There is not much doubt about the identity of this upside-down figure: it is the earth conceived as a fertile female person.

Pantheons that contain female deities are almost sure to include male forces as well. We have noticed the Indus religion's attention to male ani-

Terra-cotta statuette from Mathurā, fashioned long after the Aryan invasion of the second millennium B.C. This statuette, which exhibits the traits of a fertility figure, reveals that the religious traditions of the Indus Valley dwellers persisted despite the invasion. *Museum of Fine Arts, Boston.*

mals, in whom some degree of divinity can be assumed. A number of phalluses, or models of the male reproductive organ, have been found in the course of excavation. Their use is unknown, but it probably was cultic.

Several fascinating seals picture a male person seated in a manner that, as the "lotus posture," is fundamental in later India's meditative yoga. The figure in the seals has multiple faces pointing forward and to left and right in token of his divine, all-seeing powers. In one seal, the adoring posture of attendants on either side also suggest his divine status. In another, he is surrounded by animals of many kinds, and from the crown of his head two fronds of vegetation spring as well. The origin of life is shown in a representation of the springing of plant and animal forms from the creative mind of a meditating deity.

Because this god of the Indus people is a *yogī* (a sage who practices yoga) and is seen with many animals, many scholars believe that he was the prototype of the later Hindu god Śiva, who is skilled in yoga, who is said to face in all directions, and who has the name of Paśupati, or Lord of Beasts.

Some scholars believe that some kind of meditational yoga was already being practiced in this earliest Indian civilization. The evidence of the seals does not stand entirely alone. Other suggestions of yoga can be seen in an unusual stone bust found at Mohenjo-Daro—a representation of an adult human being of great dignity, in a posture that has yogic characteristics. He holds himself erect with head, neck, and chest aligned in a posture unusual in Indus statuary but necessary in yoga. And the position of the eyes—closed to slits—is even more suggestive of yoga. The statue reveals the existence in the Indus culture of a type of leadership peculiar to India. His introspective habits are a part of his distinction and of his qualification for leadership. Already in this image we have an exemplar of the Bhagavadgītā's ideal of the great man as "the sage of steady wisdom."

The seals show vegetable life springing from both goddesses and gods. Therefore, it would be remarkable if the religious leaders of this people did not unite these conceptions in a single theory of the creation of the universe through mythological interactions between these divine beings of the two sexes. And if the Indus thinkers were sophisticated enough to offer philosophical rather than mythological explanations of the beginning of things, they probably also conceived the world as formed, by the analogy rather than the actuality of sex, through the created interaction of two polar powers or essences. The Śāmkhya and the Śākta schools of later thought, which trace the cosmos to the interflow of such paired realities, could easily have had their beginnings here. But aside from suggesting the likelihood of a quasi-sexual dualism in their metaphysical thinking, we cannot say more about the philosophical ideas of these people.

Arrival of the Aryans

Sometime between 1900 and 1600 B.C. the Indus civilization fell into disorder. Its great cities became deserted mounds, first in the Indus Valley itself and, by 1500 B.C., in its southern border regions also. The cause of the collapse is not known. There were damaging floods during those centuries, and agricultural failures, and a breakdown of municipal regulation can be seen in the anarchic irregularities of building practices in late Mohenjo-Daro. But the end of the culture is fairly close in time to the appearance on the northwest border, in about 1500 B.C., of an aggressive nonurban people, the Aryans. During the period when Aryan hordes are known to have been on the move in the Middle East in search of new homes, some of the Indus cities came to an end in slaughter or conflagration.

Even if the Aryans were not the direct destroyers of the Indus civilization, they were surely its successors. After a short time they became the dominant people of the Indian plains, living a quite different style of life. The light-skinned Aryans were village dwellers who made their living by grazing cattle as well as by growing crops. The old, non-Aryan rural population was not eliminated, but it accepted the language of the conquerors and submitted to the dominance of their culture. The Aryans' priests became the new civilization's cultural leaders, and the Aryan religion prevailed.

In time the new Aryan India became settled and populous again. Between 1000 and 500 B.C., cities rose again on the plains and became the fortified capitals of great kingdoms. Once more, agriculture became intensive and almost the sole livelihood of the people. Surviving elements of the old religion again became relevant to the problems of a people who faced again India's persistent natural hazards and rigid social controls. After 500 B.C., the mainstream of Hinduism continued to be Aryan in name, but it became syncretistic in content. The role of the old indigenous material in this new composite religion was surely great, but its extent cannot be estimated because the Indus religion is so poorly known.

At this point we pass from inquiry into the almost unknown to the study of the almost known—the Aryans and their religion.

THE RELIGION OF THE VEDAS

The Aryans are first mentioned in Mesopotamian records of the period 1800 to 1400 B.C., during which time groups of Aryans were probably migrating also into Iran and northwestern India. Those who settled in India reveal themselves in a great body of oral literature composed and compiled by their priestly class between 1200 and 800 B.C. Whereas the religion of the Indus culture is known only from the material discoveries of archaeologists, the outlook of the Aryans has been recovered from the Vedas, the oldest of the Hindu scriptures.

The Culture of the Early Aryans

In the Vedas we discern a people who had a lifestyle quite different from that of the Indus civilization. These early Aryans built no cities, and they were less advanced than their predecessors in most of the sciences and arts. They were superior to the Indus peoples in metallurgy and weaponry, however, and they were skilled in raising horses and in using chariots in war. They grew grains in lands near their villages but they also kept large herds of grazing animals. The Aryans were divided into five tribes, each led by an independent chieftain who was responsible for defense and order. The people of all these tribes had a common ethnic identity, but they were not united under a single political rule.

The Vedas

Though the Aryans had no system of writing when they entered India and remained illiterate for a long time, they brought with them from Iran a tradition of oral poetry and took exceptional delight in their language. By about 1200 B.C. certain groups of Aryan priests had devised methods of memorization to enable them to preserve carefully the poetry then in liturgical use. By about 800 B.C. their religious poetry had been gathered into four collections (*saṃhitās*) that are commonly known now as the four Vedas. Because the texts of the poems were as firmly settled at about this time as if they had been published by a press, we may speak of these Vedas as "books," even though they were imprinted only on human memories and, even to this day, are usually recited from memory rather than read. The entire vedic age, the period during which a single cult and its literature was dominant, ranged from about 1200 to 600 B.C. We shall focus on the nature of the religion at the time the saṃhitās were collected (about 800 B.C.) because that is when the vedic cult had its greatest following.

The Sanskrit in which early Hindu literature is written belongs to the Indo-European language family. The word *Veda* is a cognate of the English *wit* and *wisdom* and means "the (sacred) wisdom (of the Aryans)." By 800 B.C. three collections already had the status and title of Veda: the Ṛigveda, Sāmaveda, and Yajurveda. The fourth collection, independent from these three in its origin and not yet quite established in its content, was already in existence and was soon to be titled the Atharvaveda. Each of these Vedas was preserved by a separate guild of priests.

THE ṚIGVEDA

The Ṛigveda was the liturgical book of the *hotars,* an ancient order of Aryan priests who originally performed sacrifices without the cooperation of any other officiant. The Ṛigveda was formed over three or four centuries, during which time special assistants were asked to take over certain parts of the performance. These cooperating specialists developed liturgical manuals of their own, and the Ṛigveda continued its development thereafter as the hymnbook of the hotars alone. When various aspects of the performance became the responsibility of the assistants, it became the special function of the hotar to recite, at the beginning and at certain key turns in the ritual, one or more hymns in honor of the god or gods. Each verse of these hymns of the hotars was called a *ric,* or praise stanza. The term gave the collection its name: the Ṛigveda (the sacred wisdom consisting of stanzas of praise). The Ṛigveda is made up of 1,028 hymns organized in ten divisions or books. Though the Ṛigveda on the whole is the oldest of the Vedas, its tenth book was added only at the very end of our period, after the Sāmaveda and the Yajurveda had already come into existence.

THE SĀMAVEDA AND THE YAJURVEDA

Compiled later than most of the Ṛigveda, the Sāmaveda is the anthology of a specialist in the musical aspects of the sacrificial ritual, called the *udgātar,* or singer. His *sāmans,* or songs, give this Veda its name. The text of the Sāmaveda consists almost entirely of verses selected from the earlier books of the Ṛigveda, arranged in the order in which the singer needed them as he performed his duties at the ceremonies. The melodies to which the sāmans were originally sung are not known.

The Yajurveda came into existence at almost the same time, to serve the needs of another new participant in the ritual, the adhvaryu. It was his duty to make all the physical preparations for the rite and to carry out all necessary manipulations of its utensils and materials, as well as to move about muttering in a low voice certain short incantations called *yajus* while making the offerings. A yajus is a short verbal formula, usually in prose, in which the priest asserts the meaning and purpose of the ongoing ritual acts in an effort to intensify their power and effectiveness. The yajus formulas give the Yajurveda its name. About half of them are fragments extracted from the Ṛigveda, and about half are new prose compositions.

THE FOURTH VEDA

After the formation of the Sāmaveda and the Yajurveda, the Ṛigveda was completed with the addition of its tenth book. For a century or two thereafter there were believed to be three Vedas, but eventually the fourth collection, which was thereafter called the Atharvaveda, was accepted as scripture.

The Atharvaveda is the collected poetry of the *atharvans,* a separate class of priests who originally had no part in the aristocratic ritual of the hotar, udgātar, and adhvaryu, which we shall now have to distinguish as the *śrauta* rites. The atharvan of the vedic age was a practitioner in a humbler domestic setting, a popular medicine man who aided individuals in their homes with rituals to alleviate personal and family crises. His rituals were usually intended for times of illness, but the atharvan also had materials for protection against demons and sorcerers, spells for securing the affection of lovers and the birth of children, and incantations for luck in throwing dice and for the expiation of sins. Although the atharvan poetry was collected later than the Vedas of the other three priests, it is poetry of a different professional circle rather than of a different age.

The atharvans also lent their services to influential people. For priests they had spells to nullify the much feared consequences of blunders in performing the śrauta sacrifices, and for royal patrons, they had spells to protect them in battle and to guarantee the security and prosperity of their rule. It must have been royal gratitude that enabled them to become, after the earliest period, the Aryan kings' household chaplains (*purohitas*), who supervised the ritual activities of the courts. This powerful office must have helped them gain, in time, their lasting position on the priestly staff that performed the dignified śrauta sacrifices.

Even before the first three Vedas were completed, it had become customary to increase the priestly staff to four. The last was a silent supervisor called the *brāhmaṇ*, who monitored and corrected the acts and utterances of the priests who used the Ṛigveda, Sāmaveda, and Yajurveda. The atharvans secured regular appointment to the office of supervising brāhmaṇ, and then they became able to win recognition of their book as a Veda. It was not possible, however, to put it to liturgical use as a full equivalent of the other three Vedas. The atharvan's poetry had been composed for other purposes and remained in use in its own special sphere of human needs.

The Vedic World View

In the vedic age Hindu India was only beginning its history of serious philosophical reflection. The great Hindu systems of thought did not yet exist. Although some of the great metaphysical questions about humanity and the universe were beginning to be asked, the answers were diverse and undeveloped, as seen in opinions of the time on major topics of concern:

1. *Humanity.* What is the essence of the human being? The vedic age was content with commonsense answers, and its probings into the nature of humanity began with anatomical observations. Seeking that organ or bodily component that is indispensable to human life, a vedic observer perceived that when breath goes, life goes. The discussion of the life essence centered on several words that referred to breath or a similar airy substance believed to permeate the living body. *Vāta,* the world wind, and *prāna,* an internal aerial current of the body, are often spoken of as the basic animating principle. But the favorite term was *ātman,* another word that is atmospheric in its connotations but less concrete in its reference. Ātman was conceived as a subtle substance existing within the human body, yet separable from it. Ātman is essential to one's being; it is one's soul. At death this subtle life-breath leaves the body and rises in the updraft of the funeral pyre to *Svarga,* the heaven above the atmosphere.

The people of the vedic age expected to reach that lofty abode where song and the sound of the flute are heard, and to dwell there after death with their ancestors in eternal light. All were confident that correct behavior and faithfulness in ritual while on earth would enable them to pass through death to Svarga, where all that was best in earthly life would continue. They did not, however, dislike their earthly bodies or long to leave the earth. On the contrary, worshipers often petitioned the gods for life spans of a hundred years and for permanent life in a similar body in an ideal but comparable world. The vedic religious practices were meant to maximize the earthly life, not to replace it with existence on a different level of being.

2. *The universe.* The substance, structure, and origin of the universe did not receive in the vedic age any extended systematic discussion like that of later times. The philosophical satisfaction of understanding the essence of the universe was not so important to the people of this age as the practical satisfaction of being able to control it. But several

basic cosmological ideas were well developed and generally accepted.

3. *The triloka.* One of the commonest analytical conceptions of the Vedas is the understanding of the universe as *triloka,* or the three realms. These realms were understood to be three horizontal strata, one above the other. The lowest was the earthly realm, *pṛithivīloka,* the disk on which humanity lived and walked. The second was the realm of the atmosphere, *antarikshaloka,* in which birds flew and the chariots of the gods were sometimes seen. Its upper boundary was the vault of the sky, impenetrable by the flight of birds or the human eye. Above this vault was a realm of mystery and eternal light, *svargaloka,* the heavenly realm, which was believed to be the home of the gods and the refuge of the blessed dead. When Yama, the Hindu Adam, died, he discovered the path to svargaloka for all men who followed him in time. There, by right of seniority, he presides over the departed fathers of us all. It was Viṣṇu, the god known as "The Preserver," who established these great divisions when he strode out and marked off the entire universe in three of his giant paces.

4. *Ṛta, the basis of order.* All natural actions in this three-layered universe are governed by an impersonal principle called *ṛta.* Ṛta enables natural bodies to move rhythmically and in balance without undergoing the disorganizing and destructive effect otherwise implicit in motion. Because of ṛta we have a cosmos, an ordered universe that undergoes change without becoming chaos. By adhering to ṛta the sun follows its daily path, setting but rising again and continuing to support the world with its light. The stars fade at dawn but twinkle again at dusk. Ṛta is a dynamic principle of order, manifesting itself in change, not in rigidity.

In social affairs, ṛta is the propriety that makes harmony possible in the actions of all living beings. In human speech ṛta is truth, and in human dealings it is justice. When ṛta is observed by human beings, order prevails and there is peace among individuals. In worship, ṛta is the pattern of correct performance. Right ritual maintains harmony between humanity and the gods, humanity and nature, and one person and another.

Ṛta is not thought to be the command of any divine being. The great vedic deity Varuṇa, the guardian of the cosmic order, is the special guardian of ṛta. He punishes those who do not speak the truth or who commit improper actions. Not even Varuṇa, however, created the ṛta. All the gods are subject to it. Ṛta is a philosophical principle, an extremely ancient Indo-European abstract idea that from the beginning was independent of theology. In India the word ṛta was eventually replaced by the term *dharma,* and the conception was modified somewhat, but the principal Indian orthodoxies still retain the original impersonality of Indian ethical theory. In no other aspect of thought are the Indian religions more different from the Semitic religious traditions than in this one.

5. *The ultimate source of things.* The composers of the vedic literature addressed themselves only casually to the problem of the world's origin and final substance. Their tentative stories about cosmic beginnings differed, though most of their speculations included two original entities: the gods, and some material stuff with which the deities worked. As to the nature of the materials the gods may have used, they had no settled answer. Ṛigveda 10.90 traces the main features of the world back to a great primeval sacrifice performed by the gods in which the body of a victim called Puruṣa (primal man) was dismembered, his limbs and organs being used to form the parts of the human and natural world. Whence this Puruṣa may have come and what he was are not explained.

Other speculators used the analogy of sexual procreation, saying that all things had been generated through the intercourse of the Sky-Father and the Earth-Mother, or by a single potent procreator. But the Vedas' scattered efforts to explain the origin of the world in terms of the vedic gods produced no generally acceptable cosmogony.

Vedic polytheism's speculations about the creation of the universe were a negative accomplishment, a realization that the *devas,* or gods, as they conceived them, could provide no answer. Each of the gods was understood to exist somewhere in nature, and many or most were defined by their association with some natural power. Conceptualized as a part of the natural world, the gods could not reasonably be understood to include the creator of the world of which all gods were parts. Even those that were not nature gods were visualized as having spatial locations, and they suffered the same limitations.

A monotheistic solution to the problem of creation was not possible within the existing ideas about divinity. So when the question of ultimate origins was at last pursued seriously in some of the latest of the vedic hymns, the Indian mind turned from personal creators to impersonal processes. At that point a necessary conclusion was drawn: If the gods could not have preceded and created the essence of things, then the essence of things must have preceded and given rise to the gods. After this conclusion was reached, impersonal treatments of the question of world origin became characteristic of Indian thought. One of the earliest and finest expressions of this tendency occurs in a hymn belonging to the last book of the Ṛigveda.

A HYMN OF CREATION (ṚIGVEDA 10.129)

We are reminded of the first chapter of Genesis as we read the Hymn of Creation. Here, too, there is mention of primeval waters and a sense of the tantalizing mystery of an event so removed from us that it is inaccessible to all the usual means of human knowing. As this daring venture of thought proceeds, however, the Indian thinker's mind reveals its own distinctive tendency as it seeks to answer the question, "What moved on the face of that mysterious deep?" Whereas the Hebrew would reply, "In the beginning God . . . ," the vedic poet considered the potentialities of all the gods and sought elsewhere for the aboriginal Reality:

1. *Nonbeing then was not, nor was there being;*
   there was no realm of air, no sky above it.
   What covered them? And where? In whose protection?
   And was there deep unfathomable water?
2. *Death then existed not, nor the immortal;*
   sheen was there none of night and day.
   Breathless That One breathed of its own nature;
   aside from that was nothing whatsoever.
3. *There was darkness hid in darkness at the outset;*
   an unillumined flood, indeed, was all this.
   That Creative Force covered by the void,
   That One, was born by the power of brooding.[4]

Contemplating the state that must have prevailed before the world existed, the seer stresses its otherness from all that is now familiar. Even the three realms (1b)* had not yet been marked out. Neither mortals nor the gods were then there (2a), nor had day and night made their appearance (2b). Where were these things then hidden, and by what (1c)? That they were sunk away in a formless watery emptiness is first suggested tentatively (1d) and then asserted (3b). Life and being were represented in that primeval waste by a solitary Creative Force, vital inasmuch as it breathed, and yet breathing as no living thing breathes now (2c). This single source of what had breath was not a personal God but a neuter It (2c). It was not even eternal but arose in the voidness of things through a natural incubating warmth or perhaps through the intense mental activity of unidentified meditators (3d).

4. *Desire came into it at the beginning—*
   desire that was of thought the primal offspring.
   The tie of being in nonbeing found they,
   the wise ones, searching in the heart with wisdom.
5. *Transversely was their severing line extended—*
   what was there down below, and what was over?
   There were begetters—mighty beings!—
   fertile power below, and potency up yonder.

Out of this pool of undeveloped life the actuality of living beings proceeded through the appearance of erotic desire and then of male and female procreators. The initiating factor again (3d) was power generated by the introspection of meditators whose identity and origin are not explained (4d). In the hearts of these sages, thought gave rise to desire (4b), and this erotic urge became the cord, so to speak (4c), by which creatures were drawn up out of the formless abyss in which they had been hidden. This primal desire was the cord also by which the line of bisexual differentiation was drawn

*The designation 1b refers to the second line of the first stanza of the hymn; 2a, to the first line of the second stanza, and so on.

across the universe (5a), distinguishing creatures into interacting males and females of great creative power (5cd).

6. Who really knows? Who can here proclaim it?
Whence is it born? Whence is this creation?
The gods are later than this world's creation
so who can know from what it came to being?
7. That from which this creation came to being,
whether created 'twas, or not created,
He who is its Overseer in highest heaven,
He only knows—or He may know not!

Here the author confesses that his picture of these remote events is not based on the knowledge of witnesses (6a); the gods, the most ancient of all knowing beings, are themselves the products of these processes and cannot testify to the beginning of things (6c). But the author is not sure that even a supreme god, the present ruler of creation, is old enough to be able to bear witness to that time (7d). His only confidence is that all life proceeded from a single divine source, which must have been of a nonphenomenal nature. Though persons were derived from it, it in itself was so different from everything known that it can be called only "That One."

At the end of the Vedas, many foundations were laid for the later Hindu monistic doctrine called the Vedānta, though the Vedānta system as a whole did not yet exist. For instance, in this hymn the One is not eternal but arose in time (3d). There is no suggestion that the plural universe is in any way illusory or that the world's generation was a devolution rather than a realization of being, and there is no religious longing to return to That One. The question of salvation is not raised.

THE DEVAS OR VEDIC GODS

Each hymn of the Ṛigveda is intended for use in the worship of one or more of the superhuman beings called *devas.* The names of these various gods of the Aryan pantheon appear throughout the texts of the Vedas. They had a central position in ritual and in vedic religion as a whole. In the mind of Aryan worshipers of the time, religion was the approaching of the devas, and if we can understand the meaning of these vedic deities, then we can understand the heart of vedic religion.

Deva is a word derived from the noun *div* (sky), an analysis of which in turn suggests a place of shining radiance. Thus the term deva implies that beings so named belong to the luminous heavens. When the vedic poets reflect on the place of the gods, they share an ancient Indo-European supposition that a celestial abode is normal to them. But the other two *lokas,* or spheres, are not excluded as possible residences of many of the deities. The gods of rain and wind, for instance (Parjanya and Vāyu or Vāta), dwell in the atmosphere; Soma is a god of the earthly realm; and Agni, or divinized fire, resides in all three spheres—earth, atmosphere, and heaven. Each god has a traditional residence in one of the realms, and all members of the pantheon are classified formally according to the realm that is their residence. This classification makes it clear that the gods are thought of as existing somewhere in nature as parts of the natural order, not its source.

Most of the vedic gods can be understood as half-personalized conceptions of the powers that underlie the various dramatic and vital aspects of the natural world. The god Vāta is the power of the wind. Vāta has been depicted as a bearded figure in a running pose. His loose hair flies backward in wild strands, and he clings tightly to the corners of his billowing cloak. Likewise, the vedic poet who speaks of the presence of Agni has in mind the physical presence of fire, whether in a luminous heavenly body or in atmospheric lightning or on the ritual altar. Parjanya is addressed in language applicable to rain and is identified by rain. Sūryā is the sun and is identified with the actual solar disk that traverses the sky. Pūṣan is the sun's light as the revealer of paths and locator of lost things. When the priest in the morning sacrifice faces Uṣas, the goddess of the dawn, it is the dawn itself that he faces as he sings:

We see her there, the child of heaven, apparent,
the young maid, flushing in her shining raiment.
Thou mistress of all earthly riches,
flush on us here, auspicious Dawn, this morning.
(Ṛigveda 1.113.7)

Even Indra, a complex deity whose basic martial character was shaped by the migrating Aryans' pre-Indian experiences, achieved a special importance in India because of his new connection there with rain. Indra was always a deity of conflict, and now, in India, his one remembered combat is his great fight with the demon Vṛtra the Withholder, that is, the withholder of the waters. Assuming that all gods operate or can operate in some sphere of nature, India has invoked this great Aryan fighter-god against the land's most threatening enemy, the evil force that withholds the monsoon.

The worshipers' petitions that one finds in the vedic hymns reveal the extent to which the gods are understood to control aspects of nature. More than reverence is involved. The adorers hope to appropriate for their own needs the extraordinary powers whose presence they apprehend. The poet-priests are quite frank in seeking material boons. In the hymn to Dawn, the composer has not failed to notice that the goddess, as the initiator of each day's hope-filled work, is the auspicious controller of the earth's treasures. A companion hymn to the same deity is explicit in its appeal for help in attaining material success:

Mete out to us, O Dawn, largesses: offspring,
brave men, conspicuous wealth in cows and horses.
(Ṛigveda 1.92.7)[5]

In other hymns we find that such requests are not exceptions, but the rule. For example, the prayer to Pūṣan is addressed to his particular function as a guiding light:

Lead us to pastures rich in grass,
Send on the road no early heat.
Thus, Pūṣan, show in us thy might.
(Ṛigveda 1.42.8)[6]

In the characterizations of the vedic gods, allusion to natural forces is constant. To a great degree, the worship of the gods can be seen to be an effort to live successfully amid the awesome nonhuman forces of the natural world.

This insight does not elucidate the entire vedic pantheon, however, nor is it a key to the concerns of all vedic religion. Particularly, the naturalistic explanation cannot be applied successfully to Indra and Varuṇa, two of the most important deities. Indeed, these two gods are mentioned mainly in connection with activities that are human and social rather than natural. If we can understand them, we can also understand how the naturalistic explanation of the vedic gods must be supplemented.

Indra is called the chief of the gods, and the fact that fully one-fourth of the Ṛigveda's hymns are dedicated to him confirms his importance in Aryan life. But Varuṇa is called the foremost of the gods in almost the same terms. Both hold the high title of *Samrāj*, or Supreme Ruler, and when one of the two is referred to as such, the other is addressed in similar terms. Together, the two form a cooperating pair of rulers whose authority is somehow complementary and comprehensive in its coverage of some important field. Taken jointly, they comprise an authority that is the Vedas' nearest approach to that of a monotheistic God.

But neither Indra's nor Varuṇa's importance rests on a connection with any vital aspect of the natural world. A seat in nature has been allotted to each of them, it is true. Varuṇa's place is the vault of the sky, and he is conceived as being present also in bodies of water. But he is by no means a personification of the sky, nor are his acts mythologizations of natural occurrences in the sky. The sky is only the vantage point from which Varuṇa surveys the deeds of human beings, and he is a water god only to the extent that he inflicts on humans diseases of the bodily fluids as punishments for offenses against truth and right. His connections with nature are too formal and superficial to give him his vast importance among the gods. His actual functions are exercised in another field.

The Indra of the Ṛigveda has a dramatic connection with the rain clouds in the single myth of his combat with Vṛtra. But Indra is in no sense a personification of rain or clouds, nor is his connection with rain old or significant in the delineation of his character. He is not a rain-giving god in any other of his known acts; his battle with the demon of drought is an isolated encounter. The established field of his operations can be found in the Vedas' references to all his other known activities and in our information about the pre-Indian cult of this god as a deity of the Aryans in Iran and Iraq. In

These North Indian coins from the early Christian era preserve the already-ancient conceptions of two vedic deities, the god of natural powers and the god whose function is social. Left, Vāta (also called Vāyu) is the divine presence perceived in strong wind; right, Indra, the old Indo-Iranian god of battles, is shown in full war dress. *British Museum.*

Iran, where Indra was known as Verethragna, he is explicitly a military god. This pre-Indian Indra is remembered and pictured, even a thousand years later, on a gold coin of the Emperor Kanishka. Indra is seen in his original character as the total warrior, in full armor, eagle-crested, and carrying both a sword and a spear. He is the Aryan battle god, a personification of the ideal powers and virtues of the Aryan warrior class (see photograph).

Unlike Varuṇa, the Indra of the Ṛigveda has nothing to do with morality, either in function or in character. Vedic mythology portrays him as a ruffian from birth: an unfilial son, a lecherous youth, and a gluttonous, drunken, and boastful adult. After consuming offerings of thousands of buffalo and after steeling his courage by drinking lakes of intoxicants, Indra lurches off to the wars and there assists his people. He protects them from the power of alien peoples and from demons that cause other gods to flee in terror. His domain is the hazardous area of his worshipers' relations with hostile outside forces. It is enough that he is immensely strong and makes the warrior class effective on the battlefield.

Varuṇa is equal to Indra in rank, but there the similarity ends. Whereas Indra represents the force of arms at the community's boundaries, Varuṇa, his co-ruler, is a force for order who defends the ṛta and guards the harmony of internal social life. His omnipresent spies examine the truth and justice of what men do, and Varuṇa catches the offenders with his mysterious noose and punishes them with disease. Whereas Indra's favor can be bought with offerings of meat and libations of strong drink, Varuṇa will accept only truthful speech and upright behavior. As guardian against anarchy, Varuṇa is the celestial patron of earthly kings, the legitimizer of their authority, and the chief deity addressed in the Aryan coronation ceremony.

Natural danger is not the focal problem in the worship of either Indra or Varuṇa. These two deal, each in his own area, with the dangers raised by the turbulence of human beings, some disrupting the community from outside and some from within. Vedic religion does not deal with natural insecurities only. Like other religions, it addresses its adherents' most acute insecurities, of whatever kind.

The worship of the vedic gods is directed toward three types of insecurity and three kinds of power. The first insecurity is natural insecurity: the danger of natural injury, disease, and want. In this area vedic worshipers supplemented normal human efforts by invoking the many nature gods and by resorting to the atharvans' more impersonal rituals. The second insecurity is moral insecurity, created by destructive individualism within the community itself. In the face of such danger, Varuṇa is worshiped as the guardian of the ṛta, the punisher of antisocial behavior, and the patron of the administration of legitimate kings. The third insecurity is military insecurity, as found in the Aryans' relations with alien political groups. Here the vedic worshipers called out to a god of unbounded force, seeking support and a rallying point in the lawless enterprise of war. In this area, they worshiped Indra, just as in economic need they worshiped the nature gods and for social stability they worshiped Varuṇa.

The gods of the Veda have varying moral natures. Varuṇa is a highly moral deity, whereas nature gods like the solar Savitar are amoral, and Indra as a personification of Aryan might is not moral at all. Because Western religions are now highly specialized in efforts to cope with the moral crises of modern societies, many Western students may find it difficult to understand how vedic worshipers were able to revere any of these deities save Varuṇa. They should remember that most religions, in the past and even now, address a wide range of insecurities. Vedic religion was as broad in its scope as the anxieties of its people.

Rituals of the Vedic Age

Religious practices often reveal further dimensions of a faith. In the rituals of the vedic age, there were three distinct types of ceremony: the family rites of the domestic hearth, the atharvan rites, and the great śrauta sacrifices. We shall attempt to describe the way they may have been practiced in about 800 B.C., a central period in the development of vedic religion. For most of our information we must work backward from literature written several centuries later. These sources are poor in quantity and quality for the first two rituals, but they tell us much about the great śrauta sacrifices.

FAMILY RITES OF THE DOMESTIC HEARTH

The father of the Aryan family performed daily rites at the domestic hearth for the welfare of all the members of his household. With the kitchen fire as his altar, he made libations of milk and offerings of food. These oblations were accompanied by short liturgies which have not survived. Though little is known about these rituals, they were probably simpler forms of the domestic practices recorded later in the *Gṛihya Sūtras* of about 600 B.C. This tradition of family ritual in its continuing evolution produced the formal rituals of Hindu personal life, including the important rites of passage called *saṃskāras.*

RITES OF THE ATHARVANS

At times of personal or family crisis, when hostile powers were believed to threaten, an atharvan was called in to perform a special ceremony at the family hearth. The early sections of the Atharvaveda contain representative spells and incantations of these "medicine men." The following are examples of the liturgical verses that atharvans recited in efforts to dispel several kinds of illness:

Born in the night art thou, O herb,
Dark-coloured, sable, black of hue;
Rich-tinted, tinge this leprosy
And stain away its spots of grey!

Just as the sun-god's shooting rays
Swift to a distance fly away,
So even thou, O Cough, fly forth
Along the ocean's surging flood.[7]

Little is known about the ritual manipulations of these priests other than what we can read between the lines, but it is apparent that the atharvan was often a priestly physician who administered herbal medicines while reciting his spells. He could also frustrate the curses of hostile sorcerers, and perform rites to conciliate enemies and to resolve quarrels between families and villages. By invoking the gods, the atharvan sought to bring into play a magical rather than a personal force. The names of the gods were uttered because the names themselves were thought to have power, not because the personal intervention of superhuman beings was sought.

THE ŚRAUTA RITES

These dignified and sonorous sacrifices were in later times called the śrauta rites because they were the main concern of the *śruti,* that is, the Vedas. This ritual also was focused on a sacred fire—not that of the hearth in a private home but one or several fires especially kindled nearby in an outdoor setting. Originally the officiant was a single priest, but by 800 B.C., a priestly staff of four was customary.

The Pattern of the Śrauta Sacrifice

Let us try to visualize a fairly simple rite as it was performed in about 800 B.C. The sacrificer (*yajamāna*) may be understood to be a rancher of northwestern India who wished to improve his relations with the superhuman powers that most affected his life. He therefore invited to his homestead a certain brāhmaṇ to organize with the help of three other priests a ceremony relevant to his needs.

On the day before the scheduled sacrifice, the adhvaryu priest arrived to make preparations for the rite, bringing in a cart all the necessary equipment: barley meal for the offering cakes, *soma* stems from which libations to the gods would be pressed, strainers and bowls for use in preparing the soma (a sacred inebriating drink), roasting spits and cooking pots, a hand drill for kindling fires, a painted post to which the sacrificial animal would be tied, and a goat.

After talking with the rancher, the adhvaryu staked out a site for the sacrifice, dug a fire pit, and prepared a *vedi,* or altar of earth. In addition, he laid down fragrant grass for the seating of the participants, and set slender poles in the ground and raised a light thatch roof over much of the area.

At dusk the priest led the rancher into this pavilion to begin a purifying seclusion called *dīkṣa*. The rancher's hair and nails were cut, and after bathing, he put on a new garment. Until the rite began, he consumed nothing but warm milk, kept his fingers doubled up like those of a baby, and spoke only with a stammer. As he passed the night watching over the sacred soma plants, he envisioned himself as undergoing rebirth into a state of purity suitable for entering into relations with the gods.

The next day, the adhvaryu with great effort kindled a fire in the fire pit. As the time for the sacrifice approached, a few neighbors gathered to watch the ceremony, though not to participate in it. The sacrifice could be watched by any Aryan, but it was essentially private in nature. The worship was the rancher's, and it was he who was expected to benefit from the ritual acts.

At the appointed hour the three other priests came: the hotar, the udgātar, and the brāhmaṇ. All took their seats on the grass along with the rancher's wife and the rancher himself, who was now allowed to open his fists and speak clearly. The adhvaryu poured into the fire pit a libation of melted butter. As the flames shot up, the hotar began the rite by reciting an invocatory hymn:

Agni I praise, the household priest,
the god and priest of sacrifice,
chief priest, bestower of great gifts.

May Agni, worthy to be praised
by sages ancient and of now,
may he bring hitherward the gods.

Through Agni may we treasure gain
and welfare get from day to day
and honor and most manly sons.

(Ṛigveda 1.1.1–3)

The fire god Agni who dwelt in all three spheres of the universe was now presumed to ascend from the fire and to carry the invitation to the appropriate gods in their heavenly abodes. The divine guests were believed to descend unseen to seats prepared

for them on the fragrant grass. There they were entertained with poetry of a lofty and flattering nature, such as the following hymn to Indra in honor of his great victory over Vṛtra:

I will proclaim the manly deeds of Indra,
the first that he performed, the lightning-wielder.
He slew the serpent, then discharged the waters
and cleft the caverns of the lofty mountains.[8]

Usually the sacrificers praised the god for deeds they wanted the gods to repeat, such as the release of rain upon the earth by Indra.

The udgātar contributed by singing his distinctive songs, the sāmans, verses from the Ṛigveda sung mostly for their pleasing and powerful sound. Meanwhile, the adhvaryu priest moved around and offered refreshments to the gods in the form of food and drink. As he did so, he muttered short prose formulas (yajuses) that explained his actions. The brāhmaṇ did not recite at all, but listened carefully and corrected any errors made by the other priests.

The libations poured into the fire by the adhvaryu for the gods included milk, water, and soma. (The soma plant is said to have been brought down from heaven to grow on certain high mountains and provide ambrosia for the gods' enjoyment. Its stems were pounded on boards, and the juice was then strained and mixed with water to make a golden drink.) When the sacrificers had drunk it, they sensed a divine presence and felt possessed of extraordinary wisdom:

We have drunk Soma and become immortal;
We have attained the light the gods discovered.
What can hostility now do against us?
And what, immortal god, the spite of mortals?
(Ṛigveda 8.43.3)[9]

The adhvaryu offered food to the gods by placing it on the grass or dropping it into the fire, and handed portions directly to the patron and the performing priests. Butter, curds, and cakes were included in the offering. At a high moment, the sacrificial goat was untied from its post, strangled, and cut up. Portions of its flesh were offered in the fire, but most of it was boiled or roasted and eaten by the participants. Every part had to be consumed, either by the sacrificers or by the fire. As the gods were being praised and entertained in these ways, they were often reminded, pointedly, of the needs and hopes of the generous.

When the ritual was completed, the satisfied gods returned to their abodes. The fee for the service (the *dakshinā*) was now presented to the priests. The customary fee was high—no less than a cow was considered acceptable. At this point the rancher bathed and put on his usual clothing. The adhvaryu gathered up the implements of the sacrifice, throwing some into the fire and others into the water. He picked up the strewn grass, tossing it into the fire. The sacrifice was over.

Many kinds of śrauta rites were devised for special occasions and purposes. The *rājasūya* sacrifice, for example, was a ritual for the ceremonial installation of a new king, and the *aśvamedha*, or horse sacrifice was used by kings to challenge any who might contest the boundaries of their realms. The modest *agnihotra* sacrifice was performed in citizens' homes at dawn or dusk in honor of Agni as the god of fire and the patron of the house and family. In the *agnishtoma* sacrifice the gods were offered their ambrosial drink, with much pouring and splashing and dripping, in hope of inducing downpours of rain.

In view of the great variety of rites that had developed as early as 800 B.C., it is not possible to offer a single description that is true to the reality of all. The box on the previous pages presents a general picture of these ceremonies, formed of elements found in many sacrifices.

THE BRĀHMAṆAS AND ŚRAUTA SŪTRAS

Beginning around 800 B.C., the priests of the śrauta sacrifices began to create compositions called Brāhmaṇas, which were loose commentaries on the śrauta sacrifices intended for use in the education of apprentice priests. Brāhmaṇas were composed in great numbers over a period of several centuries by teaching members of the priestly guilds.

After the apprentice priests had learned to recite correctly the Veda of their particular guild, the lectures now recorded in the Brāhmaṇas furnished them with the supplementary information that was deemed essential: the interpretation of obscure passages in the hymns; how to avoid certain common errors in the performances; and the extraordinary powers available through each ritual, especially as performed with full knowledge of its hidden symbolisms by the skillful and learned priests of the particular guild involved. The Brāhmaṇas set forth for the first time the view that the effectiveness of the sacrifice arose from the skill and knowledge of the priests rather than from the intervention of the gods.

Not intended to serve as manuals of performance, the Brāhmaṇas provide only patchy information about the way the sacrifices were carried out. In about 600 B.C., however, such manuals did begin to appear, written in a terse new literary form called the *sūtra*. In easily memorized prose outlines, the *Śrauta Sūtras* give detailed instructions for performing the rites. By collating the sūtras of the principal officiants, modern scholars have reconstructed the actions involved in the rites as they were practiced shortly after 600 B.C., and on the basis of this information, we can surmise what the simpler rituals of an earlier time were like.

Aims and Means in Śrauta Ritual

The liturgies of the śrauta rites reveal clearly what the sacrificers hoped to attain. They sought earthly benefits for themselves as individuals living here and now. Occasionally a king or a family head sought boons that would benefit their subjects or family members as well as themselves. At the horse sacrifice, for example, a king made the following petition:

May the cow be rich in milk, strong
the draught ox, swift the steed, fruitful the
woman, eloquent the youth. May a hero be born
to the sacrificer. May Parjanya grant rain at
all time according to our desire. May the
corn ripen.[10]

The values of vedic worshipers were practical and worldly ones, and the gods were generally regarded as favorably inclined toward dwellers on the earth. The sacrificers hoped to live a full life to a satisfying age. They expected to find acceptance in an enduring celestial home. That happy life hereafter did not preoccupy them, however; they were in no hurry to attain it. Their striving was for the improvement of this life, not its replacement.

How were the sacrifices believed capable of producing these benefits? In vedic times there was a duality of views. The hymns in the earlier part of the Ṛigveda are quite personalistic in their conception of the operation of the rituals. The ceremonies were designed to delight and stir powerful beings who could be expected to respond as pleased persons do, with actions helpful to the worshiper.

As time went by, certain weaknesses in the older theological beliefs became apparent and many priestly thinkers took a less personal view of the gods and the sacrifices. The cosmologist who composed the Hymn of Creation in about 800 B.C. was unable to believe that any of the nature gods existed at the time the natural universe was formed or could have been the initiating force in its creation. Already in this hymn, Indian speculation was shifting toward the conception that an impersonal Being was the cause of the phenomenal world.

Another weakness of polytheistic naturalism appeared when the Indians began to analyze the relationships among the various gods. Persons by their very nature are distinct from one another. But Sūryā, as the sun, could not be kept apart from the other deities that shared in the solar function, such as Uṣas (dawn), Pūṣan, Mitra, and Savitar, or even other sources of light such as Agni, the god of fire. Rain, wind, and flood also intermingle, and thus the nature gods overlapped, interlocked, and became mere aspects of a universally pervasive force when subjected to mature consideration. Under this pressure the author of Ṛigveda 1.164.46 revised the traditional vedic conception of the gods as actual persons:

They call it Indra, Mitra, Varuṇa,
And it is the heavenly noble-winged Garutman;
The Real is one though sages speak of it in many ways—
They call it Agni, Yama, Mātariśvan.

If the personal gods were seen as only the superficial appearances of an impersonal power, then what is to be believed about the reason for the effectiveness of rites in their honor? No one doubted the value of the sacrifices, but Hindus began to believe that their efficacy lay in the technical processes of the rites themselves, rather than in their influence upon divine persons. In this new impersonal view, the sacrificers' business was to understand and control hidden connections between elements of the ritual and cosmic powers that bore the names of gods. Late vedic hymns reflect this intent to manipulate those external forces in statements like "This fire is yonder moon" or "This soma is the sun." Such identifications have puzzled outsiders, who regard them as arbitrary and fantastic. We should note, however, that one of the terms in such equations refers to a cosmic power controlling a vital natural process, and the other term refers to something near at hand that is under the control of the performing priest. By manipulating the elements in the small world of the ritual, the priest tried to manipulate the forces controlling the outer universe. If the moon-shaped sacrificial fire pit, glowing with coals, was indeed the moon, then the skillful priest, while tending the fire, could influence by his manipulations the cyclic movements of the moon, and thus the passage of time, and could gain for his patron a longer life. Similarly, if soma had a secret association with the sun (because of the red crown of the soma plant or the golden color of the liquid), then through the ritual handling of soma one might ensure success in growing the season's crops.

In their search for power through the external connections of aspects of their ritual, the priests became fascinated with powers that might be exercised even through an outreach of their rituals' words. All people perceive that their words correspond to external realities, and structure them, and sometimes cause things to come into existence. Thus it came to be believed that the awesome words of the vedic hymns could have marvelous effects upon aspects of the outer world to which the words referred, and if words referring to small individual things could give one limited and particular powers, words of wider reference could yield more comprehensive powers. An obsession arose in the minds of the ritualists that there might be a word of all-embracing reference that would give them access to power over *all* things.

In this connection, there arose in the late vedic age a fascination with the term *Brahman.* It meant at first a vedic prayer or a holy spell, but in time it came to mean all such liturgical utterances collectively and the Vedas themselves as the comprehensive formulation of powerful sacred sounds.

And since Brahman referred to the collectivity of ritual words, it was assumed to have ties with the entirety of natural phenomena. By the end of the vedic age, it became a favorite term for the source and moving essence of the whole universe. Thus, "That One" of the Creation Hymn found its historic name in Brahman. In discussing Brahman, the priests had in mind practical and not merely philosophical needs. Their doctrine of Brahman as the cosmic Absolute arose in connection with their efforts to exert influence on all parts of the universe and to cope with all crises of human existence through ritual.

In vedic religion the worshipers' own identity with Brahman was not important, nor was any transfer of their being to the level of Brahman involved in their understanding of final salvation. Rather, their speculation about Brahman was the climax of an effort to ensure a successful earthly life. Since the gods could no longer be approached as persons, the worshipers sought mastery over the forces that controlled their lives by manipulating microcosmic extensions of those forces that had been discovered in the ritual. Brahman—the most comprehensive of these correspondents—was to them a mystic verbal symbol by which the whole universe could be moved.

The Vedas in Later Hinduism

The vedic religion had compiled its scriptures and established its practices by 800 B.C. Over the next two centuries, this cult achieved great currency. But by 600 B.C., disillusion had begun in many segments of the population. Those elements of the population who were still loyal to pre-Aryan cultural patterns recovered some of their power and prestige. In direct challenge to the brāhmaṇ priesthood, Jainism and Buddhism arose as independent religions. The followers of these new religions rejected the materialistic goals and the bloody sacrifices of the vedic rituals. But even those who remained attached to the Vedas criticized the animal sacrifices and became indifferent to the worldly gains promised by the vedic priests. Though few questioned the effectiveness of the sacrifices in producing the promised ends, many doubted the ultimate value of the boons ordinarily promised. Many members of the priestly guilds became increasingly fascinated by the mystical contemplation of Brahman as an omnipresent and omnipotent power.

During the sixth century B.C. the old vedic religion was in decline and a new Hinduism was emerging, which will be the subject of the next chapter. Nonetheless, some aspects of the vedic tradition have survived to the present day. The ability to perform the ancient sacrifices has never completely disappeared. There are brāhmaṇs even now who can recite the Vedas from memory. Scholars of the *karma-mīmāmsā* school have continued to debate the problems of correct performance of the rites. Periodically Hindu political leaders have revived the rites as an ancient sanction of their rule or as a symbol of their loyalty to indigenous custom. Study of the Vedas has remained the most honored form of Hindu scholarship.

Although today almost all Hindu Indians follow religious practices that originated after the vedic period, they have not rejected the services of the ancient priesthood. As the old priestly guilds died out, new organizations were formed of brāhmaṇs who were willing to serve as priests of new religious movements and to preserve their vast new literatures. The brāhmaṇ leaders of these newer movements presented them as extensions of the vedic tradition rather than revolts against the Vedas. Although the Upanishads, which will be discussed in a subsequent chapter, reflect a new religious faith with its own approach to the problems of life, they are understood to be a continuation and clarification of the vedic tradition. For this reason they are referred to as the Vedānta (End of the Vedas). The term extends recognition to the Upanishads as the last literary installation of the Vedas and as revealed scripture (śruti) of the highest order.

In time, Hinduism produced radically new scriptures such as the Hindu epics and Purāṇas, which are strikingly different in teaching from the Vedas. Such texts, too, won a place among Hindu sacred compositions, as necessary human recastings of the message of the vedic revelation. Written by historic authors, they belong to human tradition (smṛiti) rather than to vedic revelation (śruti), but they are understood to be faithful restatements with few errors, of the meaning of the revealed books. Very few currents within the broad and diversified river of Hinduism have flaunted a hostility toward the Vedas. In intention, Hinduism is still vedic, and *Vaidika dharma,* the vedic religion, remains one of the terms most widely approved by modern Hindus for the identification of their faith.

Notes

1 Bhagavadgītā 2.55–56. Unless specified otherwise, all extracts from the Bhagavadgītā in Part II were translated by Norvin Hein.

2 Sir John Marshall, *Mohenjo-Daro and the Indus Civilization* (London: Arthur Probsthain, 1931).

3 Mario Bussagli and Calembus Sivaramurti, *5000 Years of the Art of India* (New York: Harry N. Abrams, n.d.), p. 53, fig. 54.

4 All extracts from the Vedas in Part II are translated by Norvin Hein unless specifically identified otherwise.

5 Translated by A. A. Macdonell, *Hymns from the Rigveda* (Calcutta: Association Press), p. 37.

6 Ibid., p. 32.

7 Atharvaveda 1.23.1; 6.105.2. Translated by Arthur Anthony Macdonell, in his *A History of Sanskrit Literature* (Delhi: Motilal Bararsidass, 1965), p. 165.

8 Arthur Anthony Macdonell, trans., *Hymns from the Rigveda,* Vol. 1 (Calcutta: Association Press, n.d.), p. 47.

9 Ibid., p. 80. With the advantage of modern experience we perceive that soma had psychedelic properties. S. Gordon Wasson in his *Soma, Divine Mushroom of Immortality* (New York: Harcourt, Brace & World, 1968) has identified the plant with fair certainty as the mushroom *Amanita muscaria* (fly agaric).

10 White Yajurveda 22.22, translated by Arthur Berriedale Keith in his *The Religion and Philosophy of the Vedas and Upanishads,* Vol. 1 (Cambridge, Mass: Harvard University Press, 1925), p. 290.

3 Classical Hinduism: The Way of Action

In the sixth century B.C. Indian society entered a period of great transformation. The Aryans, who now occupied the entire Ganges Valley, had cleared away the thickets and plowed the fertile plains. Local chieftains ruling loosely over scattered groups of herders were replaced by kings governing from fortified cities. Over the next four centuries these regional kingdoms gave way to vast empires.

In this more settled world the dominant tensions and stresses of life also changed. As the people became dependent on their fields for their livelihood, military and social controls over them tightened, and economic and political relationships hardened into rigid patterns. The new constraints generated new stresses, which led to alterations in religious life. The old sacrifices of the vedic age were all but swept away. Curiously, the brāhmaṇs did not disappear as a priestly class, despite some resentment of the pride and greed that many of them displayed. Eventually the brāhmaṇs emerged from the centuries of transition more influential and more honored among Hindus than ever before.

In the midst of these changes was born classical Hinduism, the religious orthodoxy that has provided a framework for the life of most Indians for well over two thousand years. Indeed, despite innovations introduced by reformers in the last two centuries, classical Hinduism continues to be the dominant religious tradition of India.

New Literary Forms

SŪTRAS

Between the sixth and second centuries B.C. the vedic guilds turned to a new literary form, called the sūtra. A sūtra (literally, a "thread") contains a comprehensive discussion of a subject, expressed in a series of clipped prose sentences intended to be memorized by students in the brāhmaṇ schools. Students used these topical outlines to achieve a rote mastery of a branch of learning. First they learned to recite the sūtra accurately, and next they were taught its meaning through informal lectures.

The earliest of these compositions were the *Śrauta Sūtras*, which contained instructions for performing the vedic rites. Their appearance in this period shows that some brāhmaṇs were continuing to maintain the old vedic sacrifices. Another kind of sūtra appearing at this time were the *Gṛihya Sūtras* (Sūtras on domestic rites), which recorded for the first time the ceremonies performed by Aryans in their own homes. By teaching the correct way to conduct family rites, the brāhmaṇ authors were assuming a new responsibility for showing how persons other than professional priests should perform rites.

DHARMASŪTRAS AND DHARMAŚĀSTRAS

The brāhmaṇs' next compositions were works called *dharmasūtras*. Dharma is an abstract concept meaning "pattern of right living." The dharmasūtras go beyond describing the proper way for Aryans to carry out their ritual duties and show, for the first time in Indian religious literature, a concern for moral behavior as an essential part of one's total religious obligation. Brāhmaṇs belonging to the Āpastambha, Gautama, Vaśishtha, and Baudhāyana guilds began producing dharmasūtras during approximately the same period in which the hymns of Zarathustra and the Hebrews' prophetic books were being written. The dharmasūtras share with Zarathustra and the Hebrew prophets a new sense of the insufficiency of ritual as the sole concern of religious life. The sacredness of ceremony was not denied by the authors of the dharmasūtras, however, and Hinduism has remained to the present a religion of elaborate rites. But the dharmasūtras also stress the importance of ethical behavior and were the first to give instructions in social duty and to require conformity to sacred moral codes. In these writings the brāhmaṇs became the general arbiters of correct behavior of all kinds.

At the end of this formative age, the early codes of the dharmasūtras were recast into expanded verse compositions called *dharmaśāstras*, which were easier to memorize and understand. In time, the dharmaśāstras largely replaced the dharmasūtras as guides to ideal social behavior.

THE LAWS OF MANU

The most influential of all the dharmaśāstras was the *Mānavadharmaśāstra*. Attributed to a sage named Manu, it is known in English translation as *The Laws of Manu*. This code, which was probably compiled between 200 B.C. and A.D. 200, reflects the notions of the brāhmaṇs of that age on how Hindus ought to live. By describing the customs of the most admired classes of society of that time, *The Laws of Manu* established the public norms of classical Hindu society.

Dharma is the pattern of ideal behavior that *The Laws of Manu* and the other dharmaśāstras hold up to Hindus as a moral guide. But just what is meant by dharma? In vedic times ṛta was understood to be the universal moral principle by which all living or moving things operated harmoniously in a changing universe. Dharma is the word that became ṛta's successor in the parlance of a later society. The word ṛta is derived from a root meaning "to run" or "to go," whereas dharma comes from a verb *dhṛi* meaning "to make firm," "to restrain," or "to preserve." Dharma implies therefore a world that is and should be firmly structured. The human world of the new religious ideal of dharma is not conceived to be rightly alterable. Classical Hinduism viewed change as destructive and rejected open innovation.

The Caste System

For over two thousand years the caste system has provided the pattern for Hindu society. Castes—called in Sanskrit *jātis*, or "births"—are hereditary occupational groups that are arranged in an ascending ladder according to popular estimation of the purity and dignity of each group's traditional work.

Firmly hereditary occupational distinctions did not exist among the Aryans prior to their migration to India, and during most of the vedic age, class distinctions were few and flexible. The vedic poems, however, did mention three social classes: the brāhmaṇs or priests, the *rājanyas* or *kṣatriyas* who served as rulers and leaders in war, and the *viś* or common people. Although the sons of warriors and priests generally adopted their fathers' occupations, they were not forced to do so. Sons of commoners were not automatically barred from the priesthood or from military leadership, nor were their various crafts and trades hereditary or assigned sharply different degrees of dignity.

ORIGIN OF THE SOCIAL CLASSES

The earliest indication of a turn toward complex ranking and strong class feeling is seen in Ṛigveda 10.90. This creation hymn tells of a sacrifice in which the giant Puruṣa, a cosmic man with a thousand eyes and feet, became the victim from whose limbs and organs all the prominent features of the world were formed. The social classes of the late vedic time also were thought to have been created from Puruṣa's body:

The brāhmaṇ was his mouth,
His two arms became the rājanya
His thighs are what the vaiśya is;
From his feet the śūdra was produced.

We should note in this verse the appearance of a new, distinctly Indian order of class precedence. In Aryan societies of the Middle East and Europe, the warrior class always occupied the highest level of leadership, but in India the priesthood has from this time onward been supreme and has been the model for much that is distinctive in the standards of Hindu civilization.

In this verse, a new depth of class consciousness is shown: The moderate social differences of earlier vedic times have been sharpened. The Aryans have subjoined to their original three classes a class of menials, the śūdras, who have a lower rank than that of ordinary citizens and whose lot in life is to do the most humble tasks. There are now four social divisions or *varṇas* (literally "colors"), based on occupation. Though all four classes are part of Puruṣa, or essential humanity, they are separated by the quality of their contributions to society. The śūdras are to do the footwork, and the other classes are to carry out functions associated with the nobler parts of the body.

Scholars still have not determined the reasons for this development. It may have been a way to justify the Aryans' control of an indigenous serf population. But the four-class theory of Ṛigveda 10.90 may be only the first hint of the rising influence of surviving pre-Aryan social practice. The new hierarchical tendency may reflect social discriminations long established among the indigenous population.

DUTIES OF THE SOCIAL CLASSES

The author of *The Laws of Manu* cites Ṛigveda 10.90, making its scheme of the four varṇas the theoretical basis for the organization of Hindu society. The book's detailed description of the classical social order, however, goes far beyond the vedic ideal. The varṇas are presented as hereditary, and their inequality in dignity is proclaimed with a new emphasis. There is special stress on the superlative qualifications and rights of the brāhmaṇs, whose duty is to perform sacrifices, to study and teach the Vedas, and to guard the rules of dharma (*Manu* 1.88–101).[1] Because of their sacred work the brāhmaṇs are supreme in purity and rank, and injuries committed against them are punished more severely than offenses against persons of a lower caste. The personal service of śudras is their right at any time. If brāhmaṇs are in economic difficulty, they are permitted to take up livelihoods associated with the kṣatriya and vaiśya classes (*Manu* 10.81 ff.).

The kṣatriyas are warriors and the protectors of society. From this class arose the kings, whose duties are described at great length (*Manu* 7.1 ff., 9.248 ff.). Rulers must heed the counsel of brāhmaṇs in all matters related to dharma. The kṣatriyas may not presume to do the work of the brāhmaṇs, but in time of misfortune they may make their living in occupations designated for the vaiśyas and śūdras.

According to Manu, members of the vaiśya caste are to live by trading, herding, and farming, but trading is their most distinctive work. (In later times they turned over most of their herding and farming functions to the śūdras.) When necessary, the vaiśyas may take up the occupations of śūdras, but they are never permitted to do the work of brāhmaṇs or of kṣatriyas. Like the members of the two elite classes, however, vaiśyas are considered to be full citizens of Hindu society and are allowed to study the Vedas.

Between the vaiśyas and the śūdras is a great social gulf. The śūdras may not participate in or attend vedic ceremonies, and they are strictly forbidden to mate with persons of a higher varṇa. According to Manu, their proper occupation is to serve meekly the three classes above them. The highest possible work of śūdras is to engage in handicrafts and manual occupations. They are entitled to receive the broken furniture, old clothes, and leftover foods of brāhmaṇ households, and they are to be protected from outright starvation. It is improper for śūdras to accumulate wealth, however, and under no circumstances may they assume the work of the other varṇas (*Manu* 10.121 ff.).

PEOPLE WITHOUT VARṆA

Below the śūdras in Manu's picture is an element of Hindu society having no formal place among the varṇas. Manu called them *dasyus*. They are impure groups whose hereditary work is that of hunters, fishermen, leather workers, executioners, and handlers of corpses. Such unclean people must live outside the villages and are not allowed to enter the streets at night. They are to be given food in broken dishes placed on the ground. Hindus are not permitted to associate with them or teach them the dharmaśāstras (*Manu* 10.45 ff.). Though the term dasyu in vedic usage meant "aliens" living totally outside Aryan society, Manu refers to persons living within the brāhmaṇical culture who perform services indispensable to the Hindu communities. They are the groups that have now come to be called "outcastes."

Evidence of the importance of non-Aryan elements in the population is seen also in Manu's frequent references (e.g., in 10.8 ff.) to more than fifty hereditary groups of workers in important manual occupations which he fails to relate satisfactorily to the four-varṇa system. These groups are called jātis, or castes. Each has its own name and its own distinctive caste law (*Manu* 8.41–46). The *jātis* are the basic units of the working population.

In ingenious but unconvincing ways Manu seeks to derive all these castes from the four ancient varṇas. He describes some of their members as being the offspring of forbidden matings between men and women of different varṇas or the descendants of persons expelled from their varṇas for neglect of religious duties. It is clear that Manu and the other dharmaśāstras have tried to synthesize the vedic and indigenous social heritages by accepting the indigenous castes as subdivisions or extensions of the śūdra class of the late vedic society. These workers were added to the bottom of the original Aryan classes in such a way as to create a single social ladder whose top rungs continued to be occupied by the brāhmaṇs, kṣatriyas, and vaiśyas. Although the vedic varṇas remained the theoretical basis of classical Hindu society, the non-Aryan jātis became its core, and some unknown extra-vedic social inheritance provided its most powerful intellectual and emotional components. Thus traditions originating outside the Vedas came to dominate later Indian society.

THE FOUR STAGES OF LIFE

Even within the varṇas and the jātis recognized in traditional Hindu society, there is further distinction of rank on the basis of sex and seniority. According to the dharmaśāstras, life is an upward development through four stages of effort called the four āśramas, which are the formal age groups for males of the three upper classes. (Śūdras, outcastes, and women are not admitted to the āśramas.) Persons situated in each āśrama are expected to defer to those who have preceded them into a higher stage. The four stages are as follows:

The Student Stage Between the ages of eight and twelve a boy of any of the three upper varṇas

The cobbler follows one of the most visible of the outcaste occupations. His usefulness is great, but his social standing low: he handles leather. Because of this sanitary scruple, high-caste Hindus avoid touching shoes with their hands. *Allan L. Price/Photo Researchers.*

is expected to apply to a teacher and submit to a rite of initiation into the study of the Vedas. The student is to live with his teacher, and the teacher is to instruct the boy in the recitation of the sacred texts. In return, the pupil must obey every command of his teacher, rendering such personal services as bringing fuel and water and serving food. He must show respect to the older man, never addressing him from behind or saying anything the teacher cannot hear. He should not listen to complaints about the teacher even if they are true, and when uttering the teacher's name, he must always add an honorific title.

The Householder Stage When the young man concludes his studies, he should marry. In doing so he enters the second āśrama, that of the householder. He must beget sons, and earn a living for himself and his family by work appropriate to members of his caste. In addition, he must give alms to those who have passed into the higher āśramas.

The ideal relations between husband and wife are described in *The Laws of Manu* (5.147–158). The householder should provide the family's livelihood and try to make his wife happy. His kindness, however, is not a precondition of his wife's lifelong obligation to show loyalty and subordination to her husband. As long as he lives, she must do nothing that displeases him. After his death she must devote herself to his memory and never even utter the name of another man. "In childhood a female must be subject to her father, in youth to her husband, and when her lord is dead, to her sons; a woman must never be independent" (*Manu* 5.148). Since women are not understood to have entered into any āśrama or stage of spiritual effort, the dharmaśāstras say little about rules governing their conduct.

Forest Dwellers and Ascetics When a man has fulfilled his duties as the head of his family and sees that his skin is wrinkled and his hair white (*Manu* 6.2), he may leave his home and community and proceed into the higher āśramas of the forest dwellers and ascetics and thus into religious practices to be carried out in the seclusion of the forest. This departure from home can always be deferred until a future life. The move is actually made by only a very small percentage of the men of any generation. But sannyāsa, or the renunciation of the social world, will be necessary, in the end, for all who wish to achieve final salvation.

The distinction between the āśramas of the forest dwellers and the ascetics has never been kept clear in actual practice; the use of the two names merely recognizes that hermits pass through several stages in renouncing the life of the world and understanding mystical truth. A man who is a forest dweller may continue his habitual rituals, but when he enters the fourth and last stage, the āśrama of the ascetic, he stops performing any of the rituals or social duties of life in the world. Keeping only the most basic personal possessions and caring nothing about the comfort or survival of his body, he devotes himself to reflecting on the scriptures called Upanishads. Meditating on the soul in himself and in all beings, he attains detachment from material things and finds repose in the unity of the eternal Brahman; that is, the world soul. Hindu faith holds that this serene state continues beyond death and that those who know it will never return to this world.

For those committed to the quest for salvation, it is maturity in spiritual discipline, rather than birth, that gives them rank. But we see here again the Hindu tendency to view all beings as placed in one or another of the stations of a stratified universe. In one sense, men of the third and fourth āśramas no longer belong to the social order, but in another sense, these hermits constitute the Hindu world's highest aristocracy. Traditional Hindus honor them as advanced persons who have preceded them in doing what all one day must do. Superior to all other people, they are entitled to unique respect and to unquestioning support.

Kṛishṇapuṛ: A Modern Survival of the Caste System

The social pattern of classical Hinduism, as seen in *The Laws of Manu*, was characterized by systematic stratification and assignment of dominance, by inegalitarian conceptions of justice, and by severe restraints upon the freedom of individuals. The choice of occupation and of marital partner was restricted, and the freedoms that were allowed were extended unequally according to rank in the social hierarchy. The unequal service required of the various classes was rationalized by the provisions of divine law. The dignity and wealth of any person depended heavily upon that person's caste.

Leaving home and family behind, this elderly man has become a sannyāsī, or world-renouncer, in response to the ideal of the dharmaśāstras. They recommend that one end one's days as a spirtual seeker, living a wandering life with few possessions. *Kit Kittle.*

We are interested in knowing whether such a social order as this has been the persistent social background for the thinking and practices of the traditional Hinduism that we are about to study. The dharmaśāstras have limitations as descriptions of even the ancient Hindu society of their own time. They focus on the life of the upper castes, and to some extent they express the idealizations of the brāhmaṇs rather than the actualities of ancient life. Furthermore, we do not know, without confirmation from later ages, that the social order described by Manu has been widespread in India and long-lasting. Therefore it is of immense value to us that the general pattern of living that the dharmaśāstras describe has survived and is still available for study. Twentieth-century sociologists have found many traditional rural Hindu communities adhering to dharmaśāstra principles and sharing other ancient characteristics. We shall create from their reports an imaginary traditional village of the present day, which we shall call Kṛishṇapur. The composite will combine the features that are most often reported in sociological studies of living communities.

Kṛishṇapur, which should be thought of as located in the plains of northern India, has about fifteen hundred inhabitants who belong to some thirty castes. Varṇas exist in Kṛishṇapur not as organized social groups, but as categories of social rank with which individuals are connected only indirectly through the varṇa identification of their castes. Public opinion assigns each caste to one of four varṇas or to none. The members of some castes believe that their caste deserves a higher classification by reason of its unappreciated virtues and secret noble origins, but the general opinion of their neighbors compels them to be silent. At certain public events in the village, representatives of the castes are required to participate in the order of their precedence, thus publicly acknowledging their rank.

Most of the inhabitants have heard of the dharmaśāstras, but almost none have read, or could read, those ancient books. They do not attempt to guide their lives by the dharmaśāstras, but rather assume that the requirements of those respected books were long ago incorporated into the local rules governing village behavior. The ancient pattern of the four varṇas provides the community's broad theoretical framework, but the living and dynamic organizations of the village are the jātis that earn their livelihoods by one or another of the village's several dozen specific occupations. In ancient times only the lowest varṇas were thus subdivided, but now it is normal for all varṇas to be subdivided into castes working at specific jobs. We shall use occupational terminology to identify the castes of Kṛishṇapur's social hierarchy.

Among the brāhmaṇs we find a caste of priests who perform the rituals of childhood, a second group who officiate at the rites of adulthood, and a third whose duty is to perform the rituals of death. In addition, a village may have among its brāhmaṇs a geneologist, an astrologer, and a physician practicing the traditional Indian medicine. Most of the kṣatriyas are landowners engaged in farming, though in some villages the brāhmaṇs have taken over this occupation. The third varṇa, the vaiśyas, includes the local groups who keep official records or commercial accounts. Among the vaiśyas are also shopkeepers, moneylenders, goldsmiths, and dealers in grain and vegetable oils. The śūdra castes are the groups that perform manual tasks that are not regarded as grossly impure or morally tainted. Among them are the occupations of florist, truck gardener, mud worker (who makes bricks or looks after irrigation ditches), carpenter, blacksmith, water carrier, herdsman, barber, potter, and tailor. Finally there are outcastes, those who have no varṇa, whose jobs are thought to be sinful or grossly unclean. They include washermen, sellers of liquor, cotton carders, fishermen, leather workers, toilet cleaners, and handlers of dead bodies.

Each caste is represented by a family or a small group of families, and each governs its internal life by its own traditional caste code. The jātidharma mentioned by Manu is an unwritten code that lays down rules for relationships within families, for relations with colleagues of the same caste, and for personal habits. Matters that in many societies are left to personal taste, custom, or etiquette are firmly regulated in Kṛishṇapur. Each caste has its own rules regarding foods that may not be eaten and persons who may not join caste members at dinner or handle food for them. Restrictions on the company in which orthodox Hindus may dine are so severe that few ever eat with any but members of their own caste. Bodily contact with persons of a lower caste communicates contamination to any individual of higher rank, and from such a tainted person some degree of impurity will be spread to other members of his or her caste in the course of normal association.

When a member has undergone serious contamination, he or she must promptly remove the taint by bathing or by more drastic rites. Members must select mates for their sons and daughters from certain families of the same caste according to intricate rules. Caste rules are enforced by a council of caste elders, who punish offenders with fines and social boycotts.

Another kind of unwritten village code prescribes one's duties to castes other than one's own. It covers economic relations, describing in detail the professional services that each caste is expected to render to the households of each of the other castes, as well as the services or goods that are to be received from each of them in return. The code also specifies the bearing and speech that is proper in dealing with persons of higher or lower rank. Economically the castes fall into two broad groups: the food producers and the providers of services.

The principal food producers are of course the farmers who grow the community's grains. The second group consists of the many artisans and laborers who offer the goods and services needed to maintain farms and to equip homes. An ingenious exchange of food, goods, and services is the basis of economic life, rather than money payments. The village code outlines the duties of each worker and the share that he shall receive in the farmers' harvests.

Representatives of the town's more prominent castes make up the village council, which supervises all interactions between the castes. Workers who fail to make the traditional contributions to their clients of other castes are brought before the council. After hearing the complaint, the council can bring a rule breaker into line by ordering all castes to shun the offender and cut off all services to him.

Kṛishṇapur is a restrictive society that limits personal freedom—for example, in the choice of mates and occupations—even more severely than the ancient codes did. The caste and village codes establish an order of precedence so precise that no one in the community has an exact equal. Another person is always either one's superior or inferior. Talent and wealth ordinarily bring leadership in one's own caste, but they do not necessarily give the holder eminence in the village as a whole. Formal precedence belongs to those who are born to it, and economic advantages are distributed unequally. The freedom to enter alternate occupations, just as in the teaching of Manu, belongs to the castes of the upper varṇas alone. The brāhmaṇs and kṣatriyas of Kṛishṇapur have used this freedom to acquire and farm the land, a freedom that has helped them in their struggle to survive and hold power.

For at least two thousand years Hindus have accepted the life of communities structured in this pattern. As the persistent social background of Indian religious thought, this distinctive society has greatly influenced the content of Hindu religion. Sometimes its presence is reflected in the structure of Hindu categories of thought. Sometimes its influence is seen in provision of religious remedies for its special tensions, of compensations for its injuries, and of rational justifications for the social lots that it awards. The explanations of Hindu religious doctrine have allowed this unusual social order to survive and have enabled Hindus to live happily, generation after generation, in one of the most unequal and yet enduring societies that the world has ever known.

KARMA AND REBIRTH

The intimate connection between Hindu doctrine and Hindu society is illustrated dramatically in the case of the belief that human beings are reborn again and again to lives of varied fortune in a course controlled by the moral quality of their accumulated deeds. It is an idea central to Hinduism. With slight variations, it is accepted by Buddhists and Jains. The belief in reward and punishment through rebirth appeared at the same time that the classical Hindu society based on caste was organized. Several Upanishads that describe the concept as a new teaching belong to the period when the dharmasūtras were outlining the new society that restricted occupational choice.[2] From that time onward, karma, rebirth, and the caste system developed in a combination that became the central pillar of classical Indian culture. To understand the doctrine of karma and rebirth solely as a philosophical concept would be to understand only a fraction of its function and power.

In its most rudimentary sense, *karma* means "an action." In ethical discussions it means an action that is morally important because it is an act required or prohibited by the codes of dharma. Karma means, next, the unseen energy believed to be generated by the performance of such a dutiful or undutiful act. Long after the visible act has been completed, this energy continues in existence. At an appropriate time, it discharges itself upon the doer, causing that person to experience the consequences of the original act. Accumulated karma gives to some persons well-merited freedom from disease, sharp minds, good looks, virtuous dispositions, and long lives. It brings the opposite of these benefits to others for equally valid reasons.

Karma is believed to exert itself with particular force at those times in our individual careers when we are about to be reborn into the world. The determination of our rebirth is such an important function of karma that the Bhagavadgītā, which was composed after the Upanishads, described it as "the creative force that causes the rise of the conditions of beings" (8.3). At the moment of our conception in the womb, the moral force of our past deeds is believed to move us, with perfect justice, into a new family and a new caste. Those who have been born into a family of one of the castes of Kṛishṇapur are believed to have been brought to their lot by karma, of their own making, that justifies their rank in the village society.

Some Hindu writers conceive of karma as an energy that becomes external to the doer, hanging over one's head like a thundercloud. Without warning, like a thunderbolt out of the blue, karma descends upon the doer to effect its perfect retribution. Other Hindu thinkers describe karma as a force within the doer that operates via the conditioning of one's disposition and drives, causing those who are in wrong paths to persist in them until they are ruined by natural processes. In a somewhat similar line others have conceived of karma as a deposit of exceedingly fine material stuffs that make up a sheath—the *kāraṇaśarīra,* or causal body—that surrounds our soul. Each separate element in the sheath imparts to us a particular mental or emotional trait that entails a kind of retribution that we must eventually experience.

According to *The Laws of Manu* (12:34–51), our actions alter the balance of the three strands (*guṇas*) of our material makeup. Moral actions increase the dominance of *sattva,* the good strand, and less worthy actions increase the place of *rajas* and *tamas,* the less favorable strands. Shifts in the balance of the strands that are brought about in us by our acts bring changes also, for better or worse, in our emotional and moral tendencies, increasing the likelihood that past moral behavior will be repeated in the future. But even in the case of the wrongdoer, deterioration is not inevitable; by will power, we can resist and correct our evil tendencies. The only inevitability is that we shall undergo the just consequences of the good and evil deeds that we have already done.

Hindus who believe in one God add to such impersonal concepts the belief that good and evil acts bring their proper rewards because of God's knowledge of them. Remembering our deeds with pleasure or displeasure, God sends us at rebirth into appropriate new lives of higher opportunity or further discipline.

The Hindu belief in rebirth according to karma has convinced the people of Kṛishṇapur that their places in society are appropriate and advantageous. Each villager is understood to have a long personal history of good and evil deeds done in former lives, and each one's present situation is seen as not only just, but also as that person's best opportunity for personal betterment. But because of their past deeds and their effects, people are fit only for the particular grade of freedom and responsibility offered by their present caste and sex. To attempt to take on the duties of another social station would be not only unjust but also dangerous, since it would lead to poor performance and even more restricted rebirths in the future. The

Bhagavadgītā warns:

Better one's own duty, poorly done,
Than the duty of another, well-performed.
Doing the work natural to one's self,
One incurs no guilt. (18.47)

Through such explanations, classical Hinduism has won general acceptance of the caste system's strict controls and has made its culture a lasting one.

THE COSMOLOGY OF KṚISHṆAPUR

The horizon of the villagers extends far beyond the boundaries of Kṛishṇapur and far beyond the visible world. The geography about which they are most concerned is not horizontal but vertical, for they inhabit a universe conceived as ladderlike in structure and almost infinite in its heights and depths. They contemplate the possibility of residence, after death, in levels of the universe far beyond the highest and lowest ranks of their village society. The vedic faith in svarga has evolved into belief in many heavens and hells in which exceptionally virtuous or vicious persons will experience the agony or bliss that is their due.

The Laws of Manu (12.40 ff., 4.87–90) states that those whose bad behavior during life was dominated in various degrees by the strand of darkness (tamas) will receive appropriate treatment at rebirth. The less base are reborn as the nobler animals—elephants, horses, lions, tigers, and boars. The worse are reborn as lesser animals—tortoises, fishes, snakes, lizards, and spiders. Stealers of meat become vultures, and thieves of grain are reborn as rats. Other sinners may come back as grasses, shrubs and creepers, or in immobile states. The very sinful are condemned by Yama, the judge of the dead, to dreadful hells where they are scorched in hot sand, boiled in jars, or devoured by ravens. Manu mentions twenty-one hells, one below the other, through each of which the wicked must work their way upward.

Above the human world there are pleasant celestial realms where meritorious beings dwell, some as the superhuman *gandharvas* and *apsarases,* the musicians of the gods. Above them are the luminous abodes of the sages and ancestors, the various heavens of the ordinary gods, and finally *Bramaloka,* the heaven of Brahmā the Creator, which Hindus who believe in many deities think of as the highest heaven.

The later Purāṇas elaborate the picture of these afterworlds with endless detail, but with little consistency or authority. Popular Hinduism is united only in a general conviction that the processes of moral retribution are vast in extent and very thorough.

The Ceremonial Duties of Classical Hinduism

In the postvedic age new rituals were devised that have proved to be exceedingly durable. They may be looked upon as the counterpart in ritual of the new economic and social observances that survive in Kṛishṇapur.

THE CONTINUING TRADITION OF THE ŚRAUTA RITES

Although the śrauta sacrifices diminished in popularity during the sūtra age, they never entirely lost their following. A few priests have continued to perform them, and a few scholars have continued to study the problems of performing them correctly. The discipline of these scholars of the ritual is called *karma-mīmāṃsā,* which means the "investigation of [vedic ritual] acts." Between A.D. 200 and 1600 comprehensive works on these matters were composed by Jaimini, Prabhākara, Kumārila Bhaṭṭa, Āpadeva, and Laugākshī Bhāskara. The scholars of this school who studied the Vedas intensely for their own special purposes became the recognized Hindu experts in the interpretation of the Vedas for *any* purpose, and finally the authorities on correct methods in the study of all Hindu sacred texts. In these wider capacities they laid down some of the foundational principles of orthodox Hinduism.

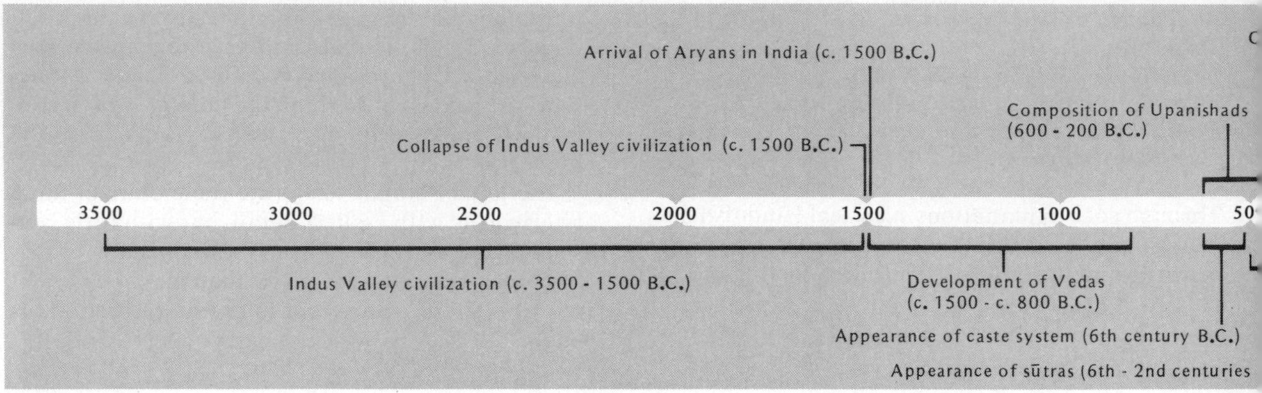

Scholars of the karma-mīmāṃsā school established the orthodox position on the nature of revelation in Hindu scriptures. As atheists, they could not understand the Vedas to be commands uttered by any God or gods; yet they did consider those scriptures to be a Word of superhuman origin, a self-existent divine Sound that reverberates eternally in the celestial realms. At the beginning of each new eon, as the world emerges again from cosmic dissolution, certain great sages hear that Word and utter it, thus introducing the Vedas again into the stream of human religious knowledge. As scriptures thus heard by the sages, the Vedas are called śruti—the "heard" or the "revealed"—and are the highest form of scripture. Because of their unique divine origin, they are infallibly true in every word.

One might expect that this insistence on the verbal authority of the Vedas would make Hinduism a fundamentalist religion, rigid in its creeds and ethical codes. But in fact Hinduism is tolerant of a wide variety of beliefs and teachings. The theorists of the karma-mīmāṃsā school took the position that the revealed scriptures had to be restated periodically by human sages in the language and terminology of postvedic times. In every cosmic age, they say, the message of the Vedas must be recast in mediating scriptures called *smṛitis,* which adapt the eternal teaching to the poorer capacities of humanity of the later ages. The religious writings of the smṛiti class, as human compositions, are not of unchallengeable authority. But they are revered as the works of ancient wise men who were learned in the Vedas. This karma-mīmāṃsā teaching explains the Hindu respect for newer writings like the dharmaśāstras and the Bhagavadgītā.

Another emancipating principle of the karma-mīmāṃsā scholars is their theory of scripture interpretation. It is called the principle of the *mahāvākyam* (the major statement). This means that when a scripture seems to contain contradictions and its teaching is unclear, puzzled students must first find the statement expressing the scripture's central message. According to the karma-mīmāṃsā scholars, the organizing theme of the Vedas and the Upanishads (which they regarded as part of the vedic literature) was the command to perform sacrifices. Portions of the Vedas and the Upanishads that appeared to have some other purpose, such as answering philosophical questions, had the actual function of preparing minds for the intelligent performance of the sacrifices. They saw such a supportive purpose also in the mythological passages of the Vedas. But Hindus of subsequent times whose interests have been utterly different from those of these ritualists have been free to perceive the heart of the Vedas in other passages of mystical or ethical or other import. This principle has often helped Hindus explain perplexing texts. More important, it has permitted Hindu thought to develop

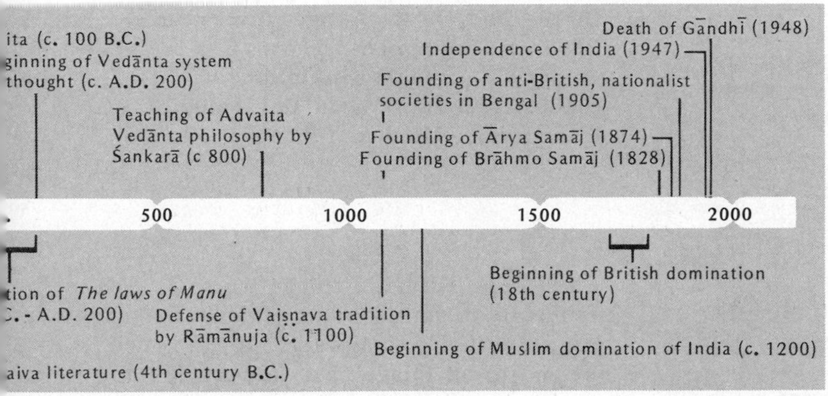

TIME LINE

HINDUISM

in any direction so long as a starting point can be found in the heritage of the past.

THE DOMESTIC CEREMONIES OF CLASSICAL HINDUISM

Soon after the sūtra style of composition had been developed, vedic guilds used this convenient literary form to record the approved ritual practices of the Aryan home in works called *Gṛihya Sūtras* (sūtras on the domestic rituals). Even today the brāhmaṇs of Krishṇapur who perform these ceremonies or instruct laypersons in how to perform them use modern compositions that cite the *Gṛihya Sūtras*. The modern manuals use ancient scriptures selectively along with amplifications introduced by commentators over many centuries. We shall describe some of the ancient domestic rites that are still in use today.

The Sandyhās (Meditations of the Twilights) The sandyhās are personal meditations designed to be performed at the important transitional hours in the sun's daily passage—dawn, noon, and evening. The dawn meditation still survives among devout high-caste Hindus, who rise for this purpose in the first light. After bathing, cleaning the teeth, sipping water, and applying to the forehead the cosmetic mark (*tilaka*) of their sect, they spend a few moments in formal breathing exercises (*prāṇāyama*). Just before the rim of the sun appears on the horizon, the worshiper stands and recites, until the sun actually rises, the lines of Ṛigveda 3.62.10:

Let us meditate upon that excellent glory
Of the divine vivifying Sun;
May He enlighten
Our understanding.

In the final moment of the rite he pours out from his joined palms an offering of water to the Sun.

The Pañcamahāyajña (The Five Great Sacrifices) Each family is asked by tradition to perform, through one of its members, daily rites in honor of five kinds of beings: the gods, the spirits, the ancestors of the family, humanity in general, and Brahman (that is, the Vedas). As prayers and bits of food are offered, worshipers are to mind their duty to revere all these venerable realities.

The Saṃskāras (Rites of the Rounds of Life) The saṃskāras mark the important transitions in the lives of Hindus of the three highest castes, from the moment of conception to death. They enable families to surround their members with affection and to try to protect them from harm at times of change. These rituals are performed in the home, usually near the family hearth. Even funeral ob-

On the banks of the Ganges River near Banāras, a worshiper performs a sandhyā, a personal meditation conducted at dawn, noon, or evening by high-caste Hindus. *Kit Kittle.*

servances, which reach their climax at the cremation site, begin and end at the home. Brāhmaṇs are usually called in to perform the most important of these rites today, but the father and the mother are the primary actors in these performances, and the father himself may officiate at them if he knows how. Apart from funerals, almost all these observances are happy occasions marked by a joyous gathering of relatives.

Today many of the ancient rites have dropped out of use. But the traditional marriage and funeral ceremonies are still part of every Hindu's career, and most of the other saṃskāras are still practiced by a minority of high-caste families. (A description of the main saṃskāras is provided in the box on the following pages.)

The Pūjā (Ritual of Image Worship) The most frequently performed of all Hindu ceremonies is a form of ritual worship called pūjā, which is addressed to an image of a deity. In the postvedic age, as dissatisfaction with the vedic sacrifices increased, pūjā took the place of the costly vedic yajña as the most common approach to the Aryan gods. The use of idols—pūjā's main innovation—is of uncertain origin. Images made of perishable materials appear to have been worshiped in shrines in the time of the *Gṛihya Sūtras,* and images of stone surviving from the second century B.C. are firm evidence of the prevalence of the new ritual at that time. In vedic times the gods were thought of as beings living on high, who might be induced to come down to visit human beings for a short time as guests at sacrifices. The innovation of which we speak arose in connection with a belief that the celestial deities, if properly approached, could be induced to adopt earthly residences and thus become more permanently available to their worshipers.

To enable a particular celestial being to descend and remain on earth, first a sculptor has to create a form displaying the known features of the deity. Then, in a special rite usually called *Prāṇa-saṃsthāpana* (establishing the vital breath), a skillful priest must invite the god or goddess to descend into the image. By means of the rite of installation, an image becomes a special locus of the divinity and a place where worshipers have easy access to the god. As long as the descended gods are cared for and honored, they are believed to remain on earth. But they cannot be neglected: They must be given personal care and be entertained with offerings of food and drink. The provision of these necessities through a daily routine of rituals is the basic activity in pūjā. If the services are not given or if the image is not protected from the weather and from affronts, the deity will abandon the image.

In pūjā as in the vedic sacrifice the object of worship is a single deity or at most a pair, and the worship is not that of a congregation, but of an individual offering worship for personal reasons or for the benefit of a household. The types of gain sought in the earliest pūjā that we know about were the same as those pursued in the older yajña: health, wealth, safety, and blessed afterlives in heavenly places. But in accordance with the new cosmology, the desire to accumulate good karma was soon added.

One of the most common sites of pūjā is the shrine of a private home. At least once a day the image, which is kept in a niche or cabinet, must be accorded the proper rites. In wealthy homes the performer may be a brāhmaṇ who is a professional chaplain, but in ordinary households a member of the family performs the function. Near the image are stored certain utensils: a vessel for water with a ladle for purifying the area with sprinklings, a bell, an open oil lamp or incense burner to be rotated before the image, and trays on which flowers, fruit, cakes, or cooked meals may be offered. In the morning the deity is roused from sleep, bathed, dressed, perfumed, wreathed with flowers, and offered breakfast. At midday a meal of hot cooked food may be offered. In the evening, supper is set before the deity, an evening song is sung, and a courteous goodnight wish is expressed.

The Hindu Temple and Its Rituals

The most exalted setting for pūjā is the public temple. For two thousand years the creation of temples and the images housed in them has been the principal outlet of Hindu artists. The great temples of India are so ornate that their fundamental plan is not easy to perceive. At the heart of a Hindu temple is a small, rectangular, windowless cell called the *garbhagṛiha* (inner or womb house). This cell houses the image of the deity of the temple and is its holiest spot. Entrance to the cell is by a single door whose threshold is crossed by few except the *pūjārīs* (professional priests) who attend the image. There is no pulpit, no preaching, and group worship is rare. Visitors wishing to make reverential circumambulations of the deity may do so by walking around the outer walls of the cell.

The second architectural feature of the Hindu temple is its *vimāna*, or spire. Usually roundish, the vimāna caps the central cell and suggests by its circularity and elevation that the sky is the true abode of the deity who now dwells temporarily beneath it. A third architectural element is the temple's porch (*maṇḍapa*). This porch may be nothing more than a small stoop to protect the doorway of the cell from the sun and rain, but it may be expanded to include standing space for visiting worshipers who come to salute the deity or to watch reverently while priests present offerings on the worshipers' behalf. At those centers of pilgrimage where there are many visitors, the maṇḍapas become waiting rooms and audience halls much larger than the garbhagṛihas.

At such great shrines there are also musicians who give concerts in the maṇḍapa for the enjoyment of the deity and the worshipers. Here the mythological exploits of the god are told in song, recitation, or pantomimes performed by dancers. At certain times of the day, the garbhagṛiha with its image is opened to the view of all visitors who have come to enjoy the blessing of *darśana*, or sight of the deity, or to offer their salutations and gifts and petitions. Other times are reserved for the god's or goddess's nap, or for "strolls" when the priests carry a small duplicate of the main image through the temple courtyard or streets.

The construction of a temple is sponsored by a single donor of great wealth, who is thought to generate very great and lasting merit by such an act. Temples remain under the control of their builders and their heirs or trustees, who have the right to appoint the head priest (*mahant*) and his staff and to receive the offerings of worshipers; but temples are public institutions in the fact that any Hindu may enter and worship there. Unlike vedic wor-

The round of the saṃskāras begins with a ceremony called *garbhādhāna* (impregnation), which is intended for the moment of a child's conception. The next rite is a *puṃsavana* (male-producing rite) prescribed for the fourth or fifth month of a wife's pregnancy and thought to ensure the birth of a male child. Also during pregnancy there is a charming rite known as the *sīmantonnayana* (parting of the hair). The husband applies to the parting line of his wife's hair a red cosmetic powder believed to protect against malignant spirits that make pregnancy dangerous. The setting is the family hearth, where the husband sits down beside his wife and uses a porcupine quill or the shaft of a spindle as a rude comb for making the required part.

The *jātakarman* (birth ceremony) includes a host of practices intended to help the mother through the dangers of labor. A brāhmaṇ comes and examines all the ropes and cords in the house, for the purpose of untying all the knots they may contain. The father is kept busy with a series of subordinate rituals to ensure that the baby will be intelligent, strong, and long-lived. The safe arrival of the child is celebrated by distributing alms at the door and giving gifts to friends and brāhmaṇs. The *nāmakarana* (naming) is a ritual that usually follows in about ten or twelve days. In consultation with a family brāhmaṇ who knows the rules of Hindu name formation, the parents select for the child a secret and a public name. The father announces the public name to an assembly of guests who include brāhmaṇs and relatives and the family ancestors, as unseen presences. All, including the ancestors, then join in a feast.

In the sixth month after a child's birth, the *annaprāśana* (feeding ceremony) is held. The principal performer is the baby, who takes its first bite of solid food. Then the gathered adults celebrate the child's accomplishment by eating an elaborate meal themselves. The first haircut, which usually takes place in a male child's third year, becomes a formal celebration known as the *cūḍākaraṇa* (queue-forming ceremony). The child is held in the mother's lap while the nervous father takes a razor and makes the first few shearing strokes. Then the firm hand of the family barber finishes the trim, leaving only the sacred tuft, the *cūḍā*, at the crown of the head. Many males continue to wear the cūḍā all their lives as a mark of a high-caste Hindu man.

The *upanayana* (initiation ceremony) is one of the great events of Hindu boyhood. It is the ritual occasion at which a boy is presented to his religious teacher to begin instruction in the Vedas. Undergoing the upanayana entitles a boy to begin the life of an upper-class Hindu. Before his initiation into vedic study his rank is equal to that of a śūdra, and if the upanayana is not performed he will remain a low person, not entitled to participate in rituals involving vedic texts or to marry a girl from a family comparable to his own. The upanayana should be performed when a boy is between the ages of eight and twelve, and it must be performed before he is twenty-four.

The essential parts of the ceremony are the meeting of the boy with his brāhmaṇ teacher and the beginning of instruction in the correct recitation of the Vedas. The boy spends the night before the ceremony in complete silence. At breakfast he sits with his mother at a meal for the last time; henceforth he will eat with the men of the family. He then bathes and is led to a canopy under which his teacher waits. The boy formally accepts the man as his guru, or personal religious preceptor. The guru drapes over the boy's shoulder and chest a circlet of sacred thread (*yajñopavīta*) to be worn always thereafter as the second necessary mark of a twice-born Hindu man.

The boy then begins his study of the Vedas, through which he will be "born again" spiritually into the heritage of vedic learning and become a member of one of the twice-born varṇas (a brāhmaṇ, kṣatriya, or vaiśya). Even if—as is usual now—his vedic studies proceed no further, he is no longer a boy in religious matters, but an adult and a member of an elite.

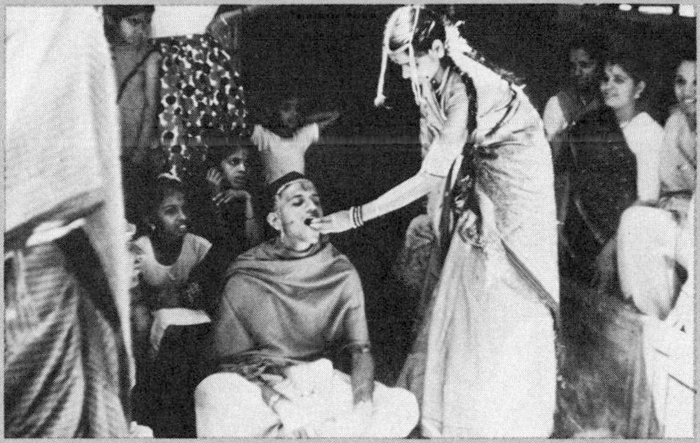

A moment in a Hindu wedding. A ceremony involves many symbols of the undertaking of new obligations. One of the wife's duties is to feed her husband and family, and this is charmingly prefigured in the episode shown here. *James Martin.*

The Hindu wedding (*vivāha*) is a group of social customs focusing on a central uniting sacrament. The first action is the parents' search for a suitable match. The parents make their choice and solemnize it in a formal betrothal of their children, and then they decide—with the help of the family astrologer—on a favorable day for the marriage ritual. On that day the bridegroom travels in procession with many friends and relatives to the bride's house, where he is received with formal honors. The rites that follow are conducted by a brāhmaṇ priest who specializes in weddings. The prominent elements in the proceedings are intended to unite the new couple visibly, to sanctify their union with a commingling of divine energies, and to assure that their life together will be long, fertile, prosperous, and undisturbed by harmful superhuman influences.

Standing before the fire that is the visual focus of the ceremony, the groom clasps the bride's hand and says, "I seize thy hand . . . that thou mayest live to old age with me, thy husband." The bride places her foot on a stone to symbolize the firmness of her resolve. The ends of their flowing garments are knotted together, and they then enter into the ceremony's climactic and binding act: walking arm in arm three times around the sacred fire, each time in seven steps. The groom then touches the bride over the heart, saying, "Into my heart will I take thy heart; thy mind shall dwell in my mind." He paints on her forehead the vermillion cosmetic mark of a married Hindu woman. To symbolize their union, they eat a common meal while sitting together, though such commensal eating will not be their general practice as husband and wife. On the evening of their wedding day the two go out under the sky and look up together at the unchanging Pole Star, their model in a marriage that is indissoluble.

When in a home a mature person has died, an observance follows that is called *aurdhvadaihika,* the rite of the translated body. Within a few hours a procession of hurriedly summoned relatives and friends starts to move toward the local cremation site, led by the eldest son of the deceased as the chief mourner. The body is carried on a litter. The sorrowing marchers cry out the name of the god Rāma or sometimes the name Hari (Viṣṇu). At the cremation ground, the body is laid on a pyre of wood constructed according to strict rules. The son then performs the difficult duty of setting the pyre aflame with a firebrand that has usually been carried from home. He prays, "O Fire, when the body has been burnt, convey the spirit to its ancestors." The mourners return in a group toward their homes, without looking back, and they bathe in their clothing before entering any dwelling.

The last of the family rites are the *śrāddhas,* postmortem ceremonies performed at home to honor and benefit the deceased. For the refreshment of departed parents, balls of rice and libations of water are offered and accompanied by the recitation of texts expressing respect and concern. Such ritual offerings are made monthly for a year. Annually thereafter on the anniversary of the death, the parent and all remoter ancestors whose names are remembered are honored in śrāddha rites. The śrāddhas support in Hindus a continuing sense that a host of unseen witnesses observes their behavior and follows their fortunes with deep concern.

All Hindu temples, both old (above) and new (right), possess the porch for shelter of worshippers and the spire rising above the cell where the icon of the deity is kept. *James McKinsey; Religious News Service.*

ship, participation in temple worship has always been open to śūdras, and since India became independent, this privilege has been extended by law to outcastes as well. But in other respects the temples do not express the collective Hindu life. As a rule, they are built by individuals, not congregations, and worship in them is the worship of individuals.

Pūjā is understood in many ways, and it is performed for many purposes, self-interested and self-sacrificing. Some seek earthly favors through the deities' goodwill, which has been won through human gifts. Others seek, by the merit of their worship, to attain after death a more fortunate rebirth on earth or in blessed realms above. When in postvedic times a longing arose for eternal liberation from rebirths, pūjā became a form of expression also for salvation-seeking persons. Those who hoped for liberation through the power of a personal God found in pūjā a means for expressing their devotion and sense of dependence. Hindu monists of the Advaita school do not hope for salvation through the worship of God or of gods, nor do they believe images to be true representations of the impersonal and all-inclusive Divine Reality; but they too have often frequented temples, seeking mental discipline in conforming to their rituals and seeing hints of the unity between self and universe in correspondences between the form of the worshiper, of the temple, and of the overarching sky above it.

Rites of the Village Godlings

In rural India another ritual tradition survives. The deities involved are minor beings unknown to Sanskrit literature, and therefore our information comes from observing Hindu life. Travelers approaching a typical Hindu village on the plains of northern India may see beside a well a pile of stones daubed with red paint. Elsewhere along a country path there may be a conical mound of earth into which a red pennant has been thrust, and fragments of coconut shell nearby indicate that the village people sense an unseen presence there that requires offerings. In central and southern India adobe cells are found, containing mud figurines. They are shrines of local godlings who must be worshiped in their own humble abodes.

These godlings are thought of by many village people as destructive natural forces that from time to time disrupt the security of village life. Human afflictions of unknown cause are believed to be the work of such local spirits who have been offended. When there is a calamity in a community because of the offenses of careless persons, someone with shamanistic gifts must be found to make contact with the irritated spirit. After the identity of the spirit and the cause of his or her anger are discovered, the villagers are told what rites and offerings must be made to appease the vengeful deity.

Many of these spirits are believed to be female. The most powerful fall into two major classes: the goddesses who protect particular villages, and the "mothers" who inflict particular diseases, blights, and other kinds of harm. The rites addressed to the village godlings are pūjās in general outline, but they belong to another tradition and differ from all the pūjā rituals described so far. The officiating priest is not a brāhmaṇ but a low-caste person, often the local washerman or toilet cleaner. The liturgical language is not Sanskrit but the local vernacular, and most of the sacrificial offerings consist of materials loathed by brāhmaṇs. The animal victims are often of species never used in vedic sacrifice, such as chickens or pigs, which are believed by the orthodox to be unclean. Deliberate cruelties are sometimes inflicted on these animals (in fact, the human participants sometimes inflict agonies on themselves) in an apparent effort to satisfy the demands of the goddesses through sufferings less grave than the loss of human life. The aim of such rites is solely to avert dangers; no notion of salvation is involved, or even of generating merit.

It may be tempting to identify these rituals with magic rather than with religion, but the rites are religious in nature to the extent that superhuman beings are addressed by ritual. Another factor is present that is often considered to be a characteristic of religion: social concern. In the worship of these deities, the usual individualism of Hindu religious activity is set aside in collective action to meet a common crisis, and local populations are drawn together in a rare unity. During the short span of these gory performances, the fragmented Hindu village becomes a community in the fullest sense of the term. Thus, although these cults are often called forms of "lower Hinduism," in one respect their achievement is high. Today, however, this village religion is on the wane, giving way to the more effective remedies of modern science.

The Place of Religious Practice in Hinduism

Hindus' religious duties, as we have seen, fall into two classes: ritual obligations and social or moral obligations. Hindus do not regard the distinction between moral and ritual duties as important; their aim is simply to fulfill the requirements of dharma, a term that covers all the acts required by tradition. All the duties described in this chapter, whether ritual or social, are alike in that they are viewed as the direct or indirect requirements of the holy Vedas. The householder's offerings of water to his ancestors, the morning worship of a wife at her domestic shrine, the activity of a king in defending his realm, and the work of a potter in shaping his clay all are sacred duties, all produce merit or demerit, and all determine the future of the doer, for good or ill.

In vedic times Hindus believed that, through the pleasure of the gods, the observance of the traditional duties would surely lead to an immortal life in the heaven of their ancestors. But Hindus in postvedic times conceived the process of reward more mechanically, in terms of the accumulation of karma, and concluded that eternal blessedness could not be earned by good deeds, however many and however great. The good karma produced by one's deeds will remain finite in quantity, no matter how long the life of virtue is continued. Final liberation is infinite in length and infinite in worth, and in a just universe, one's merit, which is always finite, cannot deserve or attain this infinite reward. Those who embrace the concept of retribution inherent in the doctrine of karma have been forced to conclude that good actions alone cannot bring final salvation from the round of births and deaths. At most, good actions can lead to blessings in this life and, in future lives, to long existences in elevated and happy worlds. Thus Hindus joined thinkers of many other religions who have held that salvation cannot be obtained by good works alone.

Desolated by this loss of hope, Hindus in postvedic times groped for new paths to a life beyond all deaths. In time they established their classical plans of salvation: the Way of Knowledge (*jñānamārga*) and the Way of Devotion (*bhaktimārga*). Those seeking eternal beatitude shifted their hope from the life of religious duty to one of these new paths. After the Way of Knowledge and the Way of Devotion were recognized as divisions of Hindu life, the older discipline of the customary duties was also thought of as a *mārga*—the *karmamārga,* or Way of Action. It is the Hinduism of the Way of Action that we have been examining until now.

The conception of the three mārgas is one of the favorite Hindu formulas for identifying the distinctive forms of Hindu religious life. We shall use its categories to outline the subject matter of the next two chapters. In using the idea of the three mārgas we should not suppose, however, that all three ways begin at the same point, or lead to the same destination. All Hindus are born into the pattern of customary living that makes up the karmamārga, and all travel on this way in their early years. Ideally, they become aware in time that the karmamārga does not end in salvation but in rebirth, and they consider taking up one of the two paths that do promise salvation.

These personal transitions from the way of duties to a way of salvation are often gradual and hidden: The status of a person is not easy to discern. It is not possible to divide all Hindus clearly into three definite groups according to mārga. Most Hindus, moreover, participate in two of them. Millions continue to perform faithfully all the duties of the karmamārga; yet they have made a strong commitment also to one of the two ways of salvation and have begun to cultivate its disciplines. And in the understanding of the Way of Devotion, the requirements for liberation can be met while remaining completely faithful to all the duties of the Way of Action. The concept of the three mārgas is more useful in distinguishing types of Hinduism than in separating individual Hindus into types.

Notes

1 All references to and translations from *The Laws of Manu* in Part II refer to G. Bühler, trans., *The Laws of Manu,* vol. 25, Sacred Books of the East (Oxford, England: Oxford University Press, 1886).

2 Chāndogya Upanishad 5.10.7 and Bṛihadāraṇyaka Upanishad 3.2.13; 4.4.5; 6.2. Unless specified otherwise, extracts from the Upanishads have been translated by Norvin Hein from the Sanskrit texts published in S. Radhakrishnan, *The Principal Upanishads* (New York: Harper & Brothers, 1953).

4 Classical Hinduism: The Way of Knowledge

The understanding that knowledge gives power is common to many religious traditions. Hindus who follow the Way of Knowledge (jñānamārga) seek an exceptional kind of knowledge, to solve an unusual problem. They observe that ordinary factual knowledge of the things of this world provides no access to eternal life, but only to things that change. The Hindu sage therefore seeks to transcend the knowledge of phenomenal things and achieve a mystical knowledge of reality as a whole, that will yield mastery over all things, and thus mastery also over the deepest problem of life. As the *Mārkandeya Purāṇa* explains it:

> One who thirsts for knowledge thinking "This should be known! *This* should be known!" does not attain to knowledge even within a thousand *kalpas* [cosmic ages]. . . . He should seek to acquire that knowledge which is the essence of all, and the instrument of the accomplishment of all objects.[1]

Esoteric Knowledge in the Vedic Age

By the end of the vedic period the priests of the vedic rituals no longer conceived of the gods as personal beings who granted favors in response to offerings. They had come to believe that the effectiveness of the vedic sacrifices sprang from their own perception in the rituals of occult extensions of important cosmic powers. They believed it was by their manipulation of these secret presences that the boons were obtained that had been thought of as gifts of the gods. In its continuing development, this tendency took two directions:

1 *The priests searched for keys that would unlock wider and wider aspects of the universe.* They were fascinated particularly with the possibility that a particular key, if found, might give access to the reality underlying the entire world. This quest for a single essence behind the diversity of the world was not only a philosophical inquiry, but also part of the struggle of a troubled age for exceptional powers for handling difficulties that were grave and deep.

2 *In the quest for control of the universe, the priests turned from the symbolic shapes of the fire pits and the esoteric meanings assigned to the external offerings and considered the possible cosmic connections of aspects of the sacrificers themselves.* The powerful liturgical words of the performing priests, the breath with which they were uttered, and the mental conceptions from which they sprang had

obvious connections with the outer world. Powers of the most comprehensive sort might be within the grasp of reciting priests who were aware of these correspondences. Fancies regarding a universal control centered particularly upon the term Brahman, which then meant the aggregate of all the Vedas' holy words. These sacred words, severally and collectively, were in the possession of the priests. If knowledge of single words gave single powers, why would not knowledge of Brahman, the collective word, give access to a total cosmic power and to the solution of the most widespread and desperate human problems?

Once the keys to power were seen as contained in the priests themselves rather than in their rituals, it was no longer essential that the rituals be performed. Meditation by the priests on their own inward being might be as effective as the performance of outward rites. As a result of such thinking, the practice of sacrifice declined and the practice of meditation increased. The spread of the new doctrine of karma further discouraged sacrifice, since ritual acts, always of finite number and therefore of strictly measured effectiveness, were now seen as unable to bring about the infinite blessing of immortality. On the other hand, knowledge was considered to be measureless, like thought, and thus infinite in its possible outreach. Even *total* reality could have knowledge as its earthly correspondence. Best of all, knowledge can be acquired, and its great power can be controlled by disciplined meditation.

Some ritualists of the late vedic age turned for power to esoteric knowledge while continuing to seek the same material gains that were the goal of the old sacrifice. But it was the seekers of the lost vedic immortality who most needed the power of secret knowledge, and they made knowledge their distinctive quest. When they abandoned ritual to pursue eternal life by means of meditation, Aryan religion developed an important new form, and the Way of Knowledge was born. It came into full expression in compositions called the Upanishads, which are the fundamental scriptures of the Way of Knowledge.

The Upanishads

The word *upanishad* means a secret teaching. The Upanishads are "secrets" in that they tell of realities not superficially apparent and express truths intended to be studied only by inquirers of special fitness. More than a hundred Hindu mystical writings of many ages are called Upanishads, but only thirteen of these are accepted by all Hindus as śruti, or revealed scripture of the highest authority. These thirteen Upanishads, the oldest, have no equal in importance in the formation of Hindu thought.

Almost all the metaphysical ideas and meditative disciplines of classical Hinduism have some root in the Upanishads and base their claim to authority on that connection. Hindus' reverence for the Upanishads rests on belief that they were revealed in the same manner as the vedic hymns and the Brāhmaṇas. The Upanishads are regarded as part of the Veda, and followers of the Way of Knowledge understand them to contain the final and full teaching of the sages who articulated the vedic revelation. Most Hindus have derived them from their impression of what the Vedas teach. In fact, the Upanishads are the most ancient books that can be understood with ease by educated Hindus. Written in classical Sanskrit, these newer scriptures were the product of the new caste society. They offer solutions to problems that have troubled members of that classical Hindu culture ever since its formation.

Although the Upanishads are not dated and their authors are not known, it is clear that those who composed them knew and used the vedic hymns, the Brāhmaṇas, and the Āraṇyakas, and it is generally believed that they began to appear about 600 B.C. The formation of the major Upanishads continued through several stages, first in prose and then in verse, probably ending about 200 B.C. The Upanishads were composed, then, in the same period as were the *Śrauta Sūtras*, the *Gṛihya Sūtras*, and the dharmasūtras. Their authors had interests that were very different from those of the authors of those sūtras, however.

THE AUTHORS OF THE NEW TEACHING

The creators of this new teaching were upper-class Aryans who had been stirred by glimpses of a blessedness more desirable than the favors promised by the vedic cult. It was an age of daring new thought and free debate. The new thinking met with the old in various settings. Sometimes the background was a royal court, where the king presided over doctrinal discussions. At other times it was an assembly of brāhmaṇs or warriors before whom famous sages debated. The scene, again, was a teacher's home where teacher or student interrupted the traditional lesson plan with new questions or surprising answers, or the setting was a family discussion during which a father or his son presented startling new ideas.

The most famous teachers of the new outlook, however, were wanderers who made rare appearances in throne rooms or assembly halls to proclaim their message but departed soon for their usual habitations in the forest. All who were deeply moved by their message were expected to leave their homes to take up the hermit's life and live on alms. The interest in the forest solitude life did not center on the practice of asceticism, but rather on the attainment of control over one's destiny by the power of knowledge.

PROCLAMATION OF BRAHMAN

The great theme of these teachers was a proclamation centering on the powerful word Brahman, which had now been given an even larger meaning. In late vedic religion the word Brahman referred not only to the recited words of the Veda, but also to the mysterious power that was felt to be present in the uttering of the vedic hymns. It was believed to be a connecting force flowing between the liturgy and the natural world, the medium through which the ritual exerted its influence upon events outside the theater of the sacrifice. The idea of Brahman as the essence of all things was not absent, but the principal vedic search was for power to move any and every part of the universe through ritual.

The authors of the Upanishads continued to conceive the Brahman dynamically, as a hidden power latent in all things, a sacred power that controls the whole world. The third chapter of the Keṇa Upanishad relates how even the greatest of the vedic gods were forced to admit that they had no power aside from their share in the power of the mysterious Brahman dwelling in them. Brahman in the Upanishads is the successor of the vedic gods as the highest and holiest Reality of religion. But this Brahman is more than a sacred power; it is the source from which all things spring, the tie that holds all things together, and the That that all things are. Brahman is not only the power but also the very essence of the vedic gods. Asked how many gods there are, the sage Yājñavalkya reduced the traditional number to thirty-three, then to three, and finally to Brahman, one and one alone (Brihadāraṇyaka Upanishad 3.9.1–10).

If Brahman is the basis of all things from the greatest of the gods to a drop of water, it followed that it was the fundamental reality of one's own self. This final turn of interpretation was not added casually for the sake of formal completeness only; it was an extension that had personal significance. In Chāndogya Upanishad 6.8–16, the sage Uddālaka Aruṇi taught his son Śvetaketu about the invisible reality that is the essence of all that exists. At the end of each phase of this indoctrination, he repeated the famous refrain that is the heart of his message: "That is Reality, That is the self (ātman), That are you, O Śvetaketu!" Nine repetitions of this phrase, coming at the climax of each of the nine chapters of this document, emphasize an identification central to the Upanishads. In the Brihadāraṇyaka Upanishad it takes the form of the famous credo "I am the Brahman" (1.4.10).

THE ANXIETY AT THE ROOT OF THE UPANISHADS

What led the sages of the Upanishads into the investigations that produced this distinctive view of life? Robert E. Hume, a respected translator of the Upanishads, believes that the authors were moved by philosophical curiosity. He points out that when a culture has attained a certain stage of mental development, it must undertake "to construe the world of experience as a rational whole." For him the Upanishads are "the first recorded attempts of the Hindus at systematic philosophizing."[2]

Indeed, the proposals in some of the Upanishads that all things originated in water, space, air, ether, the sun, or a void do remind us of similar speculations by the pre-Socratic philosophers of Greece, who were active at about this same time. The Upanishads, however, do not seek to answer life's questions by philosophical reasoning alone. Kaṭha Upanishad 2.23 and 6.10, for example, holds that Reality cannot be known "by instruction, nor by intellect, nor by much learning," for truth can be realized only "when cease the five Sense-knowledges, together with the mind, and the intellect stirs not. . . ."[3] Thus the authors of the Upanishads, despite their occasional sharp use of reasoning, were in fact mystics rather than philosophers. By stimulating imagination and intuition, they attempted to stir to life a latent capacity for vision. They were world renouncers, driven by hungers seated deeper in the emotions than the intellectual needs of the academic philosophers.

Some scholars have tried to apply the Western model of the Protestant Reformation. They have regarded the Upanishads as the outcome of a double rebellion—a rebellion of a free religion of personal experience against the formal religion of priestly rituals, and a revolt of kṣatriya religious thinkers against a brāhmaṇ monopoly of religious leadership. Those who see an overturn of leadership in the Upanishads point to the prominence, among the teachers of the new outlook, of such kṣatriyas as Ajātaśatru, the king of Banāras (mentioned in the Brihadāraṇyaka Upanishad) and King Aśvapati Kaikeya (mentioned in the Chāndogya Upanishad). Both princes are said to have had brāhmaṇs among their pupils. An attack on priestly arrogance in the Muṇḍaka Upanishad, where the sacrifices are called leaky boats in which travelers sink to their deaths, has been used in support of this view of the Upanishads as an expression of a revolt against the dominance of brāhmaṇs.

The composition of the Upanishads did entail a revolution in religion, but careful scholarship has corrected the impression that the Upanishads are the work of enemies of the brāhmaṇ class. The Upanishads do not denounce as lies the promises of the priests of the older cult; in fact, most of the leaders of the new religions were themselves brāhmaṇs. The Upanishads were preserved by brāhmaṇs. The Upanishads acknowledge that the priests' sacrifices produce the benefits promised. What they deny is that the gains obtained are of any real worth. If there was a revolt against brāhmaṇs here, it was a revolt led by other brāhmaṇs adhering to new values. It was a reform movement within the traditional religious leadership of the Aryans, refreshed by the participation of kṣatriyas and by the acceptance of some of their ideas. It did not represent the concerns of a new class of leaders, but rather the concerns of a new age.

The acute concern was death, viewed now with a special horror created by the new ideas of karma, rebirth, and caste. The death that the authors of the Upanishads dreaded was not annihilation, but a decline and collapse that was only the next in a repulsive series of lives and deaths devoid of interest and without end. They saw themselves as entrapped in saṃsāra, doomed to a wearying round of worldly lives in the cramping roles of the new postvedic society. The Way of Action no longer offered them the hope of a lasting happiness even in heaven. Their great desire was *mukti* or *mokṣa,* liberation from the bonds of karma. What they longed for was not more lives. They were already all too sure that there would be more lives. Rather, they sought freedom in a stable, unchanging existence of another nature, free from all necessity of death and birth. The solution to this problem came with the discovery of a secret bridge between the human soul and an immortal Spirit in the outer universe. The discovery was achieved in a religious quest that used the traditional Indian method of searching for correspondences.

THE DOUBLE QUEST FOR THE ETERNAL

One side of the search for something eternal was the probing of the outer universe for a possible lasting essence. Various Upanishads began the search by surmising that the visible universe originated with earth, air, water, or space as the primeval stuff. These speculations came to naught, however, and the sages found deeper insight in Ṛigveda 10.129's mysterious affirmation of "That One" lying in the waters of nonbeing, that became the single source of all that breathes. The Upanishads gave this source the name of Brahman. Brahman is one throughout the universe, and it makes the universe one. Chāndogya Upanishad 6.2.1 calls it "One only without a second." In the homogeneity of Brahman, the distressing changes of life can end completely. Those who find their existence in Brahman are immune from the unwelcome transformations of death and rebirth.

The composers of the Upanishads ventured several major statements about the nature of the world-essence. First, that Brahman is spirit—that is, it is not a material thing. As the unifier of material things, it must be an essence of a superior, nonphenomenal order that the eye cannot see. The sixth book of the Chāndogya Upanishad relates that the boy Śvetaketu had never heard of the world-soul and doubted the actual presence of a spirit that could not be seen. To explain this phenomenon, his father Uddālaka gave him a lump of salt to drop into a cup of water. Śvetaketu did so and set the cup aside for a time. Later Uddālaka asked his son to give back to him the lump of salt. The boy felt around in the cup without finding the lump and declared that the salt was not there. Instructed by his father, Śvetaketu then took several sips of the salty water from the cup and admitted that the salt, although nonexistent to touch and sight, was indeed in every part of the water. The lesson is that a reality can be present that the senses do not reveal, and the supposition that two things cannot occupy the same space at the same time does not rule out the coexistence of two realities belonging to different orders of being. Thus the fine essence called Brahman is present throughout the universe, even though all five senses fail to detect it. Through the sensitivity of the mystic its presence can be revealed.

A second great affirmation is that Brahman is generative—not a dead thing, but the source of the world and all its life. Again Śvetaketu did not understand, and his father explained by means of another demonstration. The two were standing under a banyan tree, the most widely spreading of all Indian trees. The son was told to pluck a seedpod from a branch, to open the pod, and then to crack open one of the small seeds. "What do you see there?" asked Uddālaka. "Nothing at all, sir!" Śvetaketu replied.[4] (The seed of the banyan is small, hollow, and seemingly empty.) Uddālaka then made his point: From a hollow shell with "nothing" in it, the mighty banyan tree had grown, its invisible kernel the very germ of life. And so it was with the great world tree: It had risen from an empirical nothing, from a nonphenomenal Spirit that the ignorant denied. Yet this invisible presence was a vital force that had changed itself into the endless complexities of phenomenal existence and sustained them with its life.

Brahman is indescribable. It is invisible to the eye, so how can it be characterized by adjectives relating to color or form? Beyond hearing, touch, taste, and smell as well, Brahman is beyond the power of all descriptive speech. The Tattirīya Upanishad says that we may know the bliss of Brahman, but as for knowing Brahman itself, both our words and our minds are ineffective (2.4.1). Thus in their quest for the final basis of the external universe, the sages of the Upanishads discovered an immaterial life-giving Oneness that is beyond description.

THE QUEST FOR A CHANGELESS SELF

As keenly as the Hindu thinkers searched the outer universe for Brahman, the Reality beyond the sun, they also explored the inner world. Asking, "What is the real person," they noted in detail the processes of birth, growth, decline, and death, seeking a lasting essence of the human individual. Some thought it lay in a tiny inner person, a soul the size of a thumb, that is the model from which we are reconstituted again and again for new lives.[5] Others sought it in the old vedic concept of the prāna, or life breath. Although the scrutinizing of the body that one finds in some Upanishads could be mistaken for research in anatomy, the real concern was immortality. All such attempts to find an immortal essence by external scrutiny of persons came to naught.

Finding nothing exempt from death in the material body, the sages turned to a method that proved more fruitful: a search of the psyche for nonphenomenal constituents of the human being that might be revealed by introspection. Indian thinkers have regarded the findings of inner experience as just as valid as (or perhaps more valid than) the data of objective observation. Beginning in the Upanishads, the Hindu investigations of the self have produced views that the real self, or ātman, is a nonphysical, inner presence concealed by encircling sheaths.

The array of constituents around one's true core can be visualized as a pattern of concentric shells through which one must probe to reach one's true being or self. Three such models of the human structure are traditional and have their beginning in the Upanishads. Although never brought into careful relation with each other in a single system, they all illustrate the special tendency of Hindu thinking about the person. We shall place these partial explanations of the self side by side, like three targets used in archery.

1 *The human self veiled by material stuffs.* According to this concept, the real self is hidden behind the concentric sheaths of three "bodies" of increasingly refined materiality. The outmost layer is our gross, visible body, the *sthūla śarīra.* This body is an aggregation of five kinds of gross elements called *mahābhūtas,* which are made up of smaller units called *tanmātras,* which are also of five kinds. Each mahābhūta contains one, two, or up to five tanmātras, each of which functions as the stimulator of one of the five human senses; the presence of a given tanmātra in a mahābhūta causes it to activate a given human sense. The fact that the tanmātra of taste, for example, is present in the mahābhūta of water is what makes it possible for us to taste water. (Our ability also to see, feel, hear, and smell things depends likewise upon the presence of the tanmātras of color, touch, sound, and odor.)

At death this outermost shell of the gross body is sloughed off, and at rebirth another such gross body is acquired. During death the personal and physical characteristics of the individual are preserved in a second shell, a subtle body that is the next inward from the gross body. It is in this body that deceased persons must undergo retribution in the heavens and hells. Subtle bodies are composed of the five tanmātras only, which are not perceptible to the senses. Only rarely a person of supernormal sensitivity perceives the ghostly presence of a dead person having only a subtle body.

Inward from our subtle body is our *causal body,* consisting of the aggregate of our karma. At the end of the cosmic age (*kalpa*), when the entire world devolves into the primary material stuff and the subtle bodies too are dissolved, only our causal body continues to ensheath our essential self and to preserve the record of our distinctive moral history. At the beginning of each new cosmic age, our individuality is reconstituted from the karma contained in our causal bodies, and we resume our careers in positions that are in agreement with our karma. Only in final liberation will the causal body also dissolve, and then the history of retribution will stop. Then there will be left only our inmost self, the one ensheathed by all these bodies, a being with no bodily nature at all. This is our ātman, or true self.

2 *The human self veiled by psychic organs.* According to this concept, the outermost circle that concerns us is an external ring of sense objects, the frame of material things lying just beyond the outermost boundaries of the self. Just inside this frame lies the grossest layer of an individual's psychical equipment, which consists of the ten sense faculties (*indriyas*). Five of these are the faculties for action (*karma indriyas*): grasping, moving, speaking, excreting, and procreating. The other five faculties are for knowing (*jñāna indriyas*): seeing, hearing, smelling, tasting, and feeling. Directed outward through our five sense organs, the faculties of knowing explore the objects of the surrounding

world and report on the nature of these objects to the inner faculties of our psyche.

Moving inward, the next of these faculties is the automatic mind, or *manas*. Our automatic mind identifies the objects reported to it by the five faculties of knowing. The manas, which is incapable of reflection or decision, merely transmits its recognitions to the *buddhi*, a free psychic faculty of thought, decision, and command. Buddhi is generally translated as "intellect," even though that English word does not cover all the meanings of this term. The buddhi is the seat and source of our own consciousness, but it is not the source of consciousness itself. That capacity dwells in the innermost reality of our psychic makeup, which lies at the center of this circle. Consciousness originates with ātman, the self itself.

3 *The human self veiled by states of consciousness.* The traditional accounting of our various grades of consciousness was outlined first in Chāndogya Upanishad 8.7–12. Our states of consciousness begin, at the outermost level, with our ordinary *waking state*, in which we carry out our dealings with the world. Next comes the state of consciousness that we experience when *dreaming*, a more inward condition in which we continue to perceive forms that are material but of a subtle and phantasmal grade of materiality. Next comes the advanced state of consciousness that we experience in *deep dreamless sleep*. Although in this state we are not unconscious or inanimate, our consciousness of the whole panorama of worldly things vanishes. We achieve an awareness in which there are no divisions or limits, and we have a premonition of the ultimate unity of existence. It is a blissful state; yet in this consciousness we remain aware that we are in a blissful condition and that this bliss is our own.

Because of this remnant of self-consciousness, the state of dreamless sleep is not the final condition. Further within the concentric pattern lies the ultimate state, which is blissful consciousness alone, without awareness of any object or consciousness of anything but consciousness itself. This is called simply the *fourth state*. In it all material objects, all phantasmal objects, and even the sense of having peace as an individual are gone. There is only the total peace of ātman, our true self, which is consciousness alone.

WHAT IS ĀTMAN, THE REAL SELF?

These three efforts to chart the self express one concept in different ways. All three reflect the Hindu conviction that the real person is hidden behind many veils. The real person is not the body in any of its grades; it is not the mind, the intellect, or the psyche as a whole; and it is not perceptible through the senses or known in ordinary states of consciousness. Our real self is a unique metaphysical reality characterized by consciousness. Thus wherever consciousness exists, the ātman is present. It is the unseen seer behind the eye, the unheard hearer behind the ear. Ātman is the stuff of consciousness.

Defined as the stuff and source of consciousness, the self has characteristics of immense concern to those longing for eternal liberation. For as we shall now see, its characteristics are those already found in the Brahman, the Reality behind the outer universe. Our ātman is one and not a heterogeneous thing like our body. When we continue to be conscious in meditation without being conscious of any particular thing at all, then our consciousness has no parts nor any limits. When our eyes are closed in such silent sessions, we are aware only of unbounded and undifferentiated inner space. That is the fundamental condition of our consciousness and what unifies ourselves as persons. Without this unifying consciousness we would be only an inanimate agglomeration of bodily parts, an unconscious corpse. The presence of our consciousness is the secret of our being someone, and therefore it is the ātman, our real self.

How else can we define ātman? It is spirit. This vague English term conveys at least the idea of something that is not material. The soul within us cannot be tasted, heard, or smelled as material objects can. It cannot be weighed or dissected; yet its reality is undeniable because the reality of ātman is attested by the fact of our possessing consciousness. Whereas a Westerner might argue, "I think, therefore I am," a Hindu would say, "I am conscious, therefore I am." When we cease to think, we do not cease to be, but when our consciousness is completely gone from us, we are dead. Ātman is the secret of the integrity and continuity of a human life.

Furthermore, ātman is beyond human concepts and words. Human languages were developed to describe what the senses reveal; they have no words that can truly represent the nature of the internal consciousness from which all our explorations of the world proceed. Even if our senses tried to perceive the reality of another person, they would not be able to detect anything lying deeper than the gross body of that person's outer shell. If we were to turn our own five senses back into ourselves, they would be equally useless in reaching the real person within us. This is because our senses operate only outwardly in the wrong direction for perception and cannot probe the depths within us where the ātman is. The senses are like a battery of powerful searchlights that reveal what is far away but not the operator who stands behind them and sees everything with their help. But by an extraordinary inward retraction of the consciousness that normally fills our sense organs, we can know this inmost ātman. The mystics who achieve this realization testify that no words are adequate to express what they then perceive.

Finally, ātman is germinal. It is the root of a tree of life, from which a person grows forth ever anew, time after time.[6] In the living being the ātman is thus the vital principle that sustains life and unifies the embodied self. When this spirit departs and the body is left, there is no person.

THE IDENTITY OF BRAHMAN AND ĀTMAN

Thus the answers to the two questions—What is the universe? and Who am I?—have converged. Both probes have uncovered a hidden Presence that is nonmaterial. At some fateful moment in the ardent inner searches of postvedic religion, an enlightened sage conceived that the real universe and the real self, since they possessed the same qualities, were identical in essence. The Upanishads' reasoned statements to that effect are only rational supports, however, for a conviction resting actually on a revelatory experience. The phrase "I am the Brahman!" (Brihadāraṇyaka Upanishad 1.4.10) that stimulated the creation of the Upanishads was an emotional cry of discovery. The world-renouncing hermits of the forest, striving to restore the vedic trust in a deathless hereafter, had found in their mystical experimentation a relationship between the ātman and the immortal Brahman. The opening of the fourth chapter of the Kaṭha Upanishad speaks of an original revelation:

The Creator pierced the sense-holes outward,
so one looks out, not toward the Self within.
Some wise man seeking deathlessness
with eyes inverted saw the Self direct.

Here and in other Upanishads (for example, Brihadāraṇyaka Upanishad 4.3.32 and Maitri Upanishad 6.24ff.), we have the first testimony in Indian literature, and perhaps in world literature, to the experience of oceanic trance in which the search for the real self ends in a sense of identity with a reality that is boundless in time and space. Ever since this discovery, seekers who follow this monistic path of salvation have sought to reproduce that experience and to enjoy the reassurance that it gives.

This mystical gospel brought comfort to those troubled by postvedic anxieties about death. Accomplished mystics no longer saw themselves as bodies that would deteriorate and die, then be reborn only to deteriorate and die again. In the continuing unity and absolute homogeneity of Brahman there is no possibility of change. The universal Spirit is what we are and what we always shall be.

Since there is only one Reality, annoyances and afflictions are psychological creations only. Suffering can be real only if dualities are real—for example, the duality of hammer and thumb, biter and bitten, oneself and rival, and oneself and death. Of course, the serene Oneness that absorbed all the sources of these mystics' fears absorbed their individuality as well. Satisfaction in such an immortal existence was primarily for those who were content to surrender all the values of the personal life. To those burdened by the restrictions of the caste system, individual gains and even individual existences had little worth. Many were willing to enter the peace of the universal Oneness forever, disappearing as persons like a dissolving lump of salt. Such a salvation has been the hope of millions of Hindus to the present day. As the Chāndogya Upanishad 7.26.2 expresses it:

Not death does the seer see,
nor illness nor any sorrow.
The seer sees just the All,
attains the All entirely.

The Vedānta Tradition

When the formation of the great Upanishads was completed, a new and powerful kind of religion, sometimes called the Vedānta, had come into existence. The Vedānta is based on a distinctive kind of mystical experience and on a belief in the underlying unity of all reality. Its belief in an all-inclusive unity carried with it a problem of rational consistency. The Upanishads speak on the one hand of the complex world. On the other hand, they speak of the undivided and all-inclusive Brahman, which they declare to be, alone, the true and universal Being. But how can the universe be divided and not divided at the same time? If Brahman the sole reality is one, must not the multiform world of experience be ruled out as nonexistent? And if the many things of the world are real, then must not the all-inclusive Brahman be a fiction?

Leaving little literature to reveal their thinking on this disturbing question, followers of the Vedānta tradition quietly increased in number for a thousand years. Even before the Christian Era, there were efforts to summarize in sūtras the Vedānta teaching about Brahman, but the earliest of the brahmasūtras (as the new writings were called) to come down to us is the brahmasūtra of Bādarāyaṇa, which was probably written in about A.D. 200. It is too terse to be understood without a commentary. The oldest full presentation of the Vedānta system that has come down to us is a commentary on the work of Bādarāyaṇa by the great teacher Śaṅkara, writing about A.D. 800. Śaṅkara was the founder of the important Advaita (nondualistic) school of Vedānta thought.

Śaṅkara's thought focused upon those points in the Upanishads' teaching that remained paradoxical and unclear. An ancient school of materialist thinkers known as Lokāyatas (Worldlings) had actually adopted the view that the plurality of things is real and that talk about oneness in Brahman is false. Some Mahāyāna Buddhists had come close to teaching an opposite doctrine, that the world of plurality, as ordinarily experienced, is a phantasm having no reality or substance whatsoever. Śaṅkara mediated between these extreme positions in an ingenious monistic view of the universe. We shall study those aspects of his teaching that are important to his scheme of salvation.

What is the human being? is a basic question in any Indian outlook. Śaṅkara characterized the ordinary person as being confused regarding the true answer to the question, "Who am I?" We believe ourselves to be separate individuals, each with a separate body that is real and a lasting part of ourselves. We think that the history of our changing bodies is our own history and that we undergo in our real selves unceasing decay, disease, and death. Because we all believe ourselves, as bodies, to be separate from others, each of us is filled with thoughts of "I" and "mine." Because we think of ourselves as physical beings, we think we can make ourselves happy through the pursuit of bodily comforts, pleasure, and wealth. Sometimes we fail to attain these goals and become dejected, and at other times we succeed and are elated, but only for a moment. We are never satisfied. Therefore we are miserable. But we are unaware of the reason for our misery. We want liberation from rebirth, but do not know how to attain it.

Now, what the revealed Upanishads assure us, says Śaṅkara, is that we are not individuals now winning and now losing the competitive struggles of this life. Instead, we are eternally one with the universal and immortal Brahman, the only reality. That perfect Being is always characterized by consciousness, being, and bliss. It is the Self in all of us and those are our characteristics also. In our daily life, however, we do not perceive the blessed unitary Brahman, and we do not know its bliss. Rather, we experience ourselves as bodies filled with needs and hurts, and the universal Soul, unseen, is known to us only as something referred to in the Upanishads. How then can we believe those scriptures?

ŚAṄKARA'S FOUR LEVELS OF KNOWLEDGE

In reply, Śaṅkara urged his readers to reflect carefully on the nature and value of the sense experiences on which their understanding of the world was based. Once they perceived how fallible their senses were, they would realize that ordinary experience is a poor basis for deciding what is true. Even common sense can tell us that in everyday life we know several grades of experience and several levels of so-called knowledge, and that they do not have the same value with regard to truth. Śaṅkara distinguished four levels of knowledge:

1 *Verbal knowledge.* This, the very lowest kind of knowledge, has no reality beyond the reality of words, which contain contradictions and cannot, therefore, refer to anything beyond themselves. We can speak about a square circle or the children of a barren woman, but none of us will ever experience in real life a square circle or meet children born to a barren woman. We can experience only the words. Such verbal knowledge has no objective validity. It is simply false.

2 *Deluded knowledge.* When we look out over a hot shimmering plain and see in the distance a "lake" that is only a mirage, our knowledge of the "lake" is a deluded knowledge. Again, we often catch sight of a "silver coin" on a sandy beach and on rushing to pick it up we find that it is only a silvery shell. We realize that our knowledge of the "coin" was deluded even though based on an apprehension of a reality. Such experiences may be convincing for a short time, but their erroneousness is easily detected. Soon we realize that the object of experience was mistakenly perceived. The actuality was only hot air on a plain, only a shell embedded in the sand. Such mistakes are corrected by our own later experience and by the experience of others, who laugh and tell us that we are looking at a mirage or a shell.

3 *Empirical knowledge.* This kind of knowledge comes to us when we see real lakes and real coins. We can check such data by observing them at a later time or by asking other people for their impressions of these objects, thereby confirming the "correctness" of our information. One generation passes down its empirical knowledge to its children, who find it useful and develop sciences that help them survive in this life. It is this empirical knowledge that convinces us we are all separate persons who have separate souls and bodies. It convinces us, too, that in our real selves we are bodies that suffer injuries and diseases, grow old, and die. Therefore Śaṅkara asserted that empirical knowledge, despite its worldly usefulness, needs to be corrected. It misleads us on a matter of utmost importance: our supposed individuality as separate suffering beings. Fortunately, empirical knowledge, too, can be superseded when we rise to insight of a still higher grade.

4 *Supreme (pāramārthika) knowledge.* According to Śaṅkara, there is a final and highest form of experience that yields knowledge that is absolute truth. Unlike empirical knowledge, pāramārthika knowledge is not obtained through the senses, mind, or intellect, but directly through the consciousness of the ātman alone. This supreme experience comes when our fallible senses are made to cease their operation and the conceptualizing activities of the intellect are stopped. When our psychic organs are put to rest and all our power of consciousness is concentrated in our innermost self, a unique state of consciousness called *samādhi* is reached. In this state, a distorting film is removed from the consciousness of the introverted mystic who is able then to apprehend reality as it actually is. The understanding of what is real and what is unreal undergoes a remarkable reversal:

In what all beings call night
the disciplined sage awakes;
That wherein beings awaken
that the silent one sees as night.
(Bhagavadgītā 2.69)

Direct perception reveals to the mystic that the separateness of persons is false and that the oneness of all is the truth. As the Upanishads teach, reality is one without the slightest division or possibility of change, and this one immortal Being is pure consciousness and pure bliss. This universal consciousness, timeless and immune to all ills, is what we really are. The defects of our bodies and our bodies themselves are delusions comparable to a mirage. There is liberation from all distress for those who have attained this knowledge. Those mystics are at peace now and forever who realize their oneness with the blissful Brahman.

ŚAṄKARA'S DOCTRINE OF MĀYĀ

In setting forth his doctrine of salvation, Śaṅkara found it necessary to explain why we are so seldom aware of ourselves as the changeless, blissful, and all-knowing Brahman, and why we so usually experience ourselves as individuals who age and die. Śaṅkara's solution to this problem was the doctrine of *māyā*.

We must infer, he says, that there is a mysterious impersonal force that causes an unreal pluralistic universe to be projected upon the one cosmic reality that in truth is undivided. Because its effects are undeniable, such a force must be believed to exist and operate. When operating to distort our perception of the cosmos, it may be called māyā. It is the deluding influence of māyā that causes us to project upon the universal Brahman which is the single reality the many figments that make up our everyday world. They can be compared to the "lakes" and "silver coins" we sometimes think we see. Cosmically māyā conceals unity and projects plurality, exposing all living creatures to shared delusions that are not private but social. Subjectively māyā operates in the psyche as a deluding factor that may be called *avidyā*, or ignorance. Working within us, it affects our consciousness of our own natures, making us apprehend ourselves wrongly as separate individuals, each composed of a body and soul.

Śaṅkara admitted that it is difficult to understand what the substance of māyā is and where it exists. If māyā is real, its substance must necessarily be Brahman, the sole and all-inclusive reality. But māyā and Brahman have contradictory natures: Brahman is absolute unity, changelessness, consciousness, knowledge, and bliss, whereas māyā is all plurality, the principle of change, the source of ignorance and the cause of all suffering. Māyā cannot be in Brahman, because it would cancel and destroy its nature; nor can it be a differentiated part of Brahman because Brahman has no parts. Māyā is not a reality separate from Brahman because Brahman is the only reality. Although māyā is not real, it is also not unreal because the unreal cannot produce effects, as māyā can and does with utmost power. Similarly, the products of māyā are neither real nor unreal. They are not unreal because they are delusions projected onto Brahman and have the reality of Brahman as their base. At the same time, they are not real because only ignorance gives them their apparent separate identities. The entire familiar world produced by māyā is transient and deceitful, and yet not entirely unreal.

Neither real nor unreal, not within Brahman nor yet outside of Brahman, a factor whose status cannot be explained, māyā is nevertheless a principle in whose existence we must believe. We dare not ignore it. Māyā causes the world to appear and causes us to believe worldly things that are false. It causes souls to appear and believe in their own plurality, although that plurality is false. It causes selfish behavior and a sense of individual responsibility for selfish acts. It binds illusionary individuals to illusionary bodies. It is the source of all human sin, misery, and bondage. Since māyā is the supreme impediment to salvation, all religious effort should be directed toward dispelling this ignorance (avidyā) within ourselves. Our one noble desire is our longing for the moment when avidyā will vanish from us forever along with our attachment to the things of this world. We can hope to attain this liberation if we are willing to renounce all other desires and the world itself, and adopt the arduous life of those seeking salvation through the Way of Knowledge.

RENUNCIATION (SANNYĀSA)

To attain extraordinary knowledge, extraordinary means are required; the mere study of doctrine is not enough. Those who have followed the Way of Knowledge have had to develop a sensitivity to hidden realities by retraining their entire psyche, dedicating their lives wholly to this effort.

A follower of the Way of Knowledge sits in its characteristic meditation, motionless and oblivious to the world. The forest is the ideal setting for such yoga.

Brihadāraṇyaka Upanishad 4.5 tells us that when the sage Yājñavalkya embarked on a serious search for liberation, he abandoned his family and property and went off into the forest. Throughout history, persons engaged in contemplation have found seclusion helpful to the attainment of mystical experience. For Hindu mystics monasticism was made even more attractive by the tedium of their life in an increasingly restrictive social world. While the Upanishads were being composed, Hindu spiritual seekers felt a more and more intense need to remove themselves from society. In the early and orthodox Upanishads the term *sannyāsa* (renunciation) referred to the renunciation of earthly desires, but within a few centuries sannyāsa came to mean the renunciation of the world.

In the dharmaśāstras that were beginning to be written in about this same period, such a renunciation of the world was idealized in a conception of the *sannyāsāśrama,* the fourth and final āśrama of a person's spiritual career. The religious life of an individual was to proceed through graded stages of effort arranged in a hierarchical pattern like that of the social order and the universe. As stated in chapter eight of the *Laws of Manu*, spiritual seekers were expected to pass through the stages of student and householder and theoretically through the stage of vānaprastha, or forest dweller. Then, in a consummating stage, all were expected, as sannyāsīs, to abandon the world entirely.

By making sannyāsa the final stage of spiritual effort, the religion of the Upanishads joined itself to the mainstream of Hinduism. Followers of the Vedānta tradition were henceforth convinced that they must, sooner or later, abandon the life of the householder for that of the wandering monk. For more than two thousand years, mendicants in saffron robes carrying a staff and begging bowl have been a conspicuous feature of Hinduism.

Not all of these holy men know the thought of the Upanishads or share the goals of the Advaita Vedānta. Some are adherents of bhakti religion, who have given up their worldly occupations only to spend all their time in devotion to their god. Some seek power through ancient practices of self-mortification, and some are disoriented persons with vague aspirations. The term *sādhu* (good man) tends to be applied to all religious wanderers; sannyāsī tends to be reserved for persons presumed to be learned in the scriptural traditions of the Way of Knowledge and to be serious seekers of liberation.

The decision to become a sannyāsī is a strictly personal choice. The Upanishads do not say at what age this move should be made, but it is clear that the growing influence of the Upanishads soon stirred up a massive movement to the forest of youths on the verge of manhood. The author of the

Bhagavadgītā expressed Hindu society's general dismay at the loss of the services of those who had not yet contributed the labor of their productive years. The dharmaśāstras drew up a defensive rule that world renunciation should be delayed until the declining years of one's life, "when a householder sees his skin wrinkled, and his hair white . . ." (*The Laws of Manu* 6:2). Such delaying of monastic living until old age has always been honored as the ideal, but in practice younger persons who are insistent have been allowed to enter the monastic life. The essential qualification, really, is disillusion with the pleasures of the world and a deep longing for liberation from rebirth.

Even though still living the life of a householder, Hindus committed to the Vedānta teaching may make preparations to hasten the time of their salvation. They should avoid bad conduct, which destroys serenity (Kaṭha Upanishad 2.24), and they should curb the ego and calm the mind by selfless performance of their duties. They should strive to perfect themselves in five ethical virtues that are the first steps in the formal eight-stage yoga or discipline of the Way of Knowledge. Called the five *yamas*, these five preparatory moral requirements are (1) noninjury (*ahiṃsā*), the great Hindu ideal of nonviolence toward all living beings; (2) truthfulness (*satya*); (3) honesty (*asteya*); (4) chastity (*brahmacārya*); and (5) freedom from greed (*aparigraha*).

While still members of the laity, Hindus can also cultivate the five *niyamas*—five mental virtues that constitute the second preparatory stage in the eight-stage yoga. They are (1) purity (*śauca*), cleanliness of body and diet; (2) contentment (*saṃtosha*); (3) austerity (*tapas*), the development of powers of self-denial and endurance; (4) study (*svādhyāya*), the pondering of religious texts and doctrines; and (5) meditation on the Lord (*iśvarapraṇidhāna*). Although followers of the Way of Knowledge regard the concept of a personal God as deluded, they regard theistic meditation as valuable for those who have not yet fully attained a monistic comprehension of the Divine.

Instructions for living as a layperson are often given in terms that are less formal than these lists. Śaṅkara simply says that spiritual seekers should devote themselves to constant meditation on the truths of Vedānta teaching, studying the Upanishads and contemplating such scriptural statements as "I am the Brahman."

After years or lifetimes of such preparation, it is believed, a layperson will suddenly perceive that it is time to renounce the world. The precipitating factor may be some dramatic manifestation of the transience or futility of life. A king looks into a mirror and detects in his beard the first gray hair; there is a death in the family, a domestic quarrel, the collapse of a career: such experiences may reveal to individuals the vanity of possessions and the shortness of life.

The actual departure of the would-be sannyāsī from his family and village is a solemn ritual. In a round of farewell calls the departing one gives away his prized possessions. He performs his last ritual as a householder. In a formal separation from his home, he leaves his village on foot, and his son escorts him for a stated distance on his way. Finally, at a certain spot father and son take a back-to-back position, the son facing toward the village, the father toward the unknown. Both stride off resolutely in their respective directions without looking back. The father must walk straight ahead until the end of the day without stopping. Theoretically he should never again mention the name of his village nor even think of it.

For him a completely new life begins. He becomes a wandering beggar, building no fire and cooking no food. Appearing at a house door just after the time of dinner, he eats whatever scraps he may be given. He sleeps wherever night overtakes him—ideally under a tree, but perhaps at a temple or a charitable shelter for monks. Rarely, such seekers reside for extended periods in a *matha* (monastic establishment), but no special value is attached to cloistered living. Mendicants rove as the spirit moves them, visiting temples, attending religious fairs (*melās*), stopping at places of religious pilgrimage (*tīrthas*), or lingering on mountains noted as places of meditation. The monk has no family obligations, no ritual duties, and no work to do. He is free. He will attain in his own time, alone, the liberation he is seeking.

In this spontaneous new life the irritations of a

restrictive society are eased. The former caste of the holy man is forgotten, and its restrictions no longer apply. If gifted, the holy man may become an eminent teacher or spiritual guide. Earlier confined to a life of well-defined duties in a single community, he is now his own master, free to roam and to live on alms, on the sole condition that he forever separate himself from society's concerns. Sannyāsa has been the outlet for millions of sensitive Hindus who could not endure the confinements of caste life. Sannyāsa has also been the safety valve of the Hindu caste community, siphoning off the discontent of those who would otherwise have destroyed it. The institution of the fourth āśrama, like the doctrine of karma, has been a great supporting pillar of the classical Hindu culture.

Since the skills developed in the worldly life do not help in the inner explorations of the spiritual path, the renouncer quickly seeks out a guru, a teacher who has himself made the mystical journey and reached the other shore. It is believed that destiny provides each seeker with his own true guru and that when they finally meet face to face, each recognizes the other.

Self-mortification is either a search for supernatural powers or a preparation for meditations that are the direct means of salvation. Passersby have left their coins as an offering. *Bernard Pierre Wolff/Magnum.*

The guru now administers the rite of *dīkṣa*, an irreversible initiation into the final āśrama of life. It is a ritual death to the world and a rebirth into the realm of transcendence. The teacher rips off the disciple's sacred thread and cuts off his queue, the tuft of hair that has identified him as a conforming Hindu. Henceforth the disciple will no longer be bound by the rules of any caste. The personal name by which he has been known is uttered for the last time; and the teacher confers on him a new name devoid of caste significance and pointing to some religious truth. The guru should instruct his disciple in doctrine and in the new way of life. When the disciple is judged ready, he is guided in the advanced meditational discipline which is called yoga.

YOGA

The term yoga, like its English cognate *yoke*, means "to join, to unite" and also "to harness up, to set seriously to work." Followers of the monistic Vedānta tradition understand yoga as the process that brings about conscious union of one's own soul with the world Soul. Other Hindu groups think of yoga as any systematic program of meditation. There are several systems of yoga. *Haṭhayoga* is a physical discipline used to tone the body; it may or may not be followed by deeper meditations. The Tantric schools, whose position is marginal in Hinduism, practice a *kundalinī* yoga that has its own unusual imagery. Some modern mystical movements have developed their own unusual yogic practices. But for most Hindus, yoga refers to a version of the eight-stage yoga developed by the ancient sage Patañjali, whose exact dates are uncertain.

The eight-stage yoga begins with the yamas and niyamas. The third stage is *āsana*, which means "seat"—both the site where the meditators settle themselves and the bodily posture they adopt. The site should be secluded. If possible, meditators (*yogīs*) should seat themselves on grass covered with a deerskin or cloth. They may adopt many positions, but serious meditators tend to adopt a simple posture with legs crossed and hands folded atop one another on the lap. The aim of āsana is not to strain the body, but to make it possible to forget the body so that a higher identity may become known.

Prāṇāyama, the next stage, involves special control of one's breathing. We have noted a vedic belief that a cosmic breath was and is the root of all things and that one's breath is something very near to one's own essence. By training the breath, then, one can draw nearer to the basis of one's very being. Separate attention is given to timing the inhalation, retention, and exhalation of the breath. This timing is often measured by repetitions of *ōm*, the sacred syllable symbolizing Brahman. One of the effects of severely restricting one's breathing—the rise of luminous internal experiences—is regarded as a positive step toward the attainment of the mystical goal. Śvetāśvatara Upanishad 12.11–14 lists the consequences of breath repression:

Mist, smoke, sun, wind, fire,
fireflies, lightning, crystal, a moon—
these are the preliminary forms
that manifest Brahman *in yoga.*

Breath regulation also helps mental concentration and creates calmness and a readiness for activities requiring calmness as their base.

Pratyāhāra is the retraction of the senses from attention to any external objects. Like a turtle pulling its legs into its shell, the yogī must retreat into himself and break off contact with the outer world. In this way he can concentrate all of his powers of consciousness, focusing them intensely inward upon what is at the center of his being.

Dhāranā is the steadying of the power of attention so that the meditator can concentrate on a chosen object or matter as long as he wishes. Often the guru chooses what his disciple is to focus on: perhaps an image of a favorite deity; a *yantra* (a boss or stud of metal cast into a symbolic pattern); the tip of the nose or an imagined spot between the eyebrows; or an imaginary lotus or lamp within the heart.

Dhyāna is deep and long meditation on powerful symbols of the religious faith. The yogī of Vedānta conviction may ponder the meaning of the central

Two great modern advocates of the doctrine of monism. Left, the Shankaracharya of Dwarka Peeth, the abbot of one of the monasteries founded by Śaṅkara. Right, Sarvepalli Rādhākrishnan, creative modern philosopher. In the background, the syllable *om,* the symbol of the universal brahman. *Religious News Service.*

utterances of the Upanishads, such as "Thou art That" or "I am the *Brahman.*" It is also common to use the vedic syllable ōm, a verbal symbol of the Absolute that is sometimes called the sound-Brahman:

Two are the Brahmans *to be known:*
the Brahman *that is sound, and the one above it.*
*Adepts in the sound-*Brahman
the higher Brahman *do attain.*
(Maitri Upanishad 6.22)

Reciting ōm at first aloud and then silently, the meditator continues until the sound reverberates in his inner consciousness even after his utterance has ceased, and he is carried into a realm where nothing is known but the Reality that ōm represents. The awareness of individual selfhood nears extinction, and if the yogī is bold enough to press on into this extinction, he enters into the culminating experience of monistic yoga, *samādhi.*

Samādhi (concentration) begins when the yogī's awareness, long focused on a single point, swells explosively to encompass a limitless Reality. A sense of all-reaching participation in a living cosmos sweeps over him, and his own self appears to be swallowed up in a luminous ocean. The sense of infinite oneness is understood by the mystic to be a revelation taking precedence over all earlier insight: it is the final truth about the nature of things. Plural things and plural souls are no longer seen as real. But the disappearance of individuality does not bring nothingness. The real person is found in a universal consciousness in which there are no distinctions, no possibility of change, and no sense of time. Births become phantasmal events that do not really occur, and deaths become appearances without reality. Meditators who know this experience understand themselves to be forever free.

In the assurance of immortality implicit in the unitive mystical experience, seekers of the age of the Upanishads recovered, substantially, the paradise that had been lost at the end of the vedic age. Attained by different means, it was a different paradise which could be enjoyed only by renouncing all earthly values and even personal existence itself. But millions of Hindu meditators over the centuries have judged this sacrifice to be not too high a price to pay for liberation from the bondage of the world.

People who undergo this experience are called *jīvanmuktas* (those liberated while still living). They are believed to have undergone an irreversible change. Stripped now of all sense of self and incapable of any self-serving act, they will acquire no new karma. When their old karma is expended, their bodies will die for the last time. They will then enter into final liberation in Brahman, never to be born again.

Some of the most famous Hindu saints have been natural mystics who had no need to practice yoga but achieved the unitive experience spontaneously and without conscious effort. There are some teachers today who deny the necessity of yoga and urge their disciples to await such a natural revelation.

Will all those who take up the search for mystical realization achieve it? Hindus have usually held that the chance of success is small for those who remain in society as householders, and that even renunciation of the world and a lifetime of meditational effort may not be sufficient. They feel that the outcome of yoga lies outside human control. Several Upanishads speak of success in meditation as dependent on the grace of God (Kaṭha 2.20, 23; Śvetāśvatara 3.20). Śaṅkara noted that for a monist (that is, one who believes that the Divine Being is not a person), there can be no such giver of grace; thus the matter remains a mystery, hidden perhaps in the unknown karma of former lives that assist some seekers and impede others. If realization is not achieved in the present life, however, all agree that the efforts of strivers are not lost. Reborn to more favorable situations, they will eventually attain illumination and the liberation that is their goal.

Notes

1 Manmatha Nath Dutt, trans., *A Prose English Translation of Markandeya Puranam* (privately published in Calcutta, India, 1896), p. 181, 4.18 ff.

2 Robert E. Hume, trans. and ed., *The Thirteen Principal Upanishads* (New York: Oxford University Press, 1962), p. 2.

3 Ibid., p. 350, 359 ff.; Kaṭha Upanishad 2.23.

4 Ibid., p. 247; Chāndogya Upanishad 6.12.

5 Ibid., pp. 355, 361, 401, 407.

6 Ibid., p. 126; Bṛihadāranyaka Upanishad 3.9.27.

5 Classical Hinduism: The Way of Devotion

The third of the Hindu mārgas, the Way of Devotion or *bhaktimārga,* places its hope for liberation in the power of a personal God of the universe. Two great theistic movements in Hinduism—one centered on Śiva, the other centered on Viṣṇu—have been exceedingly popular for two thousand years. Together, they probably hold the allegiance of a majority of Hindus today. These two forms of Indian religion are the most similar to the faiths of the West.

Like the Way of Knowledge, the Way of Devotion was a product of the stressful period when followers of the Vedic religion for the first time experienced a regimented social order, and when even the heavens no longer offered hope of lasting freedom. The Way of Knowledge and Buddhism offered release from karma and the unwanted round of lives, but at the cost of continuing existence as a person. Many Hindus cherished their own individuality too highly to find satisfaction in such liberations. In intellectual struggles they gradually worked out a different plan of salvation through a personal God of new stature. This development was difficult for people reared in the vedic tradition, because the comprehensive forces that control human life—ṛta or dharma, and karma—were conceived as impersonal principles. The personal gods of the Veda, on the other hand, were thought to reside in some specific region of the natural world, enjoying only limited powers and functions. Even the greatest gods were believed to control only a portion of the universe.

Speculations about a cosmic god with *universal* jurisdiction began in the late vedic hymns, but the notion of such a deity developed only slowly into a monotheism. The rise of the conception of a universal world-essence helped greatly in the emergence of monotheism when, in the Śvetāśvatara Upanishad (around the fifth century B.C.), the vedic god Rudra (now known also as Śiva) is described as Brahman, the totality of all being and all power. As the source and the essence of all material things and all souls, the Lord Śiva rules over all. He pervades persons, is present in their hearts, and as a radiance within he may be perceived by meditators who practice yoga. When we see him in ourselves as Śiva the Kindly, devotion (*bhakti*) to him is born. In response, God's grace is activated. It was he who created karma, and what he created he can break. When the fetters of karma are broken, there begins a life of freedom, including freedom from death.

A century or two later the Bhagavadgītā continued this use of the metaphysical idea of the universal Brahman to sustain a monotheistic theology. The Brahman doctrine became the foundation of the metaphysical understanding of God in all branches of the bhaktimārga. The term *bhakti* derives from a verb meaning "to divide and share," as when food is divided and shared at family and caste gatherings. The noun *bhakti* implies the unreserved loyalty and willingness to serve, combined with the special gratitude and trust found among those who share in the bounty extended by the elders who control such affectionate gatherings. *Bhaktas,* or devotees who follow the Way of Devotion, have discovered such affection at the center of the universe in "The great Lord of all the worlds, A friend of all creatures" (Bhagavadgītā 5.29). Despite this common understanding of the nature of God, the Way of Devotion has from the beginning consisted of two separate streams: the worshipers of Śiva, known as Śaivas, and the worshipers of Viṣṇu, who have long been called Vaiṣṇavas. Let us begin with the Śaivite tradition.

The Worship of Śiva

As Rudra the Howler, Śiva is known in the Vedas as a power operating in destructive rainstorms. His back is red and his neck is blue. He dwells apart from the other deities, in the mountains, and his retainers include robbers, ghosts, and goblins. His weapons include sharp arrows and the dreaded thunderbolt, which even the gods fear, and in the vedic hymns none who worship him assume that they are safe from him. He attacks many with fever, cough, and poisons; yet he is a physician also, who possesses a thousand remedies.

Those drawn to Śiva's worship have been especially sensitive to the harshness and brevity of life in this world. Seeing death as an ever-present reality, Śiva's worshipers have understood that safety can be found—if at all—only by dealing with the One who presides over such dangers. Śaivism has usually included within its fringes many small groups of alienated, morbid, and misanthropic persons drawn by the religion's stark realism who perceived Śiva as the special divine force behind all natural processes of destruction. In time, however, the worship of Śiva among some people outgrew the status of a special cult within polytheism and developed a monotheistic theology. And as the following of the deity increased, persons of more optimistic disposition entered this Śaiva circle, and the mood of Śiva-worship became more boldly hopeful.

THE LIṄGAM AND YONI EMBLEM

In the first century B.C. shrines dedicated to Śiva began to appear. In some shrines the object of worship was a stone pillar resembling the male generative organ. Śiva had come to be regarded as a source of procreation as well as of destruction. Images of Śiva in human form were also common. The worship of the *liṅgam* (phallic emblem) did not become dominant until it had evolved into a plain vertical cylinder rounded at the top, only vaguely phallic, a symbol rather than a representation of the sex organ. The four faces looking out from the sides of the shaft indicate the omniscience of the god, who faces in all directions. Within a few centuries it became customary to seat the cylinder in a shallow spouted dish. Originally this rimmed dish was a basin for catching liquid oblations poured over the liṅgam by worshipers, but soon it was thought to be a *yoni,* or female organ, representing Śiva's *śākti,* or female reproductive power. The combined icon shows the Śaivas' recognition of the importance of the feminine element in all divine activity in the cosmos (see photo on next page).

A combined liṅgam and yoni icon usually stands at the center of Śaiva shrines. Modern Hindu scholars insist that this emblem refers to metaphysical truths only, even though it uses images of the human genitals. Indeed the rites of liṅgam worship have not been orgiastic or focused on erotic interests. The icon makes a statement about the cosmos: Śiva's potent generative power is eternally at work, a force for life as well as for destruction. Because the people of the Indus Valley civilization used phalluses in their cult, many scholars believe that the liṅgam and perhaps other aspects of Śiva worship entered Hinduism from this old source, but the demonstration of a connection with that distant cultural past is not complete.

A tale about the liṅgam, told in both the *Liṅga* and the *Śiva* Purāṇas, illustrates how mythmakers

Though Śaiva artists sometimes give Śiva a human form, this simpler representation appears in the usual shrine. Śiva is seen here as the universal male power in everlasting union with his female energy. By their combined force, the world comes into being and evolves. *The Metropolitan Museum of Art, gift of Samuel Eilenberg, 1987.*

tried to express monotheistic understandings of Śiva. Once, while the universe was still in a state of dissolution, Brahmā the creator-god wandered over the primeval waters and encountered Viṣṇu. Each greeted the other in a condescending manner, indicating that each considered the other his inferior, and soon a fierce argument over seniority ensued. As they quarreled, a great pillar of flame rose suddenly out of the lower darkness and shot upward out of sight. Silenced, Brahmā and Viṣṇu decided to find out more about the pillar by searching for its upper and lower ends. In the form of a swan Brahmā flew upward out of sight, and Viṣṇu in the form of a boar pushed downward with his snout to find the pillar's base. After a thousand years the two gods returned defeated, unable to find the upper or lower end of the pillar. It was infinite. As they huddled in frustration, a humming sound began to emerge from the pillar. It was the sound of the sacred syllable *ōm,* the symbol of absolute Being. Then the great pillar opened, and Śiva manifested himself.

The pillar was Śiva's liṅgam, the eternal and limitless source of all things. Viṣṇu in his boar form bows before Śiva, and Brahmā also acknowledged Śiva's supremacy. Seeing their humble worship, Śiva extends to both deities the open palm of reassurance and blessing (see photo opposite page).

The story of the infinite liṅgam dramatizes the creativity of Śiva as a masculine force. The presence in Śiva of a corresponding feminine power is recognized in Śaiva myths about his wife, who is known as Umā, Pārvatī, or Durgā. The most vivid of all the assertions of Śiva's bisexual nature is the common image of Śiva as Ardhanārīsvara, the Half-Woman Lord. The left side of this image, always the distaff side in India, displays Śiva's feminine nature: a large woman's earring, a conspicuous breast, bangles around the wrists, and a left leg clothed in a clinging silk skirt. On the male side Śiva wears as his breech clout a tiger skin, his earring is a serpent, and in his upper right hand he holds the flaming ax that he once snatched out of the air when hostile sages hurled it at him.

ŚIVA'S DUAL NATURE

The acknowledgment of the feminine in Śiva reflected another development in the growth of his popularity: the softening of his fierce and threatening nature. As Śaivism grew in popularity during the first five centuries A.D., the mythology of Śiva developed in new directions in the epics and purāṇas. Śiva did not lose his old threatening characteristics but developed a dual nature that included a kindlier side. Showing his destructiveness still, Śiva in the purāṇas haunts the cremation grounds, his body smeared with the ashes of the dead. (Preparation for the worship of Śiva is still made by rubbing ashes over one's body and marking one's forehead with three horizontal stripes of white ash.) Śiva wears a necklace made of skulls, the skulls of the Brahmās of past eons, whom he has outlived and whose creations he has brought to an end. Stories of his wildly destructive acts continue to be told, and new names arise that stress his ferocious and terrible nature. Some orders of ancient Śiva devotees shocked their contemporaries by dwelling in cremation grounds, or by practicing bloody sacrifices, or using skulls as alms bowls.

As Śiva became a universal God, however, new myths showed him using his dreadful powers in constructive ways. In vedic times he was known as a handler of poisons, but in the new mythology his old skill with poisons reappears in the story of how he came to be called Nīlakaṇṭha (the Blue-throated). The gods, who had not yet attained exemption from death, decided to seek endless life by churning the Sea of Milk in order to extract from it the nectar of immortality. The churn was rotated by wrapping around its spindle the long body of Vāsuki, the king of serpents, which was stretched from one shore of the sea to the other. To provide a base for the spindle on the bottom of the sea, Viṣṇu took the form of a tortoise. The gods and the demons pulled on their respective ends. Just as the nectar started to emerge from the sea, Vāsuki grew sick and vomited venom from each of his thousand heads, and over the surface of the sea spread a blue black mass, the deadly Halāhala poison that could kill even the gods.

When all the gods, including Viṣṇu, were almost overcome by the poison, Śiva came to the rescue. Riding his bull Nandi, he arrived at the seashore, picked up a large shell, skimmed off the dark liquid, and drank it to the last drop. But even Śiva was not totally immune to the poison, which lodged in his throat, turning it blue. Devotees gazing at pictures of the blue-throated Śiva are reminded of the lengths to which their God would go to save his worshipers from danger. Another favorite myth celebrates Śiva's bringing down from heaven the Ganges River, whose sacred waters have ever since refreshed the land.

Śiva emerges here from the world pillar, revealing that he alone is the world's central power. Infinite in outreach, he is beyond the comprehension of the greatest of the gods. Brahmā as a swan, barely visible, upper left, and Viṣṇu in boar form try vainly to find Śiva's upper and lower limits. *Réunion des Musées Nationaux, Paris.*

ŚIVA AS THE ONE GOD

After A.D. 400 a number of groups arose that worshiped Śiva as the supreme God. Sanskrit manuals called *āgamas* were composed to guide their members in proper rituals and beliefs and in the making of images and temples. The first full-scale books of Śaiva religious philosophy were written in Kashmir between A.D. 800 and 1200. But after that time Śaiva monotheism declined in northern India, and today in most northern regions Śiva is worshiped only as one member of the general pantheon of gods.

In the south, however, the worship of Śiva as the one God expanded greatly. Since the seventh century A.D. a group of Tamil speakers near the tip of the Indian subcontinent has followed a theological tradition that came to be called the Śaivasiddhānta. In addition, the sect of the Vīraśaivas or Liṅgāyats has been popular among Kannada speakers since the twelfth century A.D.

As early as the seventh century A.D., there arose among the Tamils a series of remarkable poets, beginning with Appar and Sambandar, whose beautiful hymns are still sung. As recently as the seventeenth century there were new surges of devotion in Tamil literature, and a poet named Sivavākkiyar praised the uniqueness of Śiva in these lines:

Not Vishnu, Brahmā, Śiva,
In the Beyond is He,
Not black, nor white, nor ruddy,
This Source of things that be;
Not great is he, not little,
Not female and not male—
But stands far, far, and far beyond
All being's utmost pale![1]

The early Tamil poets' belief in a personal God was placed in great difficulty, however, by the subtle and powerful arguments of the philosopher Śaṅkara on behalf of a religion of the impersonal Brahman. Among the devotees of Śiva a need was felt for intellectual defenders of the Śaiva beliefs. The earliest Śaiva theologians in the south were Meykandār and his disciple Aruḷnandi, who taught in the thirteenth century.

By calling Śiva *Paśupati,* the Lord of Cattle, the Śaivasiddhānta theologians wished to emphasize the protective aspect of Śiva's nature. (In Western religions, worshipers have spoken of the "Good Shepherd" to express a similar understanding.) From the word Paśupati are derived the three basic topics of this theological system: *paśu* (a domestic animal and, by extension, a human soul), *pati* (owner or lord), and *pāśa* (tether or bond). These three terms are used to convey a message that the Lord Śiva feels concern for human souls and seeks to free them from the bonds that prevent them from attaining salvation.

According to the Śaiva theologians, many souls are deluded in regard to their nature, imagining themselves to be physical beings only, and beings separate from others, as all bodies are. They are not aware that God dwells in all, and that all are possessed and guided by God. Ignorant of the helping power of Śiva, they are helplessly bound by the three tethers. The tether *āṇava* (belittling ignorance) causes souls to perceive themselves as petty isolated beings existing only to serve themselves. The tether karma is the accumulated energy of past deeds that binds souls to rebirths for the purpose of reward and punishment. The tether māyā is the physical stuff of all things, including human bodies that dominate the attention of human beings and cause them to act as if physical pleasure were the purpose of life.

Śiva offers many kinds of spiritual assistance to help humans liberate themselves from these bonds. He continually creates, preserves, and destroys all things physical—both worlds and bodies—so that souls may live and learn. Śiva deliberately conceals himself so that souls will seek him, tantalized. To those who have learned to desire him, he sends, according to their advancement, first a spiritual preceptor, then visions of himself as the master of karma, and finally an Inner Light in which Śiva is known and liberation is achieved. In many shrines in southern India the principal Śaiva beliefs are expressed in images of Śiva as the supreme dancer. Śiva is worshiped there as the creator, preserver, and destroyer of life, and as a gracious guide.

The union with God of which these Śaivas speak is not like that of the Advaita because it entails no loss of one's sense of individuality nor any sense that the worshiper has become divine. Rather, it produces a feeling of being intimately supported

Śiva as the Dancer who activates the rhythms of the universe. His sending forth of the cosmos is suggested by the drum in his right hand. In his left, a flame indicates his power of destruction. At center, one hand makes the sign of reassurance, while the other points to his feet, at which worshippers may fall and receive his help. *Cleveland Art Museum.*

by a gracious and perfect Lord. After the liberating experience, devotees are expected to live joyously and freely. They frequent temples and assemblies of believers not out of obligation, but in order to engage in spontaneous worship, and to dance and sing the hymns of the ancient saints.

The Śaivasiddhānta doctrine is the living belief of millions of people today in the Tamil country, where several monastic centers of learning are maintained. Their leaders object to the Advaita doctrine, saying that it is blasphemous for human beings to identify themselves with God. But they appreciate all religions of devotion to a personal God, saying that the adherents of Christianity and Islam, because of their right religious attitudes, will be reborn into the saving Śaiva faith.

Śāktism

Śāktism receives its name from its principal teaching: that the Great Goddess who is the focus of Śākta worship is the *śākti*—the active world-creating and world-controlling power of Śiva. The Śākta religion developed in long interaction with the worship of Śiva. It is studied at this point for the advantage of viewing it in connection with Śaivism, on which it depended for two thousand years for some aspects of its growth. Śāktas accept the Śaiva symbols and myths and acknowledge Śiva to be the passive and masculine aspect of the Godhead, but they themselves prefer to worship the feminine side of the divine polarity because they conceive her to be the force that determines the course of all that goes on in the natural universe. Though they understand this ruling power to be a single personal being, they call her Umā, Pārvatī, Caṇḍī, Bhairavī, Cāmuṇḍā, Kālī, and other names connected with various acts of hers related in myths. Her primary name is Durgā, because she is known by that name in the heroic tale that her worshipers love most.

Durgā is worshiped at centers of pilgrimage throughout India. Her devotees live in significant numbers in Gujarat and Rajasthan and especially in Bengal and adjacent regions of northeast India, including the Himalayan nation of Nepal. Every year, in late September and October, the entire Hindu population of Bengal celebrates the *Durgā Pūjā,* a festival during which Durgā's deliverance of the world from the attack of the buffalo-demon Mahisha is narrated. In local pavilions, enthusiasts erect temporary clay images of Durgā brandishing her many weapons in her many hands. On each night Durgā's victories are retold by chanting the *Devī Māhātmyā* a Sanskrit narrative poem written in about the sixth century A.D. and the Śāktas' favorite scripture. On the last night of the recitations, the festival is concluded by sacrificing a goat or a buffalo as an offering to Durgā. This rite is almost the sole survival of animal sacrifice in modern brāhmaṇical Hinduism.

Śāktism is of particular interest as the modern world's most highly developed worship of a supreme female deity. The worship of Durgā has most of the characteristics of monotheism. Her power alone is understood to create, control, and destroy all phenomenal things, and thus no Śākta worship is directed to any being who is not one of her forms or appearances. But Durgā is not understood to be the whole of the divine nature; the realm of the transcendent and changeless is Śiva's, and those who seek liberation from the world (mokṣa) must seek it by meditation on Śiva in yoga. Śāktas, however, express little desire for mokṣa. As people concerned about the world, they seek from the goddess health, wealth, and general well-being. Because the goal of Śāktism is seldom salvation, this faith cannot be classified as one of the religions of the bhaktimārga, even though Śākta worship is often performed with fervent devotion, or bhakti.

ORIGINS OF ŚĀKTISM

Śāktism did not originate with the goddesses of the Vedas or directly from the cult of Śiva. Its earliest traces are seen about the time of Christ in rural areas in unorganized forms of the worship of goddesses who continued certain aspects of the mother goddess cult of the Indus Valley civilization. This matrix of ancient rural religion probably included ancient forms of the present worship of the dangerous village godlings. The brāhmaṇs first ignored these non-Aryan goddesses, but in the first few centuries A.D., a few brāhmaṇs and other Hindus who wrote in Sanskrit began to notice certain deities of the rural pantheon. In late portions of the *Mahābhārata* epic, the goddess Durgā is mentioned as receiving offerings of liquor and flesh from members of certain mountain tribes. There are also references to Cāmuṇḍā, the emaciated goddess of famine, and to Kālī, a ghoulish figure with disheveled hair who roams battlefields eating human flesh and delighting in the blood of the slain. In later literary references these goddesses have become members of Śiva's entourage, and later still, his wives. The worshipers of these goddesses made their deities not merely Śiva's wives, but also metaphysically his śāktis, or creative powers in the formation of the world. Adopting the strong Śaiva tendency toward monotheism, they too attempted to create from their feminine pantheon a more rational theological interpretation of the world than polytheism could provide.

Beginning in the first or second century A.D., preeminence was given to a group of goddesses called the Seven Mothers (*Saptamātrikā*), who were worshiped sometimes as a group and sometimes separately. They are thought to be dangerous beings, though some are kindly in appearance. Usually the goddesses in the set are accompanied by a child. They are generally represented in sculptures as full-breasted, and some look down on the child with tenderness. At the other end of the extreme stands the dreadful Cāmuṇḍā, a childless destroyer of life in general and a killer by famine in particular. Thus, the followers of the Śākta religion perceive the natural world as filled with threats and anxiously seek security.

In the *Devī Māhātmyā* Durgā is spoken of as the unification of all the feminine powers. She is proclaimed to be the eternal consort of Śiva and the sole creator and ruler of the world. The Seven Mothers and the other goddesses are said to be no more than temporary manifestations of her various powers. Even the much-worshipped Kālī became part of Durgā's essence. Yet as manifestations of Durgā, the special names and characteristics of these old goddesses continued to be remembered in worship. This complex conception of the Great Goddess allows Śāktas to interpret very different human situations in a religious manner.

Among Śākta believers two quite different moods can be found. Sometimes the furious Goddess takes the field as the champion of life. At other times Śākta believers perceive her rage as directed against themselves, and they pray that her violence may be averted, or they reflect that the Mother of the World brings suffering and death, just as she gives joy and life, and that her acts are divine and must be endured even when she inflicts horrors.

The assurance given by Śākta teaching enables believers to accept harsh experiences in a spirit of devotion. Such a calm acceptance of the tragedies of life is found in the Bengali poetry of Rāmaprasād Sen (1718–1775), the greatest modern poet of Kālī devotion, who expressed his view of his own sufferings in these words:

Though the mother beat him,
the child cries, "Mother, O Mother!"
and clings still tighter to her garment.
True, I cannot see thee,
yet I am not a lost child.
I still cry, "Mother, Mother". . . .
All the miseries that I have suffered
and am suffering, I know, O Mother,
to be your mercy alone.[2]

Although the Hindu conceptions of Durgā and Kālī are shocking, reflection will show us that the problems at the center of Śākta worship have been deep concerns in other religious traditions as well.

TĀNTRISM

A closely related form of religion called Tāntrism arose in ancient times out of the same popular goddess worship from which Śāktism was born. Tāntrists often follow Śākta patterns in their public life. They are equally feminist in their theology. But Tāntrism has mokṣa, or liberation, as its goal, and it is set off from Śāktism by erotic ritual practices and by an elaborate yoga that is sexual in its concepts. Disdained by most Hindus, Tāntrism is a marginal development with a small following.

The Worship of Viṣṇu

VIṢṆU IN THE VEDIC AGE

The second of the two great bhakti traditions has long honored the name of the vedic Viṣṇu and has taken into itself much of the lore of that kindly deity. The Viṣṇu of the Vedas is associated with the sun and is seen as promoting growth. He is present in plants and trees, provides food, and protects unborn babies in the womb. He rides a sun-eagle, wears a sunlike jewel on his breast, and is armed with a discus (*cakra*) that is clearly the orb of the sun. But he is not the sun, and thus his jurisdiction is not limited to a single part of the natural world.

Although not a great god in the vedic pantheon,

Cāmuṇḍā, one of the Seven Mothers, with her weapons and the bowl from which she drinks blood. Śāktas understand her to be a manifestation of Durgā, the universal mother, and try to accept natural destruction at her hands with trustful worship, like the figure at bottom. *Trustees of the British Museum.*

Viṣṇu in his Dwarf Incarnation plots the recovery of the earth from the demons. Modern miniature painting. *Bury Peerless.*

Viṣṇu appealed to many in postvedic times because of his deeds on behalf of humanity. When Indra, accompanied by a host of gods, drew near the mountain lair of the demon Vṛtra, the gods fled in terror, but Viṣṇu stood steadfast and helped release the waters that flowed down in seven beneficent rivers. The Brāhmaṇas recount how Viṣṇu assumed the form of a dwarf and went as a beggar before Bali, the king of the demons, and asked as alms the gift of as much space as he could mark out in three steps. The demon granted him this favor. Viṣṇu then resumed his cosmic stature and paced off in his first giant step the whole earth, as an abode for living persons. Then he marked off the atmosphere, and in the third step he established the high heavenly world as a pleasant refuge for the deceased. Viṣṇu was the one god of the vedic pantheon who was known to care about the happiness of the dead.

The cult of Viṣṇu attracted persons concerned about the problem of immortality and also those who had at heart the welfare of society. Viṣṇu worship appealed to those who saw the universe as friendly and good. Salvation seekers of the postvedic age who could not perceive the violent Rudra as their savior found an alternative in a great god who could be identified with Viṣṇu. Vaiṣṇava religion found its following among the more settled citizens and civil leaders of the Hindu world.

ORIGINS OF THE VAIṢṆAVA TRADITION

The Vaiṣṇava religion did not arise directly out of vedic circles that worshiped Viṣṇu, however. Its institutional history began in the religious life of a tribal people called the Sātvatas, who in the fifth century B.C. were already worshiping, in nonvedic rites, their special deity called Kṛṣṇa Vāsudeva. In its early phases, this religion was often called the Sātvata faith after the tribe that professed it, or sometimes the Bhāgavata faith because its great god was given the title Bhagavat, or Bounteous One. The standard term Vaiṣṇava began to come into use in the first centuries of the Christian era.

It is in the Sanskrit grammar of Pāṇini, composed about 400 B.C., that Kṛṣṇa Vāsudeva is mentioned first—already as an object of worship. A little can be learned about this deity and his worshipers in scattered references in the earliest warrior stories in the great Indian epic called the *Mahābhārata*, which was beginning to be woven together in that same period. The bards in these early epic stories refer to Kṛṣṇa Vāsudeva as a great chieftain of the Sātvatas, and it is likely that this deity arose out of the fame of a once-living ruler. The early epic materials of about 400–200 B.C. remember Kṛṣṇa Vāsudeva as much more than human, however. For many he is the God of gods, supreme ruler of the universe, worshiped not only by the Sātvatas but also by other people who had been drawn into the Sātvata religion. The Sātvata tribe, which originally had held an undistinguished position on the lower fringes of Aryan society, had by means of military success attained kṣatriya status in the eyes of most and had all but erased the memory of its plebeian origin. Established among the elite classes at the royal courts of north India, the worshipers of Kṛṣṇa Vāsudeva were in a position, after 400 B.C., to learn the Sanskrit language and its literature. For several centuries, however, they remained unsympathetic to the vedic sacrifices and showed no familiarity with the mystical religion of the Upanishads, and they made no apparent effort to explain the greatness of their God in terms of the infinite Brahman of the Upanishads.

Whatever the Sātvatas' origin might have been, after 400 B.C. they became so powerful that they were able to approach the highest classes of Aryan society. In time they developed ties with the brāhmaṇs who served as priests to the nobility. Some brāhmaṇs became adherents of the Sātvata faith and, as teachers, assisted the sect in establishing its simple monotheism upon the Upanishads' doctrine about the unification of the world in the Brahman.

The Bhagavadgītā, a work of the second or first century B.C., is the literary product of India's first creative encounter between monotheistic and monistic religious traditions. It was received with such favor that it was incorporated immediately into the *Mahābhārata* by the new brāhmaṇ editors who were beginning to recast and enlarge that epic poem at that time.

The Bhagavadgītā

The Bhagavadgītā consists of eighteen cantos of Sanskrit verse which were integrated into the sixth book of the *Mahābhārata* as a distinct unit. Often printed separately from the great epic, the Bhagavadgītā has become the most widely used of all Hindu scriptures. The kindly attitude of its unknown author toward non-Vaiṣṇava forms of religion is one reason for the work's broad appeal. The Vaiṣṇava author found positive values in other teachings and practices, and thus the text can be appreciated and used by millions who are not devotees of Kṛṣṇa at all. But the principal reason for the wide acclaim that the work received at the time of its writing was its contribution to the solution of a critical social problem: the widespread abandonment of their social stations by young men who had become disenchanted with the life of this world. The deep concern of the ruling classes had been aroused by a massive response to the proposal of the late Upanishads and other religions of the time that citizens should seek liberation by renouncing the world and becoming hermits in the forest. The Bhagavadgītā discusses this problem in detail.

The author knew the major Upanishads well and believed that Kṛṣṇa himself had revealed them (15.15). He was inspired by their message that the universe had a metaphysical unity in the nonphenomenal Brahman, but the social message of the Upanishad religion, as it was being interpreted in his own time, dismayed him. He comments on the call to the ascetic life from the viewpoint of the Sátvatas, who had just risen to responsibility for the welfare of the world and who were by no means disgusted with society or disillusioned with personal existence. Despite the author's view that all forms of Hinduism can be useful to some in the struggle for salvation, he does not regard all faiths as equally true and effective. Politely but firmly, he subordinates the impersonal Brahman of the Upanishads to the control of a personal Lord, and with great emphasis he corrects current interpretation of the Upanishads' teaching about *sannyāsa,* or renunciation. He insists that seekers of salvation need not and should not abandon the world and cease their worldly work. His method is an ingenious analysis of how the weaknesses of our acts damage us and an explanation of why external renunciation of the work of this world is not necessary for salvation.

The Bhagavadgītā opens with a scene that illustrates the crisis of the age: A sensitive warrior is contemplating the grim duty that Hindu society requires of his caste, and he recoils at the thought of the evils that will follow and of the guilt that its performance may entail. Arjuna, the despondent hero, is the chief reliance of the army of the Pāṇḍavas. He is bound by duty to fight the forces of the Kaurava prince, Duryodhana, who has committed great wrongs. But as Arjuna looks down the ranks of opponents he is expected to slay, he is moved by affection for the relatives and respected teachers whom he sees among them, and he reflects with horror on the injuries and disorder that his fighting would produce. Paralyzed by the thought of his dreadful duties, Arjuna drops his weapons and throws himself down in his chariot, saying it would be better to live by begging as monks do, than to commit such deeds (2.5). Confused about what is right, he asks for the advice of Kṛṣṇa, who is serving as his chariot driver.

Although the duty of a warrior is discussed in this story, the case of Arjuna only epitomizes the moral problem of the members of every occupation. Kṛṣṇa's message is as much a lesson for clerks, shopkeepers, and priests as it is for warriors. Must we, as the followers of the Way of Knowledge assert, abandon our worldly work with its imperfections and endless retributions if we aspire to liberation?

Kṛṣṇa responded first with conventional arguments: Disgrace descends on all who flee their duties; in using arms no real harm is done, since the soul cannot be slain. In the second canto Kṛṣṇa began to reveal the real reason why the duties of life need not be abandoned, and that is because they can be performed in a new spirit that prevents the acquisition of karma and makes them a means of liberation rather than of bondage. Our desires—our greed or aversion, our longing or loathing—are what bind acts to us and make their impurity our own. If we can perform the duties of our stations simply because the scriptures require us to perform them or simply as a service to God, and with no desire to make any personal gains, then those acts will have no real connection with us in the operation of the processes of retribution. No karma will be created by those acts, no ties with the world will be deepened by them, and no future births will ensue. After a life lived in the selfless performance of one's social role, the dispassionate soul, unfettered still despite a fully active life, is forever freed.

Kṛṣṇa explained that he himself as the Lord of the Universe creates and maintains the world in that desireless spirit: it is only to secure the welfare of the world that he carries on his eternal cosmic activity (3.20–25), and it is only to save the world from evil that he descends to mundane births age after age (4.5–15), and thus his work entails no bondage.

Human workers in the world can emulate that selflessness and share in that freedom. The renunciation that the scriptures require is not an abandonment of work—which we can never totally achieve so long as we must care for a body—but a renunciation of desires. Those who quell their desires achieve a calm that is not a mere state of the emotions but a metaphysical state of being. They attain Brahman, which is known mystically in human experience as a realization of lasting serenity (5.19 ff.). Those who know Brahman work in that serenity until the end of life, then pass quietly at death into everlasting peace, included in the eternal Brahman that is the Being of God (2.72).

Yet when Kṛṣṇa at the end of the fourth canto called on Arjuna to rise and do his warrior's duty, Arjuna still could not muster the resolve to do so. Thereupon Kṛṣṇa explained how we can employ the discipline of meditation to gain victory over desire. The heart of the Bhagavadgītā's meditation is the purposeful upward redirection of our attention. We must no longer concentrate on sense objects, as is our innate tendency; rather, looking upward, we must focus our inward eye on loftier realities—the soul, the World Soul, Brahman, and best of all, the personal supreme Lord. Beginners in the faith can struggle for an awareness of God by such humble practices as meditating on Kṛṣṇa's deeds and singing his praises, and can then move onward into deeper disciplines of meditation. The author knew advanced introspections like those of the eight-stage yoga and teaches them, but with important modifications: The genuine realization of Brahman will not come in preternatural luminous visions induced by restraint of breath, but rather in the experience of tranquility that arises from the elimination of desire.

The realization of Brahman is not an end in itself, as in the jñānamārga; rather, the realization of Brahman gives rise to a compassion for all creatures, a compassion born of the awareness of the metaphysical tie that unites all beings in a single essence, and it creates a capacity for a lifetime of desireless work. Finally, out of the realization of Brahman comes a recognition of our tie with God, the final means of salvation (18.54–56).

The eleventh canto of the Bhagavadgītā relates how the reluctant Arjuna was finally moved to devote himself to the service of God by a vision of Kṛṣṇa in his cosmic state. Overwhelmed by the revelation, Arjuna paid homage to Kṛṣṇa and proclaimed him to be the be-all and end-all of existence, even greater than Brahman (11.37), and the source of duty itself (14.27). In the last canto the climactic development of the book is reached with Arjuna's pledge to Kṛṣṇa, "I shall do your word!" (18.73). In return, Kṛṣṇa assured him that sincere strivers could turn to him for refuge, despite their shortcomings, and that he would liberate them from all their sins (18.64–66).

By adapting the Brahman concept of the Upanishads, the author of the Bhagavadgītā was able to give the simple religion of the Sātvatas a way of explaining its monotheism by using a well-established Hindu concept of the universe as a whole. In the theology of the Bhagavadgītā, the Brahman is, much as the Upanishads state it to be, the single ultimate stuff of the universe. But this universal essence is not autonomous. It is God's world-stuff, an aspect of the divine Being that is transcended and controlled by an Intelligence. The Lord has priority over Brahman (14.27) and controls Brahman (13.12 ff.). Those who have attained Brahman by means of the Way of Knowledge have attained a condition that is divine, free, and lasting, but they have not attained equality with the Lord, nor have they learned the final truth about his nature.

By entering into dialogue with vedāntic learning, the author of the Bhagavadgītā gave his sect a view of the universe that made it worthy of the attention of sophisticated persons who knew the Vedas and other Sanskrit literature. He adapted to the needs of a social and ethical religion the meditational skills that the ascetics had developed. By a positive appreciation of many other movements and sects, he created a meeting place for Hindus of many kinds. He offered to Hindu society, weakened by the alienation of its workers, an alternative to secession and parasitism, and he gave to all of Hinduism a beautiful devotional work of wide appeal. Finally, he laid the foundation for the transformation of his small sect into the most powerful stream of the bhaktimārga and into a major support of the brāhmaṇical order of things.

The Later Vaiṣṇava Tradition

The subsequent history of the Vaiṣṇava religion centered on two kinds of developments: (1) the gathering of congenial groups around the original users of the Bhagavadgītā and (2) the special responses of certain Kṛṣṇa worshippers to pressures and needs that arose in later historical periods. During a history of two thousand years the Vaiṣṇava tradition grew and became a great family of religions bound together by the common possession of the Bhagavadgītā and a few other universally accepted scriptures.

THE IDENTIFICATION OF KṚṢṆA WITH VIṢṆU

The author of the Bhagavadgītā in a few subtle statements indicated that to him Kṛṣṇa in his heavenly form was the vedic deity Viṣṇu (11.24, 30, 46). In about 150 B.C. the sage Patañjali suggested the unity of Kṛṣṇa and Viṣṇu in his *Mahābhāshya* (3.1.26) by mentioning religious dramas that recounted both the killing of Kaṃsa by Kṛṣṇa and the binding of Bali by Viṣṇu. At stake in these and other efforts to establish for Kṛṣṇa a tie with the vedic god was the orthodoxy of Kṛṣṇa's sect in the eyes of all other Hindus. The deciders of such claims were not the followers of the sect or the general population, but brāhmaṇs learned in the Vedas. By arriving at a consensus, such brāhmaṇs could retain or remove from a sect the taint of falsity of teaching. If Kṛṣṇa, even under another name, were universally understood to have been mentioned in the Vedas, his worship could be deemed to be a form of vedic religion. Brāhmaṇs might then serve the sect as priests, and citizens might adhere to it without sacrificing their orthodoxy. Bhāgavatism could be considered a revealed religion, and its scriptures could be accepted as smṛitis. In this case, full recognition came after five hundred years of pressure and accommodation.

The first group of brāhmaṇs to be won over were those who, in the period of the later development of the *Mahābhārata,* became its new reciters and revisers. In the materials of this later epic the identification of Kṛṣṇa with Viṣṇu was everywhere openly stated and accepted. The *Viṣṇu Purāṇa* of about the fourth century A.D. brings together in one book the myths of Kṛṣṇa and of Viṣṇu, marking a further consolidation of their cults. By the end of that same century, the wide use of the term Vaiṣṇava in the general brāhmaṇical literature showed that even the most hostile groups of brāhmaṇs had been won over. Thereafter, only a few dared charge that the Vaiṣṇavas were nonvedic. Respectability had been achieved, and the way had been opened for the full exercise of the great Vaiṣṇava absorptive capacity.

But in that final settlement not only the brāhmaṇs made concessions. The Vaiṣṇavas dropped the early Sātvata hostility toward the vedic sacrifice and its priesthood, such as one finds in Bhagavadgītā 2.41–44. They abandoned as well the tendency to exalt kṣatriyas as religious leaders. Their one-time tendency to minimize the importance of caste ranking was carefully contained. Brāhmaṇs and Vaiṣṇavas together became the mainstay of the caste civilization.

THE WORSHIPERS OF NĀRĀYAṆA

Early in the expansion of the Vaiṣṇava faith a sophisticated sect called the Pāñcarātrins were assimilated. The Pāñcarātrins were committed to a monotheistic explanation of the origin of the universe, and had honored as Creator their sectarian deity whom they called Nārāyaṇa. Identifying Nārāyaṇa now with Viṣṇu and with Kṛṣṇa Vāsudeva, the Pāñcarātrins ceased to exist as a separate sectarian community. The heritage of their speculations enriched this thought of general Vaiṣṇava religion.

The Pāñcarātrins performed vedic sacrifices except those that involved the slaughter of animals. Their insistence on nonviolence contrasts sharply with the position of the Bhagavadgītā, but on this point the worshipers of Nārāyaṇa were able to dominate the union into which they entered. Today, almost all followers of the Vaiṣṇava faith are vegetarians, and the objection to animal sacrifices has spread beyond Vaiṣṇava circles until now very few Hindus justify the ritual killing of animals.

The Pāñcarātrins made three other significant contributions to their new faith: (1) a pious practice called *japa* (muttering), which is the continued repetition of the name of the Deity; (2) the reintroduction into the Vaiṣṇava religion, for totally devoted persons, of a form of monastic life not dissimilar in appearance to that of the sannyāsīs of the Way of Knowledge; and (3) an expectation that as a reward for their devotion to God, worshipers might receive an actual vision of the Deity. The hope for *darśana* (a direct vision of God) is an important Vaiṣṇava aspiration today.

THE AVATĀRAS

One of the most distinctive and important of the Vaiṣṇava ideas is that the deity descends to earth and is born there in earthly forms. The first appearance of this belief was in Bhagavadgītā 4.6–8, in which Kṛṣṇa spoke of his alternation between two realms:

Though I am an eternal unborn Soul,
the Lord of Beings,
relying on my own materiality
I enter into phenomenal being
by my own mysterious power (māyā).
Whenever righteousness declines
and wickedness erupts
I send myself forth, O Bharata [Arjuna].
To protect the good and destroy evildoers
and establish the right, I come into being
age after age.

In the eleventh canto, in his awesome vision of the transcendent Lord, Arjuna addressed the Supreme Being as Viṣṇu. Most Hindus have always believed

Kalki, the tenth avatara of Viṣṇu. Like Kṛṣṇa, Kalki is Viṣṇu made manifest on earth but Kalki has yet to come.

that the god who is the heavenly source of avatāras should be called Viṣṇu, and that Kṛṣṇa Vāsudeva may be counted among Viṣṇu's *avatāras,* or descents.

The conception of avatāra is not found in the Vedas; even the essentials for its creation appeared later: the idea of a supreme deity, the idea of repeated births, and the idea of a metaphysical link between divine and human states. The Sātvata tradition probably generated the avatāra concept in order to explain how its object of worship, a well-known human being, could also be divine. This doctrine supports the Vaiṣṇavas' comparatively high appreciation of the value of worldly life and their faith in a kindly, world-concerned deity.

The number of the avatāras has never been agreed on completely. *Mahābhārata* 12.326.72–82 names seven and the *Bhāgavata Purāṇa* names twenty-two but adds that the number is really beyond counting. In the present millennium most Hindus have agreed in recognizing ten avatāras, named in this order: Matsya, Kurma, Varāha, Narasiṃha, Vāmana, Paraśurāma, Kṛṣṇa, Rāma, Buddha, and Kalki. Kalki, the tenth avatāra, is yet to come. Pictured as a swordsman on a white horse, or as a horse-headed figure, he is to appear at the end of the present evil age to unseat from their thrones the wicked barbarian rulers of the earth and to restore the righteous brāhmaṇical order. This concept of Kalki arose out of the revulsion of Hindu India, in the first three centuries A.D., to the long rule of foreign dynasties that were indifferent or hostile to the brāhmaṇs. Buddha, the ninth, is the founder of Buddhism and the one surely historical personality in the list. Rāma, the eighth of the series, is the hero of the *Rāmāyana,* an epic poem discussed later in this chapter. We already know much about Kṛṣṇa, the seventh avatāra. Paraśurāma, the sixth, may, along with Kṛṣṇa and Rāma, have been an actual person. He is said to have restored the supremacy of the brāhmaṇs by slaughtering the insubordinate kṣatriyas with his ax (*paraśu*). In the form of Vāmana, the fifth avatāra, Viṣṇu recovered the world from the demons by his famous strategy of the three steps. As Narasiṃha the Man-Lion, the fourth avatāra, Viṣṇu protected his devotee Prahlāda from persecution by a demon, whom the avatāra split open with his claws. As Varāha (the Boar), Viṣṇu as the third avatāra plunged into the sea and with his snout raised up the drowning world that lay submerged on the bottom, where it had been dumped by a demon. As Kurma (the Tortoise), the second avatāra, Viṣṇu during the great churning of the ocean stood on the ocean bottom and provided a firm base for the churn by letting its spindle revolve on his back. In his Matsya or fish avatāra, Viṣṇu warned Manu of a coming universal deluge and pulled to safety the boat that Manu built. Thus all the avatāras are conceived as benefactors of humanity.

Although the ten figures just named are recognized as divine by all traditional Hindus, only the Vaiṣṇavas feel obliged to worship any of them, and among Vaiṣṇavas it is customary to select a favorite avatāra for personal or family worship. Currently, the worship of the Matsya, Kurma, Varāha,

Narasiṃha, and Vāmana avatāras is rare. Neither Paraśurāma nor Buddha has ever attracted many Hindu devotees. Rāma and Kṛṣṇa, on the other hand, are now the most popular of all Hindu divinities. The Bengal Vaiṣṇavas and some others deny that Kṛṣṇa is an avatāra of Viṣṇu but believe, with some justification in the teaching of the Bhagavadgītā, that Kṛṣṇa Vāsudeva himself is the supreme Deity and the source of all avatāras. In the nineteenth and twentieth centuries some reform movements, particularly the Ārya Samāj, rejected as superstitious the entire list of avatāras. Other strands of modern Hindu thought moved in the opposite direction, recognizing as avatāras the extraordinary leaders of any religion, Hindu or non-Hindu.

THE MATURATION OF VAIṢṆAVA THOUGHT

Slowly the literature expressing the Vaiṣṇava outlook improved in intellectual quality and in time the Vaiṣṇava doctrine gained acceptance as a form of the thought of Vedānta, one of the six honored systems of orthodox Hindu philosophy. Early in the Christian Era, a work called the *Vedānta Sūtra,* which attempts to summarize the teaching of the Upanishads, or Vedānta, was composed by an author named Bādarāyana. Most scholars now judge that Bādarāyana was a monotheist and believed in a personal Supreme Being. The sūtra's exact meaning is seldom clear, however, without a commentary. If Bādarāyana was indeed a monotheist, then the *Vedānta Sūtra* is the Vaiṣṇavas' first systematic theology, since it covers all the major questions involved in a rounded world view. But Bādarāyana's convictions as expressed in this terse document can be variously understood.

There were ancient Vaiṣṇava commentators whose works have been lost, but the oldest surviving commentary, written about A.D. 800, is the work of the great Advaita master Śaṅkara, who alleged that the *Vedānta Sūtra,* as well as the Bhagavadgītā and the Upanishads themselves, teach that the ultimate Reality is the impersonal Brahman and that the worship of the personal God is based on a half-truth and is suitable only for the preliminary instruction of immature minds. According to Śaṅkara, those who have matured spiritually realize that persons, human or divine, are not real, but delusions arising through a cosmic ignorance called māyā.

Writing throughout a period of five hundred years, half a dozen Vaiṣṇava scholars responded to Śaṅkara's challenge and defended the Vaiṣṇava understanding of the *Vedānta Sūtra.* Their commentaries are foundational expressions of the theologies of the great medieval Vaiṣṇava sects. Rāmānuja, the first and possibly the greatest of these intellectuals, wrote in about A.D. 1100. He was not a hermit scholar, but the abbot and preceptor of a group who from at least the twelfth century were known as the Śrīvaishṇavas. That community can be traced back to a wave of devotional religion that began to sweep over the Tamil country in the sixth century A.D. and to a succession of gifted Tamil poet-devotees called Āḷvārs who then appeared over a period of about three hundred years. The Āḷvārs were of any and every caste, or none. One was an outcaste, and one, Aṇḍal, was a woman.

The teachers of this movement took up residence at the island shrine of Śrīrangam, in the Kaveri River near present-day Tiruchchirappali. The abbots of that institution raised Vaiṣṇava thinking to a new level of consistency and made it respectable in the Hindu world of intellectual discussion. Rāmānuja, the fifth abbot, produced a full commentary on the *Vedānta Sūtra* in which he criticized the theory that all plurality of things and persons has an only apparent reality, being nothing but the effect of a deluding factor called māyā on an undivided universal consciousness.

If put into direct discourse, Rāmānuja's examination of the monist argument would run as follows: Where does this māyā that you speak of—this creator of all plurality, ignorance, and evil—have its existence? Does it exist in Brahman? That is impossible for several reasons. Brahman is homogenous and can have within it no separate thing. Brahman is perfection and can have within it no evil thing. Brahman is knowledge and could accommodate ignorance within itself only by destroying itself. Brahman is the Real and contains nothing that is not real; if māyā exists in Brahman, it is real, and its alleged products—personal beings, the personal God, and the plural world—are also real, as we Vaiṣṇavas hold. Is māyā then located outside Brahman? Outside of Brahman, the sole Reality, there is only nothing. If māyā is nothing, it has produced nothing—not even the illusory world that you hold our world to be.

By these and many other closely reasoned arguments, Rāmānuja exposed weaknesses in the logic of Śaṅkara's teaching and defended the Vaiṣṇava belief in the reality of persons, human and divine. The divine, all-inclusive reality that the Upanishads call Brahman and describe as an omnipresent and omnipotent consciousness, Rāmānuja declared to be no neuter reality but the personal Lord. For Rāmānuja, Brahman was simply one of the many names of Kṛṣṇa Vāsudeva, a name that refers to him as the basis of all being.

Rāmānuja's understanding of the nature of mystical experience and its place in the religious life is a representative Vaiṣṇava view. Vaiṣṇavas aspire to darśana, a "seeing," physical or spiritual, of the beautiful form of the Lord. In its lower grades darśana can be merely a reverential viewing of an image in a shrine. At a higher stage of contemplation, darśana can become a powerful inner vision experienced in the course of devout meditative practices. Rāmānuja's comment on this higher darśana is that it is not a direct perception of the Deity, but a subjective vision shaped out of recollections of one's previous experiences. It is not a direct means to salvation; rather, its importance is that it is a powerful generator of devotion, or bhakti, which is the last human step toward salvation. Not all Vaiṣṇavas state as clearly as Rāmānuja did that such visions of deity are subjective, but all followers of the bhaktimārga agree that final liberation does not arise from the power of such visions, but from the power of God, who responds to the devotion that the visions can generate.

THE CULT OF GOPĀLA

Our account of Vaiṣṇava history has so far followed a central line of fairly homogeneous religion that evolved from models in the Bhagavadgītā. We confront the real complexity of the Vaiṣṇava movement, however, when we try to understand a mutation that occurred in the worship of Kṛṣṇa with the rise of the cult of the youthful Kṛṣṇa as Gopāla the cowherd. Though no participant in this worship of Kṛṣṇa as a cowherd boy repudiates the Bhagavadgītā, the principal scripture of this group is the *Bhāgavata Purāṇa,* a work of the eighth or ninth century A.D.

The religion of the Bhagavadgītā grew for four centuries after the time of its composition without producing any offshoots of radically new type and function. Though the Bhagavadgītā is a many-faceted work with resources for meeting many personal needs, it was esteemed in those centuries for its spiritual treatment of the causes of social disorganization. Broad in its religious sympathies and positive in its social message, it provided a spiritual rallying point during this time for Hindus who valued order and longed to realize it through the acceptance of brāhmaṇ leadership and a caste structuring of society. The resistance to brāhmaṇ dominance centered for a long time in the rich Indian lands ruled by dynasties of foreign origin—Greek, Scythian, and Kuṣāṇa—who cared little for caste ideals. The joining of the Vaiṣṇavas and the brāhmaṇs in a common cause was important in bringing down the foreign dynasties in the third century A.D. and in establishing a thoroughly Hindu social order.

The Gupta emperors (c. A.D. 320–c. 550) supported the caste hierarchy with the power of the state; the brāhmaṇs became the recognized arbiters of all social issues; and the emperors themselves often were followers of the Vaiṣṇava faith. The Vaiṣṇava religion thenceforth had few detractors, and became as securely established as the caste society. At this time of the final triumph of the restraints of caste, the worship of Kṛṣṇa produced the dramatically new Gopāla cult, with myths, metaphors, and preoccupations very different from those of the Bhagavadgītā.

The *Harivaṃśa Purāṇa,* written about A.D. 300, began the new tradition. The author says in his introduction that he is writing in order to compensate for the omissions of the *Mahābhārata,* which had failed to tell the whole story of Kṛṣṇa and his family. Then the author proceeds to relate, along with stories of Kṛṣṇa's ancestors, dozens of new stories about the early exploits and antics of Kṛṣṇa, from his birth to his unseating of his wicked uncle Kaṃsa from the throne of Mathurā. All are retold in the *Viṣṇu Purāṇa,* and again in the *Bhāgavata Purāṇa* in a full and favorite form. In a distinctive light-hearted mood, these tales tell of the child Kṛṣṇa's impudence in stealing butter from his mother's pantry and evading punishment through alibis, and of his wheedling curds from the cowherd women who were carrying their edible wares to market. In the accounts of Kṛṣṇa's adolescence, his naughtiness takes a flirtatious turn. He teases the *gopīs* (cowherd girls) shamelessly and does audacious things to excite their passion. (For further details of Kṛṣṇa's amorous deeds, see the following box.)

During the period of Muslim domination in India, large sects of worshipers of the child Kṛṣṇa were founded. They continue to have great following today. The followers of one sect are well known in the West, where they chant the name of Kṛṣṇa in public places and are therefore often called the Hare Krishna people.

The religious practices of this faith center on contemplation of Kṛṣṇa's *līlās,* or sports. The narratives of the tenth book of the *Bhāgavata Purāṇa* are read, recited, and sung, sometimes in Sanskrit but more often in vernacular versions. The escapades of Kṛṣṇa that are described in that purāṇa are enacted in an operatic style with dances in an unusual kind of miracle play, called the *Rāslīlā.* To rehearse Kṛṣṇa's līlās mentally and to envision them before the inner eye are the Gopāla cult's equivalent of yoga. Kṛṣṇa's devotees seek to obtain visions of their God in the course of private meditations, or at climactic moments of song and story in emotional religious assemblies. Mathurā and Vṛindāban, cities sacred to Kṛṣṇa, have become great centers of pilgrimage and retirement for those who wish to pursue the spiritual life in these ways.

THE WORSHIP OF RĀMA

The tradition of Rāma, the eighth avatāra of Viṣṇu, probably began with the recollection of an actual human being. Rāma's story was first written by Vālmīki in about the fourth century B.C. Vālmīki's account of Rāma's career, called the *Rāmāyaṇa,* is a great Sanskrit epic poem that has been compared to the *Odyssey.* The *Rāmāyaṇa* tells the story of Prince Rāma of the northern Indian kingdom of Ayodhyā, who fought a great war in the far south to rescue his wife Sītā, who had been abducted by the demon Rāvaṇa. Vālmīki's poem tells the tale in the spirit of heroic legend rather than of myth.

Chanting Kṛṣṇa's name on the streets of New York City. One sect that worships Kṛṣṇa has spread to the West, where its adherents are called the Hare Krishna people. *Kit Kittle.*

Kṛṣṇa and the Gopīs

The story of Kṛṣṇa's dance with the gopīs (cowherd girls) is the most sacred of the Gopāla cult's myths and the source of the principal figures of its symbolic language. The favorite version based on *Bhāgavata Purāṇa* 10.29–33 is commonly retold in popular poetic recitations, songs, or operatic performances.

On a certain full-moon night in autumn, Kṛṣṇa stood at the edge of a forest near the settlements of the cowherds. With a mischievous smile he put his flute to his lips. The flute's enchanting notes carried afar until they reached the houses of the cowherds where the dutiful wives of the herdsmen were preparing food and attending to the needs of their families. But when they heard the bewitching notes, they were helpless. Beside themselves, they dropped their wifely tasks and hurried into the dusk. At the forest's edge they came upon Kṛṣṇa. He feigned astonishment and addressed the gopīs thus:

Kṛṣṇa: O ladies, you surprise me. What service can I do you?
Gopīs: You have called us, and we have come.
Kṛṣṇa: I was playing the flute merely for my own pleasure. I have not called you. Why have you come here?
Gopīs: Why do you ask why we have come? You have called us, and it is to see *you* that we have come!
Kṛṣṇa: Now you have seen me. It is a dark night, this is a dangerous forest, and it is not a time for ladies to be roaming. Go home now to your husbands.

The gopīs protest that Kṛṣṇa is a rogue for enticing them and then rebuffing them. They hang their heads, falter in their speech, and finally are able to stammer out the real justification for their presence in the forest: "You are our *real* Husband, our only husband, the only husband of the whole human race, and it is only You that we wish to serve!"

Kṛṣṇa is pleased by this declaration and agrees to sport with the gopīs. Rādhā, their leader, joins him in organizing them for dancing. They form a revolving circle. Pleasure and excitement grow as the dance whirls on. The gopīs begin to be proud that they are in the company of the Lord of the Universe. Not content to think of themselves as the luckiest women in the world, they begin to think of themselves as the best and most beautiful women in the world. They demand services of Kṛṣṇa, saying, "Fasten my earring!," "Comb my hair!," "Carry me!" So, suddenly leaving their midst, Kṛṣṇa disappears in the forest. Forlorn and humbled, the gopīs search for him in the gloom, calling out his name as they wander through the dark glades and asking the trees and vines for hints of where he may have gone. Unable to find him, they gather in a clearing in the forest and begin to console themselves by telling each other about Kṛṣṇa's deeds. Peering through the trees, Kṛṣṇa observes the gopīs' new humility and devotion, and relents and returns to their circle. Then he begins the magnificent Mahārāsa, the rāsā dance in its most splendid form. Moving into the great circle of the dance, Kṛṣṇa multiplies his own form until there is a Kṛṣṇa at every gopī's side. As the partners whirl on, romantic feeling rises to a crescendo with the pace of the music. Every gopī's longing for Kṛṣṇa is satisfied by his special presence beside her.

This tale of Kṛṣṇa's meeting with the cowherd women uses the language of romantic love but it refers to aspects of the religious life that are not sexual.

The five original books of the *Rāmāyaṇa* were written when polytheism still prevailed in India, and thus there is no suggestion in the earlier materials of this epic that Rāma is in any way identical with Viṣṇu or is the one God. Rāma is a folk hero, an ideal warrior, and that is all. Several centuries later, an initial and a final book were added to Vālmīki's five-book composition, and the *Rāmāyaṇa* assumed its present seven-book form. In these two additions Rāma became a figure of divine stature, infused with some of the essence of Viṣṇu. The assertion of Rāma's divine status has none of the tentative and exploratory character of the avatāra idea as presented in the Bhagavadgītā, and it is already clearly understood that the avatāras descend to earth from Viṣṇu. The worship of Rāma, then, began around the time of Christ, somewhat later than the Bhagavadgītā.

Unlike the story of Kṛṣṇa, the life of Rāma was not reworked in the purāṇas. Vālmīki's fine literary narrative was from the beginning so complete and so popular that the writers of later Rāmāyaṇas (here a general term for any life of Rāma) were constrained to follow Vālmīki's basic plot and his delineation of the *Rāmāyaṇa*'s major characters. The *Rāmāyaṇa* is, above all, a tale of an illustrious royal family whose members, almost without exception, manifested the Hindu ideals of exemplary behavior in the performance of their various social roles. Finally, Rāma, after many trials, returned to his own kingdom and ruled with model righteousness in a reign remembered as a golden age of prosperity and justice.

In the first centuries of the Christian Era, this widely appreciated story became a national treasure, nourished and loved by Vaiṣṇavas, non-Vaiṣṇavas, and even non-Hindus, and the legend was carried to Java, Thailand, and Cambodia. Today also, the appreciation and use of the *Rāmāyaṇa* extends far beyond the circles in which Rāma is a principal focus of worship. Among non-Vaiṣṇavas it is loved for its moral teaching, and to ardent Rāma devotees, its moral concerns are more important than its theological ideas.

In the modern religion of northern India, Rāma became popular through the *Rāmcaritmānas* (The Mind-pool of the deeds of Rāma), an inspired retelling of Rāma's story in the Hindi language by a great poet named Tulsī Dās, about A.D. 1575. Its popularity has pushed Śāktism and Tāntrism into retreat in northern India and has made the Hindi-speaking areas predominantly Vaiṣṇava. Often called the Bible of North India, the *Rāmcaritmānas* is the most widely read of all Hindi books. Even the illiterate learn Rāma's story when local actors dramatize it annually at a great autumn festival called the Rāmlīlā, in which the entire *Rāmcaritmānas* is recited and enacted.

The relation between the cults of Rāma and Kṛṣṇa is one of mutual support. In heavily Vaiṣṇava communities today, most of the people participate in the festivals of both deities, and the worship of Rāma and Kṛṣṇa has become loosely joined in a composite religion. With theological consistency, Vaiṣṇavas can include both Kṛṣṇa and Rāma in their devotion, explaining that as different avatāras of one and the same Deity, they are identifiable with each other and are not different objects of worship. It is the difference between these two deities, however, that enables Hindus to combine their worship. As moral beings seeking self-control and social order, Hindus worship Rāma. As intellectual beings seeking reasoned understanding, they turn to the thoughtful Bhagavadgītā and to the systematic theologies of the Kṛṣṇa cult. As emotional beings oppressed by the heavy restraints of Hindu social life, they worship Gopāla Kṛṣṇa, the carefree divine prankster.

Whether the faiths of the bhaktimārga can rightly be called monotheistic is an important question for some students of religions. We have used the term "monotheism" often in this chapter. But it is also possible to consider these faiths to be polytheistic, inasmuch as both Vaiṣṇavas and Śaivas recognize the existence, as superhuman beings, of such persons as Indra, Brahmā, and the entire Hindu pantheon. But adherents of the bhaktimārga explain that these devas are no more than a superior order of created beings who are only servants of the one uncreated lord. The joint worship of Rāma and Kṛṣṇa, however, again raises the question of polytheism, reminding us of the complementary worship of Indra and Varuṇa that prevailed in the vedic period. But this combined worship of Rāma and Kṛṣṇa entails a theory of various avatāras of a single god that enables Vaiṣṇavas to consider their devotion to be monotheistic, even though two figures are honored. Does the Vaiṣṇava conception of the Divine being involve complexities of a different order from Christian belief in the existence of archangels and in distinctions within the Deity that attribute creation to the Father, guidance to the Holy Spirit, and salvation to the Son? Our difficulty in answering this question illustrates the general awkwardness of any effort to describe Hinduism by using familiar but ill-fitting Western Judeo-Christian terms.

Notes

1 Robert Charles Caldwell, trans., "Tamil Popular Poetry," *Indian Antiquary,* April 5, 1872, p. 100.

2 Quoted in Dinesh Chandra Sen, *History of Bengali Language and Literature* (Calcutta, India: University of Calcutta, 1911), p. 714ff.

6 Modern Hinduism

Familiarity with the ancient and medieval forms of Hinduism does not prepare us to meet modern educated Hindus without puzzling surprises. To help understand the radical changes that have occurred in the Hindu outlook, we shall notice the most important developments in India's political and cultural history during the past three centuries.

During the Middle Ages, Muslim invaders entered India in great force, and for five centuries they dominated the subcontinent. By 1700, several parts of India had become predominantly Muslim in religion, but the Muslim power was spent, and India as a whole had remained faithful to Hinduism. After the death in 1707 of Aurangzeb, the last great Mughul emperor, the Mughul Empire declined rapidly. For the next fifty years India lay in a state of anarchy. European merchants, protected by a few soldiers, had long operated trading posts along the Indian coastline. Now, raising mercenary armies, the Europeans began to move into the political vacuum left by the Mughul Empire's disintegration. By 1757 the British East India Company had gained control of India's most prosperous provinces, and by 1818 the British had eliminated all serious rivals for the control of the entire land.

The British Presence

The two centuries of British rule that now followed were much more disturbing to the Hindus' outlook than the five preceding centuries of control by Muslims, despite the latter's aggressive attitude toward Hinduism. There were two reasons for India's stronger reaction to the British presence. First, the British, unlike the Muslims, brought to India powerful new economic institutions. The development of Western shipping on the Indian coast drew India into a worldwide commercial network for the large-scale exchange of goods, and soon Calcutta, Bombay, Madras, and inland cities as well became huge trading centers.

This development brought with it a great increase in the proportion of the population engaged in trade and making a living outside the economic system of India's tightly knit villages. Of all caste Hindus, the merchants had always been the most free to adopt whatever forms of religion they wished, and now much larger classes of people in the new commercial centers became immune to economic pressures toward conformity. Family and caste assemblies could still bring heavy pressure on their individual members, but the termination of livelihood—the threat that had kept members of the village communities in line—could no longer be used effectively. When the Industrial Revolution reached India and factories became a major source of livelihood in the towns, millions of Hindus became free to follow radical religious leaders of their own personal choice.

The second reason for the strong reaction to British culture was the activity of the British government in promoting education. Although the network of educational institutions supported by the British government was minimal at first by present-day standards, it far exceeded the public education offered by Hindu and Muslim rulers. Early in the nineteenth century some schools began to teach Western learning as well as traditional Indian subjects. As early as 1817 the Hindu College was established in Calcutta to instruct young men in the English language and literature, and Christian missionaries soon opened similar schools and colleges.

The Hindu response was positive. In 1835 a momentous decision was made to conduct government-supported education mainly in English and to make the Western arts and sciences a principal part of the curriculum. In the same period European printing presses, set up in India in unprecedented numbers, made the literature of European culture easily available to increasing numbers of Indians who could read English.

In order to appreciate the collision of ideas that occurred, we need to examine the Hinduism prevailing in about 1800 and the shocking contrasts with which it was confronted. In the popular cults, many of the Hindu practices at the beginning of the nineteenth century concentrated on finding protection against the dangers of the natural world. On the doctrinal level, the central Hindu ideas had the function of supporting the caste system. Belief in karma and rebirth rationalized the assignment of hereditary work and unequal distribution of opportunities and honors, and justified the subjection of women in general and harsh treatment of widows in particular. The deprivations that old Hinduism imposed on many were made tolerable by teaching the evil of material desires, by offering loftier satisfactions in transcendent realms, and by denying the significance—or even the reality—of the whole physical world. Hinduism provided no rational justification for attempting to change the world. The way to happiness lay in a personal liberation from the world, not in trying to transform it into a place of freedom and bliss. Even the Bhagavadgītā, despite its recognition of the need to support social institutions, did not advise dwelling long in this world, either physically or in one's fondnesses (9.33). It was the soul, not the world, that was capable of salvation. The corporate progress of a people did not fall within the aspirational concepts of Hindu thought. Even the idea of nation had no adequate expression in the vocabulary of Indian languages.

The British brought to India in the early nineteenth century a social optimism unusual even in Western history. An advancing medical science offered the possibility of freedom from disease, and the Industrial Revolution held out the possibility of freedom from poverty. Injustices could be identified and righted, and the world could be perfected. In this Western dream of social progress, nations figured as prominently as did individuals.

From its base in biblical thinking, the Western mind conceived of the nation as a fundamental unit of moral responsibility and as a soteriological community. The British brought with them a pride and hope in one's nation that the Hindus perceived as a refreshing proposal.

The Europeans of that time were able not only to proclaim an eloquent faith in the world's regeneration but also to take actions toward that end with impressive results. The power of Western learning was as obvious to Hindu observers as the power of the new steamboats that could transport huge cargoes upstream on Indian rivers. Vaccination was clearly more effective for its purpose than offerings to the smallpox goddess. Young Hindus did not take long to decide that they wanted to learn the Western knowledge and to participate in its power.

This clear decision among the early generations of Western-educated Indians soon began to produce new movements within Hinduism. Between

1800 and 1947 there were few Hindu champions of innovation who were not also reformers of religion. The first of the Hindu movements that reflect the Western impact is the Brāhmo Samāj, founded in 1828 by a Bengali brāhmaṇ named Rām Mohan Roy (1772–1833).

The Brāhmo Samāj (Society of Believers in Brahman)

For generations Rām Mohan Roy's family had served Muslim rulers. He was sent as a boy to Muslim schools, where he learned Persian and Arabic and absorbed Muslim attitudes, including hostility toward the British. However, in 1803 he went into the revenue service of the East India Company, and under the guidance of a friendly British official Rām Mohan perfected his knowledge of English. Becoming acquainted with English literature and Western thought, he reversed his original negative opinion of Western culture and became a supporter of a temporary British rule over India and an advocate of Western education.

In 1814 Rām Mohan Roy retired from government service to promote his ideas regarding religion and morality. He denounced polytheism, idolatry, and certain Hindu social practices he deemed harmful to society. He decried the neglect of women's education and current harsh treatment of widows, and he supported, in 1829, the British government's decision to abolish by law the practice of burning widows alive at the time of their husbands' cremation. He promoted the founding of colleges and schools to teach Western literature and science.

Early in his retirement Rām Mohan studied the Bible under the guidance of Christian missionaries. He developed a lasting admiration for the moral precepts and example of Jesus but was unable to accept the Christian belief in Jesus' divinity or in the atoning value of his death. Then Rām Mohan examined the Upanishads and Vedānta sūtras and concluded that they taught a simple monotheism entirely free of polytheism and idolatry. He rested his monotheistic belief, therefore, on the Upanishads, which are counted as part of the authoritative vedic literature, and argued for the recognition of his beliefs as vedic and orthodox teaching.

In 1828 Rām Mohan founded the Brāhmo Samāj, a religious association that met weekly for a congregational style of worship that is quite unusual in Hinduism. It included prayers, hymns, and sermons expounding such scriptures as the Keṇa, Īśa, Muṇḍaka, and Kaṭha Upanishads.

The members were usually persons of high social position and good education. After Rām Mohan's death the Brāhmo Samāj was guided by new leaders whose demands for reform became increasingly incompatible with orthodox Hinduism.

Under the leadership of Debendranāth Tagore (1817–1905), the Brāhmo Samāj studied the Vedas more thoroughly and dropped its claim to orthodoxy. Taking reason and conscience rather than the Vedas as the final authority in religion, the Brāhmo Samāj taught thereafter that scriptures were to be regarded as valid only when their message was

Rām Mohan Roy, founder of the first modern movement for reformed Hinduism. Detail from a painting by Rolinda Sharples. *City Art Gallery, Bristol, England.*

confirmed by a light within the heart. In the society's earlier period its members had been urged only to make no claim to superior dignity by reason of their high caste. Now they were asked to repudiate their caste identities entirely. The society pressed for laws against child marriage. They attacked polygamy, and for the old saṃskāra rituals they devised replacements from which all references to the many gods were eliminated. Throughout the nineteenth century the Brāhmo Samāj kept the Hindu upper classes in an uproar of argument for and against their daring demands.

Sharp differences of opinion divided and weakened the group in the latter part of the century, and today the Brāhmo Samāj has only a few thousand members. The movement's theological ideas have not become dominant in modern Hinduism, but the Brāhmo Samāj won its social battles, so substantially altering public opinion that by 1900 it was no longer necessary for Hindus to join a heterodox sect and surrender membership in family and caste when they undertook to attack the inequities and extravagances of traditional Hinduism.

The Ārya Samāj (Aryan Society)

About the time when the reformist commotion of the Brāhmo Samāj was at its height in Bengal, Svāmī Dayānanda Sarasvatī (1824–1883) launched a very different campaign for change in northwestern India. (Svāmī is a title of respect given to a religious teacher.) Born to a devout Śaiva family in Gujarat, Dayānanda at an early age rejected the worship of Śiva. Becoming an ascetic at twenty-one, he wandered for some years in search of a satisfactory faith. At last in Mathurā he found his guru in a fiery and eccentric teacher named Virajānanda, who allowed his disciples to study nothing but Sanskrit grammar and a few of the oldest vedic scriptures. Virajānanda loathed the purāṇas and all the popular gods of Hinduism. In 1863 Dayānanda began his own campaigns against polytheism and idolatry. Lecturing in Sanskrit before priestly audiences, he attacked pūjās and pilgrimages, denied the divinity of Rāma and Kṛṣṇa, and asserted that the brāhmaṇs had no hereditary rights.

In 1874 Dayānanda began to address more popular groups in Hindi with much success, and wrote in Hindi his principal book, *The Light of Truth*. The following year he founded the Ārya Samāj. It spread quickly throughout the Hindi-speaking areas, making the following major proclamations:

1. India must resume its allegiance to the oldest religious literature of the land. The Vedas alone—by which Dayānanda meant the four original collections, or saṃhitās—are the Word of God. The Brāhmaṇas and Upanishads are authoritative only when they are in full agreement with the saṃhitās. Dayānanda had no use whatsoever for the purāṇas and the smṛitis—not even for the Bhagavadgītā.

2. Since the word *jāti* is not found in the Vedas, hereditary occupational castes have no place in true Hindu religion. But because the names of the four varṇas are found in the Vedas, the terms brāhmaṇ, kṣatriya, vaiśya, and śūdra may be used to refer to flexible classes to which Aryans may belong, not according to birth, but according to their level of ability. Anyone may study the Vedas. Today the Ārya Samāj promotes the education of women, permits widows to remarry, allows intercaste dining and even intercaste marriage, and denounces child marriage and polygamy.

3. The Vedas are the source of all truth, scientific as well as religious. Using an unusual method of translation, Ārya Samāj scholars find proof in the vedas that the sages worshiped only one God, of personal nature, and that they were already acquainted millions of years ago with such supposedly modern inventions as the steam engine, telegraph, and airplane. According to the Ārya Samāj, Indians who were taking up the study of Western science were merely recovering an Indian knowledge that had been lost.

4. The Vedas record the true original religion of humanity and are the ultimate source of those fragmentary truths that non-Hindu faiths sometimes retain in a corrupted form. *The Light of Truth* gives Hinduism the central place in the historical development of the world's religions. The book vilifies

Islam, Christianity, and those forms of Hinduism that Dayānanda detested, and it begins an important modern tendency toward the vehement glorification of Hinduism.

The Ārya Samāj has been bitterly hostile to foreign cultural influences in India. Dayānanda fought the resurgent Muslim movements of the mid-nineteenth century and opposed the missionary activities of Christians. For the first fifty years of its existence, the society continued to gather into its fellowship many reform-minded, middle-class Hindus. No longer seen as a shockingly radical organization, the Ārya Samāj exists quietly today as a stable religious group with about half a million members. Though the Ārya Samāj does not participate as an organization in politics, it has revived a long-lost understanding that civic concerns are religious concerns. Many of its members are important public figures.

Hindu Religious Nationalism

Svāmī Dayānanda's controlled resentment of Western influence in India was a light squall preceding a hurricane. In the late nineteenth century the sons of upper-class Indian families began to graduate from Indian universities with a new ambivalence of feeling toward Western culture. Western studies, like cut flowers transplanted from another garden, had failed to root successfully in Indian soil. Even those students who acquired a deep knowledge of the West were often offended by the aloofness of the Europeans in India, who did not grant them the dignity of full acceptance in a world culture.

About this time, the research of European scholars into India's forgotten past uncovered records of a happier and greater India of pre-Islamic times, in which enlightened Hindu rulers had patronized brilliant systems of thought and great works of literature and art. Hindu religious leaders now called on the young men of India to identify themselves with that brighter ancient heritage, and beginning about 1890 a passionate nationalism with religious overtones began to grow in the minds of many literate young Hindus. They viewed the West as a crass and worldly civilization, advanced only in the natural sciences, and saw the East as a spiritual culture destined to teach the world the art of lofty living. The rule of foreigners came to be regarded as a moral outrage. All the emotional devices of the Way of Devotion were brought into the service of a new object of devotion, the Indian nation itself, and the liberation of India became the goal of this half-religious nationalism.

India was sometimes conceived as a divine Mother in the form of the goddess Kālī. Beginning in 1905 secret societies were organized, especially in Bengal, for violent revolutionary action. At altars of Kālī, on which revolvers had been heaped, recruits vowed to bring bloody offerings to the Mother. A training manual entitled *Bhavānī Mandir* (The temple of Kālī) assured future assassins that their acts would bring the world to the light of Hinduism. Between 1908 and 1917 more than a hundred officials of the British government were killed or wounded by members of such societies. But nationalists in the Hindi-speaking areas, less accustomed than the Bengalis to making blood offerings to Kālī, cultivated a reverence for a milder figure called Bharat Mātā (Mother India).

The first great political leader of Hindu ultranationalism was Bāl Gangādhar Tilak (1856–1920), a brāhmaṇ from western India. In honor of the god Gaṇeśa, the elephant-headed son of Śiva, Tilak devised a new festival as an occasion for carrying anti-British songs and dramas to the people, and he taught the Bhagavadgītā with emphasis on such militant lines as "Fight, O son of Bharata!" (2.18). Chauvinistic nationalism reached its peak in the first two decades of the twentieth century, but it has continued to have strong spokesmen. A protégé of Tilak named V. C. Savarkar (1883–1966) organized the Hindu Mahāsabhā, a cultural society for the promotion of Hindu nationalism. The Hindu Mahāsabhā created as an auxiliary a young men's uniformed action group called the Rāshṭriya Svayamsevak Saṅgha, popularly known as the R.S.S. To extend its influence in Indian legislatures, the R.S.S. in 1951 established a political party called the Bharatīya Jan Sangh (Indian People's Party).

The basic premise of these groups is that India

Temple carving of Gaṇeśa, Śiva's elephant-headed son. A festival in his honor initiated early in the twentieth century was used to promote Hindu nationalism. *Richard Schechner.*

must be preserved in a fivefold unity: one land, one race, one religion, one culture, and one language. They believe that Pakistan and Bangladesh must be reunited with India and with Hinduism, and that all Muslim, British, and other foreign influences must be eliminated.

Mahātma Gāndhī

Fortunately for the outside world, India's independence was not won by such ultranationalists but by forces led by Mohandās Gāndhī (1869–1948). Gāndhī was a religious leader of a radically new type. Not a brāhmaṇ, he was born in a port city of Gujarat into a family of the vaiśya or merchant class. By profession Gāndhī was first a lawyer and later a social reformer and political leader. He was not learned in Hindu literature, nor was he a systematic religious thinker. Yet his religious leadership has touched to some degree all present-day Hindus, who everywhere speak of him reverentially as Mahātma (The Great-Souled One). After studying law in England, Gāndhī was admitted to the bar in India. Soon after, he moved to South Africa, where for many years he led a nonviolent movement to protect the rights of Indians living in that country. After returning to India, he became in 1920 a leader of the Indian National Congress, and thanks to his skillful direction, India at last became a free republic in 1947. The following year, while conducting a prayer meeting in New Delhi, he was assassinated by a fanatical Hindu nationalist of the outlook just described.

It is possible here to describe only a few aspects of Gāndhī's far-ranging and original personal faith. The scriptures that Gāndhī loved most were the *Rāmcaritmānas* of Tulsī Das, the Sermon on the Mount in the New Testament, and, especially, the Bhagavadgītā. His choice of scriptures reflects the centrality of moral and social concerns in his religious life. Despite his reverence for many scriptures, Gāndhī was not bound by the authority of any of them but held that one should check them against a still small voice of conscience that can speak with divine authority within one's own heart, revealing the way of right action. Though Gāndhī's assumptions about the nature of God and the universe were the general theological ideas of the Vaiṣṇavas, he was not interested in theoretical discussions and preferred the simple statement,

Mahātma Gāndhī with his spinning wheel, which became an emblem in his campaign for national self-reliance. Gāndhī called for the revival of old Indian village crafts and himself spun thread. *Margaret Bourke-White/ Life Magazine.*

"God is Truth." By this he meant that God is the basis for order and law and the force that supports moral righteousness in the world. He delighted in the precepts associated with Kṛṣṇa and Rāma without attaching any value to the myths about them. Yet God for him was not an abstract principle but a Spirit endowed with purpose, who hears prayers and supports and guides those who struggle in the cause of right in all areas of life, including politics.

Gāndhī held that all religions originate in a universal operation of the inner Voice. The precepts of the great religions vary in externals because of the differences in the languages and cultural institutions in which the impulsions of conscience are expressed. For this reason, each religion speaks with unique effectiveness to the people of its own culture. Though the religions are equal in value, they are not of equal value in all lands. The religion of another people cannot effectively replace one's own, and conversion to a foreign religion does not produce a vital and well-functioning faith.

Gāndhī's powerful and courageous tactic for social reform was called *satyāgraha* (holding onto truth). It was based on his confidence that God, in the form of Truth and the Voice that utters it, is present also in the hearts of wrongdoers. Gāndhī taught that believers in satyāgraha must seek to awaken in their oppressors their own inner voice so that they will themselves perceive their wrongdoing and voluntarily cease to do wrong. One should not seek personal victories over opponents but the victory of Truth, which belongs as much to one's opponent as to oneself. Such victories cannot be attained by violent means. Gāndhī's great campaigns for national independence were often launched under the guidance of his own inner voice; in essence they were demands that the British rulers consult the voice within themselves with regard to what was right. Gāndhī's faith so impressed the world that in the 1960s Martin Luther King, Jr., made effective use of satyāgraha techniques to advance the goals of the American civil rights movement.

Recent Religious Leaders

The religious life of most Hindus has continued in the modern period in familiar patterns under the guidance of religious leaders of old types. Some of these traditional leaders have been gifted persons of great influence.

ŚRĪ RAMAṆA MAHĀRSHI (1879–1950)

Śrī Ramaṇa Mahārshi was an authentic model of the Advaita Vedānta spirituality and one of the most famous holy men of modern times. At the age of seventeen, while a student at the American Mission High School in Madurai, he first became troubled by awareness of his own mortality, and in a trance he received assurance of his identity with a spirit immune to death. He ran away to the holy mountain where Śiva is said to have revealed himself in the infinite liṅgam, and there he remained quietly for the rest of his life. His disciples built him an āśrama (religious retreat), and aspirants from both East and West came to share the silence of his meditation hall and to receive, rarely, brief words of counsel. His doctrine was that of Śaṅkara. He was willing to allow some of his disciples to attempt the difficult eight-stage yoga, but his advice to most was merely to suppress conceptual thinking and to pursue introspectively the question "Who am I?" By following their consciousness inward to its source they would discover the soul, or universal ātman.

MAHARISHI MAHESH YOGI

A far more aggressive promoter of the Advaita outlook than Ramaṇa Mahārshi is Maharishi Mahesh Yogi, who at the time of this writing is still alive. His organization, the Students' International Meditation Society, has trained thousands of Westerners in a simple form of Hindu meditation. Mahesh Yogi has removed the aura of exoticism that formerly surrounded yoga. His extraordinary impact on Europe and America is based on his success in establishing many meditation centers and on his willingness to allow yoga to be used for the attainment of emotional equilibrium and physical health—values long appreciated in the West.

RĀMAKRISHNA PARAMAHAṂSA (1836–1886)

This many-faceted holy man has had a great influence on the course of modern Indian cultural history. Little concerned with Western ideas, Rāmakrishna was a man of visions who was familiar with many kinds of trances and apparitions. He was born of poor brāhmaṇ parents in rural Bengal and lived for most of his adult life in a temple of the goddess Kālī near Calcutta. As a young man he agonized over the death of his father and of many protectors and patrons and fell into a despair approaching madness. He appealed to Kālī to give him some token of her regard, and on one dark day he snatched a sword from the temple wall, intending to commit suicide by offering the goddess his life's blood. At that moment, Rāmakrishna later reported, the goddess emerged from her image in an ocean of light and enveloped him in wave after wave of her love. This experience ended his fears; he became a composed and effective teacher.[1]

Although Rāmakrishna was a person of Śākta outlook and a devotee of Kālī, he also had visions of many other Hindu deities, and he experienced mystical trances of the Advaita type in which personal deities had no role.

At various times Rāmakrishna had visions of Christ and of Muḥammad. These led him to believe that he had fully understood Islam and Christianity and that he had found them to be mystical religions of Hindu type. He concluded that they were valid faiths. Rāmakrishna therefore taught the unconditional equality of all religions, a position from which his followers later withdrew. Rāmakrishna's vivid testimony to direct religious experiences fascinated the educated Hindus of his time and drew back into traditional Hinduism many who had belonged to the half-Western cults.

SVĀMĪ VIVEKĀNANDA (1863–1902)

Foremost among Rāmakrishna's disciples was Vivekānanda, who organized an order of monks, the Rāmakrishna Order, to carry on the master's teaching. Vivekānanda had a university education and shared the patriotic feeling and social concern of India's English-educated elite.

In dedicating itself in India to works of social service, the Rāmakrishna Order has proposed by its example a new activist ideal for the life of the sannyāsī. The monks carry out relief work at times of famine and flood, and operate excellent hospitals and clinics. In doctrine the continuing disciples of Rāmakrishna follow the Advaita Vedānta teaching, not exactly as taught by Śaṅkara, but with a modified understanding of māyā that permits acceptance of the world as real. In interpreting Rāmakrishna's religious life, Vivekānanda and other scholars of the order ignored Rāmakrishna's preference for a personalistic worship of Mother Kālī and understood Rāmakrishna to have been above all a great exemplar of the mysticism and the doctrine of a world-accepting Advaita Vedānta.

For many educated Hindus, this Neo-Vedānta outlook has provided a new national rallying point in religion. It permits many modern Hindus to see other religions and types of religious experience as valid as far as they go, but as incomplete insights that must be completed and corrected in the end in the Advaita experience of absolute Oneness. The adherents of this view are able to recognize and yet subordinate all other forms of Hindu faith.

The Rāmakrishna Order's perception of its monism as the ultimate religion, fulfilling the aspirations of other useful but provisional faiths has become the basis for a Hindu mission to the world. In 1893 Vivekānanda represented Hinduism effectively at a World Parliament of Religions in Chicago and remained to organize Vedānta centers and to make himself the first great Hindu missionary to the West. In the United States at present there are eleven centers of the Rāmakrishna Mission, where instruction is given in Hindu meditative disciplines and where the modernized Advaita Vedānta philosophy is taught. The resident missionaries do not understand themselves to be making converts to Hinduism, but to be recalling the adherents of Western religions to the neglected monistic spirituality that has always been the hidden center of all faiths.

SARVEPALLI RĀDHĀKRISHNAN (1888–1975)

As a student, Rādhākrishnan became an admirer of Vivekānanda's modernized Vedānta, and in his mature years he developed its concepts to a new level of sophistication. He broadened its following greatly through his lucid books and worldwide lecturing. This gifted professor perceived in the Hindu tradition's sense of the oneness of all beings in the Absolute a metaphysical basis for binding together the Indian nation and eventually all humanity. He believed that Hinduism had a mission to communicate its more mature understanding of this healing unity to peoples elsewhere who in general understand this truth of Oneness less well. He anticipated that the existing religions of the world would eventually dissolve into a new monistic faith that would bring to perfection India's historic spiritual insight. In the eyes of some modern Hindus, Rādhākrishnan's Neo-Vedānta teaching has become the new Hindu doctrinal orthodoxy.

ŚRĪ AUROBINDO (1872–1950)

Śrī Aurobindo was born in Bengal and educated in England at Cambridge University, where he became a master of classical and modern European languages. Returning to India, he joined Tilak's nationalist movement and was imprisoned in 1910 for his role in inspiring an outbreak of violence in Bengal. During his confinement he underwent a mystical experience that changed his values. After his release he took refuge in the French enclave of Pondicherry and gave up his formerly Western lifestyle. He spent the rest of his life in seclusion there, practicing yogic meditation and writing in English. In the last twenty-five years of his life he did not even once descend the stairs from his upper room.

Aurobindo's interpretation of the universe, though it is substantially Indian in its concepts, includes much from the evolutionist thought of the nineteenth-century West. In Aurobindo's view of history, the world, totally real in its essence, has progressed by stages from an original condition in which nothing but matter existed. In the second stage, life appeared, and in the third and current stage, the mind emerged. The next step in evolution is now producing a higher state of consciousness in the appearance of superminds and superhumans. Through absolute mental surrender to God and through the perfection of consciousness in yoga, persons of our time can develop a transrational awareness of Śākti, the descending force of the divine in its cosmic activity. Working in the light of their integral vision, superhumans will appear and will transform the world into a place of unity and harmony. They will keep their personalities but lose their egos, and they will bring the world to its final consummation as the home of a united community of perfected human beings.

RABINDRANĀTH TAGORE (1861–1941)

Tagore was a great poet, writing in both Bengali and English, who felt the need to express his personal faith in his verse. The son of Debendranāth Tagore, he preserved from his family's Brāhmo Samāj tradition its belief in a personal God, but in time, he quietly moved away from the Brāhmo Samāj's rationalism to a mystical faith. Awareness of the divine presence came to him, however, not in the course of introversions like those of the traditional eight-stage yoga, but in moments of loving contemplation of the beauty of nature and of living beings. His compassionate view of life is beautifully expressed in his famous booklet of poems entitled *Gītānjali* (A handful of song offerings), for which he received the Nobel Prize. A cosmopolitan man with a distaste for the cultural and religious jealousies of his time, Tagore expressed in his poems, in universal language, a personal Hindu outlook that has worldwide appeal.

Rabindranāth Tagore, a noted Hindu poet who wrote in both Bengali and English. His poems have worldwide appeal. Rejecting the notion of the world as illusion, he celebrates a unifying Divine presence in nature and in humanity. *Wide World.*

Pilgrims assembled at the religious fair at Prayag, in the city of Allahabad, where the holy Ganges and Jamuna Rivers meet. Even at the lesser festival, called the Ardha Kumbh Mela, pictured here, five million people were estimated to have come together to bathe. *Religious News Service.*

For many centuries Hinduism, as both the creator and the servant of a little-changing society consisting of castes of unequal privilege, devoted itself to helping people to be content while living in a world that accommodated itself very little to individuals' desires. In modern times this highly specialized religious tradition has shown a remarkable and unexpected ability to generate new forms of religion in response to new attitudes and new and different social problems. For almost two centuries, talented Hindu religious leaders have been attempting to sweep away major parts of the world and world view of the Hindu past. As a result of their efforts, Hinduism is no longer committed to a defense of medieval cosmologies, prescientific approaches to nature, or the privileges of an ancient aristocracy.

Contemporary studies of young Hindus show that though few are well trained in their religious tradition, most are glad to identify themselves as

Hindus.[2] Educated Hindus continue to undergo traditional religious experiences. Millions still go on pilgrimages. New temples are being built all over India. The round of family rituals continues in villages and cities with modest adaptations to the altered circumstances of modern life. Hinduism appears to have been as successful as other religions in surviving in the midst of change.

Notes

1 *Life of Sri Ramakrishna* (Calcutta, India: Advaita Ashram, 1964), pp. 69–72.

2 Philip H. Ashby, *Modern Trends in Hinduism* (New York: Columbia University Press, 1974), chap. 3, "Hinduism and Contemporary Indian Youth."

PART TWO

BUDDHISM

PHOTOGRAPH BY WERNER BISCHOF/MAGNUM

Our study of Buddhism begins with the legends about the Buddha. Chapter seven describes his early life in a palace, his decision to adopt a life of poverty and meditation, his quest for enlightenment, and his preaching of a new way of life based on the four noble truths. The Buddha established a community of monks, nuns, and laypersons in northeastern India. After his death this monastic tradition solidified, and the founder's relics became the focus of a cult of veneration.

The chapter also describes the formation of early Buddhist scriptures and the emergence of the first sects. Under the Maurya emperor Aśoka, Buddhism became India's state religion. Hīnayāna Buddhism, the first of the three great Buddhist traditions, took shape between 200 B.C. and A.D. 200. Chapter eight outlines the emergence of the later Mahāyāna and Vajrayāna traditions. Mahāyāna Buddhism introduced the concept of the bodhisattva path to salvation, and Vajrayāna Buddhism created a new kind of religious text—tantras—and offered its followers new ways to achieve Buddhahood. Chapter nine discusses the expansion of Buddhism and its reactions to local needs, new religious beliefs, rites, and art forms—as well as Buddhism's attempts to adjust to the challenges and opportunities of modern times.

7 The Rise of Buddhism

Buddhism, like Christianity and Islam, originated in Asia and had a definite founder. The message given to the world by the Buddha, or the Enlightened One, became the basis for both an exalted philosophy of life, and a religion of universal appeal. Buddhist tradition is divided into three main schools, all first formulated in the Buddhist homeland of India. The first is known as the Hīnayāna or the Theravāda,* which today is the dominant religion in Sri Lanka (Ceylon) and much of mainland Southeast Asia. The second school is the Mahāyāna, or Great Vehicle, which is found chiefly in China, Korea, Vietnam, and Japan. A third school—the Vajrayāna, or Diamond Vehicle—is found mainly in Tibet and Mongolia, but also in Japan, where it is known as Shingon. Over the centuries and in many parts of the world, Buddhism has had different forms and practices, some of which contradict one another.

Life and Teachings of the Buddha

No authenticated writings of the Buddha himself have survived. In fact, the first accounts of his life were written down about five centuries after the supposed date of his death. Thus, from earliest times stories about the Buddha have been embellished with legends, and factual data about his earthly career have been difficult to establish.

According to the best modern scholarship, the Buddha probably lived from about 563 to 483 B.C., and according to some traditions, his personal or given name was Siddhārtha and his family name, Gautama. He was supposedly born in Lumbinī Grove, a spot close to Nepal's border with India, and his family belonged to the *kṣatriya,* or warrior, caste. His mother was called Māyā, and his father, Śuddhodana, was a tribal chief and a member of the powerful Śākya clan. For this reason the Buddha is often called Śākyamuni (sage of the Śākyas). His other titles include Bhāgavat (Lord) and Tathāgata, which apparently means "one who follows in the footsteps of his predecessors."

During the Buddha's lifetime, there was much ferment in India. The old order of tribal republics was breaking down, and new, territorially based kingdoms were beginning to take shape. In northeastern India—both in the Himalayan foothills where the Buddha was born and in the kingdoms of the Ganges Valley where he taught—the religious authority of the traditional Brāhmaṇic priesthood was being challenged. Groups of wandering ascetics known as *śramaṇas* or *yogīs* claimed religious authority, propounded philosophical and religious ideas, and advocated different religious practices. Buddhism was the most successful of these new religions.

*The term Hīnayāna (lesser vehicle) was applied to the Theravāda (vehicle of the elders) and other closely related schools by the followers of the rival Mahāyāna branch of Buddhism. Since the term Hīnayāna implies a pejorative comparison, the Theravādins do not usually use it in referring to their tradition, which they revere as the earliest form of Buddhism.

A recumbent Buddha (44 feet long), carved from the stone hillside, in the twelfth century A.D., at the Gal Vihara shrine, near Polunnaruva, Sri Lanka, the site of the former medieval summer capital.
George Holton/Photo Researchers.

Much of the Buddha's teaching utilized ideas current in India during his lifetime. For example, he retained the important concepts of rebirth and *karma* (the principle of moral causality) and the notion of salvation as release. The Buddha did not advocate dependence on the favor of the gods or a supreme being, and he did not conceive of his message as a divine revelation. Instead, his teaching was based on an intuitive vision achieved through meditation and described as enlightenment. Through his attainment and propagation of that vision, the Buddha changed the world for the untold millions of individuals who have accepted his insights and followed his example over the centuries.

Though it is impossible to reconstruct the details of the Buddha's original message, its spirit of religious and moral commitment has been captured in an early Buddhist scripture, the *Dhammapada:*

> Rouse thyself! Do not be idle! Follow the law of virtue! The virtuous rest in bliss in this life and in the next. Come, look at this world, glittering like a royal chariot; the foolish are immersed in it, but the wise do not touch it. . . .
>
> If one man conquer in battle a thousand times a thousand men, and if another conquer himself, he is the greatest of conquerors. . . .
>
> If a man does what is good, let him do it again, let him delight in this world, and he is happy in the next; he is happy in both. He is happy when he thinks of the good he has done; he is still more happy when going on the good path. . . .
>
> Earnestness is the path of immortality [nirvāṇa], thoughtlessness the path of death. Those who are in earnest do not die, those who are thoughtless are as if dead already.[1]

THE EARLY YEARS

According to later mythology, at his son's birth Siddhārtha's father received a prediction that his child would become either a great ruler of the world or a great teacher of humanity. Wishing his son to succeed him as chief, Śuddhodana went to great lengths to shield him from human suffering and from experiences that might lead him to embrace the religious life. Biographical accounts written long after the Buddha's time exaggerate the luxury and comfort of his early life. Siddhārtha is said to have married when young and become the father of a son. When he reached the age of twenty-nine, he went out one day in a chariot. He encountered, in succession, an old man, a sick man, and a dead man. When Siddhārtha asked Channa, his charioteer, the meaning of these sights, he was told that old age, sickness, and death were the common lot of all humanity. Finally, Siddhārtha saw a wandering hermit whose head was shaved and who wore a ragged yellow robe. Channa identified the man as a *yogī* (a follower of *yoga,* a spiritual discipline) who had dedicated himself to a life of poverty and meditation. Siddhārtha was immediately inspired to do the same.

THE GREAT RENUNCIATION

Tradition has it that that very night Siddhārtha left his beautiful palace. Passing through the pavilion of dancing girls chosen for his pleasure, he silently bade farewell to his lovely wife and son. He then ordered Channa to drive the chariot to the edge of the forest. There Siddhārtha cut off his hair and beard, and put on the yellow robe of a mendicant monk. He instructed Channa to return his hair and jeweled sword to his father. In Buddhist lore, this dramatic departure is known as the Great Renunciation.

For the next six years Siddhārtha roamed throughout northeastern India. He studied for a time with two yogic teachers of the Brāhmaṇical tradition, but left them to seek salvation on his own. For a long time he practiced self-mortification. Because of his holiness and charisma, five other ascetics chose to live at his side. One day, when Siddhārtha was near starvation, he decided that excessive fasting was a false way to truth. He began to eat again, thus offending his five companions. He ate, bathed, and sat down in the lotus position beneath a *bodhi* (or *bo*) tree at Bodh Gayā. Here the tradition recounts that he was tempted by Māra, an evil demon associated with desire and death. Siddhārtha withstood the temptations and attacks.

THE ENLIGHTENMENT

According to Buddhist tradition, the greatest event in human history took place when Siddhārtha Gautama achieved enlightenment and became the Buddha. He reviewed all his former lives and his experiences in them; he envisioned all the levels of cosmic and material existence; he grasped the cause of all rebirth and suffering; and thereby he reached Buddhahood. The Buddha had won his victory. Then, the later traditions recount, the evil Māra again came to him with yet another temptation, to enjoy his own nirvāṇa without seeking to bring his message of hope to humanity. But with the encouragement of the Brahmā Sampatti (a great deity who knew the Buddha's preaching

This temple in Bodh Gayā, India, is said to be erected on the site of the bodhi tree where Siddhārtha withstood the temptations of Māra. *Religious News Service Photo.*

would be successful), the Buddha overcame the temptation and resolved to teach all who would listen to him.

THE SERMON AT BANĀRAS

After his enlightenment, the Buddha sought out the five ascetics who had left him in disgust. Finding them in the Deer Park at Isipatana, near Banāras, he advised them that he was no longer to be addressed as an ordinary man or friend, but as the Buddha or Tathāgata. When the ascetics paid him the honor that he demanded, the Buddha accepted them as his first disciples. He then preached what tradition records as his first sermon on the Dharma,* in which he proclaimed the four noble truths:

1. All existence is suffering (*dukhka*);
2. All suffering is caused by craving (*triṣhna*);
3. All suffering can be ended;
4. The way to end suffering is by practicing the noble eightfold path.

According to tradition, the Buddha characterizes the path that brings salvation as a "middle way":

There are two extremes, O bhikkhus,† which the man who has given up the world ought not to follow—the habitual practice, on the one hand, of self-indulgence which is unworthy, vain and fit only for the worldly minded—and the habitual practice, on the other hand, of self-mortification, which is painful, useless and unprofitable. . . .

More positively, he describes the eight aspects of the path as follows:

Right views will be the torch to light his way. Right aspirations will be his guide. Right speech

*The Sanskrit term *Dharma* (in Pali, *Dhamma*) has many meanings, including law, duty, teaching, and mental state. In Hīnayāna Buddhism it means the saving truth that was lived and taught by the Buddha, but in Mahāyāna Buddhism it has a more metaphysical significance.
†*Bhikkhu* is usually translated as "monk." Nuns were known as *bhikkhunis*.

will be his dwelling-place on the road. His gait will be straight, for it is right behavior. His refreshments will be the right way of earning his livelihood. Right efforts will be his steps; right thoughts his breath; and right contemplation will give him the peace that follows in his footprints . . .[2]

THE MINISTRY

For the rest of his long life, the Buddha traveled through northeastern India, preaching the Dharma and attracting many disciples in the prosperous towns of the Ganges Valley. Two of his earliest and best known converts were Śāriputra, who became famous for his wisdom, and Mandgalyāyana, who became famous for his possession and use of magical powers. Among his closest associates, according to the legends, were his cousins Ānanda and Devadatta. Ānanda waited on the Buddha for many years, but Devadatta became a traitor, much like Judas in the Christian tradition.

Soon the Buddha organized his mendicant converts into a *saṅgha,* a Buddhist monastic order. Despite his reported reservations, women were accepted as nuns and were allowed to found a separate order. Some of the early followers were sent out as missionaries to convert others, using the following formula, which Buddhists still repeat:

I take my refuge in the Buddha,

I take my refuge in the Dhamma,

I take my refuge in the Saṅgha.

Throughout his ministry, the Buddha utilized his great personal charisma and skills in preaching and debate and was able to convince many other mendicants that his enlightenment was authentic and that his Dharma had saving power. The Buddha used his skills to guide converts along the path that he had discovered and to motivate the spiritual, intellectual, and organizational leadership his expanding community required. He laid down basic guidelines for the personal behavior of his disciples, both male and female, and saw to it that these standards were maintained. He strengthened the religion by insisting that during three months of the rainy season, his mendicant followers cease their wandering and take up residence in those localities in which they had close and continuing contact with lay supporters.

The Buddha himself spent much time in the company of laypersons, teaching the doctrine of *karma* (deeds and the law that regulates their effects) and encouraging the making of merit (the doing of good deeds to improve one's karmic condition in this life and in future lives). In this way, he was able to convert many householders into lay supporters and to accumulate goodwill in the community at large.

THE DEATH OF THE BUDDHA

After many years, the scriptures record that the great teacher had premonitions of death, and that he spoke these words to his cousin Ānanda:

The great stūpa (shrine) in the Deer Park near Banāras (Varanasi) marking the spot where the Buddha delivered his first sermon. *Stephen Borst.*

> I too, Ananda, am now grown old and full of years, my journey is drawing to its close, I have reached my sum of days, I am turning eighty years of age. . . .
>
> Therefore, O Ananda, be ye lamps unto yourselves. Betake yourselves to no external refuge. Hold fast to the truth as a lamp. Hold fast as a refuge to the truth. . . .
>
> And whosoever, Ananda, either now or after I am dead, shall be a lamp unto themselves, and a refuge unto themselves, shall betake themselves to no external refuge, but holding fast to the truth as their lamp, and holding fast as their refuge to the truth, shall not look to anyone besides themselves—it is they, Ananda, among my bhikkhus, who shall reach the very topmost Height!—but they must be anxious to learn.[3]

The Buddha is said to have become sick shortly afterward from eating spoiled pork. He died peacefully in the midst of his close disciples in the village of Kuśinagara.

After the Buddha's Death: Tradition and Doctrine

At the time of the Buddha's death, Buddhist communities had been established in several states in the Ganges Valley, and their distinctive life style set them apart from other mendicant groups and sects. Many laypersons, including rich and powerful members of the aristocracy and the merchant class, supported and encouraged the Buddhist monks and nuns. But during his lifetime, the Buddha's own personal charisma and authority had been the principal unifying factor in the communities' life and development. His death therefore required them to make several adjustments.

ESTABLISHING THE MONASTIC TRADITION

An important historical source for our knowledge of early Buddhism is the *Mahāparinibbāṇa Sutta* (Sermon of the great decease).* According to this account, the Buddha did not pass on the mantle of leadership to any of his disciples, but instead recommended that the community follow the kind of republican system used by a contemporary political group known as the Vṛjjians. Its founder emphasized the necessity of holding frequent assemblies in order to deliberate on major communal issues. He urged those who took refuge in the Dharma to use as their teacher the truth and the rules of the order.

The *Mahāparinibbāṇa Sutta* also addresses another of the disciples' problems. A monk named Subhadra was delighted at the news of Buddha's death because he assumed he and the other disciples would no longer be bound by the Buddha's strict discipline. The narrative then goes on to describe the feelings of the Buddha's renowned disciple, Mahākāsýapa. He noted that the Buddha's death was to be expected and that it only confirmed the validity of his teaching concerning the impermanence of all things and the need for the proper practice of the eightfold path. According to other sources, Mahākāsýapa then proposed holding a council of the Buddha's closest and most accomplished followers. It was convened during the rainy season in the city of Rājagṛha. Mahākāsýapa requested that the council compile and codify the Buddha's teachings so that their authority could guide the lives of the monks. The same sources describe how the five hundred *arhants* (those who had achieved nirvāṇa) proceeded. Ānanda, the Buddha's beloved disciple, recited the Dharma the Buddha had preached in the form of sermons and dialogues (the sūtras). Upāli recited the rules the Buddha had laid down to regulate the personal and communal life of his mendicant followers (the *vinaya*). Then the assembly as a whole confirmed the authenticity of both.

Many modern historians doubt that a formal council was ever convened on anything like the scale described in the later accounts. Nonetheless,

**Sutta* is the Pali word for the Sanskrit *sūtra*. As a rule, the Sanskrit form of the Buddhist term is used in this book, but here the Pali word is used to distinguish it from a later Mahāyāna text, the *Mahāparinirvāṇa Sūtra*.

it is quite certain that the process described in the narrative did take place. After the Buddha's death, certain aspects of his authority were quickly appropriated by the mendicant disciples he had chosen and trained. The authority of the arhants was generally recognized by the community as a whole. Together, disciples and arhants began the task of gathering and codifying the Buddha's teachings. His sermons or dialogues were organized into what became the core of the later scripture known as the *Sūtra Piṭaka,* or basket of discourses, and his instructions to the monks were organized into the core of the later scripture known as the *Vinaya Piṭaka,* or basket of monastic rules.

The mendicant community continued holding regular biweekly meetings, and on these occasions they recited the rules of behavior the Buddha had laid down (the *prātimoksa*) and confessed any transgressions they had committed. They continued the practice of settling in groups during the rainy season and thus maintained close ties with their lay supporters. This gradually led to the development of more permanent monastic establishments.

REACTIONS OF THE LAITY

The *Mahāparinibbāṇa Sutta* stresses that the ways in which the laity met the crisis of the Buddha's death were quite different. It reports that after the Buddha's death, the responsibility for the disposition of his remains was turned over to the aristocrats of the village of Kuśinagara. These laymen proceeded to the grove of trees where their teacher had died. For six days they honored his remains. On the seventh day they received instructions from a disciple who claimed to know the will of the spirits. Following his instructions, they took the body through the village to a local shrine.

They prepared it in the manner traditionally reserved for the body of a great ruler. The Buddha's funeral pyre was built and his remains placed on it. After the cremation, they took the relics to the council hall. For seven days they "paid honor and reverence and respect and homage to them with dance and song and music, and with garlands and perfumes."[4]

A number of neighboring groups then sent messengers to Kuśinagara demanding a portion of the relics so that they could establish an appropriate shrine within their own borders. At first, the Kuśinagara laity refused. Finally, however, they accepted the arbitration of a brāhmaṇ named Drona who decreed that the relics be divided into eight equal parts and distributed to the eight groups. Drona himself kept the relic jar. It is said that a late arrival representing the Maurya clan—the clan that many generations later produced the emperor Aśoka—received the ashes. The various messengers then took their share back to their homelands.

This narrative, like the Buddha's biography and the account of the Council of Rājagḥra, undoubtedly is in great part legend. But it does make clear that soon after the Buddha's death, the laity had established a cult of reverence for the relics of the great teacher. Moreover, some versions of the sutta composed within the first two to three centuries after the Buddha's death suggest that the mode of maintaining contact with the founder also took a second form; that soon after the Buddha died, the four sites associated with the four crucial events in his life became important pilgrimage centers. These were the Lumbinī Grove near the city of Kapilavastu, associated with his birth; the sacred site at Bodh Gayā, associated with his enlightenment; the famous Deer Park at Banāras, associated with the preaching of his first sermon; and the sacred grove at Kuśinagara, associated with his death.

Early Buddhism

We do not know the exact historical details of the various ways in which the mendicants and the members of the laity met the crisis of the Buddha's death. Yet it is apparent that both segments of the community did make a creative adjustment to the new situation and that the unity and vitality of the religion was preserved. The fourth and third centuries B.C. were a crucial period in the history of Buddhism. Many parts of the existing doctrine, symbolism, ritual life, and communal structure were developed further, and certain new patterns appeared. For example, during these two centuries,

Buddhists generally agree that nirvāṇa is the ultimate goal of religious life. But what is nirvāṇa? How can it be described in a way that is both religiously significant and philosophically appropriate? For more than two thousand years, Buddhist scholars and apologists have struggled with these questions and have come up with many different and often mutually exclusive answers. One influential attempt was made about the beginning of the Christian Era by the author of *The Questions of King Milinda*. (Milinda is the Indian form of the name of Menander, a Greek king who ruled in northwestern India in the second century B.C.) The work relates a discussion between the king and a famous monk named Nāgasena.

"Venerable one," asks the king, "Is nirvana all bliss, or is it mixed with suffering?" The monk replies:*

"Nirvana is entirely bliss, Great King, and there is no suffering in it."

"We cannot believe that nirvana is all bliss; we maintain that it is mixed with suffering. For we can see that those who seek nirvana torment their bodies and their minds: they restrain their standing and walking and sitting and eating; they interrupt their sleep; they oppress their senses; and they cast aside their wealth and friends and kinsmen.

"But those who are happy and full of bliss in the world delight their senses with pleasure. They delight their eyes with all manner of beautiful sights, and their ears with all manner of music and song; they delight their nose with the scent of fruits and flowers and fragrant plants, and their tongue with the sweet taste of food and drink. They delight their body with the touch of the soft and fine, the tender and the delicate; and they delight their mind with thoughts and ideas both virtuous and sinful, both good and bad. And they do these things whenever they like.

"But you do not develop your senses; you slay and destroy and hinder and prevent them, and thus torment your body and your mind. When you torment your body, then you feel suffering in your body; when you torment your mind, then you feel suffering in your mind. And that is why I say that nirvana is mixed with suffering."

"What you call suffering, Great King, is not what we call nirvana; it is the preliminary to nirvana, the search for nirvana. Nirvana is all bliss and is not mixed with suffering. And I will tell you why. Is there what we might call a bliss of sovereignty which kings enjoy?"

"Indeed, venerable one, there is a bliss of sovereignty."

"But the borders become disturbed, and a king must put down the revolt; and he surrounds himself with advisors and soldiers and goes sojourning abroad. He runs about over the rough ground and is oppressed by flies and mosquitoes and wind and heat; he fights great battles and is in doubt of his very life."

"But, venerable one, this is not what we call the bliss of sovereignty; it is but a preliminary in search thereof. The king seeks for power with suffering, and then he can enjoy the bliss he has sought. The bliss of sovereignty is not mixed with suffering: the bliss is one thing and the suffering another."

"Even so, Great King, nirvana is all bliss and is not mixed with suffering. Those who seek nirvana torment their bodies and their minds: they restrain their standing and walking and sitting and eating; they interrupt their sleep; they oppress their senses; they sacrifice their bodies and their lives.

"They seek for nirvana with suffering, and then they can enjoy the bliss they have sought, even as a king enjoys the bliss of sovereignty when he has destroyed his enemies. Nirvana is all bliss and is not mixed with suffering: the bliss is one thing and the suffering another. . . ."

"Venerable one, you are always speaking of nirvana: can you give me a metaphor, or a reason, or an argument, or an inference to show me its form, or its nature, or its duration, or its size?"

*From Stephan Beyer, *The Buddhist Experience: Sources and Interpretations* (Encino, Calif.: Dickinson, 1974), pp. 200–204.

"Great King, nirvana is unique and incomparable: there is neither metaphor nor reason, neither argument nor inference, which can show its form, or its nature, or its duration, or its size."

"But venerable one, nirvana is a real thing: I simply cannot accept that there is no way to make intelligible its form, or its nature, or its duration, or its size. Explain this reasonably to me."

"Very well, Great King, I shall explain it to you. Is there such a thing as the ocean?"

"Of course there is such a thing as the ocean."

"Suppose someone were to ask you how much water there was in the ocean, and how many creatures lived therein. How would you answer such a question?"

"Foolish person, I would say, you are asking me an unaskable thing. No one should ask such a question; such a question should be put aside. Scientists have never analyzed the ocean: no one can measure the water there, nor count the creatures who live therein. That is the way I would answer the question."

"But, Great King, the ocean is a real thing: why should you give such an answer? Should you not rather count and then say: There is so much water in the ocean, and so many creatures living therein?"

"But I could not do so, venerable one. The question is impossible."

"So the ocean is a real thing, yet you cannot measure its water nor count its creatures; and in the same way nirvana is a real thing, yet there is neither metaphor nor reason, neither argument nor inference, which can show its form, or its nature, or its duration, or its size. And even if there were a man with magic powers, who could measure the waters of the ocean and count its creatures: even he could not find the form, or the nature, or the duration, or the size of nirvana. . . ."

"What are the four qualities of the ocean which are found in nirvana?"

"The ocean is empty of all corpses, and nirvana is empty of the corpses of passion. The ocean is great and limitless, and it is not filled by all the rivers that flow into it; and nirvana is great and limitless, and it is not filled by all the beings who enter it. The ocean is the abode of great creatures; and nirvana is the abode of the great Worthy Ones, the stainless, the strong, the powerful. The ocean seems to flower with the vast and various blossoms of the waves; and nirvana seems to flower with the the vast and various blossoms of purity and knowledge and freedom."

"And the ten qualities of space?"

"Space does not arise, nor decay, nor die, nor pass away, nor reappear; it cannot be overcome, nor stolen by thieves; it is not supported by anything; it is the path of the birds, without obstruction, infinite. And nirvana does not arise, nor decay, nor die, nor pass away, nor reappear; it cannot be overcome, nor stolen by thieves; it is not supported by anything; it is the path of the Noble Ones, without obstruction, infinite."

"And the three qualities of the wish-granting gem?"

"The wish-granting gem grants every wish and nirvana grants every wish. The wish granting gem causes joy, and nirvana causes joy. The wish-granting gem shines with light, and nirvana shines with light."

"And the three qualities of red sandalwood?"

"Red sandalwood is hard to find, and nirvana is hard to find. Red sandalwood has an unequaled fragrance, and nirvana has an unequaled fragrance. Red sandalwood is praised by the discriminating, and nirvana is praised by the Noble Ones."

"And the three qualities of the finest butter?"

"The finest butter is beautiful in color, and nirvana is beautiful in virtue. The finest butter is beautiful in fragrance, and nirvana is beautiful in righteousness. The finest butter is beautiful in taste, and nirvana is beautiful in experience."

"What are the five qualities of a mountain peak which are found in nirvana?"

"Nirvana is as lofty as a mountain peak and as unmoving. A mountain peak is hard to climb, and nirvana cannot be reached by the passions. No seeds can grow upon a mountain peak, and no passion can grow in nirvana. A mountain peak is free of fear or favor, and nirvana is free of fear or favor."

"Excellent, venerable one. Thus it is, and thus I accept it."

controversies and schisms became central to the life of the community, and the religion received new impetus and direction when the emperor Aśoka adopted it as his own. Having enriched its understanding of the founder and his teachings as well as its own communal life, Buddhism then began to expand its sphere of influence.

DOCTRINAL DEVELOPMENT

At this time, more emphasis was placed on the Buddha's status as a *mahāpurusha*, or great being, who had synthesized and transcended the attainments of a great world-renouncing yogī and those of a universal monarch. Stories were told about the lives of previous Buddhas, and several of these legendary anecdotes appeared in the accounts of the Buddha's earthly life. These stories included Siddhārtha's discovery of old age, sickness, and death; his attraction to the life of a wandering mendicant; his renunciation of his position and wealth; his enlightenment under the bo tree; his recruitment of his first disciples; and his preaching of his first sermon at Banāras. By the end of this period, other stories relating the various miracles performed by the Buddha were also incorporated into the growing body of legends.

The sūtras containing the teachings attributed to the Buddha were classified in various ways. At one time they were divided into nine or twelve segments, each containing a particular type of material, such as sermons, predictions, verses of inspiration, and accounts of incidents in the Buddha's previous lives. Eventually they were grouped into the five *nikāyas* (in Sanskrit, *āgamas*) that make up the *Sutta Piṭaka*, or basket of sermons. There also were developments in the content of the teaching. Certain important doctrines were refined, including those associated with *anātman* (the nonexistence of any kind of self), *anicca* (the impermanence of all things); and *dukhka* (the universality of suffering). Buddhist thinkers also developed their analysis of the five basic elements of reality. The first, *rūpa*, was material form; the second, *vedanā*, was feeling; the third, *saṃjñā*, was ideas or perceptions; the fourth, *saṃskāra*, was impulse and emotions; and the last, *vijñāna*, was consciousness.

The basic insight into the simultaneous origination of all things also was important. According to the classical theory of the later sūtras, the elements of existence were contained in a twelve-part, interdependent chain of causation. Beginning with ignorance, this chain continued through the impulses and emotions, consciousness, psychological elements, six senses (the usual five senses plus the mind), contact, feelings, desire, grasping, becoming, old age, and death. This chain of causation produced *saṃsāra*, the cycle of existence in which all beings constantly endured suffering, dissatisfaction, and woe. The cycle continued until, through the practice of the Way, a key link such as ignorance or desire was broken. According to the tradition, it was this breaking of the chain of causation that finally brought the realization of nirvāṇa.

At the popular level, the same conception of reality was presented as an increasingly complex cosmology, or a way of picturing the universe, in which the destinies of all sentient beings were ordered in accordance with the principles of karma. These beings lived in a cosmos populated by a variety of divine, human, and subhuman beings. According to the teachings directed to the Buddhist laity, those who had not attained enlightenment could win merit and thereby improve their karmic destiny in many ways. The ways included the practice of simple morality and virtues, as well as the giving of gifts to support the monastic order.

DEVELOPMENTS AND DIVISIONS IN THE MONASTIC COMMUNITY

During the same period, the Buddhist saṅgha continued to change from a community of wandering mendicants into a community of followers living more or less permanently in local monasteries. The rules of the order (the *vinaya*) were adapted to accommodate these changes, and by the end of the period the vinaya had become a full-fledged constitution able to regulate the life of a large, well-established monastic community.

At the same time, the disagreements and divisions within the saṅgha were becoming more serious. For example, there is a story about a monk named Pūraṇa who was delayed in reaching the site of the council. When he was invited to join the meeting, he declined to do so, stating that he preferred to remain loyal to the teaching and discipline he had received directly from the Buddha. Whatever the historical basis for this account, it is clear that there indeed were disagreements over the religion's mythology, doctrine, discipline, and legal framework.

Over the next several centuries, the major sects took shape and a series of councils was held. Even though the traditional reports of the issues are complex and often contradictory, modern historians agree that the disputes involved both discipline and doctrines. The disciplinary conflicts were over such matters as whether the monks should be allowed to accept gifts of gold and silver and whether new rules could be added to the *prātimokṣa* (the list of monastic rules). Some of the key doctrinal disputes centered on the spiritual attainments attributed to the arhants, the ontological status of time past and time future, and the existence of a kind of personal entity called a *pudgala*.

Most Buddhist traditions affirm that an extremely important ecclesiastical gathering, the Second Council, was held in the city of Vesali during the first half of the fourth century B.C. Another council was probably held at Pātaliputra, the newly established capital of the state of Magadha, in the second half of the same century. Still another council (known to the later tradition as the Third Council) was probably held at Pātaliputra during the reign of Emperor Aśoka, whose importance to Buddhism will be discussed in Chapter 10.

The main schism in early Buddhism took place either during or shortly after the Second Council at Vesali. At this time there was a split between the *Mahāsaṅghika* (great assembly), which held liberal views, and the more conservative *Sthaviravāda* (Pali, Theravāda) or school of the elders. Later, two other groups broke away from the Sthaviravāda. The first group, the *Vātsīyaputras* (sometimes called the Sammitīyas), believed in a form of personal entity (pudgala), and the second group, the *Sarvāstivādins*, believed in the existence of a past and a future time.

Notes

1 F. Max Müller, trans., *The Dhammapada* (1870); quoted in Lin Yutang, ed., *The Wisdom of China and India* (New York: Random House, 1942), pp. 321–356.

2 "Sermon at Benares," in *The Fo-Suo-Xing-Zan-Jing*, (The life of Buddha by Aśvaghoṣa), translated from Sanskrit into Chinese by Dharmaraksha in A.D. 420 and from Chinese into English by Samuel Beal, copyrighted and published by the Open Court Publishing Company, La Salle, Ill.; quoted in Lin Yutang, *The Wisdom of China and India*, pp. 359–362.

3 T. W. Rhys Davids, trans., *Buddhist Sutras* (reprinted in Delhi, India: Motilal Banarasidass, 1968), pp. 37–38, vol. 11 of the *Sacred Books of the East*, ed. F. Max Müller.

4 Ibid., p. 131.

8 The Three Main Traditions

While the developments of early Buddhism were taking place, important political events were also occurring. Alexander the Great (356–323 B.C.), conqueror of much of the ancient world, led his troops across Persia, Bactria, and Afghanistan. In 326 his Greek army broke through the Khyber Pass into the Indus Valley. Alexander was well received by some of the Indian princes, but he still had to overcome the rulers of the Punjab. At this point his weary soldiers threatened to rebel if Alexander also insisted on invading the Ganges Valley. He was forced to turn back, and the regime he set up in the Punjab quickly disintegrated. Nevertheless, Hellenistic cultural influences began to spread throughout northern India.

Around 322 B.C., a soldier in the state of Magadha named Chandragupta Maurya seized power and founded the Maurya dynasty, which controlled most of northern India for well over a century. King Chandragupta was a successful general who built a large professional army and used it to enlarge his realm. At the same time, to fill the political vacuum left after Alexander's withdrawal from the Punjab, Chandragupta encouraged the idea of an Indian king. He supported trade and agriculture, expanded the use of currency, cleared forests, and built cities. It was a time of prosperity for the growing class of merchants.

Chandragupta was succeeded by his son, King Bindusāra, who continued the expansionist poli-

Stucco head of a bodhisattva from Hadda, Afghanistan (Gandhāra school, 4th–5th century A.D.). *Seattle Art Museum.*

cies of his father and was on friendly terms with the Greek Seleucid rulers of Persia and Bactria. Bindusāra's son and successor was the emperor Aśoka (ruled 273–232 B.C.), one of the greatest rulers of ancient India. His realm included most of the Indian subcontinent, along with Baluchistan and Afghanistan.

Several years after coming to power, Aśoka invaded the state of Kaliṅga, to the south of Magadha. Because of their stubborn resistance, some two hundred thousand Kalingans were killed or taken prisoner. Aśoka was shocked at the suffering he and his army had caused; he also seemed to realize that his realm had expanded so far that additional conquests were impractical. In any event, he was shortly thereafter converted to Buddhism. He presented himself in his inscriptions as a supporter of the Dharma who sought to establish peace, to substitute Buddhist pilgrimages for the traditional hunting expeditions, and to prohibit the practice of animal sacrifice. His role in the history of Buddhism has been compared with that of Constantine in Christianity.

Aśoka took an active interest in the affairs of the Buddhist community. From his capital at Pātaliputra, he sent missionaries all over India and as far away as Afghanistan and Southeast Asia. Among these missions the most important was that sent to Sri Lanka under the direction of Mahinda, the emperor's son or possibly younger brother. Still another mission went to Burma or central Thailand.

Throughout his vast empire, Aśoka placed inscriptions that proclaimed his message and recounted his activities. He also built many *stūpas,* or shrines, in honor of the Buddha. According to a late, obviously apocryphal legend, Aśoka divided the relics of the Buddha into 84,000 portions, which he housed in 84,000 stūpas distributed throughout India.

With Aśoka's enthusiastic support, Buddhism spread throughout the empire. What had been, only two centuries before, a small, nonconformist sect was elevated to the status of a potentially universal religion. True to the principles of the Buddha, Aśoka practiced tolerance of other religions, including the brāhmaṇs who continued to support Hinduism. Nevertheless, the Buddhists no longer

The Thuparama stūpa at Anuradhapura, which dates from the third century B.C., is the oldest in Sri Lanka. It enshrines a precious relic of the Buddha, a piece of his collarbone. *Georg Gerster/ Photo Researchers*

thought of their community simply as a monastic order complemented by a relatively unorganized laity, but rather as a saṅgha operating in tandem with a Buddhist state ruled by a Buddhist king.

Shortly after Aśoka's death, his empire began to decline. Some historians attribute this to the difficulties of maintaining communications over such a vast realm; others speak of dissensions and intrigues among members of the royal family; and still others speculate that the proclamation of Buddhist pacifism as a policy may have contributed to the decline. Whatever the reasons, the last Mauryan emperor was assassinated around 186 B.C. But the form of Buddhism Aśoka had encouraged continued to grow, both within India itself and beyond.

THE HĪNAYĀNA TRADITION

As early as the time of Aśoka, Buddhism had established the basic theoretical, practical, and sociological expressions that gave it both identity and integrity. But the Hīnayāna version of the tradition had not yet reached its full maturity, and it underwent several changes in the two centuries before the birth of Christ and in the first two centuries afterward. During this period the Hīnayānists elaborated and refined their conception of the Buddha, their understanding of the Dharma, and their style of life.

The Maturing of the Hīnayāna Tradition

DIVINIZATION OF THE BUDDHA

Within the Hīnayāna tradition there was a strong tendency for both monks and laity to divinize the Buddha. Within the monastic tradition it was asserted that, in addition to his human, physical body, the Buddha possessed a more ultimate Dharma body, or *dharmakāya*. (Sometimes this was interpreted as a body associated with his practice of the Way, and sometimes as a body associated with the truth he had taught.) The conservative schools kept such speculation in check. In the more liberal traditions the dharmic body, or body of truth, became more significant, whereas the human, physical body was reduced to the level of mere appearance.

Among the laity the tendency toward divinization was related to the growing importance of devotional activities. In the post-Aśokan period, veneration of the founder was widespread and expressed itself in a variety of new forms. During the second and first centuries B.C., several great stūpas were constructed. By the beginning of the Christian era, images of the Buddha began to appear. Through their enthusiastic participation in the veneration of these stūpas and images, the laity came to view the Buddha as a great being who had much in common with the classical Hindu gods such as Brahmā and Viṣṇu.

Although these movements brought the full historicity of the Buddha's career into question, they did not lessen the interest in recounting it. Indeed, the desire to make known the Buddha's glorious and perhaps divine actions in the world stimulated new and extended accounts of his life. Shortly after the beginning of the Christian era, the Mahāsaṅghikas and the more liberal Sarvāstivādins produced two accounts, the *Mahāvastu* and the *Lalitavistara*. These texts described the Buddha's great deeds from the period before his life as Gautama (his family clan name) through the early stages of his ministry. Other accounts produced in succeeding centuries carried the story from the period immediately before his final birth as Gautama to the time of his death and the distribution of his relics.

PAST AND FUTURE BUDDHAS

The interest in the Buddha as a divine or archetypal figure also led to greater interest in the Buddhas of the past and the future. The existence of Buddhas other than Gautama was assumed from the very early stages of Buddhist history, though it was only in the post-Aśoka period that a number of more extended enumerations of past Buddhas began to appear. Some Buddhists came to believe in a future Buddha named Maitreya, who was thought to be residing in the *Tusita* heaven (the fourth in the hierarchy of six heavens which, according to the Buddhist cosmology, constituted the upper regions of the world of desire), awaiting the appropriate time to come into the world and establish his community. In the Sarvāstivādin strongholds in northwestern India and Central Asia, Maitreya became the center of a major devotional cult. There and elsewhere the devout sought to accumulate merit so that they could be reborn when Maitreya descended into the human world. At that time, it was believed, society would be perfected, and the eightfold path and nirvāṇa would be accessible to all.

DEVELOPMENT OF THE CONCEPT OF THE DHARMA

While this movement was taking place in the Hīnayāna community, the Dharma was also being extended in various ways, probably the most obvious being the composition of some technical doctrinal treatises and the collection of sets of these treatises by the various schools. Given the name *Abhidharma Piṭaka,* or basket of the higher Dharma, these sets of treatises were recognized by most Hīnayāna schools as a third segment of teachings equal in authority to the much older Sutra and *Piṭakas Vinaya.* Though the Abhidharma collections of the various schools contained different texts, these texts grappled with the same problems. For example, they carried forward the early Buddhist effort to analyze all reality into discrete elements which, in this context, were called *dharmas.* They described the process through which the dharmas that made up the individual beings and the various levels of cosmic reality came together, and they specified the process through which human actions, despite the nonexistence of any kind of self, created their appropriate punishments and rewards. They affirmed the reality of nirvāṇa as a very different "unconditioned" dharma that was equated with release from the cycle of rebirth. Finally, they analyzed the eightfold path, including its practices of discipline, meditation, and insight. In this way they sought to describe the process through which the causes of the coming together of the conditioned dharmas (that is to say, the causes of existence and suffering) could be uprooted in order to achieve nirvāṇa, the unconditioned.

As the monks proceeded with the elaboration of the Abhidharma, they also consolidated the teachings that were directed toward the less advanced monks and the laity. For example, the ideas of karma, merit, and rebirth were grouped into a series of manuals describing the various conditions in which a human being could be reborn. These included the various hells; the realm of suffering ghosts; the realm of the *asuras,* or fallen deities; the realm of animals, the realm of human beings;

A fourteenth-century Japanese painting of the future Buddha Maitreya. *Japan House Gallery, Japan Society, Inc.*

and the realm of the gods. The kinds of deeds that could lead to rebirth in each of these realms were specified. Distinctively new practices also began to gain widespread acceptance. Some parts of the community began to practice rituals designed to transfer merit from one individual to another, particularly from a living person to a deceased relative who might be languishing in one of the various hells or in the realm of the suffering ghosts. In addition, some members of the laity began to sponsor the performance of *paritta* ceremonies in which monks recited particular sūtras to produce the magical power that would assure their patron's safety, health, and prosperity.

MONASTIC DEVELOPMENT

The continuing development of the Hīnayāna tradition also affected the saṅgha. The efforts of the monks and nuns to legitimate their position in the life of the community led to the collection of teachings on the *ārya pudgala*, or noble beings. In the Hīnayāna view, such noble beings belonged to a special group who had entered one of the four stages of the supraworldly path. These were identified as the stage attained by the stream winners, who would suffer no more than seven additional rebirths; the stage attained by the once-returners, who would be reborn no more than once; the stage attained by the nonreturners, who would not be reborn again; and the stage attained by the arhants, who had achieved nirvāṇa. Since these four kinds of noble beings had obtained the "spotless eye of Dharma" that provided authority in matters of teaching and doctrine, they could legitimately be placed alongside the Buddha and the Dharma as the third jewel or refuge for the Buddhist faithful. The later Hīnayānists believed that with the passage of time the number of noble beings in the saṅgha had declined. Nevertheless, they maintained that at least a few such noble beings remained and that they were a spiritual aristocracy which guaranteed the purity and sacred status of the community as a whole.

This same legitimating concern took a very different form in the Hīnayāna claims of the existence of an unbroken lineage of "masters of the Dharma." There was already a basis for such a view in the early Buddhist tradition, but over time the question of lineage had acquired added significance. The majority of the later Hīnayāna schools held that their basic lineage began with the Buddha himself and included Mahākāśyapa, the monk who supposedly convened the first council, three early arhants who succeeded him, and Upagupta, the legendary preceptor of Aśoka.

As these developments were taking place, there were also disputes that led to the establishment of many new schools. Before the beginning of the Christian era, the number of Hīnayāna schools had reached at least eighteen and may have been more. More important, the gap between the conservatives, associated with the Sthaviravāda (the school of the elders), and the liberals, who took their cue from the early Mahāsaṅghika (the great assembly), continued to widen. The conservatives emphasized the spiritual superiority of the monks, exalting the perfections of the arhants and other noble beings. The liberals, who questioned these perfections, were less strict in maintaining the distinction between the monastic and lay traditions. As Buddhism expanded and new elements were generated and introduced, different responses were inevitable. All of the schools, including the most conservative, accepted the rapidly proliferating lay piety. However, it was the more liberal traditions that allowed such innovations to penetrate into the monasteries themselves and even to change the monks' understanding of the inherited symbols and doctrines. In this way, some of the foundations were laid for a distinctively new Buddhist perspective—the Mahāyāna, or Great Vehicle tradition.

THE MAHĀYĀNA TRADITION

The Sātavāhana and Kuṣāṇa Dynasties

After the collapse of the Mauryan Empire in 186 B.C., Buddhism continued to flourish in the Indian subcontinent. In northeastern India, Buddhism continued to develop despite the strong Brāhmaṇic competition supported by the reigning Śuṅga dynasty. In central India and in the north (in the Indus area and on into Afghanistan and other regions of Central Asia), the Buddhist community was even more active.

During the second and first centuries B.C., a definite political and cultural order gradually took hold in central India. By the beginning of the Christian era, the powerful Sātavāhana dynasty had established political control, and for several centuries remained the dominant political and cultural force in the area. Under its hegemony the economy, which was tied to trade with Rome and the West, prospered. Buddhism—like Brahmanism—was heavily patronized. Generally, the kings supported the brāhmaṇs, whereas the women of the court took a special interest in Buddhism.

Buddhist art also blossomed. Caves, such as those at Ellorā and Ajantā, were transformed into monastic centers and adorned with Buddhist sculpture. Great stūpas and other monastic establishments were constructed at famous sites such as Amarāvatī. At the same time, other aspects of Buddhist thought and practice were creatively reinterpreted and extended. The established Hīnayāna tradition was elaborated, and new, specifically Mahāyāna patterns of Buddhist life, symbolism, and practice made their appearance.

In northwestern India the situation was quite different, but equally dynamic. During the third and second centuries B.C., the Greek political and cultural influences that had been present in the northwest since the time of Alexander remained strong. But also during this period tribes from Central Asia began to invade and eventually succeeded in establishing the Kuṣāṇa dynasty, which ruled most of northwestern India and much of Central Asia from the first to the third centuries A.D. The greatest of the Kuṣāṇa rulers was Kaniṣka, who became the king of Gandhāra sometime between A.D. 78 and 120. From his capital at Peshāwar, he controlled a vast realm which included parts of Central Asia, most of Afghanistan, and all of northwestern India.

Kaniṣka showed remarkable skill in dealing with the diverse peoples in his empire. He encouraged the advancement of the sciences and the arts. Under the Kuṣāṇa rulers, new art styles portrayed the Buddha in human form: The Gandhāra school of sculpture combined Greco-Roman elegance and natural form with Buddhist spirituality. Elegant stūpas and monasteries were erected, and huge gilt images, ivories, and fine glassware created. Through the help of Buddhist missionaries, this distinctive art style transmitted knowledge of the Buddha along the trade routes of Central Asia to the Far East. Buddhism, which was well received by the tribes living along the Oxus River and near the Pamir Mountains, soon spread also to the Tarim Basin and on to the frontiers of China.

Like Emperor Aśoka, King Kaniṣka was a convert to Buddhism and is also credited with sponsoring a great council. He reportedly summoned five hundred monks, including representatives from many parts of India and Central Asia, to a so-called Fourth Council. According to tradition, the council tried to reconcile the views of the more traditional Hīnayāna monks with the views of those who favored the newer orientation known as the Mahāyāna.

New Perspectives and New Insights

The exact line of demarcation between the Hīnayāna and the Mahāyāna traditions is difficult to draw. Many tendencies that came to full fruition in Mahāyāna were already, or later became, components of Hīnayāna life. Much of the Hīnayāna heritage, especially the later accounts of the Buddha's historical life and the vinaya tradition of monastic discipline, remained part of the Mahāyāna. Often Hīnayāna and Mahāyāna monks lived together in the same establishments, and among the laity the distinction was vague indeed. Nevertheless, the Mahāyānist movement, as it began to take shape during the last century before the Christian era, represented a significantly new departure in Indian Buddhism.

THE NEW SŪTRAS

The new perspective has been compared with that of the older Hīnayāna tradition in a variety of ways. Some scholars have highlighted the Mahāyāna emphasis on faith in the Buddha and have

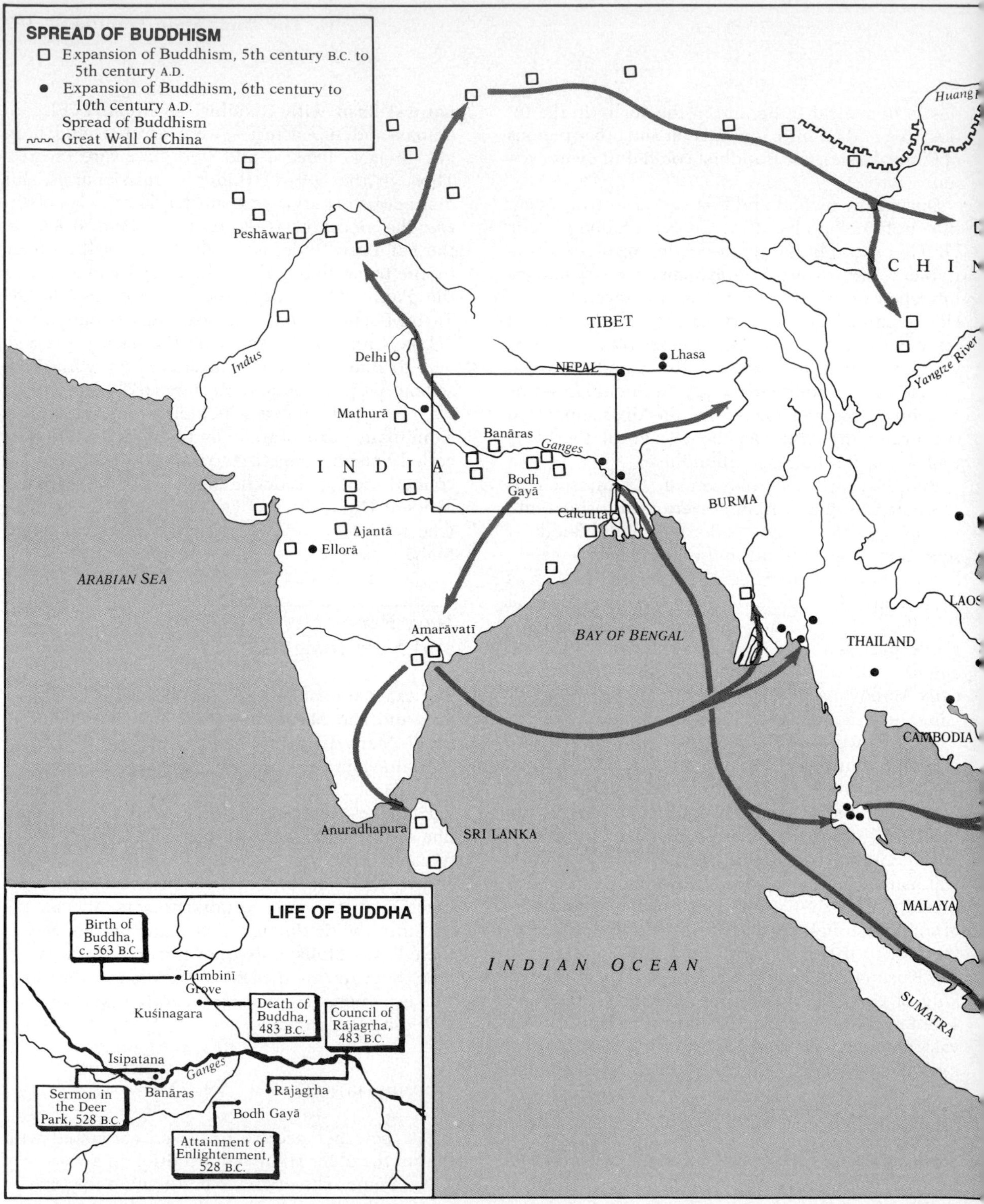

SPREAD OF BUDDHISM
Expansion of Buddhism, 5th century B.C. to 5th century A.D.
Expansion of Buddhism, 6th century to 10th century A.D.
Spread of Buddhism
Great Wall of China
Peshāwar
Indus
Delhi
Mathurā
INDIA
Banāras
Ganges
Bodh Gayā
Calcutta
Ajantā
Ellorā
ARABIAN SEA
Amarāvatī
BAY OF BENGAL
Anuradhapura
SRI LANKA
INDIAN OCEAN
TIBET
NEPAL
Lhasa
BURMA
THAILAND
LAOS
CAMBODIA
MALAYA
SUMATRA
CHIN
Yangtze River
LIFE OF BUDDHA
Birth of Buddha, c. 563 B.C.
Lumbinī Grove
Kuśinagara
Death of Buddha, 483 B.C.
Council of Rājagṛha, 483 B.C.
Isipatana
Ganges
Banāras
Rājagṛha
Sermon in the Deer Park, 528 B.C.
Bodh Gayā
Attainment of Enlightenment, 528 B.C.

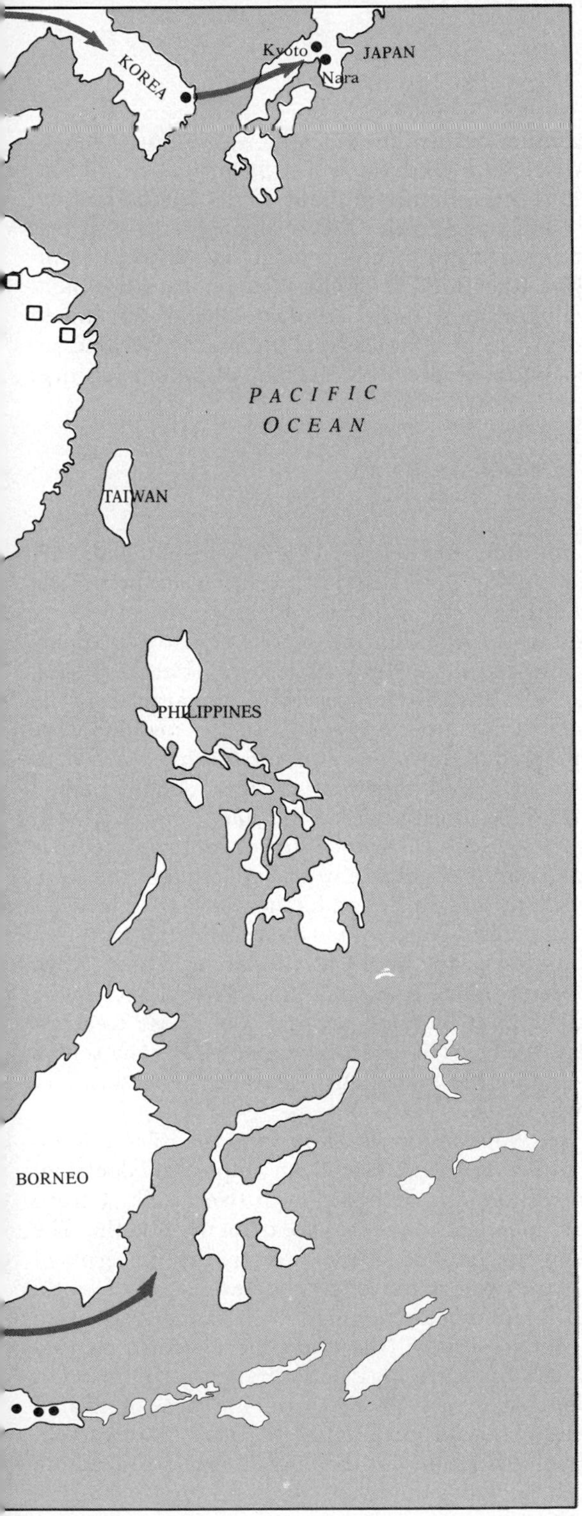

contrasted it with the Hīnayāna emphasis on self effort. Others have focused on the Mahāyāna concept of *śūnyatā* (emptiness), the understanding that the dharmas of the Hīnayānists, and therefore all reality, are empty or lacking in self-nature. Still others have concentrated on the Mahāyāna contention that monks, nuns, and laity all should follow the path of the bodhisattva—one who can achieve nirvāṇa but chooses not to do so until all other human beings can be saved. In fact, these and other ideas were expressed in the new sūtras the Mahāyāna movement produced and recognized as authoritative.

Mahāyāna sūtras were not just commentaries on the older Hīnayāna piṭakas, or "baskets" of received tradition, but purported to be the Buddha's own teaching that he had given to his most advanced disciples. Historians have found it difficult to identify the specific geographical area in which these Mahāyāna sūtras first began to appear: it may have been in the Sātavāhana domain in central India or in the Kuṣāṇa Empire in the northwest. Some have argued that they began to appear among the Mahāsaṅgkhas, a liberal Hīnayāna group, and others believe they first emerged in the nonsectarian communities that had grown up around the stūpas and their cult. In any event, texts such as the *Prajñāpāramitā* (Perfection of Wisdom), the *Vimalakīrti*, the *Sadharmapundarīka* (Lotus), and the *Sukhāvatī* (Pure Land) sūtras present the new Mahāyāna perspective.

Other sūtras that appeared during the following centuries added tremendously to the richness and complexity of the Mahāyāna tradition. In these voluminous texts the Mahāyānists refined their own understandings of the Buddha and other symbols and of the Dharma as both truth and path. They also formulated new conceptions of the Buddhist saṅgha.

BUDDHOLOGY AND THE PANTHEON

Mahāyāna Buddhism paid much attention to the various bodies of the Buddha. Early Mahāyānists took over the late Hīnayāna teaching concerning the two bodies of the Buddha (his dharmakāya and his *rūpakāya*, or physical body), and the later Yogācāra, or Practice of Yoga school, expanded the number of Buddha bodies to three. According to the *trikāya* (three body) doctrine, the Buddha continued to be identified principally with his dharmakāya. This body was considered to be ineffable and indescribable, and it was often identified with those sūtras in which this teaching was set down. The second of the three bodies attributed to the Buddha was his saṃbhogakāya, or enjoyment body, which was often associated with specially adorned stūpas and images and was a kind of intermediate, almost divine body through which the Buddha became visible to the Mahāyāna faithful. The third was the Buddha's *nirmāṇakāya,* or magical appearance body, which was identified with his epiphany as a historic human being.

This tendency to emphasize the transhistorical character of the Buddha was also reflected in the way in which the Mahāyānists interpreted his various achievements and powers. Whereas the Hīnayānists correlated the Buddha's highest meditational achievement with his attainment of nirvāṇa, the Mahāyānists focused on his special powers. They believed these powers had established a field of merit that transcended the laws of karmic retribution and remained available to those who recognized and took advantage of it. The Mahāyānists thus moved beyond the traditional Hīnayāna gospel that placed primary emphasis on self-effort. In its stead they proclaimed a gospel in which the powers of the Buddha, the recognition of those powers, and the various forms of self-effort all served as interrelated components of the path that leads to release.

Still another new aspect of Mahāyāna Buddhism was the emergence of a pantheon of celestial Buddhas and bodhisattvas. Although the Hīnayāna tradition had recognized many Buddhas, they were, for the most part, limited in number. Except for Maitreya, the Buddha of the Future, who was said to reside in the Tusita heaven, the Hīnayāna Buddhas were identified as the Buddhas of the past. The Mahāyānists expanded their view of the cosmos and recognized a plethora of celestial Buddhas, bodhisattvas, and Buddha lands.

Several groupings and individual figures assumed special doctrinal and salvational roles. For example, besides the celestial Sākyamuni (that is, the celestial Buddha whose historical manifestation was the Gautama Buddha), the Buddhas of the five and ten directions were singled out for special attention. Certain figures such as Maitreya, Amitābha (the Buddha of the Western Paradise), and Avalokitésvara (the bodhisattva who personified the virtue of compassion) eventually became independent objects of Mahāyāna piety and practice.

THE MĀDHYAMIKA AND YOGĀCĀRA SCHOOLS

In addition to creating rich mythology, the Mahāyānists also began a major revolution in their interpretation of the Buddhist teaching. A certain resistance to Abhidharma scholasticism was apparent even in some Hīnayāna schools, but this resistance was basically conservative in character. In the Mahāyāna context distinctively new insights were expressed in the *Prajñāpāramitā Sūtras,* which were then organized by an *acharya,* or doctor, named Nāgārjuna, the founder of the *Mādhyamika,* or Middle Way, school. Two centuries later yet another Mahāyāna perspective was articulated in the *Saṃdhinirmocana Sūtra* and further developed in a series of treatises attributed to Maitreyanātha (often identified as the bodhisattva Maitreya) and to two brothers named Asaṅga and Vasubhandu who taught in the fourth century A.D. These treatises were the basis of a second major Mahāyāna school in India, the so-called Yogācāra, or Practice of Yoga, school.

The *Prajñāpāramitā Sūtras* and the related Mādhyamika texts contained an important doctrinal innovation: the recognition of two levels of truth corresponding to the two bodies of the Buddha. The Hīnayāna method of analyzing reality in terms of dharmas was accepted at the lower level of truth. Other Hīnayāna teachings, such as the distinction between saṃsāra (the phenomenal world characterized by suffering) and nirvāṇa (the unconditional), were accepted as valid for those of limited insight. But proponents of the new Mādhyamika school held that at the higher level of absolute truth, all dharmas were void and empty (*śūnya*),

This bronze figure from Nepal (10th–13th century) may represent Avalokiteśvara, the bodhisattva who personified the virtue of compassion. *Seattle Art Museum, Eugene Fuller Memorial Collection.*

and all dualities, including the duality of saṃsāra and nirvāṇa, were a delusion. The *Prajñāpāramitā Sūtras* presented this position as a gospel of salvation that the Buddha had revealed in dialogues with his most advanced disciples, and the later Mādhyamika texts expressed it philosophically through a series of dialectical arguments. These late Mādhyamika texts attacked as inconsistent and unacceptable every known and conceivable interpretation of reality and maintained that every kind of mental or linguistic construction distorted the true character of reality and led to attachment and suffering. By making relative such constructions, through the "perfection of wisdom" or the use of language and reason against themselves, individuals could attain release. In the end the philosophical and religious messages were the same.

The Yogācāra sūtras and treatises preserved the fundamental Mahāyāna emphasis on different levels of truth, expanding the number to three. The third or "intermediate" level of truth corresponded directly to the third or "intermediate" body, which the Yogācārins attributed to the Buddha. These sūtras and treatises also recognized other basic Mahāyāna doctrines: the voidness or emptiness of reality, the ultimate identity of saṃsāra and nirvāṇa, and the necessity of making relative all mental or linguistic constructions in order to attain release. The Yogācārins differed, however, from the Mādhyamika tradition in that they concentrated on consciousness and its purification. In Yogācāra the void was identified with *ālayavijñāna,* or storehouse consciousness, which was taken to be the basis of all existence. The path to realization was associated with specific yogic techniques that destroyed the impure dharmas or mental constructions that distorted the storehouse consciousness. As a result of this focus on consciousness and yogic experience, the Yogācārins gradually introduced more realistic imagery. For example, the storehouse consciousness came to be considered the primal source, or womb, from which the Buddhas were born. In another closely related dimension it came to be seen as the embryo Buddha, or Buddha nature, that was present in all beings. Indeed, the Yogācārins moved to the very threshold of the kind of essentialist philosophy earlier forms of Buddhism had rejected.

Though the Mādhyamika and Yogācāra were the only schools that emerged within the Indian Mahāyāna tradition, other kinds of dharmic developments can be discerned. For example, in the fourth and fifth centuries A.D., scholastic debates led to a sophisticated Buddhist logic which was expounded in a number of technical treatises. At the same time more specifically religious changes were taking place. For example, new teachings emphasized the efficacy of faith and the possibility of rebirth in a celestial Pure Land. These were particularly popular in northwestern India and Central Asia. However, in these areas the Pure Land teachings and

The Mahāyānist "Thought of Enlightenment"

Like all the great religions of the world, Buddhism has produced a variety of inspirational works. Śāntideva, a Mādhyamika philosopher of the early eighth century A.D., extolled the religious life of the Mahāyāna in a famous devotional poem called *Entering the Path of Enlightenment.* After praising the thought of enlightenment (*bodhicitta*), Sāntideva confesses the transgressions that have, in the past, kept him in bondage to the phenomenal world of impermanence and suffering. He then launches into a great affirmation of compassion and of the central element in life for all Mahāyāna followers, the act of *bodhicittaparigraha,* or grasping the thought of enlightenment.*

I rejoice in exultation at the goodness, and at the cessation and destruction of sorrow, wrought by all beings. May those who sorrow achieve joy!

*Quotation from Marion Matics, *Entering the Path of Enlightenment* (New York: Macmillan, 1970), pp. 153–156.

I rejoice at the release of embodied beings from the sorrowful wheel of rebirth. I rejoice at the Bodhisattvahood and at the Buddhahood of those who have attained salvation.

I rejoice at the Oceans of Determination (*cittotpāda*), the Bearers of Happiness to all beings, the Vehicles of Advantage for all beings, and those who teach.

With folded hands, I beseech the perfect Buddhas in all places: May they cause the light of the Dharma to shine upon those who, because of confusion, have fallen into sorrow.

With folded hands, I beseech the Conquerors who are desirous of experiencing cessation: May they pause for countless aeons lest this world become blind.

Having done all this, let me also be a cause of abatement, by means of whatever good I have achieved, for all of the sorrow of all creatures.

I am medicine for the sick. May I be their physician and their servant, until sickness does not arise again.

With rains of food and drink may I dispel the anguish of hunger and thirst. In the famine of the intermediary aeons between the world cycles (*antarakalpa*) may I be food and drink; and may I be an imperishable treasury for needy beings. May I stand in their presence in order to do what is beneficial in every possible way.

I sacrifice indifferently my bodies, pleasures, and goodness, where the three ways cross [past, present, and future], for the complete fulfillment of the welfare of all beings.

The abandonment of all is Nirvāṇa, and my mind (*manas*) seeks Nirvāṇa. If all is to be sacrificed by me, it is best that it be given to beings.

I deliver this body to the pleasure of all creatures. May they strike! May they revile! May they cover it constantly with refuse!

May they play with my body! May thay laugh! And may they be amused! I have given my body to them. What do I care about its misfortune?

May they do whatever deeds bring pleasure to them, but let there never be any misfortune because of having relied on me.

If their opinion regarding me should be either irritable or pleasant, let it nonetheless be their perpetual means to the complete fulfillment of every aim.

Those who wrong me, and those who accuse me falsely, and those who mock, and others: May they all be sharers in Enlightenment.

I would be a protector for those without protection, a leader for those who journey, and a boat, a bridge, a passage for those desiring the further shore.

For all creatures, I would be a lantern for those desiring a lantern, I would be a bed for those desiring a bed, I would be a slave for those desiring a slave.

I would be for creatures a magic jewel, an inexhaustible jar, a powerful spell, an universal remedy, a wishing tree, and a cow of plenty.

As the earth and other elements are, in various ways, for the enjoyment of innumerable beings dwelling in all of space;

So may I be, in various ways, the means of sustenance for the living beings occupying space, for as long a time as all are not satisfied.

As the ancient Buddhas seized the Thought of Enlightenment, and in like manner they followed regularly on the path of Bodhisattva instruction;

Thus also do I cause the Thought of Enlightenment to arise for the welfare of the world, and thus shall I practice these instructions in proper order.

The wise man, having considered serenely the Thought of Enlightenment, should rejoice, for the sake of its growth and its well-being, in the thought:

Today my birth is completed, my human nature is most appropriate; today I have been born into the Buddha-family and I am now a Buddha-son.

It is now for me to behave according to the customary behavior of one's own family, in order that there may be no stain put upon that spotless family.

As a blind man may obtain a jewel in a heap of dust, so, somehow, this Thought of Enlightenment has arisen even within me.

This elixir has originated for the destruction of death in the world. It is the imperishable treasure which alleviates the world's poverty.

It is the uttermost medicine, the abatement of the world's disease. It is a tree of rest for the wearied world journeying on the road of being.

When crossing over hard places, it is the universal bridge for all travelers. It is the risen moon of mind (*citta*), the soothing of the world's hot passion (*kleśa*).

It is a great sun dispelling the darkness of the world's ignorance. It is fresh butter, surging up from the churning of the milk of the true Dharma.

For the caravan of humanity, moving along the road of being, hungering for the enjoyment of happiness, this happiness banquet is prepared for the complete refreshening of every being who comes to it.

Now I invite the world to Buddhahood, and, incidentally, to happiness. May gods, anti-gods (*asuras*), and others, truly rejoice in the presence of all the Protectors.

related practices, such as the recitation of certain magical formulas and the visualization of particular deities, did not produce special schools. Instead they became broadly diffused throughout the Mahāyāna community.

THE SAṄGHA AND THE BODHISATTVA IDEAL

The Mahāyānists also built up a Buddhist community alongside the Hīnayāna community. The older Hīnayāna groupings of noble beings and persons of great merit were accepted but were associated with a low level of spiritual attainment. For their part, the Mahāyānists saw the true Buddhist community as a fraternity of those who had understood the higher truth of emptiness and had undertaken a "higher path," that of the bodhisattvas, or future Buddhas. To be sure, the Hīnayānists had recognized the bodhisattva path as a valid and in some respects a superior way leading to release. But they had associated it with a few special beings such as Gautama and Maitreya. In the new Mahāyāna framework, the bodhisattva path was regarded as the only way to true release, as the one path that every good Buddhist should follow.

The descriptions of the bodhisattva path, which were at the very center of Mahāyāna religious life, varied somewhat over the years. Yet despite the differences in detail, these descriptions shared certain basic elements. The so-called bodhisattva ritual included praising the Buddha, offering flowers, confessing transgressions, cultivating sympathetic delight in the merit of the Buddhas and bodhisattvas, and entreating the Buddha to continue his teaching in the world. Most important, it meant grasping the thought of enlightenment (the Mahāyāna counterpart of the Hīnayānist realization of truth) and the related vow to work incessantly for the welfare and salvation of all beings.

Some Mahāyānists described the bodhisattva path as the cultivation of the ten perfections. These included the six perfections mentioned in the early *Prajñāpāramitā Sūtras* (giving, morality, patience, striving, concentration, and wisdom) and four more that were added at a later date (skill in means, the bodhisattva vows, power, and knowledge). At other times the Mahāyānists viewed the bodhisattva path as having ten stages (*bhūmi*), each of which was connected with the cultivation of one of the ten perfections. In the Mahāyāna tradition, the great heroes who persevered on this path attained the highest of all conceivable goals: they eliminated all defilements, attained enlightenment, and realized supreme Buddhahood.

Mahāyāna held open this highly attractive model of the religious life to everyone, including monks, nuns, and ordinary persons. To be sure, monastic discipline continued to be recognized as an especially important aid to the cultivation of the highest virtues. It was believed that at least some monastic experience was essential to the attainment of release. Nevertheless, the bodhisattva path was also thought to be within the reach of those who were not in a position to give up life in the ordinary world. In fact, special ceremonies were devised for the induction of lay members into the bodhisattva fraternity, and texts such as the *Vimalakīrti* and *Lion Roar of Queen Sri Mala* pay special attention to the achievements of the laity.

But despite its appeal, the grandeur of the bodhisattva ideal created serious difficulties for those who sought to practice it. As the tradition grew, the goal became increasingly distant. It came to be assumed that the usual time required to attain enlightenment was three complete eons, each nearly infinite in duration. Thus the stage was set for the emergence of a tradition that could offer both a more direct path to salvation and one that could be attained in this life. Such a tradition did, in fact, appear: the *Vajrayāna,* or Diamond Vehicle, which we describe next.

The Vajrayāna, or Diamond Vehicle

About A.D. 320, Chandragupta I (who had no connection with the grandfather of Aśoka, despite the similarity of names) rose to power in the valley of the Ganges. He was the founder of the Gupta Empire, which dominated practically all of northern India until A.D. 600 and was a period of peace and prosperity known as India's Golden Age.

The Gupta Empire was noted for its religious and cultural achievements, its advances in medicine, astronomy, mathematics, and other sciences, and its achievements in Sanskrit literature and the arts. Sculptors produced numerous images of the Buddha, bodhisattvas, and arhants in a new style that became influential throughout the Buddhist world.

The Gupta rulers, as well as their allies and subordinates to the south, generally favored the revival of the Brāhmaṇic Hindu tradition, though they also supported Buddhism. The Guptas themselves patronized the university at Nālandā, an important Mahāyāna institution in northeastern India. A large Hīnayāna university at Valabhī in the west central section of the subcontinent was also subsidized by a local dynasty that ruled between A.D. 490 and 770. And the active trade that flourished under the Guptas fostered the spread of Buddhist culture into many lands in Southeast Asia and the Far East. In the fifth century Chinese scholars visited the Buddhist pilgrimage sites in India. A later Chinese pilgrim, Xuan-zang, spent thirteen years in India and returned home with hundreds of Buddhist manuscripts and relics. During this period both the Hīnayāna and Mahāyāna schools continued to produce important scholars and teachers, and the Vajrayāna tradition began to take shape.

The final phase of Buddhist development in India occurred under the Pāla dynasty, which ruled Magadha and much of the northeastern region from the eighth to the twelfth centuries. In other areas of India during these centuries Buddhism experienced hard times, but in the domain of the Pālas, it benefited from extensive royal and popular support. Here, Hīnayāna and Mahāyāna continued to be important parts of the Buddhist community, but Vajrayāna became the most vital school.

A New Ethos: Tantrism and Yoga

The new Vajrayāna ethos had its roots in the tradition of rituals and yoga (spiritual discipline) known as *Tantra* or *Tantrism.* Tantrism was an esoteric movement that employed *mantras* (mystical words), *maṇḍalas* (circular diagrams or patterns), *śākti* (female power and deities), alcoholic beverages, meat eating, sexual intercourse, and meditation in areas associated with corpses. In many areas, the Hindu and Buddhist forms of Tantra were difficult to distinguish. But as time went by, certain groups within Buddhism assimilated a variety of tantric elements, thereby producing the Vajrayāna tradition.

THE ROLE OF THE WANDERING YOGĪS

The forerunners and promoters of this new Buddhist perspective were wandering yogīs (followers of yoga) of a most unconventional sort. Some were ordained members of the Buddhist monastic order; others were married laymen; and a few were women. The yogīs commonly wore their hair long and went about either scantily clad or stark naked.

A Fresco of a temple maiden in the Gupta style from Sigiriya, Sri Lanka.
Ceylon (Sri Lanka) Tourist Board.

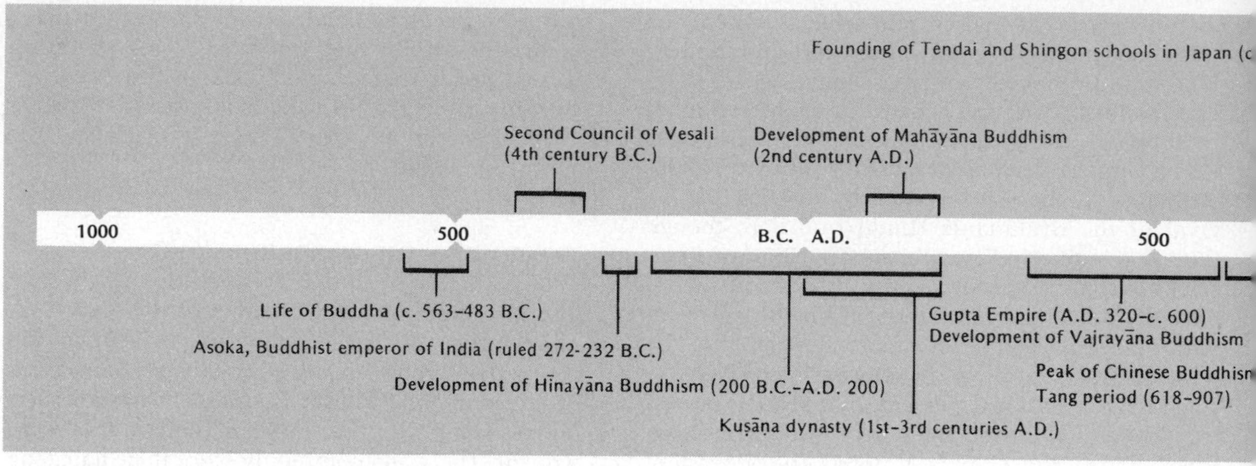

They were not attached to monastic centers, nor did they seek seclusion in the forests. Instead, they roamed the countryside and cities of India, preaching a distinctive message.

The yogīs venerated several deities, including many female deities of a highly ambivalent character. The practices of these wandering preachers were magical and focused on the importance of the human body. Various forms of yoga aimed at producing different kinds of bodily experience. The yogīs violated the customary rules of the Buddhist monastic order by advocating and practicing the ritual eating of meat, even though vegetarianism had long been as an ideal in the Mahāyāna tradition. They also drank intoxicants and engaged in rituals that included sexual intercourse. The yogīs claimed that when such activities were carried out under the guidance of an enlightened master, they could relativize or destroy the dichotomies that distorted reality, such as the distinctions between good and evil and between male and female. They believed that in this way their highest goal, fully realized Buddhahood, could be directly and immediately experienced.

THE BUDDHIST TANTRAS

The emergence of the Vajrayāna as a distinct Buddhist vehicle was associated with the appearance of new kinds of texts. These were not sūtras, but rather *tantras*, or manuals, that purported to present instructions given by the Buddha to his most receptive disciples. The Vajrayāṇists maintained their tantras had been secretly preserved during the early Buddhist centuries and were subsequently rediscovered to be used by the faithful in a time when people had lost their capacity to gain salvation in more conventional ways.

The Buddhist tantras were composed over several centuries and later classified into four different groups: the *Kriya Tantras*, *Carya Tantras*, *Yoga Tantras*, and *Anuttara Tantras*. The first two treated the more popular aspects of the tradition, generally the more mundane forms of ritual activity. The third and fourth served as guides for the new forms of meditational and liturgical practice which, according to Vajrayāna Buddhism, led directly to the realization of Buddhahood.

The Buddhist tantras were difficult to interpret not simply because they were designed as manuals for ritual and meditational practice, but also because the more advanced texts were intentionally esoteric. They used a kind of "twilight language" designed to shield the central mysteries from those who had not been properly prepared to receive them. Nonetheless, recent research has given us considerable insight into these texts, the meaning of the symbols they employed, and the character of the practices they accompanied.

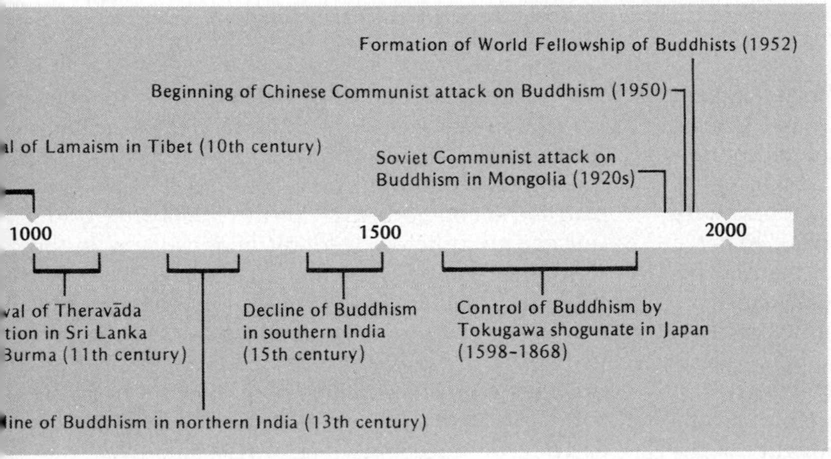

TIME LINE
BUDDHISM

THE BODIES OF THE BUDDHA AND THE VAJRAYĀNA PANTHEON

Although the Vajrayāna tradition accepted the basic presuppositions of Mahāyāna Buddhism, it made important adaptations. For example, the Vajrayānists extended the Mahāyāna understanding of the Buddha's bodies by emphasizing the importance of a fourth body (the *svabhāvikakāya* or *sahajakāya*) that constituted, from their perspective, the unity and essence of the other three. The Vajrayānists also expanded the Mahāyāna conception of the Buddhas of the five directions (Vairocana and Akṣobhya in the center and east, Ratnāsambhava in the south, Amitābha in the west, and Amoghasiddhi in the north) by adding a sixth. The sixth Buddha, they claimed, was the ultimate source and the unity of the other five. In certain offshoots of this tradition, this sixth and ultimate Buddha was called Vajradhara. Other, more theistic versions of the tradition spoke of the Adi-Buddha, or the Buddha who had been there from the beginning.

As a counterpoint to their efforts to maintain the nonduality and the nondifferentiation of absolute Buddhahood, the Vajrayānists recognized a great variety of new Buddhas, bodhisattvas, and associated deities. The Buddhas of the five directions were often identified with deities important to tantric rites. These Buddhas were also paired with feminine consorts and came to be viewed as heads of "families" into which several originally quite diverse indigenous deities were incorporated. Finally, the Buddhas in this huge pantheon often appeared in awesome and terrible forms.

Vajrayāna Buddhism was distinguished still further from its Mahāyāna roots by the variety of religious meanings associated with its pantheon. The various deities retained their traditional cosmological significance. The tradition of representing them iconographically was maintained and enriched, and they continued to receive popular veneration and propitiation. But the Vajrayānists carried the tradition further by underscoring the tantric understanding that the macrocosm was replicated in the human body. They believed that the pantheon of Buddhas, bodhisattvas, and their acolytes resided within every human being, which thus opened the way for new kinds of magical and religious practices. For example, the Vajrayānists taught that the deities could be conjured up from the depths of consciousness. Identifying themselves with the visualized forms generated in this way, the practitioners could acquire and exercise the magical powers of the gods. Moreover, by using other yogic techniques, all imaging of the world could be relativized and the deities themselves dissolved. In this way, an actual experience of the voidness, or the diamond essence, of reality could be achieved.

FOUR KINDS OF VOIDNESS AND THE USE OF MANTRAS

The Vajrayānists recognized the authority of great Mahāyāna teachers such as Nāgārjuna and Asaṅga. In addition, they devised new ways of appropriating their doctrines. For example, in certain Vajrayāna contexts four different kinds of voidness were differentiated. The first three types pertained to the three modes of truth or consciousness that the Yogācārins had affirmed: the relative, the intermediate, and the pure. A fourth mode in the series—the *vajra*, or diamond essence, of the others—was identified as the absolute void (*sarvāśūnya*).

Balancing the Vajrayāna effort to maintain the absolute nondifferentiation and nonduality of the void was the emphasis on sacred sound, or mantras. Even in the Hīnayāna tradition, the ultimate Dharma or truth had been identified with the words spoken by the Buddha. In Mahāyāna teaching (for example, in the *Lotus Sūtra*), the ultimate Dharma had been identified with a single sermon of the Buddha. It was said to have resonated throughout the entire universe and to have been heard by every human being in accordance with his or her particular capacities and sensitivities. In the Vajrayāna context, the implications of this kind of understanding of the power of sacred words was drawn out so that the entire cosmos could be seen—or better, heard—as a vast concatenation of sacred sounds and syllables.

This new concept of dharmic reality was adapted in different ways. At the level of the macrocosm, each of the various deities in the pantheon was believed to have, as its support or essence, a particular *bīja-mantra* (seed sound). In magical practice the knowledge and repetition of the special sounds that served as the essence or support of each particular deity made it possible to acquire and exercise the powers the deity possessed. Not only each of the divinized psychic forces but also each of the stages of the eightfold path was believed to have its own bīja-mantra. Through knowledge and manipulation of the appropriate sounds, the psychic forces could be brought under control, and various degrees of sanctity could be obtained. Indeed, Vajrayāna came to be known as the *Mantrayāna*, or vehicle of sacred sounds.

LIVING BUDDHAS, ESOTERIC RITES, AND COMMUNAL ORDER

The originality and distinctiveness of the new Vajrayāna orientation were perhaps most evident in its saṅgha. In the Hīnayāna tradition the great models for emulation and veneration were the *ārya pudgala,* or noble beings. In the Mahāyāna tradition the great heroes were the bodhisattvas. In the Vajrayāna context, another qualitative leap was taken by recognizing a new kind of hero and a new method of salvation. The Vajrayāna claimed that its heroes, the *siddhas* (perfected ones) and the *gurus* (masters), had attained both freedom from the bondage of existence and magical domination over it. They were recognized as "living Buddhas."

The Vajrayāna aimed at a more or less immediate attainment of Buddhahood, and never gave up the spontaneous and unconventional practices so important in its early phases. On the other hand, many later Vajrayāna practitioners followed the Mahāyānists in accepting the traditional forms of monastic discipline and practice as a useful starting point. They also believed that a thorough knowledge of the basic Mahāyāna doctrines, especially the doctrine of the void, was necessary for the higher levels of path attainment. But they extended the Mahāyāna perspective by stressing the necessity for esoteric practices powerful enough to transform theoretical wisdom and insight into an actual, bodily experience of the void.

Many new pedagogical, liturgical, and yogic techniques were used to accelerate progress toward the goal of Buddhahood. Those with less spiritual maturity might require additional rebirths. But the maximum number—set at seventeen in some traditions—was always limited. In order to achieve this comparatively rapid progress, the Vajrayāna concentrated on the relationship between the guru, who had already penetrated the highest mysteries, and the disciple, who was required to accept the guru's authority in all matters. In addition, a series of complex and symbolically rich liturgies was created to facilitate the actual experience of the void.

For example, some Vajrayānists carried out a series of ten *abhiṣeka* (coronation or baptism) rites. Each rite took place in a sacred mandala that was laid out specifically for the occasion. A particular level of consciousness was purified when the initiate became identified with a deity who represented the next higher level of realization. The first two abhiṣeka liturgies were intended to purify the physical plane (equivalent to a Buddha's nirmāṇakāya); the third and fourth were devised to purify the verbal plane (equivalent to a Buddha's saṃbhogakāya); the fifth and sixth were designed to purify the mental plane (equivalent to a Buddha's dharmakāya); and the seventh was meant to purify the ultimate plane of absolute concentration (equivalent to a Buddha's svabhāvikakāya or sahajakāya). Beyond this realization, three final rites were designed to make real the initiate's attainment by means of an actual bodily experience of Buddhahood. In their outer form, these three esoteric rites required a series of sexual activities culminating in symbolic intercourse between the practitioner and his female partner. In the inner experience of the initiate, these activities included a yogic process through which the masculine and feminine powers believed to reside in the practitioner's body were activated and reunited. This produced a kind of realization that the tradition identified with the attainment of absolute unity and voidness.

The various Vajrayāna masters, together with the disciples who accepted their authority, constituted the core of the Vajrayāna community. In addition, many Buddhists recognized the various attainments of those who practiced the Vajrayāna path, and others supported them because they believed in the efficacy of the magical powers they exercised. The Vajrayāna community included both a nucleus of elite practitioners and a much broader group of lay supporters. Throughout the period of the Pāla dynasty, which ruled northeastern India (Bihār and Bengal) from the eighth to the twelfth centuries A.D., this Vajrayāna community remained the most active force in Indian Buddhist life.

The Decline of Buddhism in India

Buddhism enjoyed a long and creative existence in India. Yet before its creativity had ended, signs of a decline had begun to appear. Around 186 B.C., when the Śuṅga dynasty took control of northeastern India, the new rulers rejected Buddhism in favor of a new form of Hinduism. Entrenched Buddhist groups were removed from power, and the more "orthodox" Hindu tradition was encouraged.

But the Buddhists were able to weather this particular crisis, and under the subsequent dynasties they even were able to make a number of significant advances (see the discussion above). However, by the third or fourth centuries A.D., it became clear that Buddhism in India was waning. It continued to decline slowly but relentlessly during the next millennium. Scholars have pointed to a variety of factors that contributed to this process, of which three are of particular importance.

ISOLATION OF THE MONASTERIES

Over the centuries many Buddhist monasteries acquired large endowments of land and other sources of wealth and thus became economically self-sufficient. This made it unnecessary for the monks and nuns to maintain their contacts with the laity, and they therefore lost the once broad popular support. Financial and other means of subsidy dried up as the monasteries became more and more remote from everyday Indian society.

THE VITALITY OF THE BRĀHMANIC HINDU TRADITION

At the same time that the monasteries were becoming isolated from the people, Buddhism was confronted by the revival of Hinduism. The Hindus created philosophical modes of thought (for example, the Advaita Vedānta system of Śaṅkara) that incorporated many Buddhist insights, and they established their own forms of monastic life. They also devised a sacramental system that was both comprehensive and directly relevant to the people's various religious and social needs. They began a devotional movement that attracted widespread popular support. Thus Hinduism was able to gain an increasing hold on the loyalty of both the elite and the people.

FOREIGN INVASIONS

In the sixth century, the armies of the White Huns swept through sections of central Asia and northwestern India. After the White Huns, other Central Asian tribes came and settled in the area between the Indus and Ganges valleys. Then, in the eighth century, Muslim Arabs arrived at the mouth of the Indus River. Gradually their armies reached eastern India, and by the thirteenth century, the Muslims had carved out an empire that included all of northern India. In the course of their raids, these various groups destroyed many of the great Buddhist centers and decimated the communities of monks and nuns. Moreover, once they had set up a system of political control, the Muslim invaders had considerable success in converting their Indian subjects, especially those who had been Buddhists, to Islam.

By the early thirteenth century, Buddhism had been almost extinguished in northern India, except in a few scattered areas. It was still practiced in southern India until the fifteenth century, when it disappeared there as well. From that time until the twentieth century, Buddhism was represented in India primarily by architectural ruins and by the dispersed remnants of its influence that had penetrated the Hindu, Islamic, and other popular traditions. But it had by no means disappeared as a living religion: in Sri Lanka; in much of mainland Southeast Asia; in China, Korea, and Japan; in Tibet and neighboring regions, Buddhism had been established and remained a vital part of everyday life.

9 Buddhism as a World Religion

EXPANSION IN ASIA

The missionary zeal that led to Buddhism's original growth and expansion within India carried the tradition into many other parts of Asia as well. The earliest known effort to preach the Dharma in a foreign land took place during the reign of the emperor Aśoka. A Buddhist mission led by Mahinda, the emperor's son or younger brother, came to Lanka (the ancient name for Ceylon, or Sri Lanka, as it is known today) at the invitation of the ruler of the island. According to chronicles written in Sri Lanka, ruler and court were quickly converted and the new religion firmly established. According to legend, Mahinda's sister Sanghamitta also came as a missionary to the island, bringing with her a cutting from the famous bodhi tree where the Buddha had received enlightenment. A descendant of this cutting is said to be still growing at Anuradhapura, a city now in ruins that was for many centuries the capital of the kingdom. Much later, in the third century A.D., a tooth of the Buddha was brought to Sri Lanka and came to be recognized as a protector of the kingdom. Still today, a relic believed to be this same tooth is kept in a special temple in the former royal capital of Kandy.

Aśoka's inscriptions and Sinhalese records indicate that the emperor sponsored other missionary voyages. One mission was probably sent to the Mon communities of southern Burma or central Thailand, and others were sent to Afghanistan and perhaps to areas even farther west. By the dawn of the Christian era, Buddhism had moved across Central Asia and was beginning to penetrate China and northern Vietnam. From China it moved to the Korean peninsula, and by the sixth century reached Japan. In the seventh century, Buddhism began to make significant advances into the Himalayan regions of Tibet. Finally, in the thirteenth century, the Tibetan form of the tradition began to spread among the Mongol population in northern China, and still later it became established in Mongolia proper and in neighboring areas of what is now southern Russia.

Without making any absolute generalizations, we should note a definite pattern in the spread of Buddhism. There is a close correlation between the Buddhist vehicle that was most active at the time of each phase of the Buddhist expansion and the traditions that have remained dominant in the new environment. For example, when Buddhism was introduced into Sri Lanka and Southeast Asia, Indian Buddhism was basically Hīnayāna in orientation, and thus the Theravāda form of that tradition, using Pali as its sacred language, has remained dominant there to the present day. In the countries of East Asia, Buddhism was accepted when the Mahāyāna was its most vital tradition, and Mahāyāna continues to attract the greatest number of adherents there. In Tibet and its neigh-

Above, drummers parade during a festival in Kandy, Sri Lanka, before the temple housing the famous Buddha tooth relic. *Ceylon (Sri Lanka) Tourist Board.*

boring areas, the process of conversion began when Vajrayāna was predominant, and the diamond vehicle has since been the major religion in that area.

Buddhist traditions outside India have been characteristically conservative. Yet in every instance they have demonstrated their own particular kind of dynamism, expressed in distinctive ways. In each case a unique historical development has affected local Buddhist perspectives and institutions, and new schools of thought and forms of practice have emerged. The Buddhist tradition in India collapsed under the pressure of competing religious and social forces, but in other Asian areas Buddhism was successful in maintaining its influence and vitality into the modern period.

Buddhism in Sri Lanka and Southeast Asia

The spread of Buddhism in India itself came about as the high culture of the northern region gradually extended its influence throughout the subcontinent. Its further expansion into the previously nonliterate societies of Sri Lanka and Southeast Asia was a continuation of this same process. Historians who have studied Sri Lanka and Southeast Asia from the third century B.C. through the end of the first millennium A.D. often describe this movement as "Indianization." Through this process the region became part of a larger religiocultural complex that they labeled Greater India.

INDIANIZATION AND THE THERAVĀDA TRADITION

The close relationship of Indian Buddhism to Buddhism in Greater India can be considered in a variety of ways. Several trade routes connected India to Sri Lanka, to the mainland of Southeast Asia, and to Indonesia. There was a continuing exchange of ideas and people, and the influence of the major Indian styles of art and architecture could be seen throughout the entire region. The waxing and waning of the three Buddhist vehicles in India was closely related to parallel developments in the various local traditions beyond the borders of India proper. Finally, the combination of Brāhmaṇic-Hindu and Islamic forces that gradually displaced Buddhism in India also became the dominant influence in Greater India and in the Indonesian islands of Sumatra and Java, thus ending the once flourishing Buddhist civilization that had produced such magnificent shrines as the great stūpa of Borobudūr.

Despite some similarities with India and Indonesia, Buddhism in Sri Lanka and the mainland of Southeast Asia followed its own course. From the beginning the Theravāda form had been important in these areas and was the first Indian tradition to become dominant in the Sinhalese royal centers. Sri Lanka chronicles describe Theravāda Buddhism as closely related to a sense of national identity. There are indications of similar patterns in Burma and Thailand as well.

During the eleventh century, as direct influences

from India decreased, a great Theravāda revival began almost simultaneously in Sri Lanka and Burma. The Sinhalese sect that emerged from the reforms of King Parakrammabahu I (1153–1186) was established in Sri Lanka, spread to Burma, and then gradually extended its influence eastward across Thailand, Cambodia, and Laos. By the fifteenth century this reformed sect had become the predominant religious force in both the major political centers, where it functioned as a royal religion, and in the villages, where it served the peasant population.

In each of these areas Theravāda Buddhism had distinctive emphases and characteristics. For example, in Sri Lanka it concentrated on maintaining the ancient historiographic tradition. The Sri Lankan saṅgha believed that the island kingdom had a unique status as the land where the Dharma had been preserved in its original form. In Burma Theravāda Buddhism stressed the study of the Abhidharma texts as a way of maintaining the purity of Theravāda teaching. In Thailand it centered on Theravāda cosmology and its implications for society and ethics. In each region the reformed tradition also had a distinctive pattern of relationships that included Brāhmaṇic and folk beliefs and practices.

BUDDHA(S) AND DEITIES

Though it was the most conservative of the Buddhist traditions, the Theravāda Buddhism of Sri Lanka and Southeast Asia evolved into a rich and complex religion. For example, the Theravādins never ceased to underscore the humanity of the Buddha, but at the same time they assembled mythic narratives of his career that went far beyond a simple recounting of his historical life. In addition, they supplemented their continuing insistence on the centrality and importance of Gautama Buddha with a willingness to accept the reality and importance of other religious figures, both within and alongside their tradition.

The Theravādins apparently did not recognize these legends about the Buddha's life until several centuries after some of the more liberal Hīnayāna sects had done so. In the versions of the stories they accepted the Theravādins were careful to omit or downplay many of the more flamboyant incidents that suggested divinity. Nonetheless, their accounts were in certain respects more complete than those in other Buddhist traditions. For example, early Theravāda commentators brought together a collection of 547 *Jātakas* (stories of incidents in the Buddha's previous lives). These stories became an important part of Theravāda preaching and artistic expression. Many of them were simply Indian folktales in which the bodhisattva had come to be identified with the protagonist. Others were more specifically Buddhist and told how the Buddha had perfected the ten virtues of almsgiving, goodness, renunciation, wisdom, energy, patience, truth, resolution, loving kindness, and equanimity.

As an introduction to this massive collection, a short account of the Buddha's career was added, beginning with his vow to achieve enlightenment and to save all humanity. It then related the Buddha's historical life after his descent from the Tusita heaven until the start of his ministry of preaching. As the biographical tradition continued to develop, the narrative came to incorporate accounts of the Buddha's later ministry and death, as well as a description of his funeral and the distribution of his relics.

Later, the sacred biography was extended to include a discussion of the progressive decline of the religion, as well as a prediction that some five thousand years after the Buddha's *parinirvāṇa* (his entrance into nirvāṇa that occurred at the moment of his physical death) it would completely disappear. When this happened, the Buddha's relics supposedly would reunite under the bodhi tree at Bodh Gayā or—according to some versions—at the site of the famous offshoot of that tree in Sri Lanka. His recomposed relics would then preach one final sermon, and with this culminating act his career would be complete.

In time the Theravādins also came to accept the ideas and practices of figures other than the Gautama. For example, the belief in the Maitreya was prevalent throughout the Theravāda community. The Theravādins held that Maitreya was residing in the Tusita heaven and that in the future he would come to earth to reestablish Buddhism and to preside over an ideal society. The Hindu gods Indra and Brahmā, as well as indigenous Indian deities such as the *yakṣas* (often associated with tree cults and sacred groves) and *nāgas* (serpent deities), also became part of the Theravāda mythology and were assigned definite cosmological abodes. Later, the great gods of classical Hinduism were incorporated into the pantheon. In addition, each local area contributed its own contingent of ancestral and territorial deities.

THE CANON AND COMMENTARIES

Just before the beginning of the Christian era, the Theravādins of Sri Lanka became the first Buddhist group to commit the three baskets of normative teaching—the *Sūtra, Vinaya,* and *Abhidharma piṭakas*—to writing. When these texts were written (in Pali), the Theravāda canon was complete. From that time onward, Theravāda interpreters concentrated on commentaries and manuals that served to explain, systematize, and adapt the canonical teachings. The most authoritative works of this kind are those attributed to a great fifth-century scholar, Buddhaghosa, and include both a massive collection of scriptural commentaries that he translated from Sinhalese into Pali and a comprehensive summary of the normative Theravāda teaching called the *Visuddhimārga* (Path of Purification). Later there were many other authoritative writings, including Pali texts such as Anurrudha's *Abhidhammaṭṭha-saṅigaha* (Compendium of Philosophy) (eighth or ninth century), and vernacular texts such as the Thai version of Buddhist cosmology known as the *Three Worlds according to King Ruang.*

The Theravāda insistence on maintaining the canonical authority of the Pali version of the three piṭakas was coupled with a strong interest in maintaining the purity of the doctrine. They were concerned with preserving the distinction between saṃsāra as the realm of impermanence and nirvāṇa as release. As a correlate to this position, they were consistent in contending that salvation could be obtained only through a process of individual effort involving moral discipline, the practice of meditation, and the attainment of insight. Nevertheless, it is clear from their commentaries and manuals that the later Theravādins introduced innovations from their own reflections and meditative experience and also absorbed and reacted to influences from various Sanskrit forms of Buddhism.

NEW FORMS OF DEVOTION

The Theravādins generally accepted new practices more slowly than did many of the other early Buddhist schools. Yet eventually they came to recognize the efficacy of a broad range of devotional, magical, and calendrical activities and rituals.

But Theravāda devotion remained focused on the Gautama Buddha, especially on the symbols that served as the traces or reminders of his career. During the earliest period of Buddhism the Buddha's human form was not represented; instead attention was centered on such symbols as the Buddha's footprint, an empty throne, or a stūpa containing a relic. But by the early centuries of the Christian era, the Theravādins had followed other Buddhists in recognizing the validity and usefulness of images in human form. The Buddha himself was portrayed as a *mahāpurusha,* or great being, who possessed the thirty-two bodily signs (for example, feet with a level tread and wheels on the soles of the feet) associated with the attainment of universal sovereignty and Buddhahood. Such images came to be housed in practically every Theravāda temple and on every sacred site. The Theravādins also came to accept the special sacredness of the relics and images of the Buddha connected with the exercise of royal power. In Sri Lanka the famous tooth relic and in Southeast Asia images such as the Mahamuni, the Emerald Buddha, and the Prabang granted protection and support to the reigning monarch.

The magical aspects of the Theravāda tradition grew in several ways. For example, Theravādins believed that the magical power acquired by monks through yogic practice could become accessible to ordinary persons who sought their aid. The blessings these monks pronounced and the amulets and other sacred objects they consecrated were believed to have special powers that could bring healing, prosperity, and the like. The Theravādins also believed that magical power could be obtained through ceremonies in which especially potent sūtras were chanted. At first the Theravādins were somewhat reluctant to recognize the validity of such rites, which were originally carried out on a rather small scale. Later, however, paritta ceremonies became important to the religious life of all Theravāda countries. Performances of rites sponsored by individuals in order to mitigate sicknesses and other personal adversities were supplemented by larger performances designed to ward off evil forces that threatened the well-being of entire villages or even kingdoms.

The Theravādins also devised a complicated cycle of rituals related to the seasons of the agricultural year. Buddhist ceremonies associated with the beginning and end of the rainy season were an integral part of the early tradition. With the passage of time and with the adaptation of the tradition to local contexts, these rites were elaborated; new calendrical observances were incorporated, and each Theravāda area followed its own cycle of ritual activity.

MONASTIC TRADITIONS AND LAY TRADITIONS

The conservative characteristic of the Theravādins was also evident in their continuing insistence on the significance of the monastic discipline, as well as their emphasis on the purity of lineage preserved through proper ordination. But divisive pressures could not be avoided, and there were different interpretations. Some Theravādins insisted on adhering to rules that forbade involvement in political activities; others felt that when the welfare of the religion or the people was at stake, such activities were justified or even required. Although some accepted the original ban on the accumulation of wealth, others found loopholes allowing individual monks to enrich themselves. Many Theravāda monasteries became powerful economic institutions. Though the monastic rules prohibited the transfer of social distinctions into the life of the monastic community, it nonetheless became a problem throughout the Theravāda world. In Sri Lanka, for example, caste distinctions became criteria for ordination in certain monastic communities—an obvious violation of the spirit of earlier Buddhist teachings.

Within the Theravāda saṅgha, each group had a different degree of organizational identity. Very early in the history of Buddhism, the few monks who continued to live as hermits or wanderers were distinguished from the great majority who lived in more settled establishments. This distinction between "forest monks" and "village monks" eventually became a basic principle in the organizational structure of the order in Sri Lanka and in the various kingdoms of Southeast Asia. There was another distinction between the monks who devoted themselves to the practice of meditation and those who were committed to the study of the Dharma. The former were often involved in the cultivation and exercise of magical powers, whereas the latter were often concerned with the acquisition and dissemination of various forms of secular knowledge.

In addition, different regional traditions produced their own particular ordination lineages. Some monks traced their lineage back through the Sri Lankan line to Mahinda, the first missionary on the island. Others traced their lineage to Sona and Utara, the Aśokan missionaries credited with establishing the tradition in Southeast Asia. Still other divisions were related to rather minute details of behavior or dress. The classic example occurred in Burma during the seventeenth and eighteenth centuries, when the order split over the issue of whether the monastic robes should be worn covering only one shoulder or both.

Differing interpretations also developed regarding the lay component of community life. Some strands of the tradition stressed karma and merit as explanatory concepts, using them to justify the traditionally hierarchic structure of Theravāda societies. Thus the king was usually identified as the preeminent man of merit within his realm. This was carried to such an extent that many of the later kings of Sri Lanka and Southeast Asia were accorded the status of bodhisattva. Other forms of power, prestige, and success, both at the court and in the villages, were also attributed to merit that had been accumulated in either the distant or the more recent past. Other strands of the tradition focused on the effect that merit-making activities were purported to have in enabling each individual to gain greater material and spiritual benefits in this life and the next.

The relation between the lay and the monastic ideals differed from time to time and place to place. In Sri Lanka an individual's ordination into the monastic life was usually a lifetime commitment. But in Burma all Buddhist males were expected to enter the order as novices for a limited period of time, and in central Thailand all Buddhist males were expected to be temporarily ordained as full-fledged monks and to spend at least one rainy season in the order. However, despite these and other variations, the basic division between the monks as a spiritual elite and the laity as a lesser but integral component of the community was characteristic of all the Theravāda traditions and remained intact throughout the entire premodern period.

Buddhism in East Asia

The spread of Buddhism from India and Central Asia into the very different civilizations of East Asia is a stunning testimony to the vitality of its message and institutions. In China the historical development of Buddhism during the premodern period can be divided into three phases: the period of importation and localization from about the beginning of the Christian era to the sixth century; the period of florescence and creativity during the sixth, seventh, and eighth centuries; and the period of persistence and assimilation from the middle of the ninth to the nineteenth century. Three phases can also be discerned in Japan: the period of importation and localization from the sixth through the twelfth centuries; the period of renewed religious vitality and its aftermath from the twelfth to the fifteenth centuries; and the period of persistence from the sixteenth century until modern times.

EARLY MISSIONARIES IN CHINA

What some historians have called the Buddhist conquest of China and others have named the Chinese transformation of Buddhism began around the beginning of the Christian era.[1] The leaders of the Han dynasty, which ruled China between 202 B.C. and A.D. 220, had established Chinese hegemony over much of Central Asia and many of its important trade routes. They also had frequent contacts with northwestern India, and travelers from Central Asia began to set up Buddhist centers in northern China. The emperor Ming (A.D. 58–75) is reliably reported to have sent messengers to India requesting Buddhist teachers. Subsequently two monks arrived at the Chinese capital of Loyang, bringing with them images of the Buddha and the sacred books of Mahāyāna Buddhism. The *Si-shi-er Zhang Jing* (Sūtra in Forty-two Chapters) and other texts were soon translated into Chinese.

The first period of Buddhist expansion into China emphasized occult meditation and ritual, as Chinese practitioners related the new teaching to the indigenous Taoist tradition. But in the Han dynasty, the monastic ideal of Buddhism met strong resistance from the Confucian precept of producing children who would honor their elders and ancestors, and the Buddhist concept of begging contradicted the Chinese tradition of hard work.

Gradually, as the influx of Buddhist missionaries continued, Buddhist ideas became better understood. Toward the end of the Han period Buddhist pagodas (stūpas) began to appear in greater numbers. Finally, after the last Han ruler was deposed in A.D. 220, the people became more receptive to the Buddhist message. At the same time the country sank into a period of social disorder and civil war. Nomadic tribes from Central Asia, chiefly Huns and Turks, raided and pillaged the lands previously protected by the Great Wall, and set up petty kingdoms of their own in northern China. As a result, many Chinese, including members of the elite, turned away from Confucianism and Taoism and sought a new orientation in Buddhism. During the same period, many of the rulers of the invading tribes also were converted.

From the fourth to the sixth centuries, the process of conversion and consolidation was accelerated. During this period China was divided into a northern region ruled by the new invaders and a southern area to which the old Chinese aristocracy had retreated. In both areas the Buddhist cause was advanced through the translation of many texts. Outstanding Chinese teachers such as Dao-an (312–385) and his disciple Hui-yuan (334–416) adapted the Dharma to Chinese modes of thought, and Chinese artists began to develop distinctive styles of Buddhist architecture and sculpture. Buddhist converts among the aristocracy generously patronized the monasteries and pursued the kind of gentlemanly piety and erudition eulogized in the famous *Vimalakīrti Sūtra*. At the same time charismatic preachers and wonder workers converted more of the new rulers and brought a large segment of the peasantry into the fold. Thus by the end of the sixth century, Chinese Buddhism had developed its own textual and iconographic idiom and become the most powerful and dynamic religious force in the Middle Kingdom.

THE BUDDHIST FLOWERING UNDER THE SUI AND THE TANG

The reunification of the country under the Buddhist-oriented Sui dynasty (589–618) and the powerful and prosperous Tang dynasty (618–907) marked the high point of Chinese Buddhism. During this period Buddhism enjoyed substantial support from the state, the aristocracy, and the populace as a whole. Many Buddhist schools flourished, including the Pure Land school (dating from the fifth century), the Chan, or Meditation, school (supposedly introduced in 520), the Tian-tai school (founded by Zhi-yi, 538–597), the Hua-yan school (founded by Fa-zang, 643–712), and the Chinese Esoteric school (introduced in the early eighth century). Buddhist influences also were felt in every aspect of Chinese culture and art, from architecture and sculpture to painting and literature.

During the Sui and Tang periods Buddhist institutions also flourished. Many temples were officially sponsored, though others were privately endowed, and they often became powerful economic and landholding institutions. Buddhist rituals, such as the chanting of sūtras or spells and the giving of gifts or donations, became important to both court ceremonials and the ordinary people. Buddhist festivals such as the celebration of the Buddha's birthday and the honoring of his relics also were enjoyed by all segments of society. However, the privileged position and popularity of Buddhism did not last indefinitely.

THE GREAT PERSECUTION

In the middle of the ninth century, a dramatic event symbolized the end of Buddhism's great influence and creativity in China. In 845 the Taoist emperor Wu-zong carried out a persecution that resulted in the destruction of thousands of Buddhist temples, the appropriation of their lands, and the unfrocking of more than 200,000 monks and nuns. Even though the persecution was short-lived and Buddhism was able to regain many of its losses, it never recovered completely.

In regard to the numbers of monks and the extent of their economic involvement, Buddhism was at least as active during the Song dynasty (960–1279) as it had been during the Tang period. But the great scholastic traditions that had provided the intellectual backbone of Chinese Buddhism had lost their vitality and influence, and the intellectual leadership was taken over by the neo-Confucian tradition. The more practically oriented Buddhist traditions that did survive (notably the Pure Land

The Buddhist influence on Chinese art is apparent in this Tang earthenware figure of a court lady (8th century). *The Metropolitan Museum of Art, gift of Mr. & Mrs. Stanley Herzman, 1979.*

and Meditation schools) melded into a Chinese cultural pattern in which Confucian, Taoist, and Buddhist elements were present. Under later dynasties Buddhism continued to function in the mainstream of Chinese religious life, and at the same time acted as a catalyst for a number of sectarian movements and rebellions among the peasants.

BUDDHISM IN JAPAN: THE NARA AND HEIAN PERIODS

Various aspects of Chinese culture began to reach Japan in the sixth century, just as Chinese Buddhism was achieving its full maturity. In about 552, Buddhist images and scriptures were introduced by a diplomatic embassy from Korea. (Buddhism had already spread from China to Korea, where it had become established at the leading political and cultural centers.) In Japan the new religion quickly gained support, and within a few decades the Prince Regent, Shōtoku Taishi, became a Buddhist and chose to model his rule after that of the Buddhist-oriented Sui dynasty in China. During the seventh and eighth centuries Chinese cultural influences continued to flourish, and Buddhism was able to solidify its position among the Japanese. At the capital city of Nara (710–781), some of the Buddhist sects imported from China formed strong ecclesiastical structures and became influential in religious and political affairs. In rural areas Buddhism also began to make its presence felt, as many Buddhist beliefs and practices were grafted onto the shamanistic traditions popular in the villages and outlying areas.

Toward the end of the eighth century, the Japanese capital was moved to the city of Heian, now known as Kyoto. Heian itself was an elegant center of the arts, and the members of the imperial court were devoted more to intrigue, literature, and the arts than to problems of government. During this period the emperors were figureheads, and the government was effectively controlled by the Fujiwara clan, which traditionally married its daughters to the emperors.

By the time the capital was established at Heian, the Buddhist sects associated with the old capital at Nara had been largely discredited by their political involvements and petty infighting. At this time, two monks traveled to China and brought back new ideas and practices that infused new life into Japanese Buddhism. Dengyō Daishi (Saichō)

(766–822) established the Tendai (in Chinese, Tiantai) school that followed the *Lotus Sūtra* and was based at Mount Hiei just outside Heian. Kōbō Daishi (Kūkai) (773–835) formed the Shingon (Chinese Esoteric) school that was the East Asian version of the Indian Vajrayāna and was based at Mount Koya, also near Heian.

During the Heian period these two schools produced a wide variety of rites, art forms, and ceremonies which predominated at the imperial court. In addition, they nurtured a broadly popular synthesis of Buddhism and Japan's indigenous religious tradition, Shinto. This synthesis was called *Sannō Ichijitsu* (Mountain-king–one truth) *Shinto* in Tendai circles and *Ryōbū* (Two-sided) *Shinto* by followers of the Shingon sect.

THE KAMAKURA AND ASHIKAGA SHOGUNATES

The second major phase in the history of Japanese Buddhism began when a bitter civil war between two rival clans ended with the victory of Minamoto Yoritomo (1147–1199). Yoritomo established the capital at Kamakura, his headquarters in eastern Japan. The imperial court at Heian with its Buddhist monasteries was left undisturbed, but military and economic policies were handled by the military government, which was known as the shogunate.

At the start of the new era, there was a burst of religious activity. As the old sects popular during the Nara and Heian periods became more decadent, a series of charismatic religious leaders arose. Eisai (1141–1215) and Dōgen (1200–1253) founded two independent forms of the Zen (in Chinese, Chan), or Meditation, tradition which were especially attractive to the military leaders and feudal warriors. Hōnen (1133–1212) and Shinran (1173–1262) founded distinctive versions of the Pure Land tradition. These new sects, known as Jōdo (Pure Land) and Jōdo Shinshū (True Pure Land), emphasized the simplest possible faith in the Amida Buddha (Amitabha), and held out the promise of rebirth in a heavenly paradise. Still another charismatic leader, Nichiren (1222–1282), founded a new and militant form of Buddhism that called for devotion to the Śākyamuni Buddha and the *Lotus Sūtra*, as well as religious renewal, political activism, and social reform.

Following the destruction of the Kamakura shogunate and the rise of the Ashikaga shogunate (1338–1573), the branch of the Zen school that had been founded by Eisai became the dominant Buddhist tradition and began to fuse with the warrior ethos of the feudal rulers. During the Ashikaga period this Zen-samurai synthesis greatly influenced Japan's visual arts, drama, and literature. The Pure Land and Nichiren traditions, along with the long-established Buddhist-oriented folk religion, also maintained a firm hold on a large segment of the people.

THE TOKUGAWA SHOGUNATE (1598–1868)

The last Ashikaga shogun was driven from power in 1573 following new power struggles among the *daimyo* (territorial lords). Finally, a gifted military leader, Tokugawa Ieyasu (1542–1616), defeated all his rivals and forced the emperor to make him the new shogun. The Tokugawa family brought peace and social conformity to Japan for the next two and a half centuries. During this time, Christianity, which had been introduced by Jesuit missionaries in 1549, was banned.

With the establishment of the Tokugawa regime, a third phase in the history of Japanese Buddhism began. The rulers sought to strengthen their political and social control by using Buddhism to create a national religion. To do this they established a hierarchy of temples within each Buddhist sect and a Buddhist temple in each administrative unit and registered each household at one of these temples. Thus the number of temples and the extent of nominal Buddhist affiliation increased substantially, but under this kind of state direction, Buddhism failed to maintain the same degree of vitality and dynamism that had characterized it during earlier periods of Japanese history. To be sure, there still were noteworthy Buddhist figures, like the Zen priest Hakuin (1685–1768) and the lay

The Equanimity of Zen Master Hakuin

Equanimity has always been one of the most prized of Buddhist virtues, and in practically all Buddhist traditions it has been associated with the most exalted levels of spiritual attainment. In the Zen context this distinctively Buddhist virtue of equanimity is highlighted in a famous story about the Zen priest Hakuin (1685–1768).*

The Zen master Hakuin was praised by his neighbors as one living a pure life.

*Quotation from Paul Reps, comp., *Zen Flesh, Zen Bones* (Garden City, N.Y.: Doubleday, 1957), pp. 7–8.

A beautiful Japanese girl whose parents owned a food store lived near him. Suddenly, without any warning, her parents discovered she was with child.

This made her parents angry. She would not confess who the man was, but after much harassment at last named Hakuin.

In great anger the parents went to the master. "Is that so?" was all he would say.

After the child was born it was brought to Hakuin. By this time he had lost his reputation, which did not trouble him, but he took very good care of the child. He obtained milk from his neighbors and everything else the little one needed.

A year later the girl-mother could stand it no longer. She told her parents the truth—that the real father of the child was a young man who worked in the fishmarket.

The mother and father of the girl at once went to Hakuin to ask his forgiveness, to apologize at length, and to get the child back again.

Hakuin was willing. In yielding the child, all he said was: "Is that so?"

Buddhist and great *haiku* poet Matsuo Bashō (1644–1694), but the general intellectual and moral quality of the monastic community gradually declined. As a part of the same process, the cultural and ideological leadership soon passed to the proponents of the neo-Confucian ideology being imported from China, and by the early nineteenth century a resurgence of the indigenous Shinto tradition also was well underway.

Buddhist Trends in East Asia

Throughout its long and eventful history, Buddhism in East Asia remained remarkably faithful to its Indian and Central Asian origins, though both the Chinese and the Japanese Buddhists made important selections, adaptations, and additions. They did so at all levels of the tradition, including their attitudes toward the Buddha, the Dharma, and the monastic discipline.

NEW ROLES FOR THE BUDDHAS, BODHISATTVAS, AND ARHANTS

The entire pantheon of Buddhas and bodhisattvas of India and Central Asia was gradually introduced into East Asia. As the number continued to grow, the new figures and the conceptions associated with them spread rapidly eastward. Besides appropriating these new figures and ideas, Buddhists in East Asia also began to introduce adaptations of their own. Not only did the appearance of the various Buddhas and bodhisattvas become more East Asian, but there were more substantive changes as well. In China the life story of the historical Śākyamuni Buddha was adapted to resemble the biographies of the traditional Chinese sages, with greater emphasis placed on filial piety. Some of the popular stories credited many of the great bodhisattvas as having previously been Chinese. Associated with traditional Chinese pilgrimage sites, the bodhisattvas were endowed with many attributes and functions borrowed from various indigenous deities.

In Japan the process of adaptation was carried still further with the assimilation of the Buddhas and bodhisattvas into the indigenous spirits known as *kami*. For example, the Shingon sect identified the Buddha Vairocana with the Shinto sun goddess who was generally recognized as the greatest of the kami.

Different figures within the pantheon came to the fore at various times and in various contexts. During the first seven or eight centuries of Buddhist history in East Asia Śākyamuni retained an important and often central position and continued to be a major focus of many of the indigenous schools such as Tian-tai, Chan, and Nichiren. But in certain traditions Śākyamuni was almost totally eclipsed: in the Pure Land sects the Amitābha Buddha of the Western Paradise was the principal figure, and in the Shingon tradition Vairocana—though a far less compelling and popular figure than Amitābha—was recognized as the primal cosmic reality.

The changes in the character and function of the great bodhisattvas are also of great interest. During the early period of Buddhist development, Maitreya was the central figure in one of the major traditions. Over time he gradually lost this position but went on to assume two other quite different and distinct identities. In continuing his early role as the future Buddha, he became the central figure in a long series of Buddhist-oriented messianic societies that continued to foment political unrest in China right up to modern times. Maitreya also came to be identified with a highly eccentric Chinese monk, Bu-dai, and subsequently was represented as a pot-bellied, innocuous figure known as the "laughing Buddha." Another example is the transformation of the bodhisattva Avalokiteśvara. In India and Central Asia this great exemplar of compassion had typically been a masculine bodhisattva and remained so during the early phases of Chinese Buddhist history. But by the second millennium A.D., Avalokiteśvara was commonly portrayed as a female figure resembling an ancient Taoist deity known as the Queen of Heaven. In this new form Avalokiteśvara (in China, Guan-yin and in Japan, Kannon) became both the focus of a popular and widespread cult and the patroness of women and childbirth.

The arhants (those who had attained nirvāṇa) were thoroughly assimilated in China, and it became virtually impossible to differentiate them from the *xian*, or immortals, of popular Taoism. In Japan there was an even more radical transformation when these arhants lost their importance and their functions were taken over by the *yamabushi* (mountain ascetics) and other figures associated with the more shamanistic aspects of the kami tradition.

NEW SCHOOLS: TIAN-TAI, HUA-YAN, AND ESOTERIC

During the centuries when Buddhism was first becoming established in East Asia, it formed direct counterparts of the various Indian schools. Thus the Hīnayāna tradition was represented by several smaller schools. The Mādhyamika tradition was also represented by Chinese and Japanese schools, as was the Yogācāra tradition. The Buddhists in East Asia, however, soon began to create different and more influential schools that were distinctively their own. These new schools can be divided into two groups: The first consisted of those with more "catholic," or comprehensive, orientations, namely, Tian-tai (in Japan, Tendai), Hua-yan (in Japan, Kegon), and the Esoteric school that came to be known in Japan as Shingon. The second group consisted of those with more "protestant," or selective, perspectives, including Chan (in Japan, Zen), various Pure Land groups, and the uniquely Japanese Nichiren sect.

Each of the three great "catholic" schools of Buddhism in East Asia had its own way of classifying the vast corpus of Buddhist texts and doctrines, as well as its own way of interpreting the Dharma. The Tian-tai system was formulated during the sixth century and classified the various strands of the tradition according to the five different phases in the Buddha's ministry. During the first, the Buddha preached the *Avataṁsaka Sūtra*, a long text presenting a variety of highly sophisticated Mahāyāna stories and doctrines. When he realized that this sūtra was too complex for his uninitiated hearers, the Buddha devoted the next three phases of his ministry to preaching sermons with a simpler content. These included the Hīnayāna piṭakas, the Mahāyāna sūtras that described the bodhisattva ideal, and the Perfect Wisdom sūtras (from the *Vaipulya sūtras*) which focused on the doctrine of emptiness and the nonexistence of all dualities and oppositions. The Buddha culminated his ministry by preaching the *Lotus Sūtra* through which he revealed the ultimate truth concerning the real identity inherent in all dualities and oppositions.

This established the *Lotus Sūtra* as the most authoritative scripture for the Tian-tai tradition, and at the same time propounded the typically East Asian Buddhist view that emptiness, or the absolute mind, was identical with the phenomenal world. It also stressed that the ultimate reality or Buddha nature was positively present in every phenomenal entity. In this way the Mahāyāna insight into the identity of saṃsāra and nirvāṇa was interpreted as giving the natural world and ordinary human activity a distinctly affirmative religious value.

The Hua-yan school, considered by many to have the most subtle and profound system of Buddhist philosophy, was organized by a monk who followed the Tian-tai practice of classifying the great corpus of Buddhist scriptures. But as the name of the school implies, he recognized the *Hua-yan* (*Avataṁsaka*) *Sūtra* rather than the *Lotus Sūtra* as the highest authority. In regard to doctrine, he extended the Tian-tai teaching on the identity of the absolute Buddha nature with each phenomenon by emphasizing the complete harmony and interpenetration among the phenomena themselves. Thus he affirmed a positive and holistic understanding of reality that had a great appeal not only for religious thinkers seeking a unifying philosophy, but also for rulers seeking to establish a totalitarian state. The Hua-yan philosophy influenced the later development of the Chan and Zen traditions.

The Esoteric (in Japan, Shingon) school was established in China during the eighth century by a series of famous Indian missionaries, and was then transmitted to Japan by the great Japanese monk Kōbō Daishi. The Esoteric and Shingon schools

"Six Persimmons" by Mu-Chi, at the Daitokuji, Kyoto, Japan. *Orion/ Editorial Photocolor Archives.*

had their own hierarchy of scriptures in which the *Mahāvairocana Sūtra* was ranked above the *Lotus* and the *Avataṁsaka sūtras,* and they also added important new liturgical dimensions. In China the Esoteric school introduced not only advanced rituals for the monks but also popular rites for the dead, which remained a prominent part of Chinese religious life even after the school itself had lost its influence. In Japan the Shingon school introduced many highly refined ritual activities that became important at the royal court, as well as other, less refined rituals that became important in the religious life of the people.

OTHER EAST ASIAN SCHOOLS: CHAN-ZEN, PURE LAND, NICHIREN

Despite the great contributions of the comprehensive Tian-tai, Hua-yan, and Esoteric-Shingon schools, they did not remain the dominant Buddhist traditions in East Asia, but were eventually displaced (in China) or reduced to a minority position (in Japan) by schools with a less scholastic attitude toward the textual tradition, as well as a narrower focus on particular religious practices. The most iconoclastic of these "protestant" groups was the Chan (in Japan, Zen) school, which first took shape in China during the sixth century. According to legend, the Chan school was begun by a famous Indian missionary, Bodhidharma, who stressed the teachings of the *Laṅkāvatāra Sūtra* and popularized the practice of distinctive forms of meditation. Eventually several other writings gained particular favor in the Chan school, including imported texts such as the *Diamond Sūtra* (one of the *Vaipulya sūtras*) and indigenous texts such as the *Liu-zi Tan-jing* (Platform Sūtra of the Sixth Patriarch), associated with a Chan teacher named Hui-neng (638–713).

As time went on, the Chan masters concentrated more on meditation to attain direct insight into the Buddha nature. For the Chan practitioners this Buddha nature was identified with one's own true self, when it was cleansed of all attachments and distortions, and with the natural world, which was thought to exhibit the Buddha nature in a pure and unspoiled way. Because of its focus on meditation and the purity of the natural world, the Chan tradition turned into a distinctive style of Buddhism that questioned the usefulness of any scriptures, images, or other such features. Thus the "sudden enlightenment" school known as Lin-ji in China and Rinzai in Japan emphasized the discipline of grappling with enigmatic riddles (in Chinese, *gong-an;* in Japanese, *kōan*).

Another, more popular "gradual enlightenment" school known as Cao-dong in China and Sōtō in Japan emphasized the practice of meditational sitting devoid of any object or goal. One simply rec-

Hands of a monk at a Zen Buddhist monastery of the Sōtō sect in Japan. In this posture of "Kyosakku," or "awakening spirit," the long stick is often held for hours.
Paolo Koch/Photo Researchers.

ognized that since one was already Buddha, there was nothing more to be done. Beyond these practices, which came to be characteristic of particular schools, the Chan-Zen tradition also developed other distinctive features, including the emphasis on the positive values of manual work, the cultivation of the arts (for example, gardening, painting, and tea ceremony), and the practice of military skills.

The other major set of "protestant" schools in East Asia, those associated with the Pure Land tradition, also traced their lineage to the early period of Buddhist development in China. In the early decades of the fifth century, Hui-yuan (334–416) introduced a devotional cult that centered on the Buddha Amitābha and promised rebirth in his fabulous Western Paradise. During the first half of the sixth century, Tan-luan (476–542), who reportedly had received the *Pure Land sūtras* directly from an Indian missionary, succeeded in establishing the Chinese Pure Land school. Some seven centuries later, related but distinctively new Pure Land sects were formed out of the Tendai and Shingon schools in Japan.

This new surge of Pure Land schools was associated with the belief that the world was in a state of decline, and that the present age was thoroughly degenerate. Thus easier methods of salvation were needed. These easier methods involved a dependence on the "other power" of Amitābha (in Japan, Amida) together with the very simplest form of devotional practice—namely, the repetition of Amitābha's name (a practice called *nian-fo* in Chinese, *nembutsu* in Japanese). In the Japanese Jōdo Shinshū (True Pure Land) school founded by Shinran (1173–1262), the emphasis on faith in Amida and his grace became so exclusive that even the usefulness of reciting his name was called into question. At this time, the older Buddhist goal of attaining nirvāṇa had been completely replaced by the distinctively Pure Land ideal of rebirth in a heavenly paradise.

Although the Nichiren school had much in common with the Japanese Pure Land groups, it displayed a character all its own. Nichiren adherents shared much of Nichiren's own militantly prophetic spirit and followed his lead in accepting the authority of the *Lotus Sūtra*. Along with religious devotion they advocated the recitation of a sacred formula, *Namu myōhō rengekyō* (Hail to the Scripture of the Lotus of the True Teaching), which was believed to be more reliable than the repetition of Amida's name. Moreover, their goal was not limited to rebirth in a heavenly paradise, but included the purification of the Japanese nation and the establishment of Japan as a "land of the Buddha."

MONASTIC ADAPTATIONS

When the Buddhist monastic community was first established in East Asia, the patterns of monastic life remained similar to those imported from India and Central Asia. But as it interacted with its new environment, several changes were made. The community soon began to adjust its ecclesiastical heritage to the more historical and biographical modes of thinking characteristic of East Asia. During the fourth and fifth centuries, Indian and Central Asian sources were used to reconstruct the history of the transmission of the Dharma in India to the first Chinese patriarch. During the Song period in China, the Tian-tai monastic community produced a treatise listing nine of its early patriarchs, and the Chan community produced its own literature, including the famous *Jing-de chuan-deng lu* (Records of the transmission of the lamp).

As Buddhism became established in East Asia, the monastic community gradually adapted itself to deeply embedded attitudes toward the primacy of family and state. The monks' and nuns' vocations and activities came to be justified primarily by their contribution to the moral and social order and by the merit they accumulated for their parents and ancestors. At the institutional level the monastic community accepted state control over such matters as the ordination, registration, and unfrocking of its members, as well as the interpretation and enforcement of the monastic rules. After Buddhism was introduced into Japan, the Chinese custom of state control was quickly adopted by the Japanese authorities, who enforced it even more stringently.

A different kind of adaptation by the East Asian monastic community involved the relaxation of prohibitions against "mundane" activities. In the Chan-Zen tradition, the rule against manual or agricultural work was rejected, and members of the monastic community were required to earn their living by tilling the soil (hence the Chan-Zen maxim "One day no work, one day no food"). Certain proponents of this requirement went even further by maintaining that such work, if collectively performed with the proper intention, could be conducive to the attainment of enlightenment.

This relaxation of prohibitions also occurred in Japan when Shinran, founder of the Jōdo Shinshū (True Pure Land) sect, legitimated and popularized the practice of allowing its clergy to marry. This practice, as well as the kind of clerical family-centeredness that it fostered, soon came to be accepted not only in Shinran's sect, but in many other Japanese Buddhist groups as well.

NEW LAY MOVEMENTS

The increasingly worldly orientation of the Buddhist teaching and monastic order in East Asia was complemented by new, predominantly lay social organizations and movements. In China many Buddhists who chose to remain outside the monasteries committed themselves to the serious practice of basic Buddhist morality and meditation, to the propagation of the Dharma, and to the publication of sacred texts. In Japan a number of laypersons formed anticlerical groups and assumed responsibility for their own initiations, communal rites, and programs of religious instruction. During the final centuries of the premodern period in East Asia, these lay movements enlivened Buddhist traditions that were otherwise rather stagnant and uncreative.

Buddhism in Tibet and Mongolia

During the early centuries of the Christian era, Buddhism was established in several Central Asian states along the trade routes connecting northwestern India and northern China. But around the middle of the first millennium A.D., there were two major developments. First, the Buddhist communities in Central Asia suffered severely from a combination of factors that included both serious competition from other religions and foreign invasions. At the same time, Buddhism began to penetrate into a new region in Central Asia, the high and isolated Himalayan kingdom of Tibet.

In this remote environment Buddhism was able to prosper, and a distinctive form of the tradition,

Lamaism, took shape. The term *lama* means a "supreme being" and is closely related to the Indian Buddhist concept of a guru (teacher). The tradition is one that has had a great fascination for many Westerners because of the aura of mystery and secrecy that has shrouded not only Tibet itself, but also the lamas and the content of their teaching. Others, however, have been scandalized by the theocratic organization of the tradition and by its attention to magical practice.

Lamaism has prevailed across a large but sparsely populated region of Asia. Today, followers of the tradition are found among the Mongols of southern Russia, western China, Tibet, and the Himalayan states of Bhutan, Sikkim, and Nepal. Its main center, however, has always been Tibet. The first dissemination of Buddhism into Tibet began early in the seventh century and continued for approximately two hundred years. A second wave of penetration was initiated in the tenth and eleventh centuries and continued through the fourteenth century. The third major phase in the premodern history of Lamaism began with the reforms of a famous monk, Tsong-kha-pa (1357–1419), and persisted well into the twentieth century.

ROYAL SPONSORSHIP

The Tibetan monarchy began in the early seventh century of the Christian era. From the outset the kings tended to favor the Buddhist cause, in opposition to the nobles who supported the indigenous shamanistic tradition of Tibet, *bon*. King Srong-brtsan-sgam-po (d. 650), a powerful ruler who established the first stable state in Tibet, was converted to Buddhism by his two chief wives, who were devout Buddhists. One was a princess from Nepal and the other a princess from China. Encouraging cultural contacts between his capital at Lhasa and northwestern India, the king set the pattern of royal sponsorship of Buddhism. With the help of Indian scholars, a script and grammar of

The immense Potala Palace, formerly the residence of the Dali Lama, overlooks the city of Lhasa, Tibet. *The Newark Museum Collection.*

A modern Buddhist worship service at Leh, India, located in a remote section of the Himalayas. *Elizabeth LeCompte.*

the Tibetan language were made. Some Buddhist texts were then translated into Tibetan, and the first Buddhist temples were erected.

During the eighth century the Buddhist cause received new support. In the early decades a Chinese princess in the Tibetan court convinced the king to make the country a refuge for monks fleeing from the Central Asian kingdom of Khotan. In addition, more Buddhist texts were brought from India and China and translated into Tibetan. Following a short period during which the power of the nobles increased and the bon tradition gained strength, Buddhism received even stronger support from King Khri-srong-lde-brtsan (755–797). According to later tradition, he sponsored a major council at Lhasa that affirmed the superiority of the Indian over the Chinese form of Buddhism, and he gave royal support to Indian missionaries. The great bSam-yas temple of Lhasa was constructed, an indigenous Tibetan saṅgha was established, and the practice of taxing the people to support the monastic community was instituted.

In the early decades of the ninth century Buddhism prospered, especially during the reign of Ral-pa-can (ruled 815–836). But when Ral-pa-can was assassinated, the first period of development in Tibet came to an end. The collapse of the monarchy followed, and Buddhism entered a state of stagnation and decay.

REVIVAL OF LAMAISM

The second major phase was the Buddhist revival in Tibet and its spread to the Mongol court in northern China. The renaissance began in the early tenth century in eastern Tibet and gradually spread to the central area around Lhasa. In the late tenth and early eleventh centuries, Lamaism was given a powerful new impetus by a famous translator, Rin-chen bzang-po. In the middle decades of the eleventh century, the revival was carried still further through the efforts of an Indian scholar, Atīṣa, who came to Tibet from one of the great Buddhist universities still open in Bengal.

The new vitality led to the gradual formation of

a number of distinctively Lamaist schools. The schools included the bKa'-gdams-pa, which retained much of the disciplined and scholarly ethos associated with the ideals of Atīsa, as well as larger, less strict, and more politically involved schools, such as the Sa-skya-pa and the bKa'-rgyud-pa. One school, the rNying-ma-pa, combined the older Tibetan heritage associated with the teachings and works of the famous eighth-century Indian missionary Padmasambhava, who had brought the tantras with him from India.

In the thirteenth century, these developments took an unprecedented turn when a Tibetan diplomatic mission succeeded in bringing about the conversion to Lamaism of Kublai Khan (1216—1294), the powerful founder of China's Mongol, or Yuan, dynasty. Thereafter Tibetan lamas were installed as religious advisers at the Mongol court in Peking, where they continued to propagate their version of Buddhist teaching and practice. At the same time, their powerful Mongol patrons granted to the lamas at Lhasa a kind of vassal status, which enabled them to establish their own political and administrative authority within Tibet itself.

THE YELLOW HATS

The third and final phase in the premodern development of Lamaism was marked by the rise of a reform movement known as the dGe-lugs-pa, or the School of the Virtuous. It was also called the Yellow Hat school because its adherents wore yellow hats, in contrast to the red hats worn by the older Buddhist groups and the black hats of the bon priests. Much of the success of the Yellow Hat movement can be attributed to the impressive scholarship and highly disciplined approach of its founder, Tsong-kha-pa. It was also strengthened by the erudition and organizational skills of his early successors.

A major turning point in Yellow Hat influence and power occurred in 1578 when one of their leaders, later known as the third Dalai Lama, succeeded in converting a powerful Mongol chieftain, the Altan Khan. (The title *Dalai Lama,* meaning "ocean" or "ocean of wisdom," is a Mongol honorific which the khan bestowed at this time, applying it also retroactively to the recipient's two immediate predecessors.) Unlike the earlier relationship between the Tibetan lamas and the Mongol rulers of China, this encounter led to the conversion of the Mongol population in Mongolia itself as well as in the neighboring regions of northern China and what is now southern Russia.

In Tibet a religiopolitical alliance was established between the Mongols and the ecclesiastics of the Yellow Hat movement. This set the stage for the emergence of a Yellow Hat theocracy which ruled Tibet during the last half of the seventeenth century and provided the model for the more permanent Yellow Hat regime which lasted from the mid-eighteenth century to the end of the premodern period. At the same time the hegemony of the Yellow Hats in Tibet persuaded several groups of Red Hat adherents to move south into the valleys along the Indo-Tibetan frontier where they established independent Lamaist outposts.

RELIGIOUS TRENDS: BUDDHAS AND THE PANTHEON

From the earliest stages of the Buddhist penetration of Tibet, the Vajrayāna tradition of late Indian Buddhism was the most important influence in the development of the new tradition. This Indian perspective received official sanction at the council of Lhasa when the Chinese Chan monks who represented its major competition were expelled from the country. During the revival of Tibetan Buddhism in the tenth and eleventh centuries, much of the inspiration and guidance was provided by Indian Vajrayānists. However the Tibetans, and later the Mongols, gradually created their own version of the Vajrayāna tradition and pantheon, their own way of understanding and expressing the Dharma, and their own patterns of religious authority and social organization.

The Buddhists of Tibet and Mongolia viewed the Buddha Śākyamuni as only one of many expres-

This painting on cotton entitled "The Wheel of Existence" (17th–18th century) illustrates the six realms of possible rebirth. *The Newark Museum Collection.*

sions of an ultimate protecting and saving power. Indeed, this power could be manifested in various forms, at various levels of cosmic and psychological reality, and in various historical contexts. They accepted from India several celestial and human Buddhas, including male and female figures as well as many other divine and semidivine figures both beneficent and demonic, and they then adapted and extended the inherited pantheon to accord with their own ideas and experiences. They devised distinctively Tibetan ways of representing the entire range of figures, from those of the Buddhas to those of the attending acolytes and worshipers, and they enriched the pantheon by incorporating the Lamaist saints who came to be recognized as full-fledged Buddhas and bodhisattvas. The female bodhisattva Tārā, who may have been imported from India, became a kind of universal protectress and the object of a cult popular among members of both the saṅgha and the laity. Some purely indigenous deities and demons were also included on the pantheon's higher levels. On the lower levels a whole host of local heroes, guardian deities, and personal familiars continued to be venerated according to local customs.

THE DEVELOPMENT OF SACRED LITERATURE

Like the Indian Vajrayānists, the Buddhists of Tibet and Mongolia accepted the idea that Buddhist truth could be expressed at different levels and in many ways. Many Sanskrit texts were translated into Tibetan. After the collapse of Buddhism in India, the translation process reached its high point when a great Tibetan scholar Bu-ston (1290–1364) edited the Tibetan texts and organized them into two great collections. The first, known as the *bKa'-gyur* (*Kanjur*), contained Hīnayāna vinayas, sūtras, and Abhidharma texts, Mahāyāna sūtras and commentaries, and Vajrayāna tantras. The second, known as the *bsTan-'gyur* (*Tenjur*), included semicanonical writings covering not only philosophical and commentarial subjects, but also more mundane topics such as grammar, logic, astrology, and medicine. In the seventeenth and eighteenth centuries, these Tibetan collections were translated into Mongolian.

Besides translating the Indian Buddhist texts, the Tibetans, and later the Mongols, wrote a sacred literature of their own. Each of the Lamaist schools produced not only its own oral traditions, but also its own sacred texts, including a systematic treatise by sGam-po-pa and various collections of famous sayings and songs. They also wrote many popular biographies of famous Indian missionaries and Lamaist saints, including great yogīs as well as more orthodox monastic leaders.

CONTINUITY AND ENRICHMENT IN RELIGIOUS PRACTICE

The affinity between the Indian Vajrayāna and the Lamaist traditions was further demonstrated by the persistent tension between the more restrained and the more exclusively esoteric Vajrayāna practices. In the Lamaist context the more restrained practice was represented by the reformist schools (notably the bKa'-gdams-pa associated with Atīsa and the later Yellow Hats associated with Tsong-kha-pa) which recognized the importance of the vinaya and the sūtras as well as the tantras. These schools encouraged adherence to the monastic discipline, and stressed the need for training in the classical Mahāyāna doctrine. The more esoteric approach was carried forward by other Red Hat schools that focused on the tantras and the oral traditions. These less inhibited schools tended to be more lax in their enforcement of the monastic rules, particularly those prohibiting marriage and the consumption of alcoholic beverages. They also tended to be more skeptical of the value of intellectual pursuits. And in some cases, they encouraged the more extreme forms of mystical activity.

Despite the schools' differing degrees of conservatism, the various segments of the Lamaist community all developed distinctive Tibetan or Mongolian practices. The Tibetan and Mongolian Buddhists drew on native shamanistic and magical traditions to enrich the inherited Vajrayāna liturgies and techniques and to acquire both spiritual and mundane power. These shamanic motifs contributed to the advancement of beliefs concerning the human soul and of rituals designed to promote healing in this life or a better rebirth in the next. It is quite probable that the Tibetan *Book of the Dead,* which claimed to be a guide through the various states and opportunities encountered between death and rebirth, was recited in this kind of ritual context. In addition, dramatic and colorful rituals accompanied both traditional monastic practices and community liturgies and festivals.

AUTHORITY IN THE LAMAIST TRADITION

The affinity between the Indian Vajrayāna and the Lamaist traditions evident in the texts and ritual practices was also apparent in matters of religious authority. The title *lama* is itself a Tibetan transliteration of the term *guru* used by the Indian Vajrayānists for revered teachers and spiritual masters. Like the Vajrayāna siddhas and gurus of India, the Tibetan and Mongolian lamas were recognized as living Buddhas or bodhisattvas of the highest order, and as such were the objects of intense veneration and even worship. Like their Indian predecessors, the lamas served as intermediaries whose magical power made it possible for them to approach the various deities and to ward off demons and other destructive powers.

The lamas lived in the same way that the Indian Vajrayānists did. The majority followed the pattern of the more conservative adherents of the tradition who had taught and practiced within the classical monastic setting. But some followed the model provided by the more radical and iconoclastic yogīs who had lived as homeless mendicants.

In the beginning, the lamas adhered to the traditional Vajrayāna belief in spiritual transmission. Like the siddhas and gurus of the Indian tradition, they transmitted their doctrines and rituals through a direct and personal master-disciple relationship. Such relationships gradually became more extended lineages, and these more extended lineages eventually became different schools or sects. However, in the new schools the Lamaists introduced an unprecedented theory according to which particular lamas of high ecclesiastical standing were held to be reincarnated in infants destined to be their successors. Thus whenever such a lama died, his reincarnation would be sought out and "discovered" among the newborn infants in the appropriate area. The chosen infant was taken to the appropriate monastery for training, and when he reached maturity, he was installed in the vacant office. (Because of this system, it is perhaps not surprising that many of the reincarnated lamas of the richer and more powerful monasteries died before they became old enough to assume their leadership responsibilities.)

As a correlate of their exalted religious status, many Tibetan lamas assumed a political and administrative authority seldom matched by Buddhist ecclesiastics in other areas. During the thirteenth and fourteenth centuries the lamas were embroiled in complicated and often violent struggles for political power. Because of the advantages provided by the special relationship with the Yuan court in China (1260–1368), the lamas were able to formalize and extend their political and administrative authority. In fact, the Tibetan government was controlled by a segment of the Lamaist community from the late thirteenth century to 1470 and from 1640 to about 1700. Around the middle of the eighteenth century the lamas again seized control and continued to rule until 1951 when Chinese Communist invaders imposed the authority of Peking over all of Tibet.

Among the Mongols of southern Russia and Mongolia, as well as among the peoples living in the small valleys along the Indo-Tibetan border, the most powerful lamas assumed similar political functions. In Mongolia this situation came to an end only when the Communists took over in the 1920s. In the Himalayan kingdom of Bhutan, Buddhist ecclesiastics have retained considerable political influence to the present.

BUDDHISM IN THE MODERN ERA

During the nineteenth and twentieth centuries Buddhists of every sectarian tradition and geographical region have been confronted by unprecedented challenges and opportunities. At the ideological level they have been faced with powerful intrusive forces, such as Christianity, Western rationalistic modes of thought, liberal democratic conceptions, and Communism. At the institutional level they have had to deal with the harsh reality of political and economic domination by Western powers that had little understanding of Buddhism or sympathy for the Buddhist cause. They have had to endure the disruption of the traditional social and economic patterns on which Buddhism has become dependent.

In addition, they have had to cope with local movements committed to limiting or even eliminating Buddhist influence. In such situations the Buddhist response has varied from conservative resistance to reform to bold new initiatives, and the results thus far have been extremely varied. In some areas the tradition has been severely disrupted. In others it has been maintained with differing degrees of vitality. And in some parts of the world, new Buddhist communities have been established.

Reform Movements

Attempts to maintain and even revitalize Buddhism in this period of rapid intellectual and social change have brought important innovations. Buddhists who were influenced by the new modes of thought and the new social forces soon began to devise new ways of appropriating and presenting the tradition. They introduced new interpretations of the figure of the Buddha, new ways of understanding his teachings, and new approaches to the life and organization of the Buddhist community. Modern reformers' interpretations of the Buddha's biography have underscored his humanity and his rational approach to the problem of human suffering. New interpretations of Buddhist teaching have been made on at least two different levels.

On the first of these levels, a number of leading intellectuals have sought to relate Buddhist thought to Christianity, to Western philosophical perspectives, and to scientific modes of thinking. In Japan this endeavor began in the nineteenth century and produced important works by sophisticated scholars. Outside Japan such efforts began somewhat later and have generally been more polemic and popular. On the second level, many Buddhist reformers have stressed the relevance of Buddhist teachings to social and ethical issues, citing their own tradition of democracy and social activism. In many countries Buddhist apologists have maintained that Buddhism can be the basis for a truly democratic or socialist society and, as a nontheistic religion, can be the basis for world peace.

On the communal level, Buddhist reformers have tried to purify the monastic order and to redirect its activities to make them more relevant to modern conditions. They have tried to discourage those monastic activities that have little immediate practical value and that require resources which might otherwise be used more effectively. They have introduced new kinds of education designed to train the monks for what they consider to be more constructive religious and social roles, and they have encouraged them to assist in providing secular education at the popular level and to perform such social services as aiding the poor and caring for orphans. In some countries—for example, in Thailand and Burma—monks have been trained to carry on missionary activities among non-Buddhists (particularly peripheral tribal populations) and to participate in government-sponsored programs of national development.

The reformers have also emphasized the importance of the laity. Laypersons have been encouraged to study the Buddhist scriptures and to practice those forms of meditation particularly suited to their own needs and situations. Buddhist associations run by lay leaders have become influential in virtually every Buddhist country. They sponsor a variety of Buddhist programs, defend the cause of Buddhism in national affairs, and provide the leadership for Buddhist ecumenical movements.

The laity in various Asian countries also has supported the Mahābodhi Society, which was organized in the late nineteenth century to reclaim and restore the sacred sites and monuments of Buddhist India. Lay leaders took the initiative in organizing the celebrations of the 2,500-year anniversary of Buddhism held in the 1950s in various parts of the Buddhist world, especially in Burma, where a major Buddhist council (the Sixth Council according to the Burmese reckoning) was convened. Lay leadership was also essential to the formation, in 1952, of the World Fellowship of Buddhists and to the quadrennial meetings of the fellowship that have continued to the present time.

The Communist Challenge

Despite the remarkable continuity in the Buddhist reformist trends during the modern era, the fates of the Buddhist communities have been very different. In the Communist-dominated regions of the Asian mainland, including Inner and Outer Mongolia, North Korea, China, Tibet, and Indochina, where for centuries the majority of the world's Buddhist population has been concentrated, the strength and vitality of Buddhism have been seriously undermined. In some of the non-Communist countries, from Sri Lanka through parts of Southeast Asia to Taiwan, South Korea, and Japan, Buddhist communities have been able to maintain their basic integrity and continue to be active. Finally, distinctively new Buddhist communities have been created in both Asia and in the Western world.

The basic pattern of Communist dealings with Buddhism has been evident since the Bolshevik takeover in Russia and the establishment of the Soviet-inspired Mongolian People's Republic in the early 1920s. In both cases the new Communist governments moved as quickly as possible to replace Buddhist teaching with Communist ideology, to weaken and then eliminate the economic privileges and powers of the monasteries, and to isolate and discredit the monastic leadership. In this way the Communist governments were able, within a few short decades, to divest the Lamaist tradition of any real power and influence. The relics of Lamaism in these areas have been preserved and are occasionally displayed to the outside world; but the vitality of the tradition has been severely curtailed.

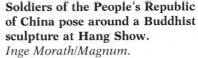

Soldiers of the People's Republic of China pose around a Buddhist sculpture at Hang Show.
Inge Morath/Magnum.

In China the Communist rise to power came much later. It was preceded by a long period of Buddhist adjustment to Western and modern influences during which many intellectual and social reforms were attempted. However, these reforms did not succeed in breaking the close and longstanding ties between Buddhism and the traditional Chinese society. When the Communists took over, Buddhism suffered severe setbacks. The traditional rights and privileges of the monasteries were rescinded. Their occupants were either defrocked or forced into materially productive occupations. The buildings were taken over and made into museums or utilized for government purposes. And the Buddhist associations that had been organized by the earlier reformers were unified and brought under strict government supervision.

The state-dominated Chinese Buddhist Association that resulted was used to foster Chinese relations with Buddhist countries but was given little opportunity to advance the Buddhist cause within China itself. During the late 1950s and the 1960s, the already weakened tradition was further decimated by the antitraditionalist campaigns mounted during the Cultural Revolution. Since the death of Mao Ze-dong, however, there have been increasing indications that the government is adopting a more moderate and encouraging policy toward all religions, including Buddhism.

During the late 1950s and the 1960s, the Chinese conquest of Tibet brought Tibetan Buddhism under an even stronger attack than the one the Maoist regime had mounted against Buddhism in China itself. Until the Chinese invasion Tibet had succeeded in maintaining an isolation that had not prepared the country for what was to happen. Following the Chinese invasion in 1959, the Dalai Lama was forced to flee, along with thousands of others. According to many reliable reports, the Chinese began their rule with a brutal repression that included the persecution of the monks who had remained. Until very recently, the Chinese did not allow outside contacts with Tibet; however, visitors are now permitted, and the repression of Buddhism seems to have abated. It is interesting to note recent rumors that the Chinese would like the Dalai Lama to return.

The Communist takeover in Indochina is so re-

The Sule Pagoda in Rangoon, Burma, enshrines several relics of the Buddha brought from India by two Buddhist missionaries, Ashin Tholla and Ashin Ottara. *United Nations.*

cent that its effects cannot yet be determined. In Vietnam, Laos, and Cambodia, the policies of the governments seem to be quite similar to those previously employed by Communist regimes in other parts of Asia. Buddhist teachings are being disparaged, Buddhist privileges are being eliminated, and the influence of Buddhist institutions is being eroded. In Cambodia, when the Pol Pot government was in control (1975–1979), Buddhist leaders and institutions were the special objects of a persecution pursued with unprecedented violence and intensity.

Buddhism in Non-Communist Asia

Outside the Communist orbit in Asia, Buddhism has fared better. For example, in Sri Lanka, Burma, and Thailand, Theravāda Buddhists have been able to retain both a dominant religious position and a strong political and social influence. The groundwork for the continued preeminence of Buddhism in these three countries was laid during the colonial period in the late nineteenth and twentieth centuries. At that time, an intimate bond was forged between the local Theravāda traditions and the emerging sense of national identity and destiny. In Sri Lanka and Burma this bond was established in the context of actual resistance to British rule. In Thailand it was cultivated by an indigenous elite engaged in a successful struggle to maintain Thai independence. But in each case Buddhist-oriented nationalism created an environment in which the Theravādins were able to retain their hold on the loyalties of leaders and people. As a result, the Theravāda community in each of these three countries has continued to be influential at every level from that of the national government to the village.

In other non-Communist areas of Asia the relationship between the traditional Buddhist communities and the broader social and political environments has been nearer to mutual acceptance and toleration than to active support. Various forms of Mahāyāna Buddhism have survived in Hong Kong and Taiwan as well as among the Chinese populations in many areas of Southeast Asia. (For the most part these communities have preserved the traditional forms of Buddhist belief and practice, though they also have instituted some reforms.) In South Korea Buddhism has persisted as a minority tradition and has given birth to several new Buddhist movements. Among these, perhaps the most important is a Zen-related reform movement called Won Buddhism, which began in the early twentieth century and now enjoys considerable support throughout the country.

The most interesting and dynamic developments have occurred in Japan. The modern period in Japan began with the Meiji Restoration (1868), which brought with it the elimination of the special privileges Buddhism had enjoyed under the Tokugawa shogunate. State Shinto became the national religion; and after World War II, Japan became a secular state. Nevertheless, despite the loss of their special position, traditional Buddhist communities have remained part of Japanese life. They have retained many of their ancient beliefs, practices, and communal organizations, but at the same time they have gradually adapted to the changing conditions.

Moreover, several Buddhist-oriented "new religions" have appeared. The most dynamic of these—for example, Reiyūkai (Association of the Friends of the Spirit), Rishō Kōsei Kai (Society for the Establishment of Righteousness and Friendly Relations), and Sōka Gakkai (Value Creation Society)—have their roots in Nichiren Buddhism and popular folk traditions. These new religions focus on the layperson and are devoted to attaining practical goals such as health and material well-being. Appealing originally to the lower middle class, they have made many millions of converts and currently exert a significant influence not only on the religious life of the country, but also on its economic and political life.

Expansion in Indonesia and India

Buddhism's survival and activity in the modern world can also be seen in the distinctively new Buddhist communities in other areas of Asia, especially in Indonesia and India. In Indonesia the Buddhist revival has been rather limited. But the revival in India represents a major development in contemporary Buddhist history.

The first stirrings of new Buddhist life in India began in the early decades of the twentieth century, when several Buddhist societies were formed by small groups of intellectuals. The members of these societies discovered in Buddhism a form of Indian spirituality that they could reconcile with both their newly acquired rationalistic attitudes and their reformist ideals of social equality. Since the late 1950s several communities of Tibetan refugees, including one headed by the Dalai Lama, have established another kind of Buddhist presence in India.

By far the most interesting and important aspect of the Buddhist resurgence in its original homeland has been the mass conversion of members of the lowly "scheduled" castes. This has taken place primarily, though not exclusively, in Maharashtra state, of which Bombay is the capital. The conversion process was initiated in 1956 by Dr. B. K. Ambedker, the leader of the Maher people. Ambedker publicly adopted Buddhism on the grounds that it was the religion best suited to the spiritual, social, and economic well-being of his followers. Initially some eight hundred thousand persons were associated with the new Buddhist movement, and the number of adherents has more than doubled during the past thirty years.

Expansion in the West

Buddhism had never seriously penetrated the West prior to the modern period. But beginning in the late nineteenth century and continuing into the twentieth century, it has become a religious and

Tibetan lamas of the Kagyü sect lead opening ceremonies for worshipers at a Buddhist monastery in Woodstock, New York. *Maggie Hopp.*

social reality in practically all parts of the Western world, particularly the United States. The primary reason for the establishment of Buddhism in the West was the establishment of immigrant communities from China and Japan. These communities have continued to grow and to develop new forms of Buddhist life suitable for a Western environment. Currently, Buddhist communities composed of Asian Americans are firmly implanted not only in Hawaii and California, but in many other parts of the United States as well. These groups include some associated with traditional Buddhist sects, such as Pure Land and Zen, and others associated with new Buddhist religions, such as Risho Kōsei Kai and Sōka Gakkai.

But the penetration of Buddhism into the West has not been limited to immigrant communities. Beginning in the last decade of the nineteenth century, Buddhist scholars and devotees have founded Buddhist societies in various European countries, Australia, and the United States. Their leaders have included intellectuals and spiritual seekers drawn to the religion and philosophy of the East. More recently, Buddhism has also become the object of widespread popular interest, particularly in the so-called counterculture, which has been stimulated and nurtured through the writings and activities of Asian missionaries such as the great Zen scholar D. T. Suzuki, Tibetan exiles such as Tarthang Tulku, and native enthusiasts such as Philip Kapleau. Buddhist influences have also appeared and been disseminated through the works of avant-garde literary figures of the 1950s and 1960s such as Jack Kerouac and Gary Snyder. With the surge of interest in Buddhism during the 1960s and early 1970s, a network of Buddhist organizations and meditation centers has been established across the United States from Honolulu and San Francisco to Vermont.

Buddhism and the Future

As a concerned observer surveys the current situations of Buddhists in various regions of the modern world, certain questions come to mind. Will the Buddhist communities that stretch from southern Russia through China to Cambodia be able to regain their strength despite devastating attacks? Will the Buddhist communities in the fringe areas of southern and eastern Asia continue to enjoy the kind of governmental support or toleration they now receive? And if so, will they be able to achieve the delicate balance between conservatism and reform that will be needed if they are to maintain their vigor and relevance? Will the fledgling Buddhist groups in India and the West be able to sustain their dynamism and become permanently established in their new environments? Different answers have been given to all these questions, by both scholarly commentators and Buddhist participants, but only the future can supply the correct one.

Notes

1 These two characterizations are the titles of books by Erik Zurcher (Leiden, Netherlands: E. J. Brill, 1959) and Kenneth Ch'en (Princeton, N. J.: Princeton University Press, 1973).

PART THREE

RELIGIONS OF CHINA, JAPAN, AND INDIA

PHOTOGRAPH BY BURT GLINN/MAGNUM

Part three covers the traditional religions of China—Confucianism, Taoism, and Buddhism—as well as the native religion of Japan, Shintō, and two faiths associated principally with India: Jainism and Sikhism. As chapter ten shows, in early China religious activities included bloody sacrifices and ancestor reverence. Later, under the early Zhou dynasty, the *Yi Jing,* a divination text, came into use. Chapter ten also examines the teachings of Confucius, Lao-tzi, and their followers. Chapter eleven focuses on the three traditions during periods of dynastic change. Confucianism became the state ideology for a time; then Taoism revived; and around the time of Christ, Buddhism arrived from India. Buddhism flourished under the Tang dynasty. Many schools were founded, and the Buddhist influence in art and literature became paramount. The final chapter on China focuses on the transition from premodern to modern times and the revolutionary changes in Chinese life this transition has brought.

Chapter thirteen traces the rise of Shintō from its obscure origin as a village religion, Shintō's role during the classical period, and the arrival of Buddhist, Confucian, and Taoist influences from China. It also covers the political and religious reorganization of Japan under the Tokugawa and the dramatic new patterns of religious life that evolved in Japan both after the Meiji Restoration of 1868 and World War II.

India, the home of two great world religions—Buddhism and Hinduism—is also the home of other traditions that are remarkable in their spiritual messages, though limited in number of adherents. In chapter fourteen we look at Jainism, whose followers do not believe in a supreme Being, practice mortification of the flesh, and seek moral perfection through nonviolence, and Sikhism, an offshoot of Hinduism that has also borrowed many concepts from Muslim mysticism.

10 Early Chinese Society: The Traditional Background

Scholars have traditionally divided the religions of China into three "isms": Confucianism, Taoism, and Buddhism. Although this is a useful classification, and one we shall also employ, it must not be allowed to obscure the assumptions shared by all three religious traditions, assumptions that make them unmistakably Chinese. We also must not lose sight of certain religious activities that do not fit easily into these three traditions, of which the most important are the state religion and the folk religion. The sacrifices on the occasion of the winter solstice are an example of the state religion, and the peasants' village and family rites illustrate the tenacious hold folk religion has long had over the great majority of the Chinese people.

THE UNITY OF CHINESE RELIGION*

The shared assumptions of Confucianism, Taoism, and Buddhism may be thought of as a common root from which a tree of many branches has sprung and which contains the following ideas about the nature of humanity and the world:

1 All parts of the universe share with humanity a degree of sentience. Human beings and "things" are thus one, without radical distinctions.

2 There is a preordained correct place and pattern of behavior for everything in the universe.

3 The ideal is achieved when all things operate in a cosmic harmony; that is, when peace and order reign supreme.

4 Humanity has a special responsibility for maintaining this harmony when it is already present in the world or for working toward its reestablishment when, because of some human tragedy, ignorance, or willfulness, it is absent.

5 Finally, the very survival of humanity depends on the establishment of this harmony insofar as this is possible.

THE DAO*

This pattern of behavior and the resultant harmony eventually came to be called the *Dao,* which means

*The Chinese terms used in this text are shown in the Pinyin system of romanization. However, quoted matter taken from translations may use the Wade-Giles system. When there is a spelling discrepancy, this fact is pointed out in a note at the bottom of the page where such a usage first occurs. For a brief explanation of the Pinyin system and a comparative listing of important Chinese terms, see box on next two pages.

**Dao* is written *Tao* in the Wade-Giles system. The words *Taoism* and *Taoist* are usually pronounced with an initial *d.*

The Pinyin System of Romanization

Many romanization systems for Chinese characters have been formulated both in China and abroad. The system most frequently employs in the English-speaking West is the Wade-Giles system. The romanization system employed in this book is known as the Pinyin system and was devised in the People's Republic of China between 1951 and 1956 on direct orders from Chairman Mao, who stated: "Our written language must be reformed; it should take the direction of phonetization common to all the languages of the world." Pinyin was adopted as the official romanization system in 1958 but has only recently begun to be accepted in the West. Since most past and present scholarship still employs the Wade-Giles system, we offer a conversion chart for some common terms:

	Pinyin System	Wade-Giles System
Dynastic Names (in chronological order)	Shang	Shang
	Zhou	Chou
	Qin	Ch'in
	Han	Han
	Sui	Sui
	Tang	T'ang
	Song	Sung
	Yuan	Yüan (Mongols)
	Ming	Ming
	Qing	Ch'ing (Manchus)
Rulers and Political Personalities	Feng Gui-fen (official)	Feng Kuei-fen
	Gao-zi (Han founder)	Kao Tzu
	Hong Xiu-chuan (founder of Tai Pings)	Hung Hsiu-Ch'üan
	Huang Di (Yellow Emperor)	Huang Ti
	Jiang Gai-shek (ruler)	Chiang Kai-shek
	Jiang Qing (Mao's widow)	Chiang Ch'ing
	Li Si (official)	Li Ssu
	Lin Zi-xu (official)	Lin Tse-hsü
	Mao Ze-dong (ruler)	Mao Tse-tung
	Ping (emperor)	P'ing
	Si-ma Qian (historian)	Ssu-ma Ch'ien
	Wu Di (emperor)	Wu Ti
	Zhang Zhi-dong (official)	Chang Chih-tung
	Zhao Kuang-yin (emperor)	Chao K'uang-yin
	Zhu Yuan-zhang (emperor)	Chu Yüan-chang
Towns and Provinces	Beijing	Peking
	Chang-an (capital)	Ch'ang-an
	Luo-yang (capital)	Lo-yang

	Pinyin System	Wade-Giles System
	Shandong province	Shantung province
	State of Lü	State of Lu
	Suzhou	Soochow
Philosophers	Dong Zhong-shu	Tung Chung-shu
	Fan Chi	Fan Ch'ih
	Fan Xu	Fan Hsü
	Guo Xiang	Kuo Hsiang
	Ju Xi	Chu Hsi
	Kong Zi or Kong fu-zi	K'ung fu-tzu
	Lao-zi	Lao-tzu or Lao-tse
	Meng-zi	Meng-tse
	Mo-zi	Mo-tzu
	Wang Bi	Wang Pi
	Xun-zi	Hsün-tzu
	Zang Shan	Tsang Shan
	Zhuang-zi	Chuang-tzu
Religious and Philosophical Terms	Dao (Way)	Tao
	Dao De Jing (*Classic of the Way and Its Power*)	*Tao Te Ching*
	de (virtue)	*te*
	he (harmony)	*ho*
	Li Ji (*Book of Rites*)	*Li Chi*
	li and *ren* (moral concepts)	*li* and *jen*
	Qi-yun (essence harmony)	*ch'i-yün*
	Tian (Heaven)	T'ien
	Wu Jing (*Five Classics*)	*Wu Ching*
	xian (immortals)	*hsien*
	xiao (filial piety)	*hsiao*
	yi (painting style)	*i*
	Yi Jing (*Book of Changes*)	*I Ching*
	yong (function)	*yung*
	you (being)	*yu*
	Yue Ling (*Monthly Ordinances*)	*Yüeh Ling*
	zhong (mean or center)	*chung*
	zhun-zi (superior man)	*chün-tzu*
	zi-qiang (self-strengthening)	*tzu ch'iang*
	zi-ran (naturalness)	*tzu-jan*
Artists	Tang Yin	T'ang Yin
	Shen Zhou	Shen Chou

"road," "path," or "way." The various religions and their schools all have differing ideas about how the Dao is conceived, known, and followed.

To the Confucians, the Dao was relatively clear and knowable and was described in the ancient texts in detailed accounts of social and ritual behavior, as well as in records of natural laws and events. This may explain the Confucians' emphasis on scholarship and learning as an indispensable means of knowing the Dao.

The Taoists saw the Dao as essentially mysterious, something best approached in simplicity and "naturalness." Followers of Taoism were suspicious of all rules, and although many of them eventually became devoted to their own forms of temple worship and private ritual, the more radical wing leaned toward more solitary pursuits as hermits and mystics.

Even Buddhism, which was introduced into China about the beginning of the Christian era, quickly adopted the term *Dao* in an effort to translate Buddhist insights into concepts intelligible to the Chinese. At an early date the Buddhists experimented with Sanskrit terms equivalent to the Dao, among which was the key idea of *Dharma*, or cosmic law. Eventually, however, the Buddhists settled on a more mysterious usage of the term Dao for the cosmic process observed with dispassionate detachment at the moment of enlightenment. The Chinese Buddhist school known as Chan (in Japanese, Zen) used for this experience an expression that means "not obstructing the Dao."

THE GOAL OF HARMONY

Harmony was the primary goal of all Chinese religious activity, though it was called by many different names and attained by many different methods. The Confucian term for harmony is *he*, which was established for the Confucian tradition in a famous passage from the *Zhong Yong* (Doctrine of the mean):

> Before the feelings of pleasure, anger, sorrow, and joy are established, there is equilibrium [*zhong:* the mean, the center]. The establishment of these feelings in proper measure of each and proper rhythm for all is called harmony [*he*]. This equilibrium is the great source of the world; this harmony is the world's universal Way [*Dao*]. With the full attainment of equilibrium and harmony comes the proper ordering of heaven and earth and the nourishment of all things.[1]

In this passage the term translated as equilibrium points to the original, true, and essential nature of things, which is here especially regarded as the essential nature of humanity and, as such, is intrinsic and potential. When human beings become active in the world and begin to act like moral beings, they are acting properly and according to their essential natures.

To describe the situation most generally, we can say that the goal of harmony has traditionally been viewed in China in two ways, each of which rests on a different conception of the powers and forces surrounding human life on which an orderly and livable world depends.

The personal view is probably the older tradition. It has persisted mainly at the folk level of society and culture and has also been most readily accepted in the religious rituals dominated by prayer and worship and in the family cult of ancestor reverence. Briefly, the personal view of religious or sacred power perceives the world as populated by personal spirits, and thus regards all things as having particular spirits attached to them. For example, human beings have souls that think, feel, and motivate them. Similarly, all things have such "souls" or spirits. This means that all things have feelings and motivations much like those of human beings. Therefore, the proper harmony with such spirits requires treating them like human beings—sometimes with flattery, sometimes with gifts such as sacrificial offerings, and occasionally with punishments—but always with respect and care.

In the ancestor cult of the family, the tablets of deceased members were kept in a special ancestral hall or alcove. Honorific names were written on each tablet, and a history was kept of the deeds of each ancestor who had brought honor to the family name. Important family events and activities were announced to the ancestors as if they were still liv-

The emperor's dragon throne was located in the Hall of Supreme Harmony, whose name suggests that attaining harmony was central to Chinese worship. *Sekai Bunka Photo.*

ing and present, and the Confucian admonition to the filial son was that he should treat his deceased parents "as if they were still living." This strong sense of living in a large, powerful, and mostly benevolent family group undoubtedly was what gave traditional Chinese their sense of comfort and well-being, and also their fear of shame and of bringing dishonor to their illustrious lineage.

The impersonal view of harmony, in contrast, regarded humanity as surrounded by numerous powers and forces, but it saw them as essentially impersonal. This view came closer to the modern scientific world view in that it perceived nature as operating according to fixed interrelationships, or natural laws. To survive, one had to be aware of the nature, potential hazards, and potential benefits each thing had and represented. One had to read the signs of coming events in somewhat the same way that scientists attempt to discover the causes of a phenomenon; but one did not talk to the powers of the world or expect them to understand one's own needs or values. This view drew a sharp line between human beings and nature, or between human society and the rest of the world. Instead of attempting to please the personal spirits, the believers in this view attempted to discover the laws of change and to analyze the forces that precipitated change in the world—to harmonize natures rather than wills.

This impersonal view was accepted by many Confucian philosophers and can be discerned in the recorded sayings of Confucius himself and particularly in the concept of Heaven as an impersonal force. The most obvious impersonalist idea in China was that of the Dao—that is, the proper Way of moral human actions that led to harmony. The Dao also determined the inevitable course of the natural world and of history.

The Shang and Western Zhou Dynasties

The first recognizable state in China, the Shang dynasty, began in about 1600 B.C. and continued until 1122 B.C. It was located in north central China, about five hundred miles southwest of the present city of Beijing. The Shang people were settled agriculturalists who were unique among the groups then living in East Asia, for three reasons: (1) They possessed a written language, which was clearly the prototype of the present-day Chinese script.

(2) They were highly skilled in the art of working metal and thus were the first people of East Asia to emerge from the Stone Age. (3) They dwelt in large fortified towns.

The Shang were highly stratified socially. The ruling classes were mainly warriors, who were probably the descendants of a once distinct group that had conquered an agricultural people. The main source of wealth in Shang China was grain crops, especially wheat and millet. The aristocrats, however, spent most of their time making war, hunting, and cultivating the arts.

ANIMAL SYMBOLISM AND SACRIFICES

The two most important Shang religious practices were concerned with bountiful harvests and devotion to ancestors. The agricultural rites and attitudes, as well as those of their Neolithic predecessors, assumed continuity. As is common among preliterate agricultural peoples everywhere, animal symbolism predominated, and sacrifices were the chief means by which the people sought to influence the powers controlling the earth's bounty. The most frequently sacrificed animal was the ox, although swine and goats also were used. Dragon and serpent designs—the symbols of abundant rainfall, abundant harvests, and the mysterious life-giving power of the earth—have been found on the surviving pre-Shang pottery.

What might be termed existential concerns—that is, concern about the survival of human groups, seems to have been uppermost in the religious practices of the common people. Their rites showed that human life patterns and plant life patterns were perceived as bound together. Human beings and plants were seen as participating in the same cosmic process of seed time, growth, and harvest. The final step in this recurring cycle was the return to the earth in order to make way for the next generation.

AGRICULTURE AND ANCESTOR REVERENCE

Besides the regularly recurring religious rites, many attempts were made to communicate with the spirits. One of the methods of divination used by the early Chinese consisted of writing down questions on tortoise shells or animal bones, which were then heated so that they would crack. The patterns of the cracks were then interpreted as answers to the questions. Although divination was the special prerogative of the aristocrats, many questions found on surviving shells and bones revealed a perhaps more mundane anxiety about a coming harvest, hope of rain or snow, or a desire for an increase in the human or animal population.

The other most significant religious concern pertained to the ancestors. Never was ancestor reverence more important to the religious life of the people than it was during the Shang. The elaborate bronze vessels of this period were used as food and drink containers and cooking pots for offerings to ancestors, and they were usually buried in richly appointed tombs for the comfort of the dead in the afterlife. The most important deity, who was called Shang-di (Supreme Ruler), was the divine ancestor of the ruling family. This royal ancestor, whose envoy was said to be the wind, was, like the king among the humans of the earth, the ruler of the spirit powers.

This pattern of ancestor reverence, familiar to students of later Chinese religious history, had already been established at this early date.

Once an ancestor died, he or she became a powerful agent who could influence the success or failure of his descendants' lives. The ancestor could reward or punish—could send bountiful harvests or famine.

The more positive side of the ancestor cult was the mutuality of the relationship. The grave furnishings and food offerings established a bond between the living and the dead. For both sides, the interruption of this contact at the moment of death was only temporary. Because the needs of the living and the dead were considered to be the same, communication between them was thought to be possible. Thus the loss felt by the living at the death of a family member was lessened. This view also helped maintain a tremendously conservative element in Chinese culture.

Bronze from the Shang and Zhou dynasties. As this set of sacrificial vessels shows, both the Shang and their successors the Zhou were expert metalworkers. *The Metropolitan Museum of Art, Munsey Bequest, 1924.*

THE EMPEROR AS THE SON OF HEAVEN

Traditional Chinese accounts place the date of the overthrow of the Shang as 1122 B.C., the year when the Zhou people under the leadership of King Wu occupied the Shang capital. The Zhou were a nonliterate farming people who had settled in the Wei River valley about three hundred miles southwest of the Shang kingdom. The Zhou had already assimilated many Shang ideas and customs, and the prestige of the Shang was still so great that their conquerors preserved much of their culture, and even adopted many Shang religious practices and laws. In fact, for eight hundred years, Zhou rulers saw to it that sacrifices to the ancestors of the deposed Shang rulers were continued. They also preserved the Shang written language, which in their hands became a vehicle for a large body of poetry, ritual, law, and wisdom.

Among the deities the Zhou brought with them were Tian (Heaven) and Hou Ji (the ruler of millet). The latter was obviously an agricultural god who controlled the fortunes of that important grain crop, and the Zhou ruling family considered themselves descendants of this deity. Tian was apparently a high god, or supreme deity, rather like the Shang Shang-di. Ultimately Tian and Shang-di were identified together in the minds of the people until the combined title *Huang-tian Shang-di* (Sovereign Heaven/Supreme Deity) became accepted. However, Tian was always more vaguely defined than Shang-di and was never identified as the ancestor of the rulers. Rather, the title for the ruler, the Son of Heaven, was understood as a term of relationship rather than of descent: The emperor reigned only because he had received the Mandate of Heaven as a reward for his virtue, not because he had been born into the position.

The ancestor veneration and agricultural rites of the Shang system were continued by the Zhou, with some modifications. As a settled agricultural people, the Zhou centered their religious and political ideas on the idea that their land was the center of the empire: here the emperor dwelled, and here the whole world had its focus. The celestial symbolism that eventually became associated with the emperor was a natural outgrowth of this attitude. The ruler was identified with the North Star, the only stationary star in the heavenly canopy constantly in motion around that fixed point.

The phoenix, tortoise, and dragon all were signs of order in the world. According to the personalist view of the world, they were sent when Heaven was pleased. "Facing south," of course, is the direction the North Star faces; we face north to see it, but it faces south toward us. The North Star is fixed and "only stands" there; yet the regular motions of the stars around it are the very model for all order and harmony.

The Wisdom Tradition: Tian, Dao, and Yin-Yang

Toward the end of the Western Zhou period, three ideas implicit in the earliest Chinese attitudes and practices were finally articulated. All three were the results of a growing tradition of religious wisdom—that is, a practical knowledge of the nature of things gained by examining their underlying causes. It was felt that beneath the surface appearance of natural and human activities there must be certain patterns and structures which, properly understood, would provide the wise with both insight into the world process and an ability to anticipate future events. All three ideas of this tradition stressed the impersonal nature of the world:

1 Tian *(Heaven) as the impersonal sacred power.* Tian was considered to be the source of the world and was a moral force that would automatically reward good and punish evil. As such Tian was usually mentioned in conjunction with the Dao, as in the expression "the Way of Heaven." In fact, for many later Confucians, Tian and Dao were often used interchangeably.

2 Dao *(the Way) as the ultimate ordering principle in the world.* The most elemental meaning of the word *dao* is a road or path. From this, it was only a short jump to using it to describe the paths of the stars through the sky and eventually the whole orderly process of change in the celestial patterns of the stars, planets, sun, and moon. Other regular patterns were associated with this meaning, notably the seasonal cycle of cold and hot, wet and dry, and growth, harvest, and dormancy. These cycles all were set down in the calendars, which were not only records of days and months, but also repositories of folk wisdom, like our almanacs. In the beginning these early calendars contained the idea of order, in which every thing and every activity had its proper time according to the season.

The ancient calendar began in our February, the month in which the onset of spring was celebrated. The emperor was directed to purify himself ritually and, together with many high officials, to "meet the spring in the eastern suburb" of the capital. The Grand Recorder, who was part astronomer, part historian, and part astrologer, was ordered to "guard the statutes and maintain the laws" and to pay careful attention to all the movements of the celestial bodies and to record them "according to the regular practice of early times." The emperor himself then was directed to pray for a good year and to plow a sacred field with his own hand in order to open the agricultural season.

3 *The interaction of* yin *and* yang *as the basis of change.* The question of why Heaven and the Dao of Heaven behaved as the calendar and other lore predicted they would led Chinese thinkers to create a theory of the structure of change—the theory of the interaction of *yin* and *yang.* Yin originally meant "covered as by clouds," hence, dark, hidden, secret, and cool; yang meant something bright and shiny, hence, light, open, and warm. These two opposites were seen as the constituents of all things, and so their relative admixture in a thing or a moment explained the events of the moment and predicted future ones. The first application probably was to the calendar itself, to the regular cycle of the seasons. Summer is bright and warm and is characterized by the active growth of plant life; winter is dark and cold and is characterized by dormancy. Eventually these ideas acquired many other meanings and served to structure all thinking. The idea of sexuality was understood from the viewpoint of yin and yang: the male is open, active, and aggressive and hence is yang; the female is hidden, passive, and yielding and hence is yin. Although sometimes yang is regarded as good and yin as bad, this is not really the case: The entire system is good because it is the Way of Heaven and thus the proper ordering of the world. True, a male-dominated society usually glorifies maleness and thus yang. In addition, most people prefer the warmth and light of summer to the cold and dark of winter. Yet those who truly understand yin and yang recommend always that both are necessary. In fact, an excess of either is considered bad.

All three ideas were clearly set forth in the classical Chinese divination text known as the *Yi Jing**

**I Ching* in the Wade-Giles system.

The yin-yang symbol. According to Chinese thinkers, change results from the interaction of these two opposing forces.

(Book of Changes). The most obvious was the theory of yin and yang, since it was the basis of the sixty-four hexagrams that make up the text. For example, Qian, the first hexagram, is composed entirely of unbroken, or yang, lines and stands for Heaven, the male and active principle; Kun, the second hexagram, is composed of broken, or yin, lines and stands for earth, the female and passive principle. An early commentary appended to the *Yi Jing* reads: "Exalted indeed is the sublime Passive Principle: Gladly it receives the celestial force [of yang] into itself, wherefrom all things receive their birth." A later Zhou commentary adds: "The Passive Principle, thanks to its exceeding softness, can act with tremendous power."[2] The Taoists, following the lead of the philosopher Lao-zi, stressed the power and virtue of acting according to yin.

The Eastern Zhou Dynasty

In 770 B.C., the emperor Ping ascended the throne. He described his feelings of dismay over the internal and external threats to his reign in these words:

> Oh! An object of pity am I, who am but as a Little Child. Just as I have succeeded to the throne, Heaven has severely chastised me. Through the interruption of the royal bounties that ceased to descend to the inferior people, the invading barbarous tribes of the west have greatly injured our kingdom. Moreover, among the managers of my affairs there are none of age and experience and distinguished ability in their offices. I am thus unequal to the difficulties of my position.[3]

The following year an army composed of non-Chinese soldiers and forces led by Zhou dissidents sacked the capital, killing the emperor and thus ending the power of the central government. This event shook the Chinese world to its foundations. But a remnant of the royal family managed to escape to the east where it established the feudal state of Lü, which became the seat of the Eastern Zhou dynasty. From the new capital at Luo-yang, in present-day Shandong (Shantung) province, the Eastern Zhou ruled for five hundred years over one of the richest and most populous areas of China.

Under the Eastern Zhou, China was divided into a number of independent states. Because of the ruthless politics and expansionist policies of most of these states, it was a time of almost constant warfare, which Chinese historians traditionally have called the Period of the Warring States.

THE AGE OF THE HUNDRED PHILOSOPHERS

The political and economic disruption of the Chinese world at that time caused thoughtful individuals to consider the meaning of human existence in a new way. This, in turn, led to a cultural crisis that resulted, during the sixth century B.C., in the age of the hundred philosophers, one of the most fruitful periods of speculative thought in all human history. A talented group of scholars and teachers began to ask questions not only about the reasons for human behavior, but also about its content. The answers to these questions tended to be both conservative and optimistic. Although many of the philosophers advanced radical new theories, the Confucian tradition that came to dominate the nation's thinking saw its tasks as making tradition more self-conscious and maintaining continuity with the past. The Chinese looked to the past for lessons on how to act responsibly. The Confucian philosophers tried to clarify and simplify these insights so that they might be more systematically and appropriately applied to everyday problems. And far from rejecting custom, they sought the wisdom hidden in it.

Confucius: The Ritualization of Life

During this period of strife and high culture, the great moral philosopher and teacher Kong Zi was born. His name has been Latinized in the West as Confucius (551–479 B.C.). According to tradition, Confucius came from an impoverished family of the lower nobility. He became a minor government bureaucrat, but possibly because of his reputation for speaking his mind, he was never given a position of high office or responsibility. He continued to criticize government policies and made a modest living as the respected teacher of many young men. In his later years he is said to have devoted himself to editing the classical books of history now known as the *Wu Jing* (Five Classics).

For the past two millennia, the teachings of Confucius have had a great influence on the thought, government institutions, literature, arts, and social customs of China. Confucianism has also been influential in Japan, Korea, and Vietnam. It is considered by many as principally a social and moral philosophy, yet as practiced by the Chinese *literati,* or the educated upper classes, Confucianism had definite religious dimensions.

LI AND SOCIAL ORDER

Confucius saw the answer to contemporary problems in the ritualization of life, which was found in the practice of *li.* Li was the most important term in Confucius's thought. It encompassed a number of ideas conveyed in English by separate words, such as *ritual, custom, propriety,* and *manners.* That li was applied to so many human activities is itself significant, because li was thought to be the means by which life should be regulated. A person of li thus was a good person; a state ordered by li was a harmonious and peaceful state.

The oldest meaning of li referred to the sacred rites of sacrifice, the heart of early Chinese religious practice. Indeed, for the early Chinese the term li was nearly synonymous with religion. Confucius took this core idea—that of activity specifically pertaining to sacred things—and enlarged it so that all activities could be viewed as sacred. On one hand, this meant that every act was conducted with the sense of mystery and seriousness hitherto reserved for sacrificial rites. On the other hand, it also meant that the *sacrificial* rites themselves were judged by Confucian society as relatively less important to religion. As Confucius himself put it, "Devote yourself earnestly to the duties due to men, and respect spiritual beings but keep them at a distance."[4] This distancing of spiritual beings, which included the ancestors, was both a sign of respect for their power and a refocusing of religious concern on human affairs. Confucius and his followers continued to perform the ancient sacrifices, but their main goal was to make the attitudes appropriate to sacrificial rites pervade all the affairs of life. For this, li was essential.

The first step in the Confucian program to establish the proper order of things (Dao) among human beings was to reform government. Confucius himself did briefly hold a position in the administration of his native state of Lü. His pupils, however, were much more successful as office seekers, and much of the discussion between master and pupil recorded in the *Lun Yu* (the *Analects;* a collection of Confucius's sayings and brief dialogues) pertained to the proper conduct of state affairs. By the time of the reunification of China in the Han period, Confucian scholars dominated the bureaucracy that ran the imperial government.

Far from favoring an egalitarian and democratic ideal, the assumed direction of influence in the Confucian view of the state was from the top down—that is, from the head of government—the prince, king, or emperor—down to the common people. Confucius believed that if the leaders could be changed, then the people would change also. The *Analects* put it this way:

> Lead the people with legal measures and regulate them by punishment, and they will avoid wrongdoing but will have no sense of honor and shame. Lead them with the power of virtuous example (*de*) and regulate them by the rules of *li,* and they will have a sense of shame and will thus rectify themselves.[5]

In the phrase "regulate them by the rules of *li,*" the term translated rather abstractly as "to regulate" had a very revealing concrete and primitive meaning of kernels of wheat filling the ear evenly. This simple yet powerful image conveyed the Confucian emphasis on order in a single economical idea: The kernels regularly and predictably filling their assigned space in an assigned pattern, over and over, conveyed both regularity, predictability, and continuity, the cornerstones of order, as well as a sense of fitness, of each thing filling its proper place. The goodness and abundance of this order was also found in the image of a good harvest.

To act according to li was to do what was right in the proper manner at the proper time; that is, to follow the Dao. This exemplification of the Dao could not help but be imitated by the people. Coercion, therefore, not only was unnecessary, but also indicated a falling away from the Dao. What replaced coercion was not an arbitrary freedom, but a voluntary participation in the rhythm of li.

The use to which Confucius sought to put li might be called a form of social engineering. It was to create an environment in which people would naturally be good, as an unavoidable consequence of the shaping power of li, just as water conforms to its container. So important was the process of shaping that Confucius saw it as the one necessary condition of civilization. A land whose people acted according to li was a civilized country; those whose people did not follow li were not civilized, and their people were not fully human in the sense that they had no means of realizing their potential as human beings.

REN AND HUMANENESS

Truly human persons were people of *ren,* that is, humanity or humaneness. To embody this quality of humaneness was the goal of Confucius's followers. But ren was more than humanity in the external sense, for it was the measure of individual character and, as such, was the goal of self-cultivation. Self-cultivation could be attained just by conforming to li, and so ren might to some extent have been understood as the ideal individual result of acting according to li. Li and ren thus were two sides of the same thing. But when Confucius spoke of ren, he emphasized in the following question the individual effort required in the proper performance of li: "If a man is not humane (*jen*)*, what has he to do with ceremonies (*li*)?"[6] This individual effort was thought of as self-control or self-mastery. As Confucius said, "To master (or control) the self and return to *li,* that is humanity (*jen*)."[7]

The psychological aspects of this doctrine, which later became important in China because of the impact of a powerful introspective Buddhist movement, were never fully resolved by the Confucians themselves. Some thought of the road to ren as the control of individual impulses and desires, an effort of the will aided by social pressure. This tended to make Confucianism a rather rigid set of uniform social rules. But others, notably the Neo-Confucian schools of thought that developed much later, saw ren as a quality of an individual's inner being: The self had been mastered in the sense that it had been transformed under the impact of li. A famous autobiographical statement by Confucius in the *Analects* supports this later view:

> At fifteen, my mind sought learning. At thirty, my character was firmly set. At forty, my doubts were at an end. At fifty, I knew the will of Heaven. At sixty, I could hear the truth with equanimity. At seventy, I unerringly desired what was right.[8]

THE CONFUCIAN SAGE AND THE GLORIFICATION OF THE PAST

Confucius did not see himself as an innovator, though in many respects his view and values were quite new. As we have seen, his view of li as an all-encompassing style of life was a radical reinterpretation. Then, too, he struggled against the entrenched power of hereditary privilege, with its tendency toward whim and selfishness, especially in the conduct of government. The strongest weapon Confucius wielded against the status quo of his day was the claim that he was trying to return to the original way of doing things. By this means he further glorified the past at the expense

**Jen* is the Wade-Giles form for *ren.*

of the present and set in motion the reform movement known as Confucianism.

The uses made of the past are best seen in the Confucian idea of the *sage* and in its emphasis on learning or scholarship. The sages, or holy men who embodied perfect wisdom, were, even to Confucius, rather remote figures. These were perfect beings who had possessed powers of knowledge, insight, and virtue far beyond those that could be aspired to by living human beings. The four sages mentioned in the Analects—Yao and Shun, legendary kings; Yu the Great, an agricultural deity/engineer of irrigation works; and the Duke of Zhou, brother of the founder of the dynasty—were divine culture heroes. They were givers of special gifts to humanity, originators of techniques that ordinary people still crudely imitated. Yao and Shun were the models for the perfect emperor. The Duke of Zhou was especially revered by Confucius because he was the ideal of the scholar-administrator Confucius himself aspired to become.

The most important quality the sages exhibited was *de* (virtue), best understood as a sacred power inherent in the very presence of the sage. It had the power by itself to change the course of history, to bring about the eagerly sought harmony. The sage-kings ruled by "inactivity." Later generations developed this idea by making the sage more nearly an ideal to which human beings might aspire here and now.

For Confucius, however, the sage was the inspiration for proper conduct and the model of behavior, and for this reason he stressed scholarship and learning, since one had to study the ancient books in order to discover and understand the Way of the great sages of antiquity: "Most exalted is [the sage] who is born with knowledge; but next is the man who learns through study."[9] It was this more modest goal to which Confucius aspired and to which he urged his disciples.

THE IDEAL MAN

The ideal man in Confucius's thought was called *zhun-zi,* usually translated now as "superior man" or "true gentleman." In his time this term meant simply a nobleman in the sense of one born to a position of wealth and privilege. Confucius changed the meaning of the term from a person honored for an accident of birth to one honored for the rewards of personal effort, of individual merit. What mattered was character, not background. To build character meant to study the Way of the ancients and to learn and scrupulously follow li.

Confucius's superior man was similar in many ways to the gentleman of Victorian England. He was cultured and reserved. He was expected to exhibit a thorough knowledge of manners (li) and to care more for his own integrity and inner development than for wealth. Specifically, the superior man had the following qualities:

1 *He was above egoism.* He looked within himself, and if all were well there, he did not worry about his relations with others. He served the common good, which was the reason he sought office.

2 *He was not narrow.* The superior man's function, his service in the world, was not to carry out any technical occupations or specific arts or crafts. As Confucius explained: "The superior man is not an implement."[10] His usefulness lay in the transforming power of his character. Even in his official duties as adviser or administrator, he did not argue or contend; he simply stated the truth without concern for the consequences, especially to himself. On the other hand, martyrdom was not to be sought for its own sake.

3 *Above all, he was a man of ren, or humanity.* On this personal level, ren is best rendered as "altruism," since it included empathy for all and concern for their well-being. But such altruism was not to be expressed indiscriminately; the goal was not an egalitarian society. Through the structure imposed by li, one was concerned with justice—that is, with seeing to it that all persons were treated as their station in life required: "Let the ruler *be* a ruler, the minister *be* a minister, the father *be* a father, and the son *be* a son."[11]

Lao-zi and the Beginnings of Taoism

Among the "hundred philosophers" of the Eastern Zhou period was one tradition has named Lao-zi

The *Analects* (*Lun Yu*) of Confucius

Confucius's disciples compiled many of their master's sayings and pronouncements into the *Analects**, which has been for 2,500 years one of China's most admired classics. Here are some of Confucius's observations of life and its problems:**

1.9 The philosopher Tsang† said, "Let there be a careful attention to perform the funeral rites to parents, and let them be followed when long gone with the ceremonies of sacrifice;—then the virtue of the people will resume its proper excellence."

1.11 The Master said, "While a man's father is alive, look at the bent of his will; when his father is dead, look at his conduct. If for three years he does not alter from the way of his father, he may be called filial."

2.1 The Master said, "He who exercises government by means of his virtue may be compared to the north polar star, which keeps its place and all the stars turn towards it."

3.11 Some one asked the meaning of the great sacrifice.‡ The Master said, "I do not know. He who knew its meaning would find it as easy to govern the kingdom as to look on this";—pointing to his palm.

3.17 Tsze-kung wished to do away with the offering of a sheep connected with the inauguration of the first day of each month. The Master said, "Tsze, you love the sheep; I love the ceremony."

7.33 The Master said, "The sage and the man of perfect virtue;—how dare I rank myself with them? It may simply be said of me, that I strive to become such without satiety, and teach others without weariness." Kung-hsi Hwa said, "This is just what we, the disciples, cannot imitate you in."

8.2 The Master said, "Respectfulness, without the rules of propriety, becomes laborious bustle; carefulness, without the rules of propriety, becomes timidity; boldness, without the rules of propriety, becomes insubordination; straightforwardness, without the rules of propriety, becomes rudeness."

12.4 Sze-ma Niu asked about the superior man. The Master said, "The superior man has neither anxiety nor fear. . . . When internal examination discovers nothing wrong, what is there to be anxious about, what is there to fear?"

12.13 The Master said, "In hearing litigations, I am like any other body. What is necessary, however, is to cause the people to have no litigations."

13.4 Fan Ch'ih requested to be taught husbandry. The Master said, "I am not so good for that as an old husbandman." He requested also to be taught gardening, and was answered, "I am not so good for that as an old gardener." Fan Ch'ih having gone out, the Master said, "A small man, indeed, is Fan Hsü!§ If a superior love propriety, the people will not dare not to be reverent. If he love righteousness, the people will not dare not to submit to his example. If he love good faith, the people will not dare not to be sincere. Now, when these things obtain, the people from all quarters will come to him, bearing their children on their backs;—what need has he of a knowledge of husbandry?"

*From *Lun Yu (Confucian Analects)* in *The Four Books*, trans. James Legge (New York: Paragon, 1966); originally in *The Chinese Classics*, vol. 1 (Oxford, England: Oxford University Press, 1893–1895). Pagination varies in the numerous reprints.

†Tsang is Zang Shan, one of Confucius's most important disciples, especially noted for his filial piety.

‡The great sacrifice was the sacrifice that the king or prince made to his remotest ancestor, and it was therefore of great importance.

§Fan Hsü is another name for Fan Ch'ih.

(in the Wade-Giles system, Lao-tzu), the "old philosopher." According to the legend, Lao-zi was the founder of Taoism and an elder contemporary of Confucius, who once consulted with him. Only one book is attributed to Lao-zi, a short work of philosophical poetry, the *Dao De Jing* (Classic of the Way and Its Power). Scholars today believe this book was probably compiled in the third century B.C. It has had great influence on Chinese thought, since it has functioned, both in the past and in the present, as a counter to the Confucian approach to life. Whereas Confucius stressed conformity and reason in solving human problems, Lao-zi stressed the individual and the need for human beings to conform to nature rather than to society.

A UNIQUE VIEWPOINT

Lao-zi opposed Confucius's view regarding fundamental issues in three important ways, and as a result Chinese thought and practice have continued to move between his and Confucius's views for more than two millennia. Lao-zi was, first of all, far more pessimistic than Confucius was about what can be accomplished in the world by human action. Much of the Confucian program he considered wrongheaded or even dangerous. Second, Lao-zi counseled a far more passive approach to the world and one's fellows: One must be cautious and let things speak for themselves. Finally, Lao-zi put the individual at the center. This meant that the Confucian concept of li, the intricate network of interconnected human ritual activities, was rejected in favor of a much more direct relationship between the individual self and the Dao.

In general, for Lao-zi existence was much more mysterious than it was for Confucius. Again and again, the *Dao De Jing* sounds the theme of the unknowableness of ultimate reality:

The Tao that can be told of is not the eternal Tao;
The name that can be named is not the eternal name.
The origin of heaven and earth is nameless;
But it may be referred to as
the Mother of all things.[12]

The mysteriousness of the Dao and the necessity of keeping the Dao as undifferentiated as possible drove Lao-zi to take a fundamentally mystical position. The Dao was thought of as far beyond any human ability to conceptualize it. It could not be thought or spoken; it could not be grasped or controlled, and no one could claim to have exclusive rights to it or power over it. Nonetheless, this Dao was present in the world and active in it, and for this reason human beings could experience it and ultimately learn to yield to it.

Those who were perfectly attuned to this Dao were the great sages of Taoism, the ones whose mystical experiences allowed them to transcend the ordinary world of human beings. And it was only in this ordinary world that there were rules for people to follow and concepts—names of things—to learn and act upon. True knowledge was possible, but it was a knowledge without words or concepts and hence was a kind of knowing very different from that of the ordinary world:

He who knows does not speak;
He who speaks does not know.[13]

One result of this mystical structure, and one that gives the *Dao De Jing* its unique poetic tone, is its reliance on paradoxical language and imagery. Paradox is endemic to mystical writings, since language is forged for use in the ordinary world. Its use to describe ultimate truths exposes its inadequacy as a vehicle, as in the formula "*x* is not *x*." In chapter sixty-four of the *Dao De Jing*, Lao-zi discusses the sage, using this formula three times: the sage desires to be without desires; he learns to be without learning; he acts without action. In this way the mysterious nature of the sage is conveyed, for the sage is one who truly "knows" the unknowable—that is, the Dao.

A more subtle form of paradox in Lao-zi's mystical philosophy is found in his extensive use of imagery. The basic lesson here is that the truth, like the Dao, is hidden and unexpected. Even in the ordinary world the wise can see that it is really weakness that eventually triumphs. Only fools seek power, and the greatest fools seek it through force. For Lao-zi, the lesson inherent in the nature of water disclosed this secret:

Incense burner from the Song dynasty, A.D. 960–1280. This bronze piece depicts Lao-zi on the back of a water buffalo. *Worcester Art Museum.*

There is nothing softer and weaker than water,
And yet there is nothing better for attacking hard and strong things.[14]

Other images include the infant, who is totally ignorant, yet unsullied by the world; and the uncarved block of wood, which is just what it is without pretentions.

NATURALNESS

The key term for understanding Lao-zi's philosophy is naturalness (*zi-ran*). In its importance and to some extent in its function, naturalness was to Lao-zi what li was to Confucius.

The natural world is in important ways the opposite of the ordinary world of human beings. Much of what we term culture is unnatural; that is, it is made by human beings. This artificiality was, for Lao-zi, the source of evil. When humans begin to think, they also begin to scheme and calculate for selfish ends. Because they do not know what is truly good—namely, the Dao—they make false distinctions between good and evil that merely serve their own petty and greedy ends. Indeed, the very doctrine of virtue is itself the result of losing the Dao, since the true sage has no need of doctrines, concepts, or self-conscious concern for virtue; he simply lives it.

Human beings living in the world of culture seek power and self-aggrandizement. Worse, once they are trapped in this unnatural world, even the best of intentions can lead only to more suffering, simply because their world is not the proper reflection of the Dao. In chapter eighty, Lao-zi outlines his vision of a utopian state in which people will be few in number and too content to be curious about their neighbors. Their disdain for human culture will lead them to ignore the use of its utensils, and their love of simplicity will cause them to give up even the use of writing.

On the personal level, naturalness means self-forgetfulness. This is the way of the sage. The sage employs naturalness not only because it places him beyond the world of culture, but also because it is the means by which the experience of the Dao can be attained. Indeed, the Dao itself is selfless and impersonal:

Heaven and earth are not humane (jen);
To them all things are straw dogs.
The Sage is not humane (jen);
To him all people are straw dogs.[*15]

Thus the Way of things is like the Way of human beings; it does not adjust to human needs and desires. Rather, the wise have to adjust to it, and in doing so, they have to shed that most human property of all, the sense of self, or ego. The sage therefore has no personal interests (chapter seven) and is impartial (chapter sixteen); he is without fixed, personal ideas (chapter forty-nine): "it is impossible either to benefit him or to harm him."[16] Since the sage has divested himself of culture, he acts only according to the Dao, that is, naturally or spontaneously.

Lao-zi makes much the same point by distinguishing between *wei* (action) and *wu-wei* (nonaction). Wei is willful, selfish action and is always harmful because it is action not in harmony with the Dao. Proper action is paradoxically called nonaction (wu-wei) because the sage in his actions merely reflects the Dao: *he* does not act; he *acts.*

THE RETURN TO ORIGINS

"Reversal is the movement of the Tao." So begins chapter forty of the *Dao De Jing.* This theme of reversal was prominent both in the *Dao De Jing* and in subsequent, more popular Taoist practices. Most obviously, this means that the true nature of Dao is the opposite of the foolish, ordinary conception of it; and this is because the Dao is paradoxical: to be weak is to be truly strong. On a deeper level this reversal points to the nature of the Dao itself as the origin of things or, as Lao-zi put it, the Mother of all things. The wise person will endeavor to return to the original source of strength in order to be nourished anew, as if again an infant.

This motif is familiar to most students of religion, since many traditions share it. The mysterious and sacred power of origins seems to be at the heart of much ritual activity, inasmuch as rituals tend to reenact events of earlier times in which the vitality of the world was greater. Divine powers create the rituals and originally performed the deeds the rituals reenact. Thus the rituals make the world and the performers new again. This revitalization is what Lao-zi sought in the approach to and experience of the Dao:

He who fully embodies the Power of Tao (te*)
Is comparable to an infant. . . .
His bones are weak, his muscles tender; yet his grasp is firm.
He does not yet know the union of male and female,
But his organ is aroused.
His vital essence is at its height! . . .
His harmony is perfect indeed![17]

The power of the infant, and thus of the Dao itself, is to be found in its quality of not-yet, its potentiality. Just as the Dao was perfect and complete in itself before the world came to be, so the wise will seek to be in their religious lives. What is potential has power because it retains the energy of creation, just as the mother possesses the mysterious power of creation before the infant is conceived. Because such power has not yet been used, it is at its maximum. And the Dao is an infinite power: It is "something undifferentiated and yet complete" which, because "soundless and formless," "depends on nothing and does not change."[18] "To be empty is to be full" (chapter twenty-two); that is, to be incomplete is to have the infinite power to become anything.

Finally, Lao-zi, like Confucius, sought harmony as the highest goal of religious activity. But his view of nature and of the value of naturalness made his route to harmony very different from that envisioned by Confucius. Virtue (de) became a mysterious power of the Dao itself rather than a social

*The traditional interpretation of *straw dogs* is that they are straw figures used in sacrifices instead of living victims. Hence there is no point in feeling compassion for inanimate objects.

*In the Pinyin system *te* is *de.*

program flowing out of the cultivation of character. For Lao-zi, the wise turned inward, not outward, to find the Dao, and there they nourished the original state of things in their maximum potency. Only when this way of life became general would the world achieve what it was looking for—that is, harmony:

Virtue becomes deep and far-reaching
And with it all things return to their original natural state.
Then complete harmony will be reached.[19]

The Confucian and Taoist Traditions

MENCIUS, DISCIPLE OF CONFUCIUS

Progress toward the peaceful and harmonious way of life advocated by both Confucius and Lao-zi was slow in the fragmented China of that period. The Confucian scholar Meng-zi, whose name has been Latinized in the West as Mencius (ca. 372–289 B.C.), led a life very much like that of his great teacher. According to tradition, he briefly held a minor government post but did not have much influence in official circles. Mencius constantly urged the rulers of several petty states to adopt Confucian principles, but his advice apparently went unheeded. Mencius taught that it was the duty of rulers to promote their subjects' happiness. Kings whose conduct was good would enjoy the Mandate of Heaven. Those who followed evil ways, however, would lose Heaven's protection, and their subjects would have the right to depose them.

Mencius venerated Confucius, and at one point he is said to have exclaimed: "There never has been another Confucius since man first appeared on earth."[20] Again, he classed his master with the best of the ancient sages: "Confucius alone was the one among the Sages with a sense of the appropriateness of the occasion. In Confucius we have what we would call the quintessence of harmony."[21]

Like all disciples who are remembered by subsequent generations, Mencius not only accepted his master's teachings and example, but also amplified and added to them. Yet although he agreed with the whole program of li, Mencius concentrated on a more narrowly conceived ethic. He was also much more of a theoretical psychologist than Confucius. Mencius was concerned with the essential nature of humanity, with righteousness, and with the plight of ordinary people.

Mencius's effort to delineate human nature seems at first to have led him to a conclusion even more optimistic than that of his master: Humanity was essentially and originally good, and all else followed naturally from this inborn tendency. The kernel of this goodness was the quality of ren, which needed only to be nurtured, rather than established by the mastery and control emphasized in the *Analects*. Ren was seen by Mencius more as love, in the sense of familial affection, and needed only to be tempered by righteousness for a man to become a sage in the personal realm or to build the ideal society in the public realm.

There is a hint here of Lao-zi's doctrine of the importance of origins, coupled with the enduring Confucian concern for human affairs (the arena of righteousness). Also, rather like Lao-zi, Mencius believed that all people could become sages if they applied themselves to the task of nurturing their own best impulses.

Mencius adopted what might be called an organic metaphor to explain his psychology:

> Bull Mountain was once beautifully wooded. But, because it was close to a large city, its trees all fell to the axe. What of its beauty then? However, as the days passed things grew, and with the rains and the dews it was not without greenery. Then came the cattle and goats to graze. That is why, today, it has that scoured-like appearance. On seeing it now, people imagine that nothing ever grew there. But this is surely not the true nature of the mountain? And so, too, with human beings. Can it be that any man's mind naturally lacks Humanity [*ren*] and Justice? If he loses his sense of the good, then he loses it as the mountain lost its trees. It has been hacked away at—day after day—what of its beauty then?
>
> However, as the days pass he grows, and, as with all men, in the still air of the early hours his sense of right and wrong is at work. If it is barely perceptible, it is because his actions during the day have disturbed or destroyed it.[22]

Like the trees, the true nature of human beings must be allowed to grow. The soil out of which ren grows is "a feeling common to all mankind that they cannot bear to see others suffer."[23] On this precept, Mencius's ethic and political thought were based. For when this inborn trait came to fruition, especially in the mind of the sage, it became the guiding principle by which the empire was governed and all human interaction regulated.

XUN-ZI AND THE SCHOOL OF LAW

Mencius's idealistic and optimistic assessment of human nature was repudiated by another important Confucian teacher, Xun-zi (ca. 300–238 B.C.) who, like Mencius, was for a time a member of the philosophical academy in the state of Qin. Xun-zi believed human beings were basically inclined toward evil, although like all Confucians he strongly advocated the doctrine of human perfectibility. But because the state believed that strict laws and punishments were needed to control people and to maintain order, Xun-zi reinterpreted the doctrine of li as a control function of the state. As a political philosopher, Xun-zi was pragmatic; he saw the impersonal, naturalistic side of the world as paramount. As a religious teacher, he believed in the power of a strict and disciplined system of li to transform those who applied themselves so that their natural evil inclinations could be overcome.

Although more influential in his own time than Mencius, after the Han period Xun-zi was nearly forgotten. This can be explained partly by the very success of many of his ideas of statecraft, which bore a close resemblance to those advocated by the Fa-jia, the School of Law or the Legalists. The probable founder of this school, Shang Yang, who died about 338 B.C., became a powerful adviser to the king of the state of Qin. Qin had become a Legalist state perhaps because of its position on the periphery, where the cultural traditions identified by the Confucians as li were less strong.

Under the Legalist policy, all subjects were forced to work hard and to share mutual responsibility for law enforcement. A person who knew of a crime and failed to report it might receive the same punishment as the criminal did. This authoritarian concept of government, which resembled the totalitarian regimes of the twentieth century, contributed substantially to the expansion of Qin. As we will see in the next chapter, the rulers of Qin eventually absorbed through conquest all the remaining Chinese states and created the first Chinese empire.

MOISM, THE RELIGION OF MO-ZI (ca. 471–391 B.C.)

A near contemporary of Confucius, Mo-zi (whose name in the Wade-Giles system is spelled Mo-tzu), remains an enigmatic figure in the religious history of China. Little is known about him except that he founded the movement that bears his name. But the mystery is not due merely to a lack of information. The movement Mo-zi founded seems so diametrically opposite to Confucianism, and indeed to the very cultural and religious patterns distinctive to China, that its very existence and power in Zhou times seem impossible to understand.

Moism is perhaps best understood as a movement of the upper strata of the peasant and working classes. It drew on what later became elements of folk and popular religion, especially by insisting that Tian (Heaven) was a personal deity who watched over the affairs of human beings and meted out rewards and punishments through lesser spiritual beings whose shrines and altars dotted the Chinese landscape. Mo-zi's curious acceptance of a heavenly hierarchy, coupled with his adamant rejection of an earthly hierarchy, appealed to those with little social prestige, worldly power, and wealth.

The most strikingly un-Confucian doctrine of this stemmed from their rejection of elitist values and their assertion of the doctrine of universal love. The only law that was to govern human interaction was universal altruism. People were to treat other people as they would treat themselves, and they were to cherish other families and other states as if they were their own. Their reward would be prosperity and peace, for Heaven would enrich those who practiced this way of life. Thus the system of

Moism might be described as one of enlightened self-interest, presided over by a stern but benevolent god, as this statement from a surviving work of Mo-zi indicates:

How do we know that Heaven wants righteousness and dislikes unrighteousness? I say: With righteousness the world lives and without righteousness the world dies, with it the world becomes rich and without it the world becomes poor, with it the world becomes orderly and without it the world becomes chaotic.[24]

In its emphasis on compassion and altruistic love, Moism resembles the teaching of Jesus, especially the Sermon on the Mount. But perhaps because Mo-zi's teaching was incompatible with the Chinese spirit or because it failed to capture any enduring allegiance among the educated and powerful, Moism ceased to exist by the close of the Zhou period.

ZHUANG-ZI AND RADICAL TAOISM

Tradition ascribes to Zhuang-zi (ca. 369–286 B.C.) the book that bears his name, although it is clearly the work of several hands. In the core of this work, a number of brilliant and original essays show him to have carried on the tradition of Lao-zi, though he did not share his teacher's concern for good government and a utopian society. Instead, he was a complete mystic who was intoxicated with the Dao. His wild flights of fancy and utter disregard for custom have both fascinated and repulsed the Chinese to the present day. He was a poet, and quite unlike Lao-zi, he was also an accomplished philosopher. Zhuang-zi used reason and logic against each other. He made fun of Confucius's rational conceptual framework, and Confucius often appeared as an ironic figure in Zhuang-zi's works, uttering outrageously un-Confucian statements. Zhuang-zi was far more interested in the practical consequences of living the Taoist life than Lao-zi. Zhuang-zi often described everyday events to illustrate his points, and his favorite literary form was the parable. A famous example in section nineteen of the *Zhuang-zi*, entitled "Mastering Life," tells the story of a carpenter named Qing who won praise for making a bell stand so perfect that it seemed fashioned by supernatural power. Qing denied any real artistry and apologized for his technique:

When I am going to make a bell stand, I never let it wear out my energy. I always fast in order to still my mind. When I have fasted for three days, I no longer have any thought of congratulations or rewards, of titles or stipends. When I have fasted for five days, I no longer have any thought of praise or blame, of skill or clumsiness. And when I have fasted for seven days, I am so still that I forget I have four limbs and a form and body. By that time, the ruler and his court no longer exist for me. My skill is concentrated and all outside distractions fade away. After that, I go into the mountain forest and examine the Heavenly nature of the trees. If I find one of superlative form, and I can see a bell stand there, I put my hand to the job of carving; if not, I let it go. This way I am simply matching up "Heaven" with "Heaven."[25]

The exercises of nourishing one's nature, fasting, and concentrating one's attention became standard Taoist religious practices. They were intended to result in so perfect an agreement with the Dao that amazing feats of artistry could be accomplished effortlessly. Not only was this Taoist life effortless because the adept was able to act with things rather than against them; it also was effortless because the person so purified his thoughts of egocentric desires that the "desired" goal itself was abandoned, even though it was rather mysteriously accomplished all the same.

Perhaps the most striking difference between Lao-zi and Zhuang-zi was the latter's expanded and enlivened view of the Dao. Zhuang-zi did accept Lao-zi's mysterious Dao as the powerful source of all things, the intimate experience of which was the only way to the good life. Yet for Zhuang-zi, the Dao was far from quiet; in fact, the best description of his Dao would be "change." The *Yi Jing* (Book of Changes) seems to stand behind this development, but that text emphasizes the regular order of changes. Zhuang-zi still subscribed to an almost wild, capricious universe that the wise should seek less to predict than to celebrate. Followers of the Dao should not so much adjust themselves to the orderly nature of things as they should joyously ride on a cresting wave of constant transformation. As Zhuang-zi put it, the follower "chariots upon the Dao."

Another story from the *Zhuang-zi* illustrates both the nature of change and the proper attitude toward it:

> Suddenly Master Lai grew ill. Gasping and wheezing, he lay at the point of death. His wife and children gathered round in a circle and began to cry. Master Li, who had come to ask how he was, said, "Shoo! Get back! Don't disturb the process of change!"
>
> Then he leaned against the doorway and talked to Master Lai. "How marvelous the Creator is! What is he going to make out of you next? Where is he going to send you? Will he make you into a rat's liver? Will he make you into a bug's arm?"[26]

It was not so much that there was no order in the process of change; rather, Zhuang-zi's point was that the sage need not be concerned, since this would take care of itself. The sage had to learn to forget knowledge, to forget the distinctions on which the value systems of the ordinary world were based. Such persons would be not so much the innocent children Lao-zi described as those who would see all things as they really were—that is, as a part of a single organic whole and separate from the arbitrary, distinct compartments into which ordinary knowledge had divided them.

Zhuang-zi's name for this exalted state of mind was *wu-nian,* literally "no thought" or "no mind." This term was later adopted by the Buddhists, who used it to describe the state of enlightenment within the world characteristic of the Chan (Zen) school.

The sage's state of "no thought" was also one of self-forgetfulness: "I have lost myself." When the world was seen as a whole and when the distinctions among things were no longer perceived, the distinction between the self and all things also disappeared. The subjective result was a state of tranquility, of quiet delight in all things equally. The sage was unaffected by sorrow or joy, and his mind functioned like a mirror: it reflected events without holding onto them. It had a kind of joy in them, but it was a peculiarly egoless joy, a joy and acceptance of things without attachment to them. All things had become equal.

Zhuang-zi's sayings, "the Great Man has no self" and "from the point of view of the Way, things have no nobility or meanness,"[27] have served many Chinese both as words of consolation in times of adversity and as an inspiration in the pursuit of mystical experience.

Notes

1 *Chung Yung (Doctrine of the Mean),* 1:4. Translated by Alan L. Miller.

2 John Blofeld, trans. and ed., *I Ching (Book of Changes)* (New York: Dutton, 1965), pp. 90–91. (*I Ching* is *Yi Jing* in the Pinyin system.)

3 Clae Waltham, ed., *Shu Ching (Book of History),* document 28 (Chicago: Henry Regnery, 1971), pp. 238–239.

4 *Lun Yu (Confucian Analects),* 6:20, in *A Source Book in Chinese Philosophy*, trans. and comp. Wing-tsit Chan (Princeton, N. J.: Princeton University Press, 1963), p. 30.

5 *Lun Yu* 2:3. Translated by Alan L. Miller.

6 *Lun Yu* 3:3, in *A Source Book in Chinese Philosophy,* p. 24.

7 Ibid., 12:1, p. 38.

8 Ibid., 2:4, p. 22.

9 Ibid., 16:9, p. 45.

10 Wing-tsit Chan, *A Source Book in Chinese Philosophy,* 2:12, p. 24.

11 Ibid., 12:11, p. 39.

12 *Tao Te Ching,* in *A Source Book in Chinese Phi-*

losophy, chap. 1, p. 139. (*Tao Te Ching* is *Dao De Jing* in the Pinyin system.)

13 Ibid., chap. 56, p. 166.

14 Ibid., chap. 78, p. 174.

15 Ibid., chap. 5, p. 141.

16 Ibid., chap. 56, p. 167.

17 Ibid., chap. 55, p. 165.

18 Ibid., chap. 25, p. 153.

19 Ibid., chap. 65, p. 170.

20 W.A.C.H. Dobson, *Mencius* (Toronto: University of Toronto Press, 1963), p. 88.

21 Ibid., p. 163.

22 Ibid., p. 141.

23 Ibid., p. 132.

24 Wing-tsit Chan, *A Source Book in Chinese Philosophy,* p. 218.

25 Burton Watson, trans., *Chuang Tzu: Basic Writings* (New York: Columbia University Press, 1964), p. 127. (Chuang-tzu is Zhuang-zi in the Pinyin system.)

26 Ibid., p. 81.

27 Ibid., p. 100.

11 Dynastic Change and the Three Traditions

Unification under the Qin

Around the middle of the third century B.C., a disciple of Xun-zi named Li Si became the major adviser to the king of Qin. Li Si, who was a great Legalist scholar, was also one of China's most effective statesmen. With his advice the Qin ruler was able to consolidate his power over all of northern China. After the collapse of the Zhou dynasty in 221 B.C., the prince of Qin grandly assumed the title *Shi Huang-di* (first sovereign ruler/deity). He extended the Chinese Empire to the north, west, and south, even occupying Tonkin in what is now Vietnam.

To eliminate opposition to the new dynasty, the emperor, at Li Si's suggestion, ordered the destruction of all nonpractical and nontechnical books, including Confucius's sayings. Fortunately, many of the Chinese classics were hidden by scholars who admired them, and thus this precious heritage was saved for future generations.

Before the deaths of the first emperor in 210 B.C. and of Li Si in 208 B.C., the Qin dynasty introduced many changes into Chinese society. A centralized bureaucracy and the pattern of imperial rule that was to last for more than two millennia were established. Much of the Great Wall had been built to keep the barbarian nomads of Central Asia out of the settled lands of the Chinese. A vast network of canals and roads had been constructed, radiating out from the capital, and the various systems of writing had been standardized into a single, uniform system.

The Han Dynasty (202 B.C.–A.D. 220)

The ruthless and inhumane methods which had so rapidly brought the leaders of the Qin dynasty to power also led to the dynasty's destruction. Soon after the death of its founder, discontent with the harshness of the regime resulted in armed rebellion. One of the rebel leaders was a peasant who had risen to the rank of general in the Qin army. He proclaimed himself emperor of the new Han dynasty and gave himself the name of Gao-zi (High Ancestor). Moving the capital to Chang-an, Gao-zi began a reign of territorial expansion, economic prosperity, and political unity.

The Han continued the centralizing and Legalist tendencies of the Qin. Since the accent was on uniformity in politics and in culture, this was not a particularly innovative time; the stimulating and dangerous period of the hundred philosophers was over. Under the Han the Chinese had time to consolidate their past gains and to weave the complex and disparate elements of their society into a brilliant but rigid pattern. The excesses of the Qin period were discarded, but many of its best features were kept: uniform weights and measures were decreed; the standardized system of writing developed under the Qin was maintained; and paper was invented. Intellectually, too, it was a time of consolidation. Editions of the Chinese literary classics were prepared, especially those valued by the Confucians; a national bibliography was compiled; and a national university was founded. The first official historian, Si-ma Qian, was appointed.

Religious events and trends were tied to the cultural and social patterns of the period. For example, the Han saw the dramatic rise of a new social class—the literati, or scholar-officials. These were highly trained civil servants who, by virtue of their learning, took an increasingly larger responsibility for running the empire. The literati were drawn from a new kind of landowning gentry who had largely replaced the old aristocracy. Landowning gave to some of the gentry the economic base required to support the lengthy process of their education. Education at this time was the key to government service and government service became a sure avenue to social prestige.

During the centuries of Han rule, China enjoyed stability and prosperity. The armies of Wu Di and other martial emperors conquered the nomads of the Gobi (desert). The Great Wall was extended far into the Tarim Basin, and thousands of Chinese colonists moved into that area. Southern Manchuria and northern Korea were subdued. The power of the Han dynasty has been compared with that of the Roman Empire, which was reaching its apogee about this time, and in fact, the Chinese carried on a lively trade with foreign lands. The Romans, who were eager for Chinese silks and other textiles, exchanged Roman gold and silver for Chinese goods in the markets of India. In addition, much trade between China and the West moved overland along the Old Silk Road of central Asia.

In the third century A.D. both the Roman and Han empires began to crumble as a result of internal dissension and renewed attacks from the barbarian peoples living outside their borders. Although the destruction of the Roman Empire took longer to accomplish, it was more complete and permanent. But even after the deposition of the last Han ruler in A.D. 220, Chinese civilization did not disappear. For nearly four hundred years (220–589) there were civil wars and invasions. Nomadic peoples like the Turks and Huns founded petty kingdoms in the north, but refugees from northern China were able to preserve the old Confucian traditions in central and southern China. Nanjing, on the Yangzi River, became the capital of a Chinese ruler who still claimed to hold the Mandate of Heaven.

In time the non-Chinese conquerors of northern China adopted Chinese ways and were absorbed

The Great Wall of China. The many embrasures in the wall show that it was built to protect China from invaders. *Eastfoto.*

into the indigenous population. This ability of Chinese civilization to conquer its enemies by absorbing them into its culture rather than by overcoming them militarily dates from the days of the Zhou conquest over the Shang.

Many changes took place after the collapse of the central authority. The uniformity demanded by the Han gave way again to a great diversity of thought and religious practice. This, more than anything else, allowed Taoism not only to achieve a hold on the intellectuals, but also to become an organized religion in its own right, distinguishable from both the mystical leanings of the educated class and folk practices. At the same time the diversity and confusion of the period also allowed a foreign religion, Buddhism, to take root in the Chinese soil.

THE THREE TRADITIONS

The Triumph of Confucianism

Religion was intertwined with the state in two ways:

1 The education required to pass the difficult civil service examinations was overwhelmingly Confucian, consisting of the *Wu Jing* (Five Classics), which Confucius was traditionally said to have either written or edited. The Five Classics were the *Chun Jiu* (Spring and Autumn Annals), the *Yi Jing* (Book of Changes), the *Li Ji* (Book of Rites), the *Shi Jing* (*Book of Poetry*), and the *Shu Jing* (Book of History). All of these had Confucian interpretations which were more important than the literal readings of the texts. The cultured elite who held positions of power in the imperial government were therefore steeped in Confucian learning, values, and attitudes.

2 The official duties of the government administrators included the actual performance or overseeing of religious matters in the state cult. There was no independent priesthood: officeholders were expected to perform rituals on the local level as well as to assist the emperor at court.

Confucianism triumphed as the imperial ideology mainly because it provided a firm basis for cultural unity and stability without requiring the harsh methods characteristic of the Qin period. Rather, the Confucians attempted to govern themselves and their empire by means of *de* (exemplary virtue) and *li* (ritual). Their failures, which were numerous, were not so impressive as the general level of their successes; in fact, only a surprisingly small number of imperial officers (about 140,000 civil servants) were needed to administer the huge and diverse Chinese nation. Since the literati controlled the government, they were able to thwart the ambitions of would-be aristocratic or military adventurers. In addition, Confucianism gave both support and prestige to the throne by reviving court ceremonies and emphasizing the role of the emperor as a mediator between heaven and earth.

THE MING-TANG PHENOMENON

The interaction between the Confucian interest in ritual and the imperial concern in solidifying its temporal and spiritual power can be seen in the phenomenon of the Ming Tang, or calendar house. Confucians had long admired the Western Zhou period for the purity of its ritual observances. The Han scholars reconstructed an idealized building in which the Son of Heaven would imitate the path of the sun through the zodiac, and perform many of the rites intended to ensure the abundance of crops and the peace and harmony of the empire. The most impressive of the Ming Tangs actually constructed during the Han was built right into the imperial palace.

THE WORK OF DONG ZHONG-SHU

Confucians of the Han period not only contributed to ritual practices themselves, but also gave them and the imperial establishment a philosophical justification. The greatest and most representative of the Han philosophers was Dong Zhong-shu, who lived during the second century B.C. His thought combined the dominant Confucian concern for li and de with Taoist ideas and folk elements.

Dong Zhong-shu emphasized the ancient notion of yin and yang found in the *Yi Jing* (Book of Changes).

Dong Zhong-shu combined this idea of yin and yang with a theory that explained the pattern of natural and historical events as resulting from the varying dominance of one of the five elements or agents (*wu-xing*), wood, fire, earth, metal, and water. Yin and yang were still the basis of all change, but now the perceptive person could explain more complex phenomena by means of the five agents. A complex system of correspondences was developed in which various phenomena (for example, colors, tones, directions, and seasons) were explained in terms of the five agents. The basis of this system is as follows:

> Heaven has Five Agents: the first is Wood; the second, Fire; the third, Earth; the fourth, Metal; and the fifth, Water. Wood is the beginning of the cycle of the Five Agents, Water its end, and Earth is its center. Such is their natural sequence. Wood produces Fire, Fire produces Earth, Earth produces Metal, Metal produces Water, and Water produces Wood. Such is their father-and-son relationship. . . . It is the Way of Heaven that the son always serves his father. Therefore when Wood is produced, Fire should nourish it, and after Metal perishes, Water should store it. Fire enjoys Wood and nourishes it with yang, but Water overcomes Metal and buries it with yin.[1]

These correspondences were designed to explain everything, and therefore to provide a frame of meaning in which all events could be seen as part of a cosmic pattern and process. It is difficult for people today to understand such a comprehensive and unified world view and to recognize its significance to the culture and to those who lived within it. What might appear to many of us today as an impersonal and inevitable cycle of events in which the ability of individuals to aid or thwart such events was strictly limited might have seemed to the people of the Han period a comfortable and predictable world. Even disasters like wars or earthquakes made sense as parts of a well-functioning system that was, in the long run, benevolently disposed toward humanity.

Dong Zhong-shu's philosophy centered on the doctrine of the Mandate of Heaven. In his commentary on the *Chun Jiu* (Spring and Autumn Annals), this mandate was to be made known through the harmony and prosperity of a reign; the removal of the mandate would be recognized by the absence of these elements. It thus became important that the people take note of any unusual occurrences that might signal the will of Heaven. Dong Zhong-shu argued that an official means had to be provided for interpreting such events. An institution like the position of the Grand Astrologer in the imperial government was created, whose duties included watching the heavens for portents and signs, as well as the study of history as a means of systematizing the meaning of celestial observations.

Dong Zhong-shu's theory also supported the widespread belief among both the common people and the members of the upper classes in omens, portents, geomancy, and divination. At this time the *Yi Jing* found its way into official Confucianism as a practical guide to divination. Strictly, however, the *Yi Jing* is neither a Confucian nor a Taoist book; it is a complex divination manual which grew over the centuries and reached its present form at the end of the Han period. Since that time it has been admired by educated Chinese as a uniquely Chinese combination of practical wisdom and esoteric lore. Its religious significance is clearly indicated by the ritual surrounding its handling.

Reflecting and supporting Dong Zhong-shu's philosophy, the *Yi Jing*—like the Bible in Judaism and Christianity and the Qur'ān in Islam—is to be treated with respect. The procedure for consulting the *Yi Jing* is designed to place questioners in a receptive and meditative frame of mind. Its accuracy is said to be dependable only if questioners compose their minds and open themselves to the mysterious Dao, which is the ongoing flow of events. Even in favorable circumstances, serious thought is needed for the proper understanding of the text within the context of a particular moment. (The presentation of Chinese divination in the box

Chinese Divination: The *Yi Jing*

The hexagrams of the *Yi Jing*. Various combinations of the broken and unbroken lines yield configurations that are used to predict the future.

The figures (hexagrams) of the *Yi Jing* are made up of unbroken and broken lines. The first hexagram is composed entirely of unbroken lines ䷀ ; the second entirely of broken lines ䷁ . All possible combinations of these two diagrams result in sixty-four hexagrams. Each one has a descriptive name and has attached to it two interpretive statements, known as the "judgment" and the "image." Also, each of the six lines of the hexagram has separate interpretive statements.

Let us assume that you are spending the summer far from your home. You fall in love and wish to ask the *Yi Jing* what course you should follow. You must toss either coins or sticks from the yarrow plant in such a way as to form a hexagram. In the process you also will create some moving lines, which will direct you as the seeker to a specified line text and will also make a secondary hexagram. If you have your specific question in mind as you make the toss and have the proper attitude, then theoretically your present situation will be described by the hexagram you form. The changes you may expect in the future will be indicated by the secondary hexagram shaped by the moving lines. Let us assume that the toss of the coins or sticks produces the following hexagram:

No. 56, Lü the Wanderer: ䷷
above, the clinging, fire
below, keeping still, mountain
The Judgment:
The Wanderer. Success through smallness. Perseverance brings good fortune to the wanderer.
The Image:
Fire on the mountain: The image of the Wanderer. Thus the superior man is clear-minded and cautious in imposing penalties, and protracts no lawsuits.*

There are moving lines in both the fourth place and the top place in the hexagram. This leads you to the line texts:

Nine in the fourth place means: The Wanderer rests in a shelter. He obtains his property and an ax. My heart is not glad.

Nine at the top means: The bird's nest burns up. The Wanderer laughs at first, then must needs lament and weep. Through carelessness he loses his cow. Misfortune.†

The moving lines also lead to a second hexagram, which indicates the more distant future of the situation evaluated in the initial hexagram:

No. 15, Ch'ien, Modesty: ䷎
above, the receptive, earth
below, keeping still, mountain
The Judgment:
Modesty creates success. The superior man carries things through.
The Image:
Within the earth, a mountain: The image of Modesty. Thus the superior man reduces that which is too much, and augments that which is too little. He weighs things and makes them equal.§

That is the full answer for you to ponder. The decision is left to you as the questioner. You should make your decision only in meditative interaction between the often enigmatic text and your own mind.

*From Richard Wilhelm, trans., the *I Ching* or *Book of Changes* (Princeton, N.J.: Princeton University Press, 1967), pp. 216–217.
† Ibid., pp. 218–219.
§ Ibid., pp. 63–64.

on the opposite page supplies fuller details on how to consult the *Yi Jing*.)

Taoism and the New "Dark Learning"

During the Han period, many Taoist beliefs and practices gained widespread popularity, either openly or with the tacit approval of the Confucian establishment. Among these were alchemistic experiments aimed at producing either immortality or a long life for the practitioners. Other Taoist rites were intended to bestow magical powers, such as the ability to fly through the air, to heal the sick, or to control spirits. Loosely connected to the belief in alchemy was the devotion to the *immortals* (*xian*)—mysterious and capricious figures who were thought to have achieved immortality through a combination of alchemy, asceticism, and meditation. The xian reputedly had extraordinary magical powers that could be invoked by the prayers of the living. This belief in the immortals was shared by Chinese of all social classes. One of the great military leaders of China, the emperor Wu Di (141–87 B.C.), sent a group of explorers into the eastern sea (the East China Sea) with instructions to find the home of the immortals and bring back the elixir of eternal life.

Sacrifices to famous individuals were also officially instituted by the Han dynasty. In A.D. 59 ceremonies honoring Confucius and the Duke of Zhou were decreed for all the schools, and in A.D. 164 the emperor built a temple to Lao-zi in the capital, using in it rituals based on the official sacrifices to Heaven.

The philosophical side of Taoism was developed by disappointed scholars and court officials who fled the corrupt petty states of the fragmented empire in search of a simple life far from the political world. As might be expected, this new form of Taoism was much influenced by Confucian values, and its political and social theories were essentially those of the orthodox Confucianism of the Han period. Within this practical framework was contained a philosophy based on the teachings of Laozi and Zhuang-zi.

THE NEW PHILOSOPHERS: WANG BI AND GUO XIANG

Wang Bi (A.D. 226–249) wrote influential commentaries on the *Yi Jing* and *Dao De Jing* in which he sought to understand all things in terms of being (*you*) and nonbeing (*wu*). Nonbeing was seen as powerful and whole—that is, containing all things in embryo. Nonbeing thus became the description of the original Dao. In accordance with this view, Wang Bi tried to transform the *Yi Jing* into a philosophical work. Each hexagram, he believed, had a single controlling line that was to be understood as having a specific relationship with the original nonbeing.

In contrast, Guo Xiang, who died in 312, based his philosophy on the *Zhuang-zi,* which he interpreted according to the *Yi Jing* as showing the impersonal and inevitable nature of change. His primary category was thus *zi-ran,* the spontaneity of naturalness.

NEW GROUP LOYALTIES

These new aspects of Taoism, which were called the *dark learning,* dominated Chinese thought after the fall of the Han. The dark learning provided not only a basis for rigorous philosophizing, but also a justification for casual gatherings of "retired" intellectuals which were referred to as the Pure Conversation Movement. Scholars, poets, and painters who disdained official positions would meet to discuss their respective pursuits and to enjoy one another's company. Taoism provided them with a sense of participation in the mysterious and dark life of the cosmos, and no doubt it helped compensate them for the loss of their influence in the political world. At the same time, these intellectuals were unconsciously forming a pattern of behavior and lifestyle that would henceforth become available to educated persons who went into retirement either voluntarily or involuntarily. As time went on, Buddhism—especially the Chan sect, known as Zen in Japan—also became part of this pattern.

At the same time, Taoism was becoming an im-

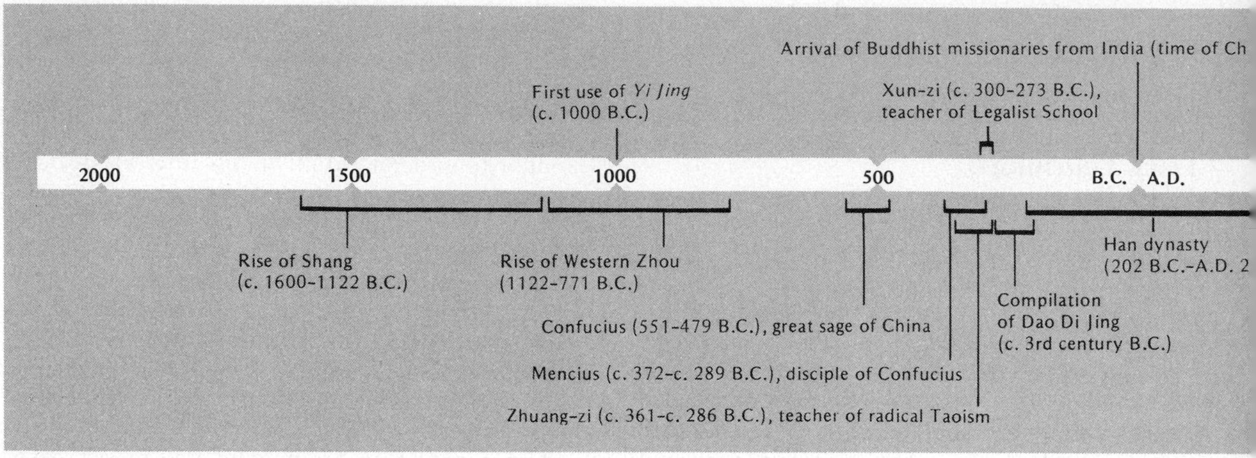

portant influence among the common people. Its political and ritualistic elements coalesced in such a way that Taoism achieved a separate sectarian existence. A new phenomenon appeared in Chinese religious history, namely, the religious group. Heretofore the people of China had participated in religious activity according to their membership in different kinds of groups, for example, the family, the village, or the scholarly profession. These new Taoist sects were voluntary organizations that cut across earlier organizational lines and forged a new kind of group loyalty. Again, the pattern set at this time greatly influenced China's subsequent religious and political life. Chinese *secret societies,* which have often been the nuclei of political uprisings as well as religious devotions, date from this time and have continued this pattern to the present. Among the famous secret societies were the White Cloud Society, which was founded in the twelfth century by Buddhist monks, and the White Lotus Society, which in the fourteenth century helped overthrow the Yuan dynasty.

TAOIST SECTS

Two major Taoist sects were active after the fall of the Han dynasty. The first was the Celestial Masters group, which was formed in about the middle of the second century in western China, where it carved out an autonomous theocratic state. The second was the Yellow Turbans group, which began in Shandong province and eventually controlled some eight provinces before it was put down in bloody battles at the end of the second century. Both sects emphasized the art of healing, the confession of sins, and magic; and both were led by charismatic leaders who functioned as magical healers and military leaders.

They also shared an essentially utopian vision of life, which taught that the future would be a time of peace and prosperity during which people everywhere would live in harmony with themselves and the spiritual powers of the cosmos. This hope was held most fervently by the Yellow Turbans, who called themselves the followers of the *Tai Ping Dao* (Way of the Grand Peace). They believed they could achieve this blessed state through purification rites and rituals expressing the harmony inherent in the nature of things.

These two Taoist sects, as well as the many others that followed them, established a circle of religious concerns that included both the individual and the collective poles. The element holding the two poles together was a common concern for healing. To the individual, healing meant freedom from

TIME LINE

RELIGIONS OF CHINA

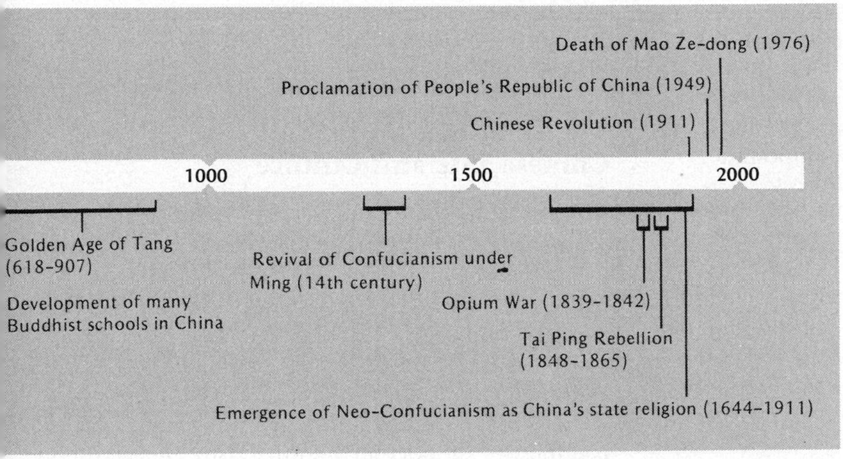

physical and mental disease. But the assumptions of the Chinese popular world view led to theories of disease that were closely tied to the various divine powers—some malevolent, others benevolent—which were thought to control the phenomena of the world. Individuals who wished to be truly healed and protected from future dangers had to bring about a state of harmony between themselves and these largely unseen powers. In turn, this would place them in a network of relationships that also included other humans, thus introducing the collective element. On the collective side, parishes were organized around a priesthood and a regular round of ritual observances with congregational participation. On the individual side, Taoist priests acted as healers by distributing potions and magical formulas and in traditional priestly roles as intermediaries between individuals and the spirit world.

The concern for healing also bound together other elements in sectarian Taoism. Strong moral elements were greatly strengthened as the Buddhist influence in China increased. To fail to live up to the moral code was regarded as a major cause of suffering and disease, and to confess one's transgressions and ask for forgiveness was often seen as a prerequisite to healing. In the Celestial Masters sect, for example, misdeeds and repentances were written on three pieces of paper; the first paper was buried; the second was placed on a mountaintop; and the third was thrown into a river. The purpose of this ritual was to inform all the cosmic powers of one's repentance. In addition, some Taoists were convinced that the human body was divided into three regions, each inhabited by a divine being in the shape of a worm that gnawed away at a person's vital organs to the extent deserved by his or her transgressions. On one night a year the three divinities were thought to ascend to the celestial powers to advise them of the person's misdeeds and to secure permission to shorten his or her life span in accordance with the judgment of the gods.

Healing served to bind the quest for a long life and even for immortality to the popular Taoist sects. The cult of the immortals and the practice of alchemy had become a part of Chinese religious practices during the Han regime. Those beliefs were now incorporated into organized Taoism. Individuals themselves could become adept at such practices or use the powers of experts. They might also seek the elixir of immortality or some other means of prolonging their lives.

There were many techniques for achieving a long life. Alchemy often combined ritual and meditative preparations in a sort of rite of purification. One of the most famous compilers of alchemist lore set down the following rules for preparing the "medicine of immortality":

> The medicine should be prepared on a famous mountain, in a lonely spot. . . . The compounder should be on a diet for one hundred days previously and should perfect the purification and anointment of the body with the five perfumes.[2]

In this example, purification preceded the compounding and taking of the elixir. A special kind of Taoist ritual elaborated the purification rite into a meditative, even ecstatic discipline. In such practices, Taoist mysticism took a major step beyond what was hinted at in the works of Lao-zi and Zhuang-zi. Henceforth a direct and ecstatic experience of the Dao was not only a matter of literary speculation and hope, but also a practical possibility. Taoist mysticism had removed the obstacles.

Taoist meditation techniques were just as much based on the popular notions of healing as they were on Lao-zi's ideas of the Dao. Nonetheless, Lao-zi formulated the belief that the microcosm (an individual human being) and the macrocosm (the world of nature and the Dao that lay behind it) could be brought into harmony with each other. This harmony was the key to success in life, whether it was a long life, tranquil contentment, or the thrill of ecstatic experience. But practical meditation techniques took this idea much further by assuming a very detailed set of correspondences between what might be called the inner and the outer worlds. A person carefully chose the proper substances, times, and attitudes from the outer world in order to sustain the inner world.

The deeper the Taoist mystics probed, however, the more preoccupied they became with appropriating the sacred power of the many Taoist deities. While meditating, people could apprehend these divine powers inside them and communicate with them. In this way they could, by means of visualization exercises, experience themselves as internally identical with the divine powers of the cosmos. Purification rites and the nourishment of the spiritual essence within the individual became ways to live in perfect harmony with these powers, which were regarded as the manifestation of the Dao in the inner world.

The Buddhist Contribution to Chinese Life and Culture

Buddhism began to enter China about the beginning of the Christian era when it was still a strong, living religion in India. Missionaries followed the trade routes across Central Asia during the Han dynasty, and soon centers of Buddhist learning appeared in northern China. After the fall of the Han, Buddhism flourished under the patronage of the various petty states established by the non-Chinese conquerors of northern China. But the common people knew nothing of this exotic foreign practice, and Chinese intellectual circles had only a distorted picture. From its elaborate rituals, rich visual art, and complex philosophies, many saw Buddhism as a variant of Taoism. The tendency to identify Taoism with Buddhism during this period can be seen in the following excerpt from a Confucian scholar's memorial to the throne, in which he admonished the emperor to reassume his proper duties:

> Moreover, I have heard that in the palace sacrifices have been performed to Huang-lao and the Buddha. This doctrine [teaches] purity and emptiness; it venerates non-activity [wu-wei]; it loves [keeping] alive and hates slaughter; it [serves to] diminish the desires and to expel intemperance. Now Your Majesty does not expel your desires; slaughter and [the application of] punishments exceed the proper limit. Since [Your Majesty] deviates from the doctrine, how could you [expect to] obtain the happiness resulting from its [observance]? Some people say that Lao-tzu has gone into the regions of the barbarians and [there] has become the Buddha.[3]

The first Buddhist enclaves in China were centers of learning whose primary function was to translate into Chinese the vast and abstruse Buddhist literature of India. But soon the most exotic feature of the new religion became known—namely, the organization of its adherents into monasteries and

"Buddhist Monastery by Stream and Mountains," ink on silk, attributed to Chü Jan (active 960–980), Northern Song dynasty. *Cleveland Art Museum, Gift of Katharine Holden Thayer.*

convents. The monastic institution was not only the heart of early Chinese Buddhism, but in many ways it was also the greatest obstacle to acceptance. Filial piety was too deeply ingrained at all levels of Chinese society for the easy success of an institution that, symbolically at least, required its members to turn their backs on the world, abstaining from not only its pleasures, but also its responsibilities. Buddhist monks and nuns were celibate and could not carry on the family line. In the monasteries and convents they lived in new "families," and their duty was no longer to their parents or to human society.

Despite this handicap, Buddhism did gain many adherents, especially among the educated gentry, many of whose sons sought a haven from the uncertainties of official life where they could live in an atmosphere of quiet contemplation in which scholarly and esthetic pursuits could be cultivated along with the more strenuous disciplines of ritual performance and meditation toward the experience of enlightenment. They filled the ranks of the growing Buddhist saṅgha, the community of the Buddhist faithful who strove for the ultimate harmony that came with loss of self.

For the Buddhists, nirvāṇa, the final goal, required the experience in meditation of the truth of nonself—or, as they often put it, the detachment from the false notion of self. Detachment from self and detachment from the world were simply the same thing stated from different points of view. This seems to have struck a chord among many Taoists of that day, because not only were many Buddhist ideas interpreted using Taoist concepts, but the Taoists themselves began to build monasteries and convents. The Taoist tendency to produce recluses or hermits adapted itself to the example of Buddhism to produce "communal hermits" whose common goal of enlightenment was sufficient to bring together those seeking individual religious experiences. In this period too, there began the mutual borrowing that eventually enriched the Taoist meditation techniques and helped produce that most Chinese of all Buddhist schools, Chan.

The Golden Age of the Tang

After more than three hundred years of internal weakness and foreign domination, China again achieved political unity during the short-lived but important Sui dynasty (A.D. 581–618). The Sui embarked on an ambitious program of canal building in order to link the traditional Chinese centers on the northern plain to the developing areas in the

Seated Buddha, an eighth-century statuette dating from the Tang dynasty. Buddhism was finally accepted in China under the Tang emperors and predominated until the emergence of the Song. *The Metropolitan Museum of Art, Rogers Fund, 1943.*

Yangzi River valley. After an unsuccessful war in Korea, however, the Sui fell from power.

The Tang dynasty (618–907), which followed the Sui, gave China a long period of opulence. The Tang completed the canal system, broke up many large estates in order to distribute lands to the peasants, and reformed the administrative machinery of the central government. The civil service was improved. Areas in the expanding empire inhabited by non-Chinese groups were allowed to retain their local princes, provided they respected the Tang emperor as their overlord. This prosperous period, China's golden age, was marked by creativity in literature and the arts. Tang culture radiated throughout all of East Asia and was widely imitated in Korea, Japan, and Vietnam.

Two unusual aspects of the Tang state should be noted: (1) Its intellectual and artistic circles were dominated by Buddhism, which had been imported. (2) Its culture was extremely cosmopolitan. Caravans crossing Central Asia linked the markets of India and the Mediterranean ports with the Chinese capital of Chang-an, which became a center of foreign ideas as well as foreign goods. Missionaries of various Christian denominations, especially the Nestorians, built churches there. In addition, there was a Jewish community and, in time, a Muslim community as well. Preachers from Tibet brought the Vajrayāna, or diamond, tradition of Buddhism, with its magical rites based on the tantras.

At first Buddhism received the enthusiastic official support of the emperors. Its adherents were from all classes of Chinese society, and thousands of Chinese men and women retired to monasteries and convents to meditate on the Buddhist Dharma, which was known to the Chinese, of course, as the Dao, or Way. But in 845 a nativist reaction swept across China. Powerful Taoist forces convinced the emperor that the followers of foreign customs, especially the Buddhists, posed a threat to the political stability and economic security of the nation. Thousands of monastic centers were shut down or destroyed, and tens of thousands of monks and nuns were forced to resume their lay status. Under the succeeding Song dynasty, Confucianism slowly regained its old position of prominence. Meanwhile, however, Chinese Buddhism had made lasting contributions to the life of the Chinese people.

The impact of Buddhism on China's religious life was discussed in part three. Here we consider some of the Buddhist contributions to China's cultural life.

Religion and Esthetics in the Tang and Song Periods

In China both literature and the fine arts have been closely tied to religion. A survey of the arts from the Tang to the Ming shows how religious ideas permeated cultural life during the premodern period as Confucian, Taoist, and Buddhist ideas merged into an artistic life style that became an influential model for generations of Chinese.

The relationship between a graphic representation of a person or thing and that very person or thing has long fascinated the Chinese. In the early days they believed that a painting somehow captured reality itself; so, for example, viewing a portrait of an emperor was the same as being in his presence. Literature was also influenced by this idea, especially since the basis of Chinese ideographic writing is a pictorial representation of a concrete thing or an abstract idea.

This belief in the close association between reality and its image or representation gradually became broader and more subtle as Taoism became a separate religion and as landscape painting developed into a definite art form. Nature was seen more and more as the ground of the real and as the source of the profound and abundant life in the Dao. A landscape was a representation not of a single thing, but of all reality. It was a world picture. Both the thrill of religious experience and its sense of truth and profundity were associated with painting.

Besides the effect of a painting on the viewer, the creation of the work of art was also important. The artist who produced such a mysterious and powerful object also had to participate in the depicted reality in a special and especially intimate way. Under the influence of Buddhism, this idea came to dominate Chinese esthetic circles from the Tang period onward. Particularly Chan Buddhism, in wedding itself to Taoist notions of painting, produced a long period of preoccupation with the life and life style of the artists, which even Confucianism came to accept.

Prior to the Tang period, the canons of artistic

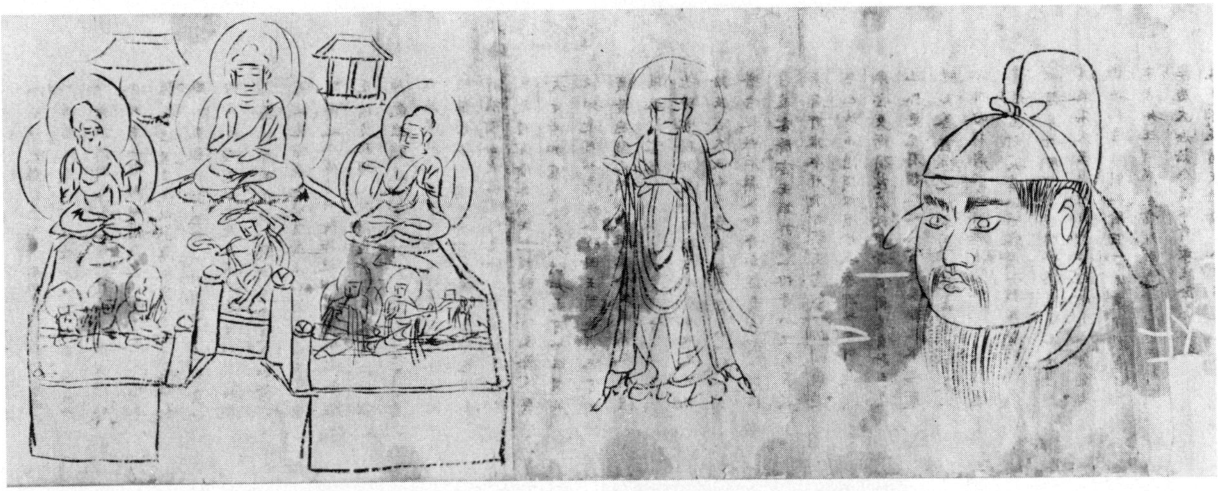

Sketches on the back of a sūtra fragment, hand scroll dating from A.D. ninth to tenth century; appended by an anonymous artist to a religious text. By the end of the Tang dynasty, religion powerfully influenced all aspects of Chinese cultural life, including artistic creation. *William Rockhill Nelson Gallery of Art—Atkins Museum of Fine Arts.*

"Bodhisattva Ksitiar" (left), painting dating from the Tang dynasty, when the strict conventions that had dominated the fine arts began to give way as a new style emphasizing spontaneity emerged under Buddhist influence. "The Sixth Patriarch Cutting a Bamboo" by Liang Kai dates from the Southern Song dynasty. Its use of empty space shows a strong Buddhist sensibility. *Tokyo National Museum.*

theory centered on the Taoist notion of *Qi-yun*, or "essence-harmony." *Qi* (essence or life-breath) was the term used to refer to the pure, self-existing thing itself, a thing's own reality. To paint a proper picture of a thing, the artist had somehow to apprehend and experience this essence as it existed in harmony with all other things. To do this meant going far beyond mere skill with brush and ink; it required an intimacy with the objects depicted that approached a mystical identity. Not only did the artist have to experience the harmony inherent in the existence of a thing, he had also to establish a harmony with that preexistent harmony.

CLASSES OF PAINTINGS

According to this ambitious understanding of the artistic process, scholars before the Tang period classified paintings according to the following schema (the four steps are listed in a descending order of religious and artistic excellence):

1 First came the sacred or divine paintings (*shen*), which were produced "without effort"; that is, they were expressions of the artist's perfect harmony. Since the artist had already expended effort to achieve the necessary technical ability to produce such paintings, their actual production was inevitable.

2 Next came the profoundly mysterious paintings (*miao*), which could admit observers to only a glimpse of the true reality.

3 Then came the paintings that were merely clever.

4 Finally came the paintings that revealed only technical skill.

DEVELOPMENT OF THE YI STYLE

In the Tang period a new classification was added to the traditional list. The rising tide of Buddhism had made the *yi* style important. *Yi* means "to deviate," and an yi person was a hermit, or one who had retired from public life. Artistically it implied one who did not follow the established canons of style and taste, and its defenders identified it with the spontaneity of artists who worked under the pressure of an inner compulsion and not under the falsifying constraint of convention. During the Tang and Song dynasties the yi style was usually first in importance, or occasionally second. Some critics spoke of it with awe and suspicion, since such a disregard for convention would probably bring out extreme qualities in the artists, producing either great excellence or great failure. One critic in the Song period put the problem in these words: the artists' "intentions may often have been noble, but they fell into vulgarity."[4]

By the Song period the Chan influence on the developing Chinese theory of painting had become significant, contributing the following three ideas:

1 The spontaneity of the painter in the quick and effortless creation of a painting is seen as equivalent to the sudden enlightenment of the Chan school. This enlightenment, which is known as *wu* in Chinese and *satori* in Japanese, is a moment of sudden insight into the nature of things, especially the meaning of nonself. It is sudden in that no matter how much study and meditation may have gone into the effort to achieve it, the experience itself always comes without warning. A painting or a poem has to be constructed quickly, with great economy of strokes or syllables, since such a work of art is also sudden and momentary. The result is often thought of as a fossilized remainder of an actual enlightenment experience.

2 The prominent use of nothingness, or empty space, appears as a result of the Chan attempt to portray graphically its central doctrinal tenant, the essential emptiness of all things. Things are not reality themselves; in enlightenment the mind becomes a mirror that reflects the endless stream of thing-events. Reality is the empty awareness itself and not the content of that awareness. Chan paintings of the Song period, as well as those of subsequent periods, rarely fill the framed area. A sense of transcendence, mystery, and loneliness is apparent. Since reality is formless, what has form is needed only insofar as it is through form that one

can grasp formlessness. Put another way, without forms, how can one see the spaces between them? The loneliness motif performs a twofold function. First, it communicates the poignancy of relinquishing the emotional ties to this world, such as those to home, family, and worldly success, which for most people make life worth living. Second, it emphasizes the formless, empty nature of that otherworldly goal: It is without either one's own self or other selves.

3 Poetry and painting are two complementary expressions of the profound experience of enlightenment. Long before the Chan school began, Buddhist monks had traditionally written *gathas*, or songs celebrating the wonders of Buddhist truth. These were an outlet for feelings of joy and awe, and especially in the Chan context in which actual enlightenment was actively sought, they became a means of celebrating that mysterious event—they performed the same function as Chan painting.

Notes

1 Wing-tsit Chan, trans. and comp., *A Source Book in Chinese Philosophy* (Princeton, N. J.: Princeton University Press, 1963), p. 279.

2 Lu-ch'ang Wu, trans., "Ko Hung on the Gold Medicine and on the Yellow and on the White," *Proceedings of the American Academy of Arts and Sciences,* 70 (December 1935), 239.

3 E. Zürcher, *The Buddhist Conquest of China* (Leiden, Netherlands: E. J. Brill, 1959), p. 37.

4 Teng Ch'un, "Miscellaneous Sayings," in Osvald Siren, *The Chinese on the Art of Painting* (New York: Schocken Books, 1963), p. 89.

12 Traditional Patterns: From Premodern China to Revolutionary Change

Over the centuries China has oscillated between periods of strong centralized control and periods of internal weakness, foreign invasion, and civil war. Despite changes in the ruling dynasties, however, life for the great majority of the Chinese people continued to follow the age-old patterns, even into modern times.

PREMODERN CHINA

The Revival of Confucianism

One of the dominant philosophical developments of premodern China was Neo-Confucianism. To trace the rise of this important movement to its position of dominance as the state religion during the Yuan, Ming, and Qing (Manchu) dynasties (1644–1911), we must return to the crucial Song dynasty (960–1279). The dynasty that had preceded the Song on the throne of China, the Tang, had disturbed the literati by adding the study of Taoist and Buddhist texts to the school curriculum required of all candidates for the government bureaucracy. Since they all had to pass civil service examinations based on this curriculum, this "battle of the books" was not an idle matter.

After the fall of the Tang, Zhao Kuang-yin, the first Song ruler, called on the literati to help him bring stability to the administration. Acting on their recommendations, the conservative emperor dropped the Taoist and Buddhist texts from the school curriculum and reinstated the Confucian classics. Although most Chinese continued to follow popular religious cults that included elements of Taoism and Buddhism, members of the official and scholarly classes turned back to the Confucian classics and their commentaries for workable theories of government and insight into the human condition.

Although Neo-Confucianism had been launched in official circles somewhat earlier, it did not attract a wide following among intellectuals until the appearance of highly respected commentaries on the Confucian classics written by two philosopher brothers, Cheng Hao (1032–1085) and Cheng Yi (1033–1107). Some time later two other philosophers gained prominence. The first of these masters, Ju Xi (1130–1200) consolidated the earlier writings, prepared a standard commentary on the classics, and drew up a compendium of Confucian philosophy. The second, Wang Yang-ming (1472–1529), was greatly influenced by Buddhist thought.

Perhaps the most striking aspect of Neo-Confucianism was its debt to Buddhism. Indeed, even though this new point of view revived the past by returning to Confucius and Mencius, it nonetheless asked new questions, questions learned from Buddhism. As one modern historian describes this situation:

> The molders of neo-Confucianism lived in a climate suffused with Buddhist influence. Even the language and the modes of discourse at their disposal had developed in the ages of Buddhist dominance. The new dimensions of meaning they discovered in the ancient Chinese classics were dimensions which experience with Buddhism had taught them to seek and to find.[1]

The most pervasive Buddhist influence has been found in the Neo-Confucian insistence on an absolute metaphysical basis for thought and reality. This absolute functioned much as the Buddha nature was thought to function, since it was both the means by which all knowledge was gained and the organizing principle of that knowledge. The Neo-Confucians called this absolute *li* (principle). (The term is pronounced like *li* [ritual] but means reason, principle, or order.) The Confucian classics had used this idea merely to refer to the orderliness of things that li (ritual) had established. But in the Song period, li (principle) became a metaphysical entity, or reality itself.

Cheng Yi spoke of this li with the same tone of awe and celebration with which the Buddhists spoke of the Buddha nature as emptiness: "Empty and tranquil, and without any sign, and yet all things are luxuriantly present."[2] Ju Xi referred to li more prosaically but no less exaltedly when he said, "The Great Ultimate is nothing other than Principle." He went on to explain this meant that even heaven and earth existed by means of principle and that principle was even before them. Indeed, it was by means of principle that the yin and yang were generated.[3]

Neo-Confucianism did not begin with an activity (li, ritual) that established interrelationships and order; rather, it began with the relationships that themselves existed in a purely ideal realm before these activities could embody them. Outward observance could only serve to exemplify these absolutes, which were collectively called principle.

Another debt to Buddhism was the concern for the psychological insight into and the descriptions of the mental mechanisms by which human beings function. For example, a seeming paradox that bothered Ju Xi and Wang Yang-ming was the need to affirm both the essential tranquility of the mind

"Silent Angler in an Autumn Wood," by Shen Zhou. Whereas the inscription expresses Confucian sentiments, the painting itself reveals the Buddhist desire to turn from the world. © *Wan-go H. C. Weng.*

in its ideal state and its ability to deal actively with the everyday world. It is similar to the state of tranquility in activity that the Chan Buddhists seek to experience in *wu* (enlightenment), and for this the image of the mind as a passive mirror was developed.

This psychological concern also thrust the Confucian notion of the sage again into the foreground. The sage, like the Buddhist bodhisattva, was an actual being, or state of being, and an ideal actively sought by the faithful. Again, like the Buddhist bodhisattva, the Neo-Confucian sage was spoken of as having achieved enlightenment. Unlike the Buddhist counterpart, however, the sage, though tranquil in the ability to dwell in contemplation of the eternal principle, was nonetheless active in the world of affairs and therefore exhibited the typical Confucian array of attitudes, including very un-Buddhist emotions. According to Ju Xi:

> [Man's] original nature is pure and tranquil. Before it is aroused, the five moral principles of his nature, called humanity, righteousness, propriety, wisdom and faithfulness, are complete. As his physical form appears, it comes into contact with external things and is aroused from within. As it is aroused from within, the seven feelings, called pleasure, anger, sorrow, joy, love, hate, and desire, ensue. As feelings become strong and increasingly reckless, his nature becomes damaged. For this reason the enlightened person controls his feelings so that they will be in accord with the Mean. He rectifies his mind and nourishes his nature.[4]

New Political Trends: The Mongols and the Ming Dynasty

The once powerful Song dynasty gradually crumbled under the repeated attacks of barbarians from Mongolia. By 1127 the Song were forced to retreat to the south, abandoning northern China to the Mongol invaders. Between 1260 and 1368 all of China came under Mongol rule (the Yuan dynasty). Its greatest ruler, Kublai Khan, controlled China and Mongolia between 1260 and 1294 and established his capital in a new city, which was later called Beijing, "northern capital."

When Kublai Khan's successors grew effete and relaxed their grasp, Buddhist-influenced secret societies began to plot against the hated foreign rulers. In 1368 a former peasant and Buddhist novice named Zhu Yuan-zhang led a popular rebellion, seized Beijing, and either destroyed or expelled the Mongols from China.

Zhu Yuan-zhang became the first emperor of the Ming dynasty (1368–1644), which preached a return to the old Chinese way of life. All traces of Mongol rule were rooted out, and Confucianism again became the state religion. With the assistance of the literati, the civil service examinations were reinstated, and the commentaries on the Confucian classics of the Neo-Confucian philosopher Ju Xi became the main course of studies in the school curriculum.

No other Neo-Confucianist stressed the experience of enlightenment more than the Ming period philosopher Wang Yang-ming. An extraordinary biography of this man has been preserved, detailing his youthful immersion in both Buddhism and Taoism. For example, he passed a Taoist temple on the day set for his ceremonial betrothal and, sitting down to meditate, forgot all about his ritual duties. Finally he gave up his Buddhist-Taoist yoga practices. Nonetheless, both the content of his philosophy and the dramatic way in which he discovered it are strongly reminiscent of Buddhism. On one occasion he went into retreat with a few disciples temporarily out of favor at court. There he lived the life of a Chan monk, meditating on life and death, humbly chopping wood and carrying water for his students. He was plagued by the question of what a sage was, and he devoted himself to becoming one. His biography describes the decisive moment in these words:

> The great object of his meditations at this time was: What additional method would a sage adopt who lived under these circumstances? One night it suddenly dawned upon him in the midnight watches what the sage meant by "investigating things for the purpose of extending knowledge to the utmost." Unconsciously he called out, got up and danced about the room. All his followers

were alarmed; but the Teacher, now for the first time understanding the doctrine of the sage, said, "My nature is, of course, sufficient. I was wrong in looking for Principle in things and affairs."[5]

Wang was thus "enlightened" about his own nature, in which he discovered nothing less than principle itself. This set him on an intellectual course in which he identified both mind and principle and thought and action. He was strongly influenced by Buddhism in the theoretical basis of his thought, although he remained Confucian in his emphasis on practical affairs in statecraft and ethics.

Traditional Patterns of Religion

We have surveyed the three great religions of China and their respective developments up to the end of the premodern period. Let us now try to make some generalizations about the role of Chinese religion in the past.

Our analysis has been based largely on the assumption that it is possible to analyze traditional Chinese society and its religions by referring to the different symbols and social levels shared by the Chinese. Human groups tend to have their own sets of identifying symbols which determine, at least theoretically, their similar status, power, and function. In China this has been especially important because of what has been called the diffusion of religion throughout Chinese society. This means that the religious institutions and religious functionaries have tended not to be independent of other social groups, but rather to be a part of institutions like the family, state, and village. Religion has been an expression of a quality felt to be inherent in all human endeavors, rather than a specialized activity more or less insulated from the rest of life.

This point of view was strongly implied in Confucius's idea of li as the quality of life that makes humanity truly human. In addition, both the Confucian system and the whole Chinese religious pattern were based, in part, on the concept of hierarchy—that is, on the existence of inequality among human beings and human groups with respect to status, power, and function. This is seen particularly in the traditional Chinese family, with its system of unequal but mutually advantageous relationships. Just as the father nurtured his son, the emperor nurtured his subjects; and just as the son revered his father, the nation revered its emperor.

The two major groups in traditional Chinese society were the imperial state and the family. Because of the social diffusion of Chinese religion, these institutions were both secular and religious. There also was an intermediate level, which included the popular activities in the village and the religious ceremonies in the neighborhood. Finally, there were religious groups that did not follow this diffused pattern—namely, such specifically religious institutions as the Buddhist saṅgha, some Taoist groups, and the secret societies. Because these institutions did not fit the pattern of Chinese life, they were viewed for centuries as threats to China's religious and political stability.

THE IMPERIAL OR OFFICIAL LEVEL

In the past there were three elements at the imperial, or official, level of religion in China:

1 The imperial cult was the set of religious activities under the direct control of the court. Rituals included the seasonal sacrifices in which the emperor himself played a central, priestly role. The cult of the imperial ancestors was maintained with regular rituals on the first day of each new season. Here the division of religious labor inherent in the hierarchical principle was exemplified to the most extreme degree: The people were not permitted even to witness the rituals that were carried out on their behalf and that most clearly expressed the common identity of the Chinese nation. The emperor was the people's representative to the deities.

2 The Confucian cult formed the ritual life of the literati, the powerful bureaucrats who ran the government offices, as well as all the would-be officeholders, most educated persons, and most members of the rich gentry class. The cult served to

The Imperial Palaces, Beijing. Walls and a moat surround this group of palaces, which were in the possession of the Chinese emperors for over five hundred years. *Eastfoto.*

reinforce both the group's loyalty to the state and its responsibility for disseminating the traditional Chinese culture. Twice a year local officials offered prayers, incense, and food at the temples of Confucius and his ancestors. The most elaborate and solemn rituals in honor of Confucius were performed by members of the Imperial University, the center of Confucian learning in the capital.

3 The *yamen* was the judicial, clerical, and cult center of the imperial presence at the lowest level of Chinese society. Local officials were expected to preside at many rituals throughout the year. They followed a book of ceremonies in which were prayers not only to Confucius, but also to the god of war (Guan Yu), the god of literature, the local city god, and the deities of the land and grain. There were prayers for special occasions. Those elements of Buddhism that had become part of Chinese popular belief were also included; prayers were offered to "Father Buddha" and the bodhisattvas Guan yin and Di zang.

THE POPULAR LEVEL

The intermediate popular level of religious activity consisted of the village or neighborhood ceremonies celebrated throughout the year, usually on the birthdays of the gods being honored. Many of these deities were the same as those included in the official cult, but several other popular powers and gods were added, drawn from Taoism and Buddhism.

Also at this popular level were those individual religious activities not carried out within the family group. They included personal petitions to local shrines, campaigns for personal moral rectification, and individual participation in yogic and hygienic practices.

THE FAMILY LEVEL

At the family level, the center of religious activity was the ancestral cult. Of course, many village festivals had their familial counterparts, but the ancestors received the most solemn and regular attention. All important family events were ritually announced to them, and marriages were performed in their presence. The great ancestral remembrances were occasions for the many branches of a family to gather, so they strengthened the authority of the head family and its patriarch. Filial piety kept alive this feeling of solidarity, and all family members felt responsible for the family's wealth and honor. Value and status were shared, first by members of the family and then, by extension, by the imperial establishment.

The intermediate levels were quite weak in traditional Chinese society. State officials might frequently be posted to different areas, precluding the formation of any strong local ties; yet an official would, with little hesitation, resign his position and return home to nurse an ailing parent or to perform the prescribed and lengthy mourning rites at the death of a parent.

SPECIFICALLY RELIGIOUS INSTITUTIONS

The Buddhist saṅgha was probably the oldest and best-organized of the religious groups that did not fit the pattern described above. The primary motivation for the persecutions visited upon the various independent religious groups by the central government was always political. In times of persecution, the Buddhists claimed—more or less convincingly—that the saṅgha was otherworldly and hence without political ambitions. All the same, the tightly knit organization of the monastic institution was greatly admired by many groups operating outside the imperial consensus. Impressive rituals of initiation and commitment were a part of becoming a monk or nun, and the division between the monks and nuns and ordinary persons was constantly reinforced by marked differences in life style and dress. Indeed, such strong group loyalties are known to have weakened loyalties to the distant imperial establishment. Buddhist secret societies, in fact, helped undermine the hated Yuan (Mongol) dynasty.

Some insight into the fears of the central government can be found in the laws the imperial court promulgated under the Qing (Manchu) dynasty. Severe punishments were prescribed for:

> . . . religious instructors and priests who pretend to invoke heretic gods, write charms or pronounce them over water [to cure sickness], or carry around palanquins with idols in them, or invoke saints, calling themselves true leaders, chief patrons, or female leaders; further, all societies calling themselves at random White Lotus societies of the Buddha Maitreya, or the Ming-tsun religion, or the school of the White Cloud, and so on . . . finally, they who in secret places have portraits and images, and offer incense to them, or hold meetings which take place at night and break up by day, whereby the people are stirred up and misled under the pretext of cultivating virtue. . . .[6]

Certainly the imperial government recognized the strength of religious loyalty and the power inherent in the invocation of sacred sanctions or symbols. These, it saw clearly, could be used to promote the status quo—the official orthodoxy and the family system—or to undermine it. The frequency of rebellions led by secret societies underscored the reality of this threat. Indeed, several Taoist secret

Buddhists receiving instruction at Beijing's Fayuan Monastery. Complex initiation rites were required of monks and nuns. Throughout Chinese history, the Buddhists' commitment to the communities they joined helped undermine the authority of the Chinese emperors. *Eastfoto.*

societies were instrumental in the final overthrow of the imperial establishment in the revolution of 1911. Before that happened, China would endure several centuries of change brought on by contact with the expanding West.

CHINA IN A PERIOD OF REVOLUTIONARY CHANGE

Contact with the West

The Mongol conquests in Asia and eastern Europe that culminated in the Yuan dynasty (1260–1368) in China made possible fairly free communication between China and the West. Bent on adventure and trade, several European travelers made the long overland journey from the rich commercial center of Venice to the Mongol court in Beijing. The most famous of these Western adventurers was Marco Polo, who spent almost seventeen years (1276–1292) collecting impressions of this exotic land. Little trade resulted, however, and even the Franciscan mission established in 1305 at Beijing failed to survive the fall of the Yuan. This first contact served primarily to fire the imagination of Europe concerning the fabulous wealth and strange customs of Cathay, the name by which China was known to the people of medieval Europe.

Further contact had to await the development of sailing ships, which by the end of the sixteenth century were carrying trade goods, colonial armies, and missionaries to Asia, from the Indian Ocean to the Sea of Japan. At first the Chinese court regarded these "Western barbarians" as only another group of the pirates who from time to time harassed the merchant ships and coastal settlements on the frontiers of the empire. The Ming leaders, having just purged their nation of foreign influences left by the Mongols, had little curiosity about more strangers.

From the Chinese point of view, this attitude is understandable. China had always encountered cultures that were its social, philosophical, technological, and artistic inferiors. The very prestige of Chinese culture—its customs, thought, and values—had eventually subdued China's conquerors, and it had maintained its historical and cultural continuity. The Chinese saw themselves as the center of civilization: All others were barbarians, and barbarians had nothing to offer the civilized.

THE JESUIT MISSION

By the mid-sixteenth century, the Portuguese trading enclave at Macao on the south China coast made Christian missionary work in China again possible, and one of the most effective elements in the Catholic Counter-Reformation, the Society of Jesus, carried the main burden of this effort. From the first the Jesuits adopted a policy of deemphasizing their strangeness in a land that had little use for strangers. So successful were they that some were given official posts and the protection of the emperor.

The Jesuits did their homework well: They learned Chinese, studied the Confucian classics, and impressed the literati by entering into philosophical discussions. They praised the Confucian morality and love of learning not only to the approving Chinese, but also to their distant colleagues in Europe. No less a figure than the French philosopher Voltaire was influenced by their accounts of China, which seemed to be an almost utopian land ruled by enlightened philosophers who had long since banished superstition and had installed a high-minded morality. The literati perceived Christianity mainly as a moral system consistent with Confucianism. Even more important perhaps were the interesting and useful sciences of Western mathematics and astronomy associated with the representatives of Christianity.

But storm clouds began to gather. The very policy of accommodation to Chinese culture and forms that had served the Jesuits so well brought disagreement and dissension within the Church. The missionaries had allowed Chinese Christians to continue to participate in the state cult and ancestor veneration, classifying these practices as nonreligious "civil ceremonies." The famous Rites Controversy, as it was called, culminated in 1706 when the angry Manchu emperor ordered that the Jesuit practices must be followed. Soon afterward, however, a papal decree was issued countermanding the emperor's order and threatening excommunication to those who did not comply. The line between religion and culture—between what is seen as essential and what is seen as merely customary—had been redrawn, and all the Christian missionaries were expelled from China. The strangeness of the foreign religion had come into conflict not only with the deeply held attitudes of the Chinese people, but also with the power of the emperor as upheld by the Confucian literati.

THE OPIUM WAR

Early attempts by Western merchants to establish trade relations had been frustrated by more than the Chinese refusal to take the West seriously. To this was added the West's new appetite for Chinese silks and tea. The Chinese, however, were not tempted by the mechanical curiosities the West offered in return. Most Europeans made up the ensuing trade deficit with silver, but the British encouraged the use of opium. Grown in the British-controlled areas of India, the drug could be shipped to Canton cheaply. So successful was this program that soon China saw its store of silver dwindling.

Chinese objections to the opium trade were both economic and moral. After many attempts to restrict its use, the emperor finally sent one of his ablest officials, Lin Zi-xu (1785–1850), to Canton with instructions to stop the trade once and for all. In March 1839 Lin seized the opium from the merchants and dumped it into the harbor. But Lin was a good Confucian as well as a man of action, and after apologizing to the waters for the pollution he had caused, he sent the British queen, Victoria, a letter in which he appealed to her sense of morality to intervene and stop the trade at the source. "The wealth of China is used to profit the barbarians," Lin protested, and he asked:

> By what right do they then in return use the poisonous drug to injure the Chinese people? Even though the barbarians may not necessarily intend to do us harm, yet in coveting profit to an extreme, they have no regard for injuring others. Let us ask, where is your conscience?[7]

Lin's ignorance of the West was as profound as his knowledge of Confucianism: The power of the West was invested in trade and empire. Nor was the British monarch a Manchu autocrat. The British replied by going to war, and their weapons and organization proved vastly superior to the Chinese defenses. The Treaty of Nanjing (1842) ending the hostilities was the first of many "unequal treaties" that humiliated the Chinese and compromised their sovereignty.

CULTURAL AND RELIGIOUS CRISIS

The restless and some would say reckless creativity of the West had produced by the middle of the nineteenth century not only superior armaments and economic exploitation through colonialism, but also intellectual and religious movements of far-reaching consequences. New secular trends were visible in the scientific world view, and new secular ideologies such as socialism and communism were being formulated. China had not so much joined the world as the world had joined China. And the world was in ferment.

The Confucian elite attempted to keep the West's intellectual influence at a distance, just as the imperial government had tried to do in the economic and military spheres. One of the more persuasive spokesmen for the traditionalists was Feng Gui-fen (1809–1874). A devoted student of the classics, he had also distinguished himself as an assistant to Lin Zi-xu and other high officials.

Feng coined the term *zi-qiang* (self-strengthening) as the proper attitude of the Chinese toward the Western threat: Western science and technology had much to offer, and in fact, translation centers should be set up and the best students sent there to learn Western mathematics, physics, chemistry, and medicine. But the Chinese must be very selective in their borrowings from the foreigners: According to Feng, "What we then have to learn from the barbarians is only the one thing, solid ships and effective guns."[8] Apart from this, the West had little: "Those [books] which expound the doctrine of Jesus are generally vulgar, not worth mentioning." In 1860 Feng clearly set down the formula that was to dominate Chinese thinking until the end of the century:

> If we let Chinese ethics and famous [Confucian] teachings serve as an original foundation, and let them be supplemented by the methods used by the various nations for the attainment of prosperity and strength, would it not be the best of all procedures?[9]

By 1898 China had fought and lost short wars with Britain, France, and Japan and had lost territory or spheres of influence to Russia, Japan, Germany, France, and Britain. But the attempt to preserve the Confucian foundation of Chinese culture and government only grew stronger. Zhang Zhi-dong (1837–1909) was the most eloquent spokesman for the second generation of this movement. His slogan "Chinese learning for the fundamental principles, Western learning for the practical application" was more than a popular rallying cry; it was also an attempt to use Neo-Confucian philosophy to confront the new situation.

Ju Xi in the Song period had made much of the distinction between *ti* (essence or substance) and *yong* (function). An idea or an emotion had both ti and yong, an inner or theoretical aspect and an outer application. Put another way, thought and action were seen as two sides of the same thing. But Zhang's use of this distinction drastically changed its meaning: How could Western action (function) be a natural or inevitable expression of Chinese thought (essence)? For now there was neither a necessary nor a close connection between thought and action.

With the conclusion of the Opium War and the increased economic and military penetration of China by the Western powers came a renewal of Christian missionary activity. This time it was predominantly Protestant and was carried out principally by the British and Americans. Schools, orphanages, and hospitals as well as churches were built by the various Christian groups. But it was perhaps through the schools that Christianity had its most noticeable impact on the Chinese. Zhang Zhi-dong was nonetheless optimistic about this kind of Western incursion. If the Confucian essence were truly strong, such secondary problems would disappear by themselves:

Facsimile from an album illustrating the Boxer Rebellion, published in China in 1891. Xenophobia reached its height during the Boxer Rebellion as conservatives in Chinese society sought to rid China of foreign influence. The rebellion was suppressed by the Western powers *Snark/ Editorial Photocolor Archives.*

L'ILLUSTRATION

LE NATIONALISME EN CHINE

Les supplices de l'enfer réservés aux chrétiens. — On y voit un porc chrétien scié en deux, un autre pilé dans un mortier — des démons à têtes de cheval et de bœuf président à la torture, tandis que d'autres chretiens y assistent derrière une grille, en attendant leur tour. Parmi ceux-ci, des étrangers en costume européen. « Malheur aux convertis! dit le texte, tels sont les supplices qui les attendent, eux, leurs femmes, leurs enfants et leurs petits enfants! »

Pour fêter la naissance d'un enfant, sacrifiez un porc et une chèvre. — « Quand l'enfant aura trois jours, nous vous tuerons. Quand l'enfant aura un an, nous les mangerons. » Vous, ce sont les porcs, les chrétiens; eux, ce sont les chèvres, les étrangers. Cette image se répète sous diverses formes en s'appliquant à tous les événements de la vie de famille. Dans celle-ci, le sacrifice est figure au premier plan; on aperçoit au fond la famille du nouveau-ne.

Rendez aux porcs ce qui vient des chèvres. — Des étrangers, en costume européen, apportent une chèvre à la porte d'un temple surmonté de l'inscription *Hing-Tan*, nom d'une ecole célèbre fondée par Confucius. Leurs presents sont repoussés avec mépris et la morale de cette image, dit le texte, est que les disciples de Confucius ne veulent rien apprendre des chretiens. A remarquer la couleur verte dont est toujours enluminée la coiffure des étrangers.

A bas les étrangers! Au feu leurs livres! — A gauche, en bas, un *autodafe* que des patriotes contemplent en se bouchant le nez, car les livres étrangers empoisonnent : la religion dépravée qu'ils enseignent ne prêche-t-elle pas le mepris des traditions, des ancêtres et des sages, de Bouddah et des Genies? Au premier plan, un portefaix apporte au bûcher une charge de livres chretiens. Plus haut, des patriotes assomment des étrangers à coups de bâton.

Les pirates étrangers mis en déroute par l'éventail sacré. — Allusion à la légende d'après laquelle Chu-Ko-Liang, ministre de l'empereur Liu-Pei, ayant régné de 181 à 234 de l'ère chrétienne, mit en déroute une flotte ennemie, après avoir obtenu par ses prières un vent favorable. L'image représente le grand patriote monté sur une jonque de guerre et brandissant l'éventail qui souffle l'incendie sur le vaisseau des barbares occidentaux. L'incendie détruit le navire, ajoute le texte chinois, et les pirates meurent tous dans les flammes.

Soumission générale des porcs et des chèvres. — L'animal fabuleux représenté au milieu du groupe est le Kilin, roi des quadrupèdes. Les porcs sont, comme toujours, marqués des signes *Jésus*, *missionnaire* et *converti*; les chèvres, du signe *occidental* ou *étranger*. Tous les étrangers réfractaires, tous les chrétiens incorrigibles ont été exterminés des différentes manières représentées précédemment. Les survivants reconnaissent la suprématie de la Chine; ils se prosternent devant sa gloire et célèbrent l'apothéose du fils du Ciel.

Fac-simile d'un album d'imagerie populaire prêchant la guerre contre les Etrangers, publié en 1891 à Tchang-Cha, province de Hou-nan.

When our national power becomes daily stronger and the Confucian influence increases accordingly, then the foreign religions will be merely like the Buddhist monasteries and Taoist temples which we may leave to their natural fate. What harm can they do us?[10]

The armament of Confucian ti was also sufficient to deal with the Western religious challenge. After all, it had worked before.

The flaw in this reasoning was not merely that it misused thc Nco-Confucian philosophical tradition, but also that the Neo-Confucians of the Song and Ming had considered unity necessary not only for the human psyche but also for human cultures.

The Tai Ping Rebellion

While the literati were wrestling with the impact of Western learning on the elite levels of society, a synthesis of East and West was being formulated on the popular level out of elements of Christian and Chinese religiosity. Instead of the esthetic and detached humanism of early Confucian flirtings with Christianity through the offices of the Jesuits, it was the popular culture, in which religion and action were not mediated by esthetics and which was expected to produce immediate results, that was affected. This led to the Tai Ping Rebellion, which devastated China and almost toppled the Manchu dynasty.

The leaders of this revolt (Tai Ping means "great peace") believed that the Christian God's kingdom could and would be established on earth. Furthermore, without being restrained by the tradition of interpretation of Christian teachings and a culture based partly on them, the Tai Ping leaders applied Christian concepts to their own society with revolutionary zeal. They tried to establish their religious utopia by military force, and they very nearly succeeded.

The Tai Ping vision of a heavenly kingdom on earth was derived as much from centuries-old peasant frustrations as from the Christian gospel. Its leaders sought radical egalitarian social structures: All people would be equal, including women. The old hierarchical system would be abandoned, and property would be held in common. All would be members of the same family, and for this reason sexual activity would be prohibited. Confucian notions of the world as a family were mingled with Christian millennialism and popular Taoist ideas of a struggle against demonic forces. The form of organization of the old Buddhist secret society was given a Christian content: Instead of the future Buddha (Maitreya) who would establish a pure land on earth, a new messiah would appear—in fact, he had already appeared.

Anthropologists are familiar with the sort of phenomenon in which a culture threatened by outside disruption often responds by creating a new synthesis. Elements of the old and new are incorporated into a "revitalization movement" that seeks to reestablish the old religious and cultural values, but in fact accommodates to the new ones. In North America the new religion of Handsome Lake among the Iroquois and the Native American church centering on the peyote cult are classic examples of such movements.

The founder of the Tai Ping movement was Hong Xiu-chuan (1814–1864). As a young man he had come to Guangzhou to take the imperial examinations. Though he had failed once, he made another attempt in 1837. He failed once more, and then he fell ill. Awakening after an extended period of nervous collapse, he recalled a vision of divine beings and heaven. Eventually he encountered some Christian missionaries and, after reading some of their religious tracts, was able to interpret his experiences. Hong came to believe that he was the younger brother of Jesus who had been called on to complete Jesus' work as a second messiah. He believed he had been escorted to heaven by angels and given new internal organs in a manner typical of the initiatory visions of Asiatic shamanism. He was instructed that the great evil in the world was the Confucian teaching, and having successfully struggled against Confucius and the various demons in heaven, he had been sent down to earth again with a sacred sword to restore the true teaching of Christ. Hong came to view the religion of the threatening West as having been originally Chinese.

The splendor of the imperial court (above) contrasts sharply with the bare existence of the common people like this shopkeeper's family. A desire to right this inequality was a leading cause of the Tai Ping Rebellion.
Religious News Service.

Curiously, the Westerners were for Hong not the so-called barbarian demons against whom his sword was sent: The true enemies of the Chinese people were the Manchu rulers who had taken China from the Chinese and thus perverted God's heavenly kingdom. The Great Peace (Tai Ping) would come with the overthrow of the Manchus, and God's kingdom of perfect brotherhood for all would ensue.

From 1850 to 1864, when the Tai Pings were finally crushed, Hong and his generals were at constant war with the Manchu regime. It was a double irony that native Chinese troops under native Chinese leadership finally stopped the Tai Ping advances after the Manchu troops had failed, whereas the intervention of the "Christian" powers of the West, notably Britain, led to the rebels' ultimate destruction. The great dream of peace had brought death to an estimated twenty million people.

China in the Twentieth Century

The first half of the twentieth century was for China a time of trial. It was a period of feeble government alternating with anarchy and civil war which culminated in the Communist victory in 1949. During this period one event stands out as significant to later Chinese history: the emergence of Mao Zedong* (1893–1976) as the leader of the Communists in the famous Long March of 1934. The national government under Jiang Gai-shek (1887–1975) began its notorious "bandit extermination" campaigns against the Communists in 1927, and later its forces surrounded the Communist guerrilla bases in southeastern and south central China. But the Communists managed to break out and escape to the north. Although thousands died on this six-thousand-mile Long March, the result was a strengthening of the Communist movement.

In 1932 Japan commenced in earnest its attempt

*Mao Tse-tung in the Wade-Giles system becomes Mao Ze-dong in Pinyin. Chiang Kai-shek becomes Jiang Gai-shek.

to conquer all of China by attacking Shanghai. It became a three-way struggle: Jiang's forces resisted the Japanese when possible and sought out and fought the Communists. The Communists under Mao organized the people into guerrilla units to harass the advancing Japanese and tried to dodge Jiang's "bandit exterminators." After the defeat of Japan in the Pacific War, the Communist armies were able to sweep Jiang Gai-shek's forces out of the mainland and into exile on the island of Taiwan. In October 1949, before cheering throngs in Beijing, Mao Ze-dong proclaimed the People's Republic of China.

RELIGION UNDER THE COMMUNIST REGIME

The official attitude of the Communist government toward traditional religion has come as no surprise. Karl Marx wrote in the nineteenth century that religion was the opiate of the masses, an instrument used by oppressive regimes to divert the attention of the people from their true enemies and even to enlist them in the willing service of their own exploiters. Therefore religion did not exist in a truly Communist society and was at best tolerated in a society in the process of transformation.

In theory, then, there is freedom of religion in the new China; in fact, the government has mounted a number of campaigns against those who practice it. Sometimes these campaigns have been verbal, such as identifying Confucianism with a repressive "feudal" system designed to exploit the masses. The people in their study sessions should "struggle against Confucius." Some campaigns went further, denouncing many popular Taoist practices as base superstition. Some acts of the government have been crassly manipulative: At times it has wooed the international Buddhist community by showing off a carefully nurtured Chinese Buddhist lay movement, while at the same time shutting down Buddhist centers. Often, religious institutions have been closed, churches and temples destroyed or confiscated, and priests and ministers sent to forced labor camps. But most indicative of the prevailing atmosphere in China is the fact that former monasteries are now shoe factories, and temples have been abandoned or converted into showpieces to bolster national pride. But traditional religion still has an ideological function in modern China: Its fossils are useful in teaching the masses about the evils of the past.

THOUGHT REFORM

Perhaps the most fundamental attack on religion in the years of revolutionary fervor was the attempt to "convert" religious leaders to Marxism. Here Marxism has tried to *replace* religion.

Thought reform, as it is known in China, or "brainwashing," as it is called in the West, is an advanced and effective technique. Prisons are seen not as places where habitual criminals are sent to be rehabilitated or where people are punished; rather, they are viewed as psychiatric clinics where those with improper ideas are sent to be reformed. Crimes are said to be caused by improper values—in other words, by heterodoxy. It is in the thought-reform prisons that the overwhelming thrust toward self-transformation is felt by the most recalcitrant. The "struggle sessions" constantly underway among the masses also utilize the prison techniques, albeit in a less intense and brutal way.

The basic technique of thought reform is what a noted psychohistorian has called "milieu control," or the careful manipulation of a person's entire environment so that he or she is forced to incorporate alien beliefs. A person's value system and notion of reality may be permanently changed by this technique. China has always used milder forms of milieu control: The Buddhist and Taoist monasteries for centuries have attempted, toward very different ends, to provide an environment conducive to the achievement of a different kind of self-transformation—spiritual enlightenment. In Maoism, however, the combination of guilt and self-dissatisfaction plus physical abuse is used to gain the cooperation of the person being converted. Often a great sense of relief and joy accompanies the final conversion. Robert Jay Lifton, a psychiatrist at Yale University, describes the heart of the thought-reform process as follows:

> The milieu brings to bear upon the prisoner a series of overwhelming pressures, at the same time allowing only a very limited set of alternatives for adapting to them. In the interplay between person and environment, a sequence of steps or operations—of combinations of manipulation and response—takes place. All of these steps revolve about two policies and two demands: the fluctuation between assault and leniency, and the requirements of confession and re-education. The physical and emotional assaults bring about the symbolic death; leniency and the developing confession are the bridge between death and rebirth; the re-education process, along with the final confession, create the rebirth experience.[11]

MAOISM AS A RELIGION

For some time scholars of religion have pointed out that any modern, supposedly secular ideology functions much as a traditional religion does. Thus an ideology like Marxism provides a world of meaning for its followers: It organizes their energies, defines what is worth doing, sets up a system of good and evil, and establishes rituals designed to reinforce these values. For this reason many scholars have called Marxism a pseudoreligion. But it might be more accurate to call it simply a modern, nontheistic religion. Like the traditional religions it seeks to replace, Marxism attempts to transform people into its own image of perfection. When it is successful, it engenders in the faithful a familiar sense of awe and reverence, of exhilaration or guilt, in the presence of what it establishes as sacred and of ultimate value.

Therefore, Marxism, especially in its Chinese form, is an enemy of traditional religions precisely because it is itself a religion that seeks to replace the others. Maoism has established as its ultimate values unlimited material progress and strong nationalistic power with which to confront the rest of the world. Evil is found first in the outside world, seen as imperialist enemies, and second within the body politic of the Chinese people themselves, as atavistic tendencies toward individual privilege and pride.

An enumeration of religious or quasi-religious elements within Maoism might begin with the often repeated holy history. The Moses-like figure of Mao is seen as leading the Communist armies on the Long March. They encounter many difficulties along the way, with enemies on every side. Many holy martyrs fall during this period of "salvation history" until the victory is finally won. The foreign devils (imperialists) are thrown out of China, and the domestic demons (landlords and capitalists) are punished. Once the victory is won, Mao himself emerges as a holy person. A poem celebrates his new position in a parent's advice to a child:

> *Chairman Mao saved us from our sea of sorrows,*
> *Never forget it, good child of mine.*
> *Neither mountains of knives nor seas of fire*
> *Should stop you from following Chairman Mao.*[12]

The holy person of Mao became truly cultic during the emotional upheaval known as the Great Proletarian Cultural Revolution, which began in 1966. The salvation history was not by itself adequate for the task of transforming the hearts of the people:

> The thought of Mao Tse-tung is the sun in our heart, is the root of our life, is the source of all our strength. Through this, man becomes unselfish, daring, intelligent, able to do everything; he is not conquered by any difficulty and can conquer every enemy. The thought of Mao Tse-tung transforms man's ideology, transforms the fatherland . . . through this the oppressed people of the world will rise.[13]

Here too emerges into prominence the holy book of Maoism, the famous little red book that contains the thoughts of Chairman Mao. This includes all wisdom and replaces all philosophies and theologies as well as all scriptures. During the Cultural Revolution, bookstores offered for sale *only* the writings of Mao. In every spare moment throughout the workday people were expected to read, memorize, and ponder his thoughts. The People's Liberation Army, which "had the deepest love for Chairman Mao and constantly studied his works," helped organize family study sessions on the holy book. Typically, families held regular meetings to

National Day Parade, October 1, 1950. Workers celebrate the first anniversary of the founding of the People's Republic of China by marching through the streets with posters of their leader, Mao Ze-dong. Like traditional religion, Maoism provides its adherents with a set of values and inspires in them a sense of awe and dedication. *Eastfoto.*

study and implement Mao's teachings and "make self-criticisms and criticisms of each other."[14] One possible result of all this is described in ritual terms: A meal was prepared of wild herbs and ordinary food, the former to represent the past and the latter "as a token of our present happiness":

> After the meal the whole family stood before a portrait of Chairman Mao and made this pledge: "From now on we will conscientiously study Chairman Mao's writings, follow his teachings, act according to his instructions. . . ."[15]

MAOISM AND THE TRANSFORMATION OF CULTURE

Holiness, or ultimate value, was found not only in the person and works of Chairman Mao, but also in the Chinese masses. It was the people, especially the peasants, who instinctively knew the correct doctrine and who felt the need for communism long before the actual organizers and leaders of the movement emerged. And it was to these same people that the leaders, including Mao himself, always had to return. As Mao once stated: "Our god is none other than the masses of the Chinese people. . . . When we say, 'We are the Sons of the People,' China understands it as she understood the phrase 'Son of Heaven.' The People have taken the place of the ancestors."[16] The people revered and imitated the chairman, and the chairman revered and learned from the people. The study of Mao's thoughts became an exercise in self-understanding, or in the conformity of the individual to the collective wisdom.

This view has had far-reaching consequences for modern China, and the Maoist vision of cultural transformation took its first step here: Culture begins with the masses; what is correct comes from the masses. But they are inarticulate, so Mao must interpret for them. Furthermore, no amount of mere study of words or abstract ideas can substitute for actual experience. Intellectuals and urban youths must be sent to the countryside and live the life of a rural peasant in order to grasp and internalize the true mass perspective. The famous May Seventh schools attempted to do this with study sessions at school alternating with periods of agricultural work.

The ongoing task of each generation, then, is the transformation of the individual's personal, selfish, and urban outlook to the peasant's collective, self-sacrificing attitude. The artificial environment of the thought reform prison is—in a milder and more benign form—naturally present in the Chinese countryside. But this mass culture is present elsewhere also: All artistic and literary activity must show this same peasant attitude and must therefore be socially relevant and "correct." The editorial policy of a new Chinese literary magazine which began publication in 1973 shows this policy in action. Its editors solicited:

> . . . all novels, essays, articles, works of art which present in a healthy way a revolutionary content. They must: (1) exalt with deep and warm proletarian feelings the great Chairman Mao; exalt the great glorious and infallible Chinese Communist Party; exalt the great victory of the proletarian revolutionary line of Chairman Mao; (2) following the examples of the Revolutionary Model operas, strive with zeal to create peasant and worker heroes; (3) on the theme of the struggle between the two lines, reflect the people's revolutionary struggle. . . .[17]

Maoism's quest for purity of attitude has sometimes met with resistance, even within the ranks of the faithful. The Communist revolution in China was not merely a victory of the peasants and workers over their former exploiters, but also an outpouring of nationalism. The strengthening of the nation and national pride required dedication to a strong military establishment and a strong economy. This meant the creation of a modern industrial state, with its modern technology and need for management skills. This need for expertise or modern skills could and often did run counter to the desire for revolutionary purity. The usual way of discussing this problem has been to distinguish between being "red" and "expert." Officially it has been necessary to be both red and expert: One must be politically correct and follow the "mass line," but one must also learn the skills required to be productive. In fact, since 1949 China has oscillated between these two poles, emphasizing one and then in reaction swinging to an emphasis on the other.

The most zealous, emotional, and disruptive period of emphasis on ideological purity ("redness") was during the Cultural Revolution. During this time (from 1966 to the early 1970s), the production of goods was allowed to suffer greatly in the service of purity. Purges not only of intellectuals and managers but also of Communist Party bureaucrats were carried out on an immense scale by roving bands of youths known as the Red Guards. Clearly, to be "red" was of supreme importance, and all had to be sacrificed for it. This chaotic rite of purification stopped only when the army finally stepped in to restore order.

The death of Mao Ze-dong in 1976 has not meant a significant change in direction for China or for Maoism. The emphasis of the Cultural Revolution on "red" at the expense of "expert" already had begun to wane, and the late 1970s saw a further shift away from the emphasis on ideological purity. The hated Gang of Four led by the "evil" Jiang Qing (Mao's widow) has been blamed for all the excesses of the Cultural Revolution. The West has been quick to celebrate this thaw in relationships with China, and there have been more trade and cultural exchanges. Meanwhile, more than 4 million people each year still visit the mausoleum of Chairman Mao. "The religious intensity of that experience," wrote one Western observer in 1978, "cannot be matched by any Christian shrine anywhere in the world."[18]

The 1980s have seen an increase in China's willingness to open itself to the world. A limited degree of private enterprise is now possible, and the press is less rigidly controlled by the government. But still the spectre of the red vs. expert dichotomy broods over China as the leadership tentatively experiments with increased individual freedom while at the same time attempting to maintain state control for the sake of stability and ideological purity. Maoism is for the moment quiescent—even a limited amount of criticism against Mao has been permitted. Christianity once again can be practiced openly, although severe restrictions still prevail against expansion of church buildings or membership. Taoism, except for the most elementary folk beliefs, has been destroyed. Buddhism is still a presence: some temples have been allowed to reopen, and perhaps with help from abroad the monastic tradition, now in utter ruin, may be rebuilt. And today, even for the intellectuals, Confucianism, once virtually synonymous with Chinese identity, is but an historical curiosity.

Notes

1 Arthur F. Wright, *Buddhism in Chinese History* (New York: Atheneum, 1965), pp. 90–91.

2 Attributed to Ch'eng-I by Chu Hsi in his *Chin-ssu Lu (Reflections on Things at Hand)* 1:32 in *A Source Book in Chinese Philosophy,* trans. and comp. Wing-tsit Chan (New York: Columbia University Press, 1967). (Ch'eng-I becomes Cheng Yi, and Chu Hsi is Ju Xi in the Pinyin system.)

3 Chu Hsi, *Chin-ssu Lu* 49:8b–9a in *A Source Book in Chinese Philosophy,* p. 638.

4 Ibid., 2:3.

5 Frederick Goodrich Henke, trans., *The Philosophy of Wang Yang-ming* (La Salle, Ill.: Open Court Publishing Company, 1916), p. 13.

6 Quoted in C. K. Yang, *Religion in Chinese Society* (Berkeley and Los Angeles: University of California Press, 1967), pp. 204–205.

7 Ssu-yu Teng et al., *China's Response to the West* (Cambridge, Mass.: Harvard University Press, 1954), p. 25.

8 Ibid., p. 53.

9 Ibid., p. 52.

10 Ibid., pp. 173–174.

11 Robert Jay Lifton, *Thought Reform and the Psychology of Totalitarianism* (New York: W. W. Norton, 1963), p. 66.

12 Donald E. MacInnis, comp., *Religious Policy and Practice in Communist China* (New York: Macmillan, 1972), p. 367.

13 Robert Jay Lifton, *Revolutionary Immortality: Mao Tse-tung and the Chinese Cultural Revolution* (New York: Random House, 1968), p. 73.

14 MacInnis, *Religious Policy,* document 109, p. 341.

15 Ibid., p. 340.

16 Ibid., pp. 16–17.

17 Quoted in Simon Leys, *Chinese Shadows* (New York: Viking, 1977), p. 137.

18 Michael Lee, "Searching for Sin in China," *Christian Century,* 13 (December 1978), 1199.

RELIGIONS OF JAPAN

13 Japan's Religions: From Prehistory to Modern Times

THE NATURE AND MYTHS OF SHINTŌ

Shintō, the native religion of the Japanese people, is a set of traditional rituals and ceremonies rather than a system of dogmatic beliefs or a definite code of ethics. The term *Shintō* is the shorter (Chinese) pronunciation of *kami no michi* and is generally translated as "the way of the gods." To the early Japanese the *kami* were the supernatural beings who animated the world around them. In the Japanese tradition, most kami are associated with nature and include the deities of heaven, earth, seas, and underworld. Usually well-disposed toward humanity, many kami are thought of as protective spirits.

The origins of Shintō are lost in the mists of prehistory. It has no founder, no all-powerful deity, no sacred scripture, and no organized system of theology. Although peculiar to Japan, it has been somewhat influenced over the centuries by Confucianism and Buddhism. Nevertheless, certain attitudes and practices have persisted from earliest times to the present. In many ways Shintō occupies in Japan a position similar to that of Taoism in China. Like Taoism, it has incorporated many concepts from Buddhism and shares today with Buddhism the allegiance of most of the Japanese people.

Shintō as a "Little Tradition"

Scholars seeking to reconstruct the history of Shintō are forced to use fragmentary and uneven evidence. There were no documents written in the most important formative period, the third to the sixth centuries A.D. Historians have had to draw on folklore, archeological findings, and oral traditions written down long after their original formulation. Even in more recent periods the development of Shintō has been difficult to ascertain beyond its broadest outlines. This is because of the very nature of Shintō, which has been for much of its history what some scholars call a "little tradition" lived by the common folk rather than by the learned and powerful. The anthropologist Robert Redfield describes this situation:

> In a civilization there is a great tradition of the reflective few, and there is a little tradition of the largely unreflective many. The great tradition is cultivated in schools or temples; the little tradition works itself out and keeps itself going in the lives of the unlettered in their village communities. The tradition of the philosopher, theologian, and literary man is a tradition consciously cultivated and handed down; that of the little people is for the most part taken for

granted and not submitted to much scrutiny or considered refinement and improvement.[1]

In its role as a village religion Shintō has not been concerned with great historical events; it has continued year after year and century after century to meet the daily and immediate needs of believers. They do certain things because their parents have done them and because others do them. As a little tradition, Shintō does not have laws; it has customs. It does not have general and abstract philosophies; almost all of Shintō is particular—only this festival, that habit, this act.

This does not mean Shintō has no structure or internal coherence: There are many common assumptions about the nature of the world and human life and destiny, and it is with some of these that we begin our discussion of Japan and its religions.

The Nature of the Kami

The scholar Motoori Norinaga (1730–1801) derived the term *kami* (often translated into English as "god") from a word written with a different character but pronounced the same, which means "above," "high," "lifted up"; by extension it also means something unusual, special, and powerful; finally, it also can connote something august, awe-inspiring, mysterious, divine. This understanding accords well with the modern Western notion of the most elemental form of religious experience: the discovery of *mana*—that is, an undifferentiated power inherent in all things that gives each its peculiar nature, efficacy, and attributes.

When this power becomes concentrated for some reason, it is believed to manifest itself as a sacred object or event, which in turn gives rise to special

Japanese women coming to pray for the well-being of their families at the Shintō-shrine Mitsumine Jinja, as their ancestors have done for nearly two thousand years. *Religious News Service.*

activities called religion. Certainly, the Japanese have responded to the manifestation of kami in their midst by the creation of many *matsuri*, or festivals, to which the kami are invited. The undifferentiated character of kami may be seen in the fact that many local shrines house kami whose names are not known and about whom no myths exist. Such shrines are more local places of reverence than attempts to establish a relationship with a particular deity. There are three main types of kami:

1 *Clan ancestors, or ujigami.* In the beginning these were probably the most important kami. The most famous of the *ujigami* is Amaterasu, the sun goddess, who has her primary shrine at Ise. Closely associated with Japan's ruling family, Amaterasu at one time had an imperial princess as her priestess. To be close to the center of political power, the Fujiwara, one of the most powerful of Japan's clans during the Nara period, moved their clan shrine from the countryside to the capital at Nara, where the shrine still remains.

2 *Deification of a power of nature or humanity.* Besides the ujigami, there are also other kami with quite different responsibilities. Indeed, Amaterasu herself, whose name is translated as "the heavenly shining one," is a manifestation of the sun. Often the names of the kami indicate the deification of a natural or a human force. Examples are the creative (*musubi*) kami called *takami-musubi* and *kami-musubi,* who are identified with the powers of growth and reproduction; the "straightening" kami who are responsible for setting things right; the "bending" kami who bring misfortune; and the "thought-combining" kami (*omoikane-kami*) who confer wisdom. Other kami are associated with such natural objects as heaven and earth, the stars, mountains, rivers, fields, seas, rain, wind, animals and insects, trees, grass, and minerals.

3 *Souls of dead leaders.* The third type of kami is the souls of great emperors and heroes. In more recent times these kami have also included anyone who has died in unusual or pathetic circumstances. Those deities who were formerly human beings (*hitogami*) reflect the influence of Taoism and Buddhism and also reveal the dark side of the kami nature. Perhaps the most famous of these is Tenjin, who is revered at the Kitano shrine in northwestern Kyoto. In life Tenjin (Sugawara Michizane) was a powerful court figure during the late ninth century. Through intrigue Michizane was discredited and exiled to the southern island of Kyushu, where he died. Some years later, after a series of natural disasters culminated in the emperor's death, a female shaman was possessed by Michizane's angry spirit and announced that he had become a deity of disasters and was the chief thunder demon. At this revelation, Michizane's name was cleared of all disgrace. Eventually the Kitano shrine was constructed in his honor, and a festival associated with this shrine became an annual ceremony at the imperial court.

Shintō Mythology

Early in the eighth century A.D., inspired by Chinese historical writings, Japanese scholars collected their oral myths and historical traditions into two important official "histories," the *Kojiki* (Records of Ancient Matters), which appeared in 712, and the *Nihongi* (Chronicles of Japan), which appeared in 720. These are the best and most complete sources of information on primitive Japanese beliefs regarding the nature and origin of the cosmos, kami, and humanity.

The adoption of the *Kojiki* as the official version of the origin of the Japanese state in the early eighth century conferred on Shintō mythology the status of a great tradition. Shintō's position was later overshadowed by Buddhism, although Japanese intellectuals began in the seventeenth century to revive Shintō by associating reverence for the sun goddess and the other kami with loyalty to the Japanese state. By the end of the nineteenth century, this movement had resulted in the establishment of Shintō once again as the dominant religion of Japan.

CREATION MYTHS

Creativity in the Shintō myths took many forms: sexual union, cutting up or subdividing existing kami, and releasing the blood of a kami. Each drop of this sacred life fluid was believed to have the power to generate new kami. Certainly a sense of *mana* is overwhelming in these early myths, in which even a kami's most casual activity produced new deities. As we shall see, three of the major Shintō divinities were created as the result of a purification rite, thus prefiguring the later importance of these rites as a means for humans to gain divine power. There are four myths about the sun goddess becoming the ancestor of the Japanese imperial family.

The Primordial Parents According to the *Kojiki*, the first kami arose from the primordial chaos and dwelt on the high plain of heaven. Next were created the kami of birth and growth. Finally, the original parents—Izanagi, the male principle, and Izanami, the female principle—descended from heaven along a rainbow bridge. Standing on the tip of this bridge, Izanagi thrust his jewel-like spear into the ooze below. When an island emerged, the two kami stepped down to it, mated, and produced the eight great islands of Japan. In this cycle the male-female love that turned to hate was the dominant theme and was never wholly resolved.

Many kami were born to the couple, but only after the dominance of the male was recognized. When the male god of fire was born to Izanami, his mother was killed by the flames. Izanami thus went to *Yomi*, the land of the dead beneath the earth, and in his grief Izanagi followed his wife. Despite the warning of Izanami, whose body was now corrupt, he could not keep himself from looking at her. They quarreled, and Izanagi fled back to the upper world, pursued by the polluting forces of decay, disease, and death. These forces turned into the thunder demons, kami who bring disease and death to humanity. Seeking to repair the harm he had inadvertently caused, Izanagi vowed to create life even faster than the thunder demons could destroy it. Thus the present balance between death and life was established.

The Sun Goddess and Her Tempestuous Brother At this point Izanagi formed the most august of all the kami through a purification rite designed to cleanse him of the pollution of the lower world. From his left eye was born Amaterasu, the sun goddess, who was given power over the high plain of heaven. Out of his nostril emerged Susano-ō, the god of storms, who was placed in charge of the earth. And from Izanagi's right eye came Tsukiyomi, the moon god, who had power over darkness.

The cycle of Amaterasu and Susano-ō is the most decisive of the Shintō myths. Amaterasu, who represented the principle of order, busied herself with weaving in a dwelling place known as the "pure house." By contrast, her brother was an impetuous deity who committed many offenses against the Shintō concept of divine order. Some of these offenses were of a polluting character: Susano-ō tried to visit his mother in the land of the dead, thus running the risk of contact with death. He killed living things by flaying them alive. Finally one day he defecated in the "pure house." Other offenses were associated with agriculture: Susano-ō broke down the boundaries between rice fields and was responsible for a double planting of the rice crop, which resulted in poor harvests. Disorder in heaven was reflected in disorder on earth.

Disgusted and angered by her brother's deeds, Amaterasu hid in a rock cave, bringing darkness to heaven and earth. In dismay the heavenly kami attempted to entice her out of the cave by inventing music in order to arouse her curiosity. When she peeked out to see the entertainment, the kami dazzled her with a mirror and jewels, the sacred objects of Shintō. Amaterasu finally emerged, restoring the brilliant light of the sun to the world, a classic symbol of life and divine order.

At the end of the cycle, Amaterasu and Susano-ō had a final confrontation to test each other's purity and good intentions. Significantly, Susano-ō was vindicated. He had *intended* no evil, and his heart was as pure as Amaterasu's. Shintō views evil not as malevolent, but rather as the unintended result of ignorance and error. Banished from heaven, Susano-ō settled at Izumo in western Japan. Here he slew a many-headed snake, married the daughter of a local chieftain, and founded a dynasty. Eventually he even recovered the favor of the other kami through his good deeds.

The story of Susano-ō's offenses forms a major portion of the purification rites (*harai*) at every Shintō ritual. In earlier times a great purification rite was held twice each year to purify the emperor as the symbolic head of the nation.

The Descent of the Heavenly Grandson Okuninushi, a descendant of Susano-ō, was the chief priest and ruler of the Izumo area. One day Amaterasu's grandson, Ninigi, was instructed to descend from heaven to earth to take over power in Japan, which meant that Okuninushi and his forces had to be subdued. As Ninigi left heaven, he was given a sword as well as the mirror and jewels used to lure Amaterasu from her cave. In this legend—known as the Descent of the Heavenly Grandson—Ninigi was successful. The heavenly kami came down with him and negotiated in his favor with the kami of Izumo, who promised to protect Ninigi. Significantly, neither Okuninushi nor his sons were killed in the struggle, but instead were enshrined as kami either at Izumo or on the Yamato plain. This arrangement is in keeping with the Shintō view that the kami must be treated properly. If this is done, what is experienced as evil can turn into good.

The Myth of Jimmu Ninigi's great-grandson Jimmu became the first human emperor of Japan. According to later Shintō historians, the date of this event was 660 B.C. During Jimmu's reign, the final establishment of the proper order of things on earth was accomplished. Shintō theoreticians maintain that this mythic event marked the origin of the Japanese state and that the Japanese imperial family is directly related to Jimmu. Amaterasu's shrine at Ise is said to contain Jimmu's mirror, jewels, and sacred sword. Though in this myth Jimmu functioned in some sense as a kami, he also appeared as a man. He prayed to the kami for help and guidance and was able to overcome difficulties only with the help of Amaterasu.

This cycle established Jimmu in the normal world of human beings without mentioning the creation of humanity as being different from that of the kami. The inescapable conclusion is that followers of Shintō believe in a continuity between the human and the divine: Men and women are simply kami with very little of the kami nature. Yet a human being might become a kami, since the difference is superficial—a matter of degree.

Although the destructive power of some kami is noted in the myths and is also a prominent feature of many Shintō rituals, Amaterasu and her descendant on earth, the emperor of Japan, are conceived as more concerned with peace and order. The emperor is charged by the sun goddess to pacify the world; thus Shintō is cosmocentric in orientation. It maintains a life- and world-affirming way of life that follows the rhythms of nature, especially through the changes of season and the activities associated with farming. The beauty of nature is emphasized, a view perpetuated by the Japanese today in the strong love they feel for their native land.

The nature of the kami is fundamental to this view, since the kami stand behind all natural phenomena. Just as James Joyce remarked of Ireland that "every hollow holds a hallow," we might also say of Japan more prosaically that the cosmos is permeated with the kami nature. For the followers of Shintō, the good life consists of living in accord with the natural rhythms of our existence in the here and now.

MYTHIC STRUCTURE AND INTERPRETATION

There are two main elements in Shintō mythology. First is its emphasis on sacred time—that is, the "age of the kami," when marvelous events occurred. Its chief distinction from our present time is that then the kami were still actively creating the world. Indeed, the age of the kami can be regarded as an elaborate etiology, or a story of how things "got the way they are." Besides investing these stories with the prestige associated with origins, this time element allows the myths to function as models or paradigms.

Anything done by the kami is not only the first occurrence of this event, but also the establishment of a pattern humanity is bound to imitate. Especially important are ritual precedents. The first purification rites are associated with the creation of Amaterasu, Susano-ō, and Tsukiyomi. The first

Eleventh-century statue of the Shinto God of Good Fortune. Whereas some kami are seen as destructive by Shinto worshipers, most are believed to have a positive influence on the course of events. *Sekai Bunka Photo.*

shamanic rite is said to have been performed in heaven in the attempt to coax Amaterasu out of the rock cave.

The second element is Shintō's tendency to divide all things and powers into pairs of contending opposites. The pattern of the sequence moves from a period of opposition to decisive events that bring about some kind of a resolution or synthesis. In the *Kojiki* the synthesis achieved nearly always results in the victory of Amaterasu's forces over the contending parties. Thus Amaterasu as the chief kami and the imperial ancestor was identified with the forces of good and order. Susano-ō was obviously among the forces of disorder as the founder of a rival cult and political center. The struggle was continued until final victory was won by Jimmu, the first human emperor. What has ceased is the mythic struggle among the kami powers in the age of the kami. Order has been established in the world, although disorder is still present. As a result, the struggle continues in the world of human beings by means of ritual action, and the myths have become relevant to the ritual concerns of humanity.

This system of contrasts functions on many levels in the Shintō myths. On the political level, it is represented by the struggle to establish the imperial clan as sovereign over all the Japanese islands. On the ritual level, the opposition is between the center established by Jimmu at Yamato near the Inland Sea, where Amaterasu is the chief kami, and the earlier center at Izumo on the Sea of Japan, where Susano-ō's cult is located. There also are other rivalries: that between the heavenly kami, who protect Ninigi, and the earthly kami, who protect Okuninushi; that between male and female; between land and sea; between elder brother and younger brother.

Ritual

Ritual performance in Shintō is fundamentally a matter of ordering the cosmos through human action. Just as Amaterasu sought to promote order through her descendant the emperor, all humans seek to aid this process through ritual. In early times the emperor himself was the most important ritual personage. Rituals were performed in his name and especially for his benefit as the representative of the whole nation.

This emphasis on order is found in several places in the ritual texts, including the *norito* (prayers, words of praise) collected in the *Engishiki* (Statutes of the Engi Era), compiled in A.D. 927. Here, again and again, the story of the creation and establishment of the world is referred to or is actually retold from the mythic texts. The central moment was the descent of Ninigi, the grandson of Amaterasu, who came down from heaven as the divine emperor to establish the proper ordering of things and to build his palace, a symbol of the divine presence on earth. This prototype of all Shintō shrines was a place of communication between heaven and earth, since a kami dwelt there:

Because in the bed-rock below, where you hold
sway, the palace posts are firmly planted,
And the cross-beams of the roof soar high towards
the High Heavenly Plain,
And the noble palace of the Sovereign Grandchild is
constructed,
Where, as a heavenly shelter, as a sun-shelter, he
dwells hidden,
And tranquilly rules the lands of the four quarters
as a peaceful land.[2]

Before Ninigi could safely descend, however, the land had to be "pacified." The rituals recount this part in some detail and in so doing present the early Shintō idea of disorder with elegant clarity. A messenger was sent out from heaven to reconnoiter:

The Land of the Plentiful Reed Plains and of the
Fresh Ears of Grain [*that is, Japan*]
During the day seethes as with summer flies,
And during the night is overrun with gods [*kami*]
which shine as sparks of fire.
The very rocks, the stumps of trees,
The bubbles of water all speak,
And it is truly an unruly land.[3]

Disorder was rampant, and things were not right: Whoever heard of rocks, trees, or water speaking?

COMMUNICATION WITH KAMI

The creation was not yet complete; the world was not yet prepared for humanity, and peace must be literally quiet. This first and therefore most powerful act of purification or ordering is invoked in the rituals of classical Shintō.

The process of ritually ordering the cosmos requires communication and even communion with the kami and is the goal of much ritual action, of which there are five major parts:

1 *The sacralizing of time and space.* The shrine area itself is a sacred space, established by its *torii,* or gates. The rituals take place in the middle of this area, hidden from public view, and the shrine itself, the dwelling place of the kami, is not entered even for ritual performances. Purification rites precede all Shintō rituals and are performed by the priests, who must shut themselves away from the world, eat special foods, and abstain from sexual intercourse. These rites include bathing ceremonially, rinsing the mouth, and transferring pollutants from the priest to a special wand, which is then thrown away. Even the day of festival is chosen according to either the established calendar or divination. All this is done in preparation for the presence of the kami.

2 The kami are called to attend the ceremony in their honor. The motif of the Descent of the Heavenly Grandchild is also used to reinforce this request.

3 Offerings are made of food and drink, usually rice, fruits and vegetables, water, *saké,* and fish. Thus "we [the worshipers] give to you the products of the earth." The prayers "give to you our praises."

4 Then the kami's blessing is given through a branch of the sacred *sakaki* tree, a kind of evergreen.

5 Finally the priest shares with the kami a meal made up of the food and drink previously offered.

The ideal result of ritual performance is not a specific gift or blessing, but a sense of living with the kami in a world permeated by kami and hence at peace and in harmony with the powers so close at hand. This relationship is often compared with that between parent and child.

SHAMANIC RITUALS

One type of ritual activity that has persisted in Japan is the practice of shamanism, a way of communicating with the kami by falling into a trance. The kami is considered to possess the shaman or, in Japanese, the *miko.* Most miko are women, and

The Great Torii of Itsukushima shrine. The gate to this shrine, dedicated to the three daughters of the Shinto god Susano-ō, stands offshore of the sacred Miyajima Island and is inundated at high tide. *Consulate General of Japan, New York.*

this has been so from the very earliest times, when shamanism seems to have been more important to Shintō worship.

The earliest historical account of Japanese shamanism is contained in a Chinese chronicle dated about A.D. 297, the *Wei-shi* (The History of the Kingdom of Wei). It tells of the country of Wa (Japan) which was ruled by Queen Himiko from her capital of Yamatai. The queen is said to have been a sacred person and able to communicate with the gods. She lived alone, and only her brother was permitted to see her in order to carry out her commands. This account resembles the political organization of the island of Okinawa, whose inhabitants are thought by scholars to have preserved usages common to Japan in archaic times. There, until recently, the

Contemporary Shintō Ritual

It is a misty morning in spring. Kyoto, the ancient capital of Japan, is unusually quiet. Ahead of us is a large parklike area, with a central walkway lined by weathered stone lanterns. The walk leads through a simple wood gate (a *torii*) that designates this place as a Shintō shrine. It is sacred to the kami whose special dwelling place is here. Just beyond the torii stands a stone tank, before which a woman and her child pause to rinse out their mouths with water, purifying themselves before coming into the presence of the kami. On each side of the path are numerous small, thatch-roofed buildings, many large old trees, and side paths. A white-robed priest walks slowly by and, at a crossing of two paths, faces toward each of the four directions in sequence, clapping his hands and bowing to each direction.

Matsuri, or public festival, at Tsurugaoka Hachiman shrine. Most Shintō worship is carried out by individuals in private, but elaborate public festivals do occur and are conducted by priests. *Sekai Bunka Photo.*

The woman and her child have now stopped before the largest of the shrine buildings. There she throws some coins into an offering box. Pulling a rope attached to a bell in front of the structure, she claps her hands, bows to the main shrine, and then prays silently. To one side of the large open courtyard in front of the main shrine a small stand has been set up. Here the woman buys a printed oracle, which tells of good or bad fortune ahead; its message is related in her mind to the prayer she has just offered to the kami. She ties the paper to the branches of a tree, among many other papers left by previous worshipers, either in gratitude for the promise of future gifts from the kami or in order to help avert a bad prognostication.

Most of the elements of Shintō worship are present in this simple act of piety we have just described. Much of Shintō consists of just such private acts, for the religion has little philosophy, offers little in the way of ethical strictures, and only occasionally is associated with public, congregational services. The larger shrines have a regular calendar of ritual events, which are tied mainly to the agricultural year and are concerned with good harvests or other bounties of nature as well as freedom from such calamities as earthquakes, floods, and diseases. The large public festivals called *matsuri* are much more elaborate than the acts of individual worship and are carried out by the priests. On such occasions the offerings take the form of food and *saké* instead of money. The prayers are much longer, and they often are formally chanted to the accompaniment of music.

rule was divided between a female religious specialist and her brother, the secular king. Even today shamanism is still the center of religious practice on Okinawa.

The *Nihongi* preserves what may have been standard practice during Japan's archaic period in the curious tale of Emperor Chūai, who held a kind of shamanic seance with his wife in which she acted as the miko. The emperor played the *koto,* a stringed instrument, to call down a kami who took possession of the empress and spoke through her. This story was a warning to those who disobeyed the commands of the kami, since refusal to believe the kami's words and to act on them resulted in the emperor's death. Not surprisingly, the shaman empress ruled in his stead.

Shamanic rituals, unlike the matsuri, are always performed for and at the instigation of individuals. Many people seek out the miko in order to ask the kami for advice on important decisions, such as the choice of marriage partners or the outcome of business or agricultural endeavors. Many seances are requested to determine the cause of disease or other misfortune. The answer is usually that the individual has offended some kami by an improper ritual performance or simply by neglect. An account of a shamanic seizure during a mountain pilgrimage was recorded at the end of the nineteenth century: two pilgrims paused partway up the slope, one holding a Shintō sacred wand, the other chanting a prayer:

> All at once the hands holding the wand began to twitch convulsively; the twitching rapidly increased to a spasmodic throe which momentarily grew more violent till suddenly it broke forth into the full fury of a superhuman paroxysm. It was as if the wand shook the man, not the man it. It lashed the air maniacally here and there above his head. . . . The look of the man was unmistakable. He had gone completely out of himself.[4]

The chanter then asked about the pilgrimage, whether it would be propitious and whether "the loved ones left at home would all be guarded" by the kami. Through the mouth of the possessed the kami answered: "Till the morrow's afternoon will the peak be clear, and the pilgrimage shall be blessed."[5]

THE JAPANESE STATE: YAMATO, THE CLASSICAL PERIOD, AND THE MIDDLE AGES

The origins of the Japanese people are obscure. It is believed that in prehistoric times many groups migrated to the islands of Japan, and from linguistic and mythic evidence, two primary groups have been identified. First is the proto-Malay group from Southeast Asia and the Pacific islands who were chiefly fisherfolk who settled in coastal areas and practiced a type of possession shamanism. In Japan they mingled with an aboriginal agricultural group that cultivated rice in the coastal lowlands, and their combined culture is probably reflected in the legend of Queen Himiko.

The second main wave of settlers was a warlike, semi-nomadic people from northern Asia. They were predominantly Mongoloid, and their religion was an ecstatic type of shamanism and a belief in a divine land in the clouds and/or on mountaintops from which the divine power and presence would come to aid the people. In times of trouble the shamans were believed to be able to travel on spirit journeys to this land to find cures for disease or other distress.

The Rise of the Yamato State and the Imperial Institution

By the fifth century A.D., the area around the Inland Sea was under the control of the descendants of the Mongoloid conquerors. All memory of their foreign origin had been forgotten, and the people were divided into autonomous groups whose dominant branches were believed to be descended from the kami. These groups were called *uji,* or clans, and their leaders controlled their economic, social, and religious functions. The clan religion focused on the ancestors who were identified with or held some

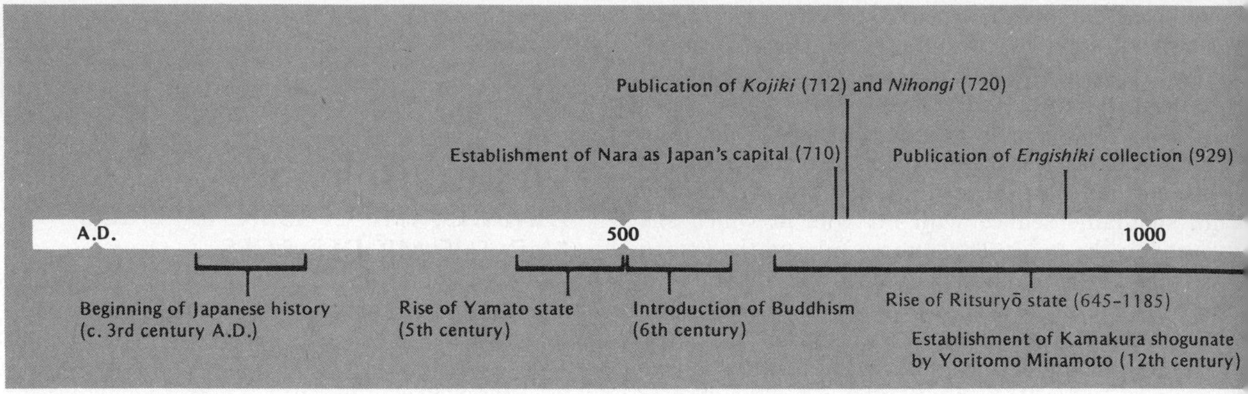

power over the forces of nature. Through shamanic possession and agricultural and social rituals, they communicated with the divine powers.

There are two hypotheses regarding the origin of the imperial institution. First, the Tennō (imperial) clan may have led the invasions of the Altaic, or Mongoloid, people, a theory supported by Shintō mythology in the story of Jimmu, who conquered the Yamato area. But Japanese cultural history records the Tennō clan and its "emperor" as having had only religious, ceremonial functions. This suggests a second hypothesis, that the emperor and perhaps the empress originated in archaic shamanism rather than in warfare. If so, the stories of the seances in the *Nihongi* are also tales of the original purpose of the imperial institution: The empress as the *miko* could become possessed by the important kami who guided the destiny of the group. The emperor then became the interpreter of her utterances and the kami's messenger. There is, however, some question as to whether or not the emperor actually did rule, in the sense of occupying himself with the day-to-day matters of government. By the beginning of the seventh century A.D., the important Soga clan seems to have wielded most of the actual power in the state as the primary "advisers" to the emperor.

During the sixth century Buddhism was introduced from mainland China, eventually bringing with it the splendor of Tang civilization. The prince regent of this period, Shōtoku Taishi, did all he could to promote Buddhism and Chinese culture at the Yamato court.

Classical Japan: Nara and Heian

Shortly after Prince Shōtoku's death, there was a bloody revolution in which the Soga clan was virtually annihilated by the combined efforts of the Nakatomi clan and an imperial prince named Tenji. The victors represented a pro-Chinese faction that sought to reorganize the state, and through the Taika Reform, they imposed Chinese law and social customs. The state they created survived from A.D. 645 to 1185. (In Japanese history this long period is divided into the Asuka, Nara, and Heian eras.) Because Shintō attained the status of a great tradition at this time, it was also the period of classical Shintō.

The power of the clans was theoretically broken by a radical centralization of economic power in the hands of the emperor. Clan lands were confiscated by the throne and parceled out as rental (taxed) property directly to the peasants. A system of provincial administration replaced the old clan structures, although neither the clans nor their traditional cults were abolished. Instead, the clans be-

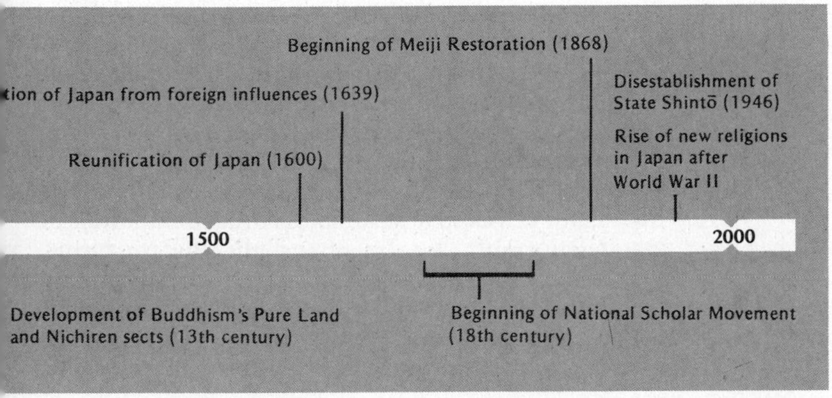

TIME LINE

RELIGIONS OF JAPAN

came nonofficial organizations whose loyalties and cohesion kept them at odds with the central authority. The development of an official mythology and cult life that focused on the imperial court reflected the government's efforts to centralize national life.

The Chinese notion of a sovereign combining both religious and secular political functions and supported by an elaborate system of ritual and graphic symbols of centralized power was slow to grow in Japan. Sacred and secular functions were not assumed by a single reigning emperor until 668 when Tenji, the imperial prince who had assisted in the coup of 645, ascended the throne. For twenty-three years he had been content to wield the real power behind the scenes as the crown prince. But now the sacred descendant of Amaterasu had to cope with the ordinary affairs of government.

THE COURTS OF NARA AND HEIAN

As the emperor became, to some extent, a practical politician, his symbolic value was also enhanced. In 710 a capital city, Nara, was established for the first time, which meant permanence as well as a monumental statement of the new order. The emperor in his palace was the pivot around which the rest of the universe revolved. Both Nara and the later capital at Heian (present-day Kyoto) were laid out in the Chinese fashion in a grid pattern oriented to the four compass points. The palace was situated at the northern end of the city, and clustered around the palace were the houses of the aristocracy. The courtiers, increasingly separated from the land and their old clan seats, became the bearers and co-creators of the new culture. The result was a flowering of poetry, pottery, weaving, architecture, gardening, elegant dress, and court ritual—both sacred and secular.

Many artisans were brought from Korea and China, and in nearly all things, China and the Chinese way became the touchstone. Learning was primarily Confucian learning. A Confucian national university was established. Poetry was written in Chinese, as were the official histories and government documents. Japan at this time took its place within the greater Asian cultural sphere whose center and source was China.

But the native traditions were not forgotten. Indeed, the introduction of Chinese writing enabled the preservation of much of the old Japanese culture that otherwise might have been lost. It was perhaps the fear of this that prompted the court to order the compilation of the two great myth collections, the *Kojiki* and the *Nihongi*, as well as a collection of ancient Japanese poetry, the *Manyōshū* (Collection of Myriad Leaves), which was completed in 766.

THE MEETING OF SHINTŌ, BUDDHISM, CONFUCIANISM, AND TAOISM

During this period many cults flourished, mostly under the patronage of the court and noble families. The ritual calendar of that time reveals many Shintō and Buddhist festivals, as well as several Confucian rites and Taoist festivals. Shintō was the favored religion. The government was divided into two equal parts, the various civil departments and the department of Shintō affairs. (The latter was revived during the Meiji Restoration of imperial power in the nineteenth century, when Shintō once again achieved a position of national importance.) Again, with few exceptions, the Buddhist rites, though supported by the court, were conducted not in the palace itself, but at various temples around the city. By contrast, most Shintō festivals under imperial patronage usually had separate celebra-

Illustration attributed to Iwasa Matabei (1578–1650) of *Genji Monogatari* (Tale of Genji), an eleventh-century novel by Lady Murasaki Shikibu. Both the novel and the artwork accompanying it reflect the refinement of court life at that time. *Freer Gallery of Art/Smithsonian Institution.*

Aoi Matsuri, a Shintō procession dating from the Heian era (794–1185), when the religions of China gained adherents in Japan but the native religion predominated. *Sekai Bunka Photo.*

tions within the palace in the presence of the emperor.

Taoism was also important in this period and offered a structure for the monthly festivals of the Chinese calendar, beginning with the first day of the first month, followed by the second day of the second month, and so on throughout the year. Of course, Taoist ceremonies often also contained native Japanese themes.

Perhaps the most revealing document of this period is Prince Shōtoku's Seventeen Article Constitution. Not really a constitution in the legal sense, this brief edict set forth a fundamental philosophy of government and life. It urged allegiance to Shintō, Confucianism, and Buddhism under the assumption that they were not incompatible and that each represented a valuable specialty or division of labor. Confucianism provided the ethics of family cooperation and national loyalty; Buddhism was concerned with the future of the individual in the next world and promoted the stability of the state in this world; and Shintō was the best means of handling the immediate environment to ensure abundant harvests and a minimum of natural disasters.

For the common people, these changes came much more slowly, and there is evidence that the imperial court sought to prevent Buddhist elements from reaching the peasants for fear that these religious powers might be used against the central authority. Nonetheless, by the middle Heian era (794–1185), the more practical elements of both Buddhism and Taoism had filtered down to the peasants. But even here the native Shintō tradition remained paramount, and these foreign elements were usually integrated into Shintō and considered simply as adding force to the already established practices. For example, *onmyōdō* (the way of yin and yang) divination—a Taoist practice—used a Shintō miko to communicate with the native kami and sought to deal with the same spiritual problems as did Shintō. The Pure Land Buddhist chant (*nembutsu*) invoking the name of Amitabha (in Japanese, Amida) was used in a similar way to cure ills and to ensure the chances of a good harvest.

Classical Shintō

ISE AS A CULT CENTER

The legends preserved in the *Nihongi* describe the establishment of the center of Amaterasu's cult at Ise, far from the Yamato Plain and the seat of the emperors. Ostensibly this was the spot where Amaterasu first descended from heaven, though just when it was established as a cult center is not known. It is probable, however, that its isolated location was connected with the increasing involvement of the emperor in secular affairs. But Amaterasu was too important to be left to the possible neglect even of the emperor, and thus the famous Ise shrine was built for the yearly round of rituals. The emperor as the direct descendant of Amaterasu and the head of the Tennō clan had to be represented at these rituals, so an imperial princess, called the *saigu,* was appointed to live at Ise and to be the imperial presence there. Restricted by many taboos and subject to the most rigorous standards of purity, she was an idealized form of the emperor in his capacity as priest.

INARI AS THE CHIEF AGRICULTURAL DEITY

While Shintō was uniting around the imperial institution, the official mythology, and the cult at Ise, elements of the folk religion began to take form. One manifestation was the cult of Inari, the chief agricultural deity of Japan from early times to the present. Although the name Inari probably comes from an ancient place name associated with an especially powerful sacred manifestation, one ingenious folk etymology attributes its meaning to *ine,* "rice plant," and *naru,* "to grow." Certainly Inari did eventually draw into his cult many of the diverse elements people associated with successful harvests, abundant food, and fertility.

Legend has it that the first and most important

Amida Nyorai Zazo, a row of nine statues dating from the eleventh century, in the Jōruri-Ji temple in Kyoto. Each statue represents the Amida Buddha, whose name was chanted regularly by Japanese Buddhists. *Sekai Bunka Photo.*

Inari shrine was founded in A.D. 711 at Fushimi, which is located in what became the southern outskirts of Kyoto. The story was that a certain rich man was using a ball of rice as a target for practice in shooting arrows. Suddenly a white bird emerged from the ball and flew away to a mountaintop (at Fushimi) and there perched on the branches of a cryptomeria tree. If the mysterious appearance of the bird were not enough to signal the presence of a kami, the roosting place of this particular bird would have done so, since the cryptomeria was and is one of several evergreen trees upon which kami often descend. The man realized he had failed to show proper reverence for food as the special gift of the kami. To make amends he had a shrine built at the spot indicated by the bird, which was regarded as a manifestation of Inari.

Presumably the cult of Inari, or something very much like it, had existed for some time in the daily religious life of the common people. But with the founding of the shrine at Fushimi and the creation of the new capital nearby, Inari became more important in the religious life of the court. Throughout the Heian period the Fushimi Inari shrine rose in prestige until it was classified as one of the three most important shrines of the nation. Imperial patronage began in A.D. 823 when the first large shrine building was erected in gratitude for successful prayers for rain. Then in 908 the shrine's fortunes were greatly enhanced when the prime minister had built three shrines on separate hills. The three kami enshrined at this time were Ugatama, the female kami of food and clothing, Sarudahiko, the earth kami also associated with the monkey, and Ameno Uzume, also known as Omiya no Me. All three figure in several myths in the *Kojiki* and *Nihongi*. Thus Inari, the kami of the common people, was identified with the official mythology and legitimized and made more prestigious.

As the Fushimi Inari shrine became more important, branch shrines and autonomous Inari cults were established. Merchants and artisans adopted Inari as their special kami. Like a whirlpool drawing into itself much of the free-floating material nearby, the Inari cult attracted more and more folk elements. Foxes became associated with Inari, probably first as the kami's special messenger. Eventually, foxes became identical with Inari and were seen to be the kami itself. Inari shrines are still decorated with fox figures as guardians or attendants.

Also associated with Inari shrines was the traditional Shintō *torii,* or gate, which in all shrines marks the entrance to the sacred precincts and symbolizes the separation of sacred and profane. But Inari shrines use the torii itself as a sacred object in such a way that each minor shrine and sacred spot may have red-painted torii around it. Sometimes, as at Fushimi, there are so many of these gates that the paths leading to the various shrines become torii tunnels. No one knows how this tradition began or what it means.

Another folk element in the Inari cult is the ancient worship of the phallus. This is often represented by the foxes' stylized tails, which are shaped like the male organ. The ambivalent character of the fox throughout East Asian folklore also suggests an association with sexual potency and sometimes uncontrollable sexual passions. Especially in Japan, foxes are thought to be able to possess human beings and drive them to dangerous excesses.

But although the phallus is the most common and obvious sexual symbol at the Inari shrines, the emphasis is neither exclusively nor even predominantly on male sexuality. The presence of rounded stones and the copious use of red paint indicate a balancing presence of the feminine element. This is especially obvious in the case of the paint, since most of the other shrines use no paint at all. The color red is associated with feminine sexuality and fertility in nearly all primitive societies: here it is associated with agricultural abundance. The life and fruitfulness of plants are believed to be intimately and mysteriously bound up with that of animals and of humans. The blood associated with menstruation and birth is also believed to be the source of the life force of the rice plant.

All this was derived from folk traditions, of course, but the association of the food kami, Ugatama, from Shintō reinforces these ideas, since several myths tell of her murder and thus suggest that it was from the spilling of blood that the various foods and food plants were primordially derived. We might further speculate that the mysterious to-

Fukiage Inari shrine. Many Inari shrines are entered through a series of torii, which are themselves considered sacred. *Sekai Bunka Photo.*

rii of the Inari shrines symbolize the entrance to the womb of the earth, the source of the most powerful lifeblood as well as of all plants.

Shintō–Buddhist Syncretism

Buddhism was part of the Chinese cultural heritage that Japan sought to borrow and adapt to its own ends. This meant two important things. First, Buddhism was carefully regulated and restricted by the new central government. Prince Shōtoku and others saw Buddhism as a powerful civilizing force that would bring education and the literary arts to Japan, as well as more imponderable benefits in the form of efficacious intervention with the sacred powers. Second, Buddhism, like other Chinese cultural and religious elements, was imposed on the people from above. It was a part of official policy, and its temples, monasteries, and art were intended in part to support the centralizing of the culture.

Nara, besides being the capital, also became a temple city and the headquarters of Japanese Buddhism. Its elaborate and powerful Buddhist establishment was as much a political, intellectual, and artistic institution as a religious one. During the reign of Emperor Shōmu (ruled 724–749), the Buddhist influence became especially strong. A government-sanctioned Buddhist hierarchy was established in an attempt to control Buddhism and to unify the nation under Buddhist dominance. Also to this end, work was begun on the Tōdai-ji in Nara, the temple which eventually housed the Daibutsu (Great Buddha) statue still to be seen there today. Completed in A.D. 752, this forty-five-foot statue is of the Vairocana Buddha (Dainichi), the great sun Buddha, and thus fits in well with the cosmic symbolism of the city itself, as well as the imperial identity with the sun through Amaterasu.

Perhaps more significant in the longer view was Shōmu's establishment of the *kokubun-ji,* the official Buddhist temples built in each province throughout the nation. The main work of these temples was the preservation of the nation: its peacefulness, its harvests, and its emperors. Prayers without cease were offered here. In addition, these temples became centers of learning and training grounds for future Buddhist leaders. But they were not supposed to be centers for the dissemination of Buddhism among the common people, since Buddhism at this time was officially the business only of a small monastic elite.

The power of Nara Buddhism reached its apex with the appointment of a Buddhist monk as the chief minister in the reign of Empress Kōken (ruled 749–758). Eventually this led to disaster for both the monk and those Buddhists who had hoped to make their creed the national religion of a theocratic state. Dōkyō was thwarted in his attempt to usurp the throne in 769, and it was probably fear of the Buddhists' power that motivated Emperor

Horyuji temple near Nara, a city of numerous temples. Built in A.D. 607 by Prince Shōtoku, who promoted Buddhism in Japan, this temple and the artwork it houses are among the earliest examples of Japan's cultural heritage. *Consulate General of Japan, New York.*

The Daibutsu, or Great Buddha, statue in Kamakura, a city near present-day Tokyo, which was the seat of an early medieval warrior government. Completed in the thirteenth century A.D., this statue depicts the Buddha Amida, the central figure in Pure-Land Buddhism. *Sekai Bunka Photo.*

Kammu (ruled 781–806) to move the capital to Heian (Kyoto) in 794.

But Buddhism could not be safely contained within the kokubun-ji, and throughout the Nara period (710–781), it grew to become the principle religious practice of the Japanese aristocracy. The temples were opened to the upper classes, and the rituals became elaborate and esthetically pleasing. In addition, priests were able to offer powerful Buddhist charms and other techniques for curing or averting disease and calamities. Gradually Buddhist assumptions about the nature of human life and destiny became commonplace, and such ideas as karma and the possibility of life after death were generally accepted. Even among the common people, illegal missionary activity was carried on to some extent by the wandering priests called *hijiri*.

The impact of all this Buddhist activity in and around Nara and Kyoto, and especially on the aristocracy, was tremendous. But since few people saw religions as exclusive, Shintō continued to flourish, with many Buddhist elements. Then too, Buddhism had a long history of assimilating non-Buddhist elements, both in its native cultural setting in India and during its centuries in China. Many Hindu and Indian folk elements had been integrated into Buddhism, and some of the Hindu vedic gods were represented in the myths and legends transmitted to Japan. So there was room for Shintō figures as well.

THE JINGH-JI SYSTEM

The mixture of Shintō and Buddhism proceeded along several paths. Perhaps the earliest attitude held by those caught up in the Buddhist world view was that the Shintō kami should be taught the Buddhist Dharma and eventually led to enlightenment, just like human beings. To this end Buddhist sūtras were chanted at Shintō shrines, and eventually it became a common practice to establish a small Buddhist temple within the shrine precincts with its own complement of priests. Typically nothing was lost, nothing was thrown away; the old was supplemented by the new in this *jingu-ji* (literally "shrine temple") system.

It was a small jump from this position to the notion that the kami were already enlightened and were in fact disguised manifestations of the various Buddha and bodhisattva figures mentioned in the sūtras. This notion of identity or of equivalence was easy and even natural at the folk level, since kami were known more for their location than for their theological definition. Since even the names of the kami enshrined at a particular spot might not be known or agreed upon, they might as well be thought of by Buddhist names as by any other.

HONJI-SUIJAKU

Chinese Buddhists had already developed a philosophical justification for this last approach, known in Japanese as *honji-suijaku*—that is, "original substance, manifest traces." In Japanese application the *honji,* of course, was the Buddhas and bodhisattvas, and the *suijaku* were the kami. But when coupled with the Buddhist doctrine of *upaya* (sufficient means), the *honjaku* (as it was often shortened) theory gave the kami a status equal to that of the Buddhas. Bodhisattvas, especially, were thought to employ sufficient means by manifesting themselves in whatever form would be most effective in a given situation to bring about the conversion or enlightenment of the people. Eventually not just kami but also famous ascetics and priests were believed to have been manifestations of bodhisattvas, as were famous people such as Prince Shōtoku and several emperors.

One important reason for expounding the honjaku theory was, of course, to gain popular acceptance of Buddhism. But this attitude was not entirely based on concern for the spiritual well-being of the people: The Buddhist temples and monasteries were becoming the owners of more and more land, and as administrators of large estates, they needed the cooperation of the peasantry. At the same time it is clear that many devout Buddhists sincerely believed in the reality and power of the Shintō kami. As early as the middle of the eighth century an emperor had built a shrine to the local kami within the precincts of Tōdai-ji in order to pacify the local spiritual powers. This eventually became common practice in many Buddhist temples.

THE MOUNTAIN SECTS AND THE YAMABUSHI

With the establishment of the new capital at Kyoto came the introduction of new forms of Buddhism which hastened the integration of Shintō and Buddhism. The so-called mountain sects of Buddhism that came to dominate court life by the end of the ninth century had their headquarters on the peaks of sacred mountains. We know that mountains had been sacred places to Shintō before the introduction of Buddhism, and their choice as temple sites was no accident. First, the sponsors of the mountain sects wished to rejuvenate Buddhism by removing it from the political intrigue and secular ambitions that dominated the capital. The founders of mountain Buddhism also sought the special protection of the powerful kami whose special province was the mountains. Dengyō Daishi (Saichō, 762–822), the founder of Tendai Buddhism on Mount Hiei (which can be seen in the distance from Kyoto), was a sincere believer in the Shintō kami. Before he left Japan on his travels to Tang China, he prayed at several shrines in Kyushu for the success of his journey to study with the Chinese Buddhist masters and to return with a fuller understanding of the Dharma. And when he founded his temple, Enryaku-ji, on Mount Hiei, he dedicated several shrines to the native kami of the mountain. Similarly, when Dengyō Daishi's contemporary Kōbō Daishi (Kūkai 774–835) founded his Shingon sect on Mount Kōya, he is said to have had a vision of the kami Nifu Myōjin, whom he recognized as the guardian of the mountain. In addition, the Shingon temple in the southern part of Kyoto, the Tō-ji, was placed under the care of the kami of the Inari shrine.

Both Tendai and Shingon Buddhism came to be dominated by Buddhist forms of tantrism, usually referred to as Esoteric Buddhism (in Japanese, *mikkyō*). This tradition provided a great stimulus to Japanese iconography, and its elaborate rituals appealed to all levels of society. Whereas Nara Buddhism can be characterized by its emphasis on philosophy, Heian Esoteric Buddhism can be said to have sought religious power and spiritual achievement through ritual. This also made possible new forms of Shintō-Buddhist amalgamation. The use of the *mudra* (ritual hand and body gestures) became popular, as did the *dharani* (ritual chanting of sacred formulas, often in Sanskrit or garbled Sanskrit) and the *maṇḍala* (the sacred diagram).

Whatever the philosophical justification for these

Head of a Buddhist temple guardian from the Kamakura period (A.D 1185–1392), fashioned of Hinoki wood. During this period, Buddhism flourished in Japan and the influence of both the Shintō tradition and the imperial court with which it was associated declined. *William Rockhill Nelson Gallery of Art—Atkins Museum of Fine Arts.*

practices that the Tendai and Shingon monks and nuns might have had, the popular conception of them encouraged a faith in their objective efficacy. Salvation came to be a matter more of external activities than of any internal, personal transformation. For Shintō, which had always stressed ritual and which had never had an unworldly, personal notion of salvation, this development was natural and easily assimilated. The most significant result at the folk level was the formation of a Shintō-Buddhist combination centered on the old Shintō cult of sacred mountains.

The *yamabushi*, or mountain priests, did not live according to monastic rules or in monastic communities. Rather, they met only occasionally to journey to various sacred mountains to conduct their own esoteric rituals there. The sacred sites were Shintō, as were the priests' costumes and some austere practices such as ritual purifications in mountain waterfalls. But most of the deities whose names were invoked and the content of the rituals themselves were derived from Buddhism. Both Tendai and Shingon eventually established special branches to serve and influence the yamabushi cults. One of these, later known as Shugendō, still exists today.

The Medieval Period

The traditional Japanese era names of Kamakura and Ashikaga correspond to the medieval period, which lasted from 1185 to about 1600. By the beginning of this period Japan had become a collection of more or less autonomous agricultural estates called *shoen.* Not taxable by the central government, the shoen themselves came to exercise all the actual functions of government. The imperial court at Kyoto continued to carry out ceremonial activities, but was no longer a political force. In 1185 a great naval battle was fought at Dan no Ura, the strait between Kyushu and the main island of Honshu, and in it the child emperor Antoku died, along with many of the Taira clan, who had controlled the court. The victorious clan was the Minamoto, or Genji, and its leader, Minamoto Yoritomo, established a military government at Kamakura, near the present city of Tokyo. But the prestige of the old court, the emperors, and the old aristocracy was still great, and Yoritomo eventually was given an official title (*shōgun*) to rule in the place of the emperor. Many of the newly powerful military men (the *samurai*) were given court titles.

The Kamakura government did not survive for long, however, and in the power vacuum that resulted, Emperor Go-Toba in 1333 attempted to restore direct imperial rule. His coalition of court aristocrats and dissident samurai proved to be too weak, and he was driven into exile in 1336. A new military government was established by Ashikaga Takauji with its headquarters in the old capital. The imperial establishment suffered the indignity of a rival (northern) court set up by the Ashikaga with a puppet "emperor." Symbolic of the difficult times faced by the court and by Shintō, in 1336 the last *saigu* at Ise retired and became a Buddhist nun, thus ending the tradition of the imperial presence at Ise.

But the nadir of imperial power and prestige was undoubtedly reached at the conclusion of the Onin War (1467–1477), which was fought mainly within the city of Kyoto itself. Afterward, no effective central authority remained, although the Ashikaga shoguns remained the nominal heads of the administrative structure. The old court aristocracy was impoverished, the city was in ruins, and the reigning emperor had to support himself by selling samples of his calligraphy. Fighting was continuous throughout Japan as rival feudal lords (*daimyo*) contended for advantage.

Curiously, this period of political chaos was one of vitality for Buddhism. Out of the rich and varied life of Tendai came new popular movements known as the Pure Land (Jōdo) and Nichiren sects. These benefited greatly from the lack of central authority and gained wide acceptance among the common people. Their messages were simple and their practices were easy to perform. Faith would lead to rebirth in a Buddha's paradise, for which chanting and acts of piety were sufficient. The Nichiren sect, although similar in many ways to Pure Land, was much affected by the prevailing militaristic tone of the times and sought national unity under the banner of a Buddhist utopian ideal.

Also in the Kamakura period, Zen Buddhism was reintroduced to Japan from Song China. Particularly attractive to the new elite, the rising samurai class, was the austere practice of the Sōtō Zen school founded by Dōgen (1200–1253). It was the influence of Zen that brought about a new flowering of Japanese culture: Artists saw in Zen's quest for the meaning of Buddhism in discipline and simplicity an inspiration for new esthetic canons.

Although in this period Zen was restricted to the elite, the Pure Land and Nichiren sects at last brought Buddhism to the people. At the village level Shintō now had to share the loyalties and energies of the people with its powerful rival. Particularly important was the rise of a religious division of labor which gave popular Buddhism its special function in the conduct of funerals and concern for the dead. The so-called *nembutsu-hijiri* were especially popular for dealing with the fear of evil spirits of the dead, belief in which the chaotic times seem to have promoted. People reasoned that if the chanting of the Buddha Amida's name (nembutsu) could result in personal salvation for the faithful, then a skilled practitioner should be able to do the same vis-à-vis evil spirits.

Despite the dominance of popular Buddhism and the eclipse of Shintō as a great tradition as represented by the imperial court, Shintō did not die out. It may be that the same forces that enabled Buddhism to create new forms as the central authority diminished also affected Shintō.

State Shintō with its elaborate mythology, interacted with popular religious sentiments to create the myth dramas called Kagura, which can still be seen today. Kagura performances at Shintō shrines were the precursors of the Zen-dominated Nō dramas, as well as the farcical Kyogen and the melodramatic Kabuki. They utilized court music and dancing as well as the myths of the *Kojiki* to popularize what had been the official cult. Such themes as the creation of the world by Izanami and

Diary of a Pilgrim to the Great Shrine at Ise

Religious pilgrimages in Japan were made in early times by both Shintō and Buddhist faithful. Whether sought as a reinforcement of piety, an ascetic exercise, or a religious experience, the pilgrimage has been the source of a considerable literature. Pilgrim diaries were often preserved as inspirational devices and contain much introspective piety as well as travel descriptions and elegant poetry. Among the most highly valued of such diaries is that of the Buddhist priest Saka, from which the following excerpts are taken. Note especially the nostalgia for the vanished classical past and the ambivalence of a Buddhist toward the Shintō deities. At this time (1342), Japan was slipping into the medieval period of political disintegration.

And as to the Way of the Deities, in primaeval days they reached out from on high and created land and gave it the name of Onokoro Island, and on to it the two Deities [Izanami and Izanagi] descended from Heaven. . . . [For many thousands of years] the deities alone protected the land and dealt graciously with the people, for the virtuous assistance of Buddhism in governing the country was not yet.

But after many years, when people had ceased to trust in the Way of the Deities, Prince Jōgū (or Shōtoku-taishi) appeared and not only spread the Knowledge of Buddhism but also was a manifestation of this Way. After him came Dengyō-daishi. . . . So Buddhism did not remain an exclusive faith: it made friends with the Way of the Deities. And though its sects have various doctrines they all have the one principle of perfecting the intuitive soul and revealing the jewel of the enlightened mind. . . . For, though one's inward conviction may have a profound assurance of the reality of the Nirvana state, it is difficult for those born in folly and delusion to be saved. Whereas these deities manifest themselves outwardly among the unsaved worldly minded and it is easy for the unenlightened to profit by them. . . .*

*A. L. Sadler, trans., *The Ise Daijingū or Diary of a Pilgrimage to Ise* (Tokyo: Meiji Japan Society, 1940), pp. 48–59.

Izanagi, the struggle between Amaterasu and Susano-ō, Amaterasu's withdrawal into the cave, Susano-ō's slaying of the monster, and Ninigi's descent have been reenacted countless times for villagers. To these Shintō elements were added others, such as the Inari kami and the fox messengers.

As with the sophisticated Nō drama, the meaning of Kagura is not communicated only by its recitation. Its more mysterious language of gesture is also important, as is its setting and music. It may be that folk tradition sees in these plays a drama more timeless and universal than that in a particular mythology. These timeless aspects are structuring elements, such as the struggle between man and woman, the ambiguity of evil and good, and the continuity between the human world and that of the kami. Some sense of the universality of Kagura may be seen in the three basic character types. According to American folklorist A. W. Sadler:

> First, there is the *kami*, who is, with rare exceptions, the heroic figure in the play. Next, there is the *modoki* role. He is usually the servant of the *kami* (the feudal footman, as it were), and his actions in a sense echo those of his master; that is to say, in carrying out his master's orders, he appears to parody the swashbuckling mannerisms of the heroic lead—much to the delight of the crowd, who must feel closer to the *modoki* than to his lord. The third character is the enemy of the *kami*, usually a demonic creature of some sort. But there are . . . *modoki* elements in the performance of the demonic lead, suggesting that a demon is essentially the backwards reflection of a *kami*. For the heroic lead's servant and his enemy have this much in common; they are both doers of mischief. The demon's mischief is destructive, and must be stopped; the servant's mischief is harmless (though time-consuming), and in the end he is always loyal to his master. . . .[6]

Although it is dangerous to assume that these twentieth-century attitudes are the same as those of long ago, a modern Shintō priest explained the continuing appeal of these religious dramas: "You must try to get the spirit of the dance. *Kagura* is one of the ways of giving pleasure to the *kami* at *o-matsuri* time; so origins do not matter, only the spirit."[7]

The Reunification of Japan

In the second half of the sixteenth century Japan once again had a strong central government. It began with the consolidation of the Nagoya area in 1560 by the powerful daimyo Oda Nobunaga (1534–1582), who then marched into Kyoto (1568) and drove out the last Ashikaga shogun (1573). Although Nobunaga failed to establish a new dynasty of military rulers, he went far toward the military conquest of the disparate power centers, including not only the strongholds of the daimyo but also the temples, such as the great Buddhist complex on Mount Hiei, which he burned in 1571, and the fortified headquarters of the Ikkō sect (a branch of Pure Land Buddhism) at Ishiyama, which he finally overcame in 1580.

Nobunaga's successor was Toyotomi Hideyoshi (1536–1598), a poor farmer's son who had risen to power as a military man. By 1590 Hideyoshi had subdued the rebellious daimyo in the outer provinces and settled down to reform Japanese society. He continued Nobunaga's policy of restoring the prestige of the imperial court, partly to enhance his own status, and he also promoted Neo-Confucianism as the organizing principle of the nation. On the basis of this model, he bound the peasants to the land and established rigid class distinctions among the samurai, farmers, and merchants.

Hideyoshi's death brought on a bloody power struggle to determine his successor. The Battle of Sekigahara in 1600 was a decisive victory for Tokugawa Ieyasu (1542–1616), who was given official recognition by the imperial court with the title *Seii-Taishogun* (military dictator), which his descendants held until the restoration of direct imperial rule in 1868. The Tokugawa ruled Japan from the fortress of their clan at Edo (modern Tokyo), which was converted into a virtually impregnable center of power.

THE TOKUGAWA REGIME AND MODERN TIMES

The tumultuous period of unification also saw the first contacts with the West. First to appear were Spanish and Portuguese traders and the Jesuit missionaries. The Japanese at first were interested mostly in trade and in European firearms and viewed Christianity as a symbol of technological and cultural advancement. In the beginning, the Jesuits under the leadership of Francis Xavier (1506–1552) conveyed their message using the indigenous cultural and religious forms, as they had in China. Under Nobunaga's rule Christianity enjoyed a privileged position because he sought to use the new faith as a counterpoise to the entrenched power of the Buddhist sects that threatened his own.

But by the end of the sixteenth century, religious differences between Catholics and Protestants, as well as bitter rivalry between Jesuits and Franciscans, helped undermine the Christian cause. In addition, rumors of Western imperialistic intentions had reached the Japanese leaders. In 1587 Hideyoshi issued an edict prohibiting foreign missionaries from operating in Japan and interfering with the Shintō and Buddhist teachings. Little effort was made to enforce it until 1597 when twenty-six Japanese and European Franciscans were crucified at Nagasaki. Then in 1614 the Tokugawa regime, in an attempt to tighten its grip on the reins of power, issued an edict banning the practice of Christianity. This led eventually to a Christian uprising in Kyushu, where several Christian daimyo had constructed strongholds. The defeat of the Christian rebels in 1638 destroyed this threat to the central authority, but in 1639 the rising tide of European expansion led the shogun to close Japan to all foreign trade. Only the Dutch were allowed a limited trade concession on an island in the harbor of Nagasaki. Japanese Christians were hunted down and forced to recant or to suffer martyrdom.

The Closing of Japan

The closing of the nation to foreign trade and ideas had far-reaching consequences. The Tokugawa regime had adopted Neo-Confucianism as its official ideology and had imposed on the nation a rigid social, political, and economic policy. The Confucian insistence on loyalty to superiors and family ties was especially enforced. Buddhism was used as an arm of the state to keep watch on the people through a "parochial system" in which every household was ordered to affiliate with a particular Buddhist temple. By government order every Japanese became a Buddhist at a single stroke.

The effect on Shintō of this extraordinary policy was at first negative. Even Shintō priests had to become Buddhists, and some chose to leave the priesthood altogether. But certain Shintō-Buddhist groups profited greatly. The mountain priests, for example, expanded their influence by becoming Shintō priests; many married *miko*, the Shintō shamanistic practitioners, and practiced a syncretistic religious system that combined mountain asceticism, Esoteric Buddhist rites, and native shamanism within the context of the old village shrine cults.

One result of the imposition of Buddhism as the de facto state religion was the proliferation of Buddhist temples and the establishment of new academies for training priests. Yet in the long run Buddhism suffered greatly from this deceptive windfall. Buddhist religious life tended to become a hollow, formalistic observance, and many priests were attracted to their profession not by piety or zeal, but by the financial security it offered. The consequence was that the prestige of Buddhism steadily decreased. Among the elite, Buddhism was seen as inferior to Confucianism, and the people turned increasingly to Shintō to express their true religious feelings. Among the educated classes, however, the study of Confucian philosophy had an additional and unexpected result: It reawakened an interest in classical literature and history, at first the Confucian classics and then Japanese history, culture, thought, and religion. Thus the stage was set for the Shintō revival of the Tokugawa period.

The National Scholar Movement

In 1728 a priest of the Inari shrine in Kyoto submitted a petition to the Tokugawa rulers in which he pleaded for patronage to establish a school of "national learning" (*kokugaku*) for the study of Japanese classical literature. This was the beginning of a renewal movement that sought to strip Shintō of its foreign (that is, Chinese) elements and establish it as an intellectual force rivaling the dominant Buddhist and Confucian schools of the time. In the beginning the program was concerned only with religious and philosophical matters. National scholars Motoori Norinaga (1730–1801) and Hirata Atsutane (1776–1843) succeeded in organizing a set of scriptures as a basis for Shintō theory and produced careful textual editions of such Japanese classics as the *Manyōshū*, the *Kojiki*, and *Genji Monogatari* (Tale of Genji), an eleventh-century novel of Japanese court life by Lady Murasaki Shikibu. These works were presented as the sacred scriptures to the newly awakened Shintō intellectuals.

An early work by Motoori called *Tama Kushige* (Precious Comb Box) became the manifesto of the movement. In it Motoori refers to the descent of the imperial prince, Ninigi, in the myth about the establishment of the sun goddess's descendants as Japan's emperors:

> In the Goddess' mandate to the Prince at that time it was stated that his dynasty should be coeval with Heaven and earth. It is this mandate which is the very origin and basis of the Way. Thus, all the principles of the world and the way of humankind are represented in the different stages of the Age of Kami. Those who seek to know the Right Way must therefore pay careful attention to the stages of the Age of Kami and learn the truths of existence.[8]

Hirata made even stronger claims for nationalism, and his views on the uniqueness and superiority of the Japanese *kokutai* (national spirit) were later made the basis for the ultranationalist ideology of the 1930s. In 1811 he wrote his *Kodō Taii* (Summary of the Ancient Way), in which he asserts:

> People all over the world refer to Japan as the Land of Kami, and call us the descendants of the kami. Indeed, it is exactly as they say: our country, as a special mark of favor from the heavenly kami, was begotten by them, and there is thus so immense a difference between Japan and all other countries of the world as to defy comparison. . . . We, down to the most humble man and woman, are the descendants of the kami.[9]

During the Tokugawa period, when this statement was written, the emperor, as the standard bearer of the old tradition, was an obscure figure living in seclusion in Kyoto: the real seat of government was four hundred miles away at Edo in the hands of samurai. To express such ideas at that time was not only religiously innovative, but also possibly politically subversive. It was no accident that in the nineteenth century the leaders of the Meiji Restoration, who swept away the feudal regime, did so in the name of the emperor and kokutai.

The Pilgrimage and Preaching

While the national scholar movement was getting underway among the elite, popular religious movements were started in which Shintō elements predominated or were mixed with Buddhist or Confucian ideas and practices. One of the most important of these was the religious pilgrimage. Although its origin in Japan is obscure, it probably began as part of the ancient mountain religion. By the Nara period emperors and aristocrats are re-

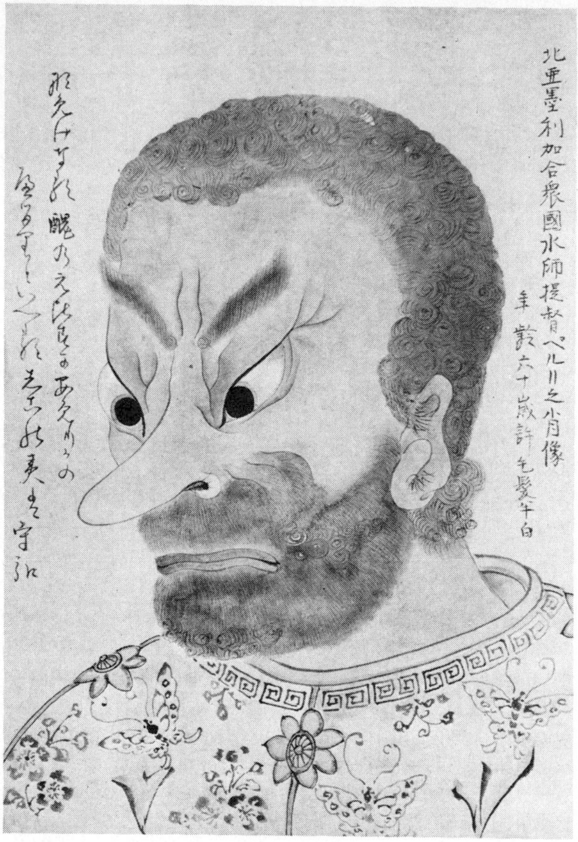
北亜墨利加合衆國水師提督ペルリ之肖像
年歳六十歳許毛髪半白

"Peruri No Shozu." This unflattering portrait clearly reveals Japanese sentiment regarding U.S. Commodore Matthew C. Perry, who opened up Japan to the West in the nineteenth century. *Sekai Bunka Photo.*

corded as having made journeys into the Yoshino mountains south and east of the Yamato Plain. Later the yamabushi conducted mountaineering exercises as part of their ascetic training. In the Ashikaga period pilgrimages to important shrines were organized by priests who sought in them a way to help counteract the inroads made by popular Buddhist sects. By the Tokugawa period the pilgrimage had become an important religious activity among both Buddhists and Shintō believers.

Motives for pilgrimages were complex. The edict binding peasants to the land meant that only on a religious pilgrimage could one leave the farm and see something new. Also, the yamabushi tradition of gaining religious merit or spiritual power through asceticism was still strong, and the rigors and privations of pilgrimages to sacred shrines or temples or other sites were thought to be especially efficacious. The social and esthetic enjoyment of visiting a famous waterfall or mountain also cannot be discounted.

To support the common people's desire for a pilgrimage, local village societies were formed to pool the resources of members so that every year a few might be subsidized to make these pious journeys. Out of these societies sometimes grew large organizations of like-minded devotees of a certain shrine. These movements developed into Shintō sects devoted to pilgrimages to certain places. In late Tokugawa times, the most popular destination of Japanese pilgrims was the Shintō shrine at Ise.

Another important aspect of popular religion in Tokugawa times was the development of the Shintō preaching movement. Movements like the Shingaku (Heart-learning) founded by Ishida Baigan (1685–1744) and the Hōtoku (Repayment of blessings) founded by Ninomiya Sontoku (1787–1856) began partly in response to the new middle class's religious aspirations. For the most part these movements were strongly influenced by Confucian ideas of reverence and loyalty and were caught up in a mounting tide of nationalism and modernization that focused more and more on the imperial institution as the symbol of unity and identity.

The Meiji Restoration

The modern period of Japanese history began in 1868, and since then there have been dramatic changes, changes that have affected all aspects of Japanese culture. Like the Taika Reform of A.D. 645, it has been a period of cultural disruption and innovation brought about by the rapid assimilation of foreign elements, this time from Western civilization. By the early years of the twentieth century Japan had become both a technologically advanced industrial nation and a strong military power with colonial possessions. To understand this rapid transformation, we need to examine the situation in Japan in the middle of the nineteenth century.

At that time the power and prestige of the Tokugawa had greatly diminished. The rise of the merchant class, the decline of agriculture, and the burgeoning imperial prestige all combined to make enemies for the military rulers. Furthermore, the superiority of Western military and commercial power increasingly highlighted the inability of this conservative regime to protect the nation. When the American naval commodore Matthew C. Perry sailed his ships into Tokyo Bay in July 1853, his arrival precipitated a crisis that had been building for years. Treaties opening ports to trade were quickly negotiated with the United States, Britain, Russia, and other Western powers. The reluctant and almost defenseless rulers of Japan were forced to accept the same arrogant treatment from the Western powers as China had, including unequal treaties and extraterritoriality.

Out of the political chaos that resulted from their fear and outrage emerged a coalition of the Tokugawa regime's traditional enemies, daimyo long out of power, court nobles, and the imperial family itself. The last shogun resigned in November 1867. The Meiji emperor, who had succeeded to the throne only a few months before, became the actual ruler of Japan. The new Meiji era was proclaimed in January 1868.

Meiji Japan

The new government soon launched attacks on Buddhism, which quickly gained popular support. In the reform edict of 1868, Shintō shrines were required to purge themselves of all Buddhist influences. Buddhist priests attached to Shinto shrines were forced to return to lay life. The Shintō-Buddhist priesthood had to choose one or the other religion, and in 1872 it became illegal for Buddhists to teach that kami were manifestations of Buddhist figures. Many Buddhist temples were destroyed out of a public zeal to purify the national life.

MODERNIZATION

Much of Meiji life was dominated by the one thought: modernization. This led to many excesses, among them an often superficial and faddish imitation of things Western. But because of a basic distrust of Western nations as political rivals as well as a fearful pride that drove its people to catch up with the West, Japan felt obliged to prove that it was the equal of the West both culturally and militarily. In these two aims, which were intimately connected in the minds of many Japanese, can be seen the seeds of important developments in the late nineteenth and early twentieth centuries. The Japanese observed that Western nations had constitutions, modern law courts, religious freedom, mass production, strong military forces, and empires, and in imitation of the West, they sought and achieved all of these in half a century.

Yet modernization did not always prove compatible with the Japanese kokutai. Religious freedom and democratic government had to be modified to meet Japanese conditions, and both modifications introduced Shintō traditions and values.

As the direct descendant of Amaterasu, the emperor was a divine person who symbolized Japan's national origins and unity. He could not rule directly and could not demean himself to the level of everyday political affairs. Yet a parliament as a deliberative body could hardly be thought of as being able to perceive the imperial will. Thus the constitution drawn up in 1889 provided for both an emperor and a parliament, but gave the real power to neither. Rather, real power was held by a few oligarchs who acted in the name of the emperor.

There was a dilemma similar to this in the matter of religion. Shintō had been made the national religion, although the constitution guaranteed religious freedom. The problem was "solved" by separating what was termed State Shintō from Sectarian Shintō. The former was declared to be nonreligious and the duty of every loyal citizen. The latter was organized into several sects that did not receive government patronage. Reverence for the emperor and respect for his authority, as well as reverence for many national heroes and the mythic kami, was required of every Japanese and was taught in the government schools.

The nationalistic spirit, combined with the official Shintō ideology, can be seen in the following excerpt from *Kokutai no hongi* (Fundamentals of our national polity), a book issued in 1937 by the Ministry of Education for training schoolteachers:

> Our country is established with the emperor, who is a descendant of Amaterasu Omikami, as her center, and our ancestors as well as we ourselves constantly have beheld in the emperor the fountainhead of her life and activities. For this reason, to serve the emperor and to receive the emperor's great august Will as one's own is the rationale of making our historical "life" live in the present; and on this is based the morality of the people. . . . An individual is an existence belonging to a State and her history which forms the basis of his origin, and is fundamentally one body with it. . . .[10]

The success of this educational policy can be seen in the events of modern Japanese history, many of which stem from the fact that the Japanese people, by 1941, had been molded into a powerful technological and military force. United in national purpose, they were amenable to almost any policy that their leaders, wrapped in the cloak of imperial authority, cared to initiate. Most impressive of all perhaps is the fact that the leaders themselves seemed to have genuinely believed they were carrying out the will of the emperor and expressing the Japanese kokutai. It is significant that when the nation lay in ruins in 1945 and the war was already lost, the leaders of Japan feverishly tried to negotiate a peace that would respect that same mysterious and vital principle.

STATE SHINTŌ

The official position of the Japanese government from the beginning of the Meiji Restoration to 1945 was that State Shintō was not religious—which was, of course, intellectually untenable. It was a legalistic ploy to enable the government to claim its place among the Western nations as a supposed guarantor of human rights, including religious freedom. This so-called civil cult had four main components:

1 *The shrine complex at Ise dedicated to Amaterasu.* This institution was especially important, as it was the seat of the ancestor of the imperial clan. It had become a popular pilgrimage site as well. It was and is considered the first of all of Japan's shrines.

2 *Three shrines located within the grounds of the Imperial Palace in Tokyo (since 1869).* Closely related to those of the Ise cult, their rites were carried out in the palace by the emperor and the imperial family. The shrines were dedicated to Amaterasu, the deceased emperors, and all the kami of the nation.

3 *Shrines throughout Japan for those who had done special service to the nation.* These gradually became memorials to those who had died in battle. The most important is the Yasukuni Shrine near the Imperial Palace in Tokyo. By 1945 there were 148 of these shrines.

4 *Shrine Shintō.* This accounts for 97 percent of the more than one hundred thousand shrines all over the country, including village shrines as well as those traditionally maintained by the central government.[11]

The civil cult as outlined above became, in fact, a system in which the ancient religion of Japan was used by the central authority to promote loyalty to itself, social solidarity, and patriotism. It was a powerful tool in the hands of those who in the nineteenth century had undertaken the difficult task of creating a modern nation out of the feudal domains of the Tokugawa period. By the twentieth century it had become the tool of the militarists who brought the nation to ruin in World War II.

Japan's New Religions

During the nineteenth century many new religious groups sprang up in Japan in response to the rapidly changing cultural and political situation. These new religions were closely knit sectarian groups emphasizing group solidarity and combining Shintō, Buddhist, Christian, and Western elements.

For some decades, anthropologists have been studying religious movements that characteristically arise in times of extreme cultural and social disintegration. Most often these have occurred in nonliterate societies colonized by the West. Anthony F. C. Wallace, an American anthropologist, in writing about the Iroquois people of North America, describes what seems to be a typical dilemma facing such societies:

> They faced a moral crisis: they wanted still to be men and women of dignity, but they knew only the old ways, which no longer led to honor but only to poverty and despair; to abandon these old ways meant undertaking customs that were strange, in some matters repugnant, and in any case uncertain of success.[12]

Perhaps the single most important characteristic of such cultural disintegration is the individual's feeling of having been cut off from his or her origins, and thus from the source of life's meaning. This absence of continuity is particularly injurious to ritual activity that depends heavily on past models which are then repeated, imitated, and celebrated. In Japan as elsewhere, the response to the destruction of traditional models has been to establish new ones. But because religious authority does not follow the same laws that other types of authority do, no parliament or executive decree could suffice to gain the allegiance of the people. The religious category for innovation and devising new models is revelation, and the model must have sacred origins. In the Japanese case, the Shintō pattern of communication with the sacred kami was employed by many new sects, most often in the form of shamanic possession.

One of the most dramatic examples of modern shamanic possession in the service of new revelation comes from Tenrikyō (religion of divine wisdom). Its founder, Nakayama Miki (1798–1887), was possessed by Tentaishogun and nine other kami, who proclaimed through her:

> Miki's mind and body will be accepted by us as a divine shrine, and we desire to save this three-thousand-world through this divine body. Otherwise, and if you all refuse our desire, the Nakayama family shall completely cease to exist. . . .[13]

Among Miki's most impressive achievements are the many poems she composed under the inspiration of the kami. Taken together, they constitute a new mythology—that is, a new understanding of the origins and meaning of the cosmos.

Although hundreds of new religions have appeared, especially since the defeat of 1945, they all have similar characteristics. Besides their dependence on shamanic revelation, they include (1) an emphasis on healing the ills of body and mind; (2) a dependence on myth rather than philosophy as the locus of meaning; (3) an appeal to the nonintellectual and lower socioeconomic levels of society; (4) a propensity for congregational worship and other group activities; and (5) a strong allegiance to a single founder or to later charismatic leaders.

These characteristics can be found whether the new religion is of Shintō, Buddhist, or Christian origin, although Shintō accounts for more new sects in Japan than any other religion. Of the

Extract from the Doctrinal Manual of Tenrikyō

One of the first and still the largest of the Shintō new religions is Tenrikyō.* The doctrinal manual of this sect, from which the following excerpts are taken, was compiled from the revelatory experiences of its founder, Nakayama Miki, in the latter part of the nineteenth century. Portions of these texts are used in Tenrikyō's daily rituals and are chanted or sung together with dancelike gestures. Note that the mythological elements, though inspired by the classical Shintō creation story, diverge considerably from it.

I, the foremost and true kami, have descended at this time from heaven to this house [of the Nakayama family] in order to save everyone of the world, and intend to dwell in the person of Miki as my living shrine. . . .

I am going to perform something which is just as marvelous as the creation of the world by me. What I am going to initiate is a brand new type of a religious service. . . . Salvation, which to be sure depends on the sincerity of your heart, will not only enable you to prevent sickness but also death and decay. Indeed, if everyone united in mind should perform this service, all the problems of the world will be solved. Even the gravest sickness will be eliminated by the rhythmic breathing and hand gestures [of the sacred dance].

In the beginning of the world there was only an ocean of muddy waters. The divine parent, known then as the Moon-Sun, bored with the state of chaos, decided to create man in order to enjoy himself by looking at man's joyous life. . . . Now, the moon element of the divine parent entered the body of Izanagi, while the sun element entered the body of Izanami, both teaching them the art of human procreation. . . . The first group of offspring . . . as well as their father Izanagi died. Then Izanami, following the art of procreation which had been given her before, conceived the same number of seeds and delivered them after ten months. . . . Looking at them, Izanami smiled and said that they would eventually grow into human beings of five feet. She then died, and her offspring without exception followed her footsteps. Subsequently, human beings went through 8,008 stages of rebirth, including those of the worm, birds, and animals, and eventually died out, leaving only one female monkey behind. From her womb, five men and women were born. . . .

"Lending and borrowing things." Inasmuch as we borrowed our life from the divine parent, it is essential that we use it to follow his will. . . . But, human beings, not realizing this principle, tend to think that they can do everything according to their selfish desire based on their limited human minds. Preoccupied by their own suffering, happiness, and profit, human beings often think contrary to the will of [the divine parent] who wishes the harmony and happiness of all mankind. The divine parent warns men against such selfish concern by using the analogy of dust [which can easily accumulate and clouds our minds]. . . . He cautions us to reflect on the eight kinds of mental dust—vindictiveness, possessiveness, hatred, self-centeredness, enmity, anger, greed, and arrogance. . . .

*Wing-tsit Chan et al., eds., *The Great Asian Religions* (New York: Macmillan, 1969), pp. 302–303. The doctrinal manual was translated by Joseph M. Kitagawa.

Shintō groups, Tenrikyō is both the oldest and the largest, though Konkokyō is also important. The largest and certainly the most obtrusive of the new religions, however, is Sōka Gakkai (Value-Creation Society). It is also known as Nichiren Shōshū to emphasize its affiliation with the medieval Nichiren sect of Buddhism. This group claims millions of followers, both in Japan and abroad, and its po-

Sho-Hondo complex in the foothills of Mount Fuji, south of Tokyo. The Sōka Gakkai, the Buddhist sect that built this complex, is the largest new religion in Japan and is growing rapidly. Pictured above is The Mystic Sanctuary. The High Sanctuary (below) is one of the largest religious structures in the world. *Religious News Service.*

litical party, the Kōmeitō (Clean Government party), has managed to elect several of its members to the Japanese Diet. Along with its authoritarian internal organization and its militant conversion tactics, Sōka Gakkai has a utopian scheme to convert Japan into a Buddhaland.

Clearly, the appeal of the new religions, and this is especially apparent in the case of Sōka Gakkai, stems in large measure from their genius for providing a sense of group solidarity. In a world increasingly typified by the breakdown of traditional family and community ties in the face of urbanization and industrialization, this ability to give the individual a sense of belonging is all-important. The Japanese, so close in time to a very traditional society and even more fragmented than most modern nations as a result of their defeat in war, are obviously attracted by such religious developments. Individuals can find in the new religions the reinforcement of like-minded people who together create a small world of their own, a world in which each person has a role and a meaning in relation both to the kami or other deity and to the community as a whole.

Yet another significant characteristic of many of the new religions of contemporary Japan is the importance of women in their creation. We have already discussed Tenrikyō and its founder Nakayama Miki. We might add three groups in the Shintō tradition. One is Ōmotokyō (Teaching of the Great Origin), jointly founded by a husband and wife. The wife claimed to be possessed by the kami Konjin. Next is Jiyūkyō (Freedom Religion), founded by former Ōmoto devotee Nagaoka Yoshiko, who announced that she was the incarnation of Amaterasu. And third is Tenshō Kōtai Jingūkyō (named after a deity), which was established by Kitamura Sayo. This last group is especially interesting from the viewpoint of women's studies, since its founder has a strong personality and proposes an increased role for women in religion and society.

Kitamura Sayo (1900–) was the wife of a poor farmer and faithfully served her husband and tyrannical mother-in-law for twenty years. Then she experienced personality changes and shamanic possession and proclaimed herself the living shrine of the "Heavenly Father" and his consort Amaterasu. In 1946 she announced the foundation of a new Age of God in which she would be the instrument of God to save the nation and establish his kingdom. This new age is closely identified with the original kami age in which traditional Shintō mythology began. The name of her sect is revealing, since Tenshō is another name for Amaterasu and Kōtai Jingū is the name of the inner shrine at Ise. Sayo considers herself to be a living shrine. Furthermore, both Sayo and her deity have androgynous features, and Sayo has become very aggressive in speech and manner, sitting cross-legged and wearing masculine clothing. She no longer is a wife to her husband, although she continues to be a devoted mother to her son. Sayo's teachings regarding life's purpose and practical behavior also reveal strong feminist inclinations:

> Sayo's advice to her women followers also reveals some ambiguity toward womanhood. She taught that women who, like herself, have known many trials are very close to the Kingdom of God. In the coming Age of God, women would play a role more significant than the role they had played in the preceding era. This, she said, is a man-centered age in which power rules the world, while the coming age will be a wholesome one in which women will march in the vanguard on the road to the Kingdom of God.[14]

Although Sayo seems to lean toward equality with or even superiority over men, she herself has remained conservative about the family. This plus masculine resistance within Tenshō Kōtai Jingūkyō have largely blunted the feminist thrust here as in other religions. Despite the unusual heritage of a female deity at the head of the pantheon and strong feminine representation in the founding of many new religious sects, Shintō remains representative of the male-dominated Japanese culture.

Shrine Shintō since World War II

After 1945 events moved quickly in Japan. The Allied Occupation, which lasted until 1952, was from

Priests at Mitsumine Jinja, a Shintō shrine in the Saitama prefecture. Religion and the state have been officially disassociated in Japan since the end of World War II, but the Japanese still sense a strong connection between religious practices and the office of the emperor. *Religious News Service.*

the beginning largely dominated by the United States, and the revolutionary changes it brought bore an unmistakably American stamp. The constitution that took effect in 1947 tried to make Japan a bastion of democracy and individual freedom in the Western pattern. War was made unconstitutional, as was any but self-defense armed forces. The Shintō Directive of 1946 disestablished State Shintō with a sweep, converting the many shrines into independent, private religious institutions relying solely on private and voluntary contributions for their continued existence. Public officials were prohibited from participating in religious ceremonies in their official capacities, and the emperor was made to deny publicly his divinity.

This imposition of the American insistence on strict separation of religion and state has been a continuing problem for the Japanese as a nation and for Shintō believers. To this day, the position of the emperor and the meaning of the imperial institution have resisted clarification because these concepts clearly run counter to the American scheme. To pretend that the emperor is not a religious figure is as misleading as it would be to pretend (as did the prewar government of Japan) that Shrine Shintō is not religious.

Events since 1952 have steadily led government and people to recognize the special relationship between Shintō and the Japanese national identity. Soon after the issuance of the Shintō Directive in 1946, the Association of Shintō Shrines was formed to coordinate the programs of the newly independent shrines. This group has been active in setting up educational programs, raising money, and providing an effective united voice for Shrine Shintō. The association managed to prevent the destruction of the Yasukuni Shrine in 1946, and it even helped arrange for the emperor and empress to be present at ceremonies there in 1952.

Since 1969 the association has attempted again and again to reestablish the Yasukuni as a national shrine. Similar efforts have been made for Ise, especially in connection with the traditional rebuilding of the structure, an enormously expensive undertaking that is all but impossible without government aid. With much less success the association has also attempted to have the constitution rewritten in order to safeguard the position of the emperor as the head of state and to have the imperial household rites recognized as national religious ceremonies. But it has been successful in litigation to permit the performance of Shintō ceremonies at the various traditional points in the construction of government buildings. And the association has induced the government to underwrite the maintenance of certain Shintō ceremonies as important "cultural properties." What cannot be done in the name of religion can sometimes be accomplished in the name of culture.

Another development that might indicate the future direction of this religious tradition is the attempt by some to formulate a Shintō theology and to promote Shintō as a universal religion. Foremost among these scholars is Ono Sokyo of Kokugakuin University in Tokyo, the intellectual center of Shintō since its founding in 1890. Ono has been active as a lecturer for the Association of Shintō Shrines and has been involved in political discussions within that body. A summary of his thought may be read in English in his *Shintō: The Kami Way* (1962). Although recognizing the unique historical development of Shintō as the national or ethnic religion of Japan, Ono argues for its universal insight. Potentially at least Shintō is a world religion: Its ethic of loyalty and its appreciation of nature, together with its belief in the "immanental sacred," are applicable to all humanity and are an important message to everyone. As a dramatic gesture in support of this view, the Conference on Shintō held in Claremont, California, in 1965 closed with a traditional Shintō ritual in which George Washington and the American Founding Fathers were invoked as kami.[15]

On the other hand, as a voice of moderation and universalism within Shintō, even Ono argues that nationalism, the imperial institution, and Shintō ceremonies are inextricably bound together. In a secular context the Japanese (and Shintō) dilemma reappears, still focused on the mysterious person of the emperor. A modern Japanese business leader can admit that the emperor is a rather ordinary man but adds:

> The Emperor goes back to the very beginnings of our history. One dynasty. And every Japanese is finally of that blood—related to the Emperor. He's not a god. He's hardly a temporal power. But even in 1975 he is our *source.*[16]

Notes

1 Robert Redfield, *Peasant Society and Culture* (Chicago: University of Chicago Press, 1960), pp. 41–42.

2 Donald L. Philippi, trans., *Norito: A New Translation of the Ancient Japanese Ritual Prayers* (Tokyo: Institute for Japanese Culture and Classics, 1959),

pp. 18–19. From the Grain-Petitioning Festival.

3 Ibid., p. 73.

4 Percival Lowell, *Occult Japan* (Boston: Houghton Mifflin, 1895), p. 6.

5 Ibid., p. 7.

6 A. W. Sadler, "O-Kagura: Field Notes on the Festival Drama in Modern Tokyo," *Asian Folklore Studies,* 29 (1970), 281–282.

7 Ibid., p. 300.

8 Ryusaku Tsunoda, William T. de Bary, and Donald Keene, *Sources of Japanese Tradition,* 2 vols. (New York: Columbia University Press, 1964), 2:16–18.

9 Ibid., 2:39.

10 Ibid., 2:280–281.

11 Wilbur M. Fridell, "The Establishment of Shrine Shinto," *Japanese Journal of Religious Studies,* 2 (June-September 1975), 139–140.

12 Anthony F. C. Wallace, *Religion: An Anthropological View* (New York: Random House, 1966), p. 31.

13 Hori Ichirō, *Folk Religion in Japan* (Chicago: University of Chicago Press, 1968), p. 237.

14 Nakamura Motomochi Kyoko, "No Women's Liberation: The Heritage of a Woman Prophet in Modern Japan," in *Unspoken Words: Women's Religious Lives in Non-Western Cultures,* ed. Nancy A. Falk and Rita M. Gross (New York: Harper & Row, Pub., 1980), p. 185.

15 Wilhelmus H. Creemers, *Shrine Shinto after World War II* (Leiden, Netherlands: E. J. Brill, 1968), p. 183, n. 16.

16 Melvin Maddocks, "Why Japan's Emperors Have Lasted," *Christian Science Monitor,* 1 (October 1975), 19.

14 India: Jainism and Sikhism

THE FOLLOWERS OF THE VICTOR

Jainism appeared more or less in its present-day form in northeastern India about 2,500 years ago as a reaction to the domination of Indian religion by the Hindu brāhmaṇs. Jainism is based on the teaching of Vardhamāna, who is known as *Mahāvīra* (Great Hero) and *Jina* (Victor). His disciples are called *Jains* or *Jainas*, "followers or children of the victor." The Jains' goal is to overcome the impermanence of earthly life and to be released from the eternal cycle of existence. To do this, Jainism focuses on (1) asceticism, or the mortification of the flesh, a feature common to many currents of Hinduism and other Indian religions; and (2) individual striving toward moral perfection by means of ahiṁsā (nonviolence). Jains especially avoid harming any living creature, as they believe that every manifestation of nature has a soul.

The Indian Background

Jainism began as a monastic faith and then developed a lay movement. Though Jains pray to the Hindu gods for earthly favors, such as long life, a male heir, and prosperity, the true objects of their devotion are the *Tīrthaṅkaras*, or the Jain saints. The term *Tīrthaṅkara* means "makers of the river crossing" or "finders of the ford," those who went beyond the gods and found a way to save humanity. Indeed, Jainists revere the Tīrthaṅkaras as models of spiritual victory who found their way across the river of life and won release from the eternal cycle of karma. (Karma is the actions that affect a person's present and future life.) To Jains, the law of karma determines human destiny. According to Heinrich Zimmer, an expert on Indian philosophy, Jainism is transtheistic; that is, it does not deny the existence of the gods but goes beyond them.[1]

Like Buddhists, early Jains regarded the vedic sacrifices of the brāhmaṇ priests as cruel. Unlike the Buddhists, who generally deny the existence of substantial reality, Jains have remained faithful to an archaic form of realism based on a common-sense acceptance of the surrounding world. Human destiny is the center of Jain teaching. Although people need to be guided along the right path, they must rely on themselves to seek the moral elevation that will save them from the domination of matter. The British scholar Ninian Smart calls Jainism "a moving testimony to constructive pessimism."[2]

Possibly because of Jainism's asceticism and doctrinal rigidity, it failed to acquire the large following that Buddhism won within and beyond India. Jainism is limited to the Indian subcontinent, though it did survive the rise and fall of Buddhism in India as well as attacks from Hinduism and Islam. Today there are about 2 million Jains, including scholars, bankers, and traders.

They still practice Mahāvīra's teaching with comparatively few changes. They are strict vegetarians; they not only refuse to eat meat, but also

This eleventh-century statue of Mahāvīra, the last maker of the river crossing, shows him surrounded by the other Tīrthaṅkaras. *Seattle Art Museum. Eugene Fuller Memorial Collection.*

to use leather. A Jain monk covers his face with a gauze mask or handkerchief to guard against breathing in (and thus destroying) insect life. He carries a broom to sweep the path ahead of him to avoid stepping on any living beings. At night Jains refrain from drinking water for fear of unintentionally swallowing a gnat.

Makers of the River Crossing

Jains reject Western scholars' claims that Mahāvīra was the founder of Jainism and instead trace the Tīrthaṅkaras to prehistoric times. According to Jain theory, there were twenty-four Tīrthaṅkaras in all, beginning with Ṛṣabha, who lived for 8.4 million years. The nineteenth Tīrthaṅkara, Mallinātha, is said to have been a woman. The twenty-second Tīrthaṅkara, Nemi, lived for 1000 years; Pārśva, the twenty-third, for 100 years; and Mahāvīra, the last maker of the crossing, for 72 years. Modern scholars believe the biographies of the first twenty-two Tīrthaṅkaras are mythological, but they do accept Pārśva and Mahāvīra as historical figures.

Pārśva, who is often referred to as Pārśvanātha (the Lord Pārśva), was born in about 872 B.C. in what is now the city of Banāres. His father was the local ruler, King Aśvasena, and his beautiful mother, Queen Vāmā, dreamed that her child would be a great spiritual leader. Pārśva was a brave warrior who defended his father's domain and married the daughter of a king. But he was not interested in the luxuries of the court, and at the age of thirty he renounced worldly pleasures and began a life of austerity.

On this occasion Pārśva's evil brother Saṁvara tried to kill him by summoning a great rainstorm. Undisturbed, Pārśva continued his meditation while two cobras spread their hoods above his body to protect it from the downpour. For seventy years Pārśva wandered India, gathering disciples and teaching them to observe the four vows: not to take life, not to lie, not to steal, and not to own property. At last he finished his karma and achieved liberation (*mokṣa*) on Mount Sammeda in Bengal, which is revered by Jains today as the Hill of Pārśvanātha.*

*Heinrich Zimmer has pointed out (*Philosophies of India*, pp. 60, 196) that Pārśva, who was praised for the blue-black color of his skin, represented the survival of the dark-skinned Dravidian stock and a way of life that antedated the arrival of the Aryans. After the vedic period Aryan and non-Aryan beliefs were synthesized into a recognized Indian system of thought which was accepted by classical Hinduism, Buddhism, and Jainism.

Pārśva's successor Mahāvīra lived between 598 and 526 B.C. or, according to some sources, between 599 and 477 B.C. Mahāvīra was born at Vaisālī, a city in northeastern India, into a Jain family belonging to the warrior caste. As was the case for Pārśva and the Buddha, Mahāvīra's birth was surrounded by portents of future greatness, and his mother had many dreams predicting that her son would be a religious savior. Mahāvīra's name at birth was Vardhamāna, which means "Increasing," and he was the second son. According to most accounts, Mahāvīra married and became the father of a daughter. Though drawn to the religious life, he remained in his parents' house until their death and then secured his brother's permission to become a Jain monk. After tearing out his hair by the roots, Mahāvīra put on a monk's robe. Thirteen months later he stripped off his robe and began to go about naked: Nudity for Jain monks is a sign of devotion and renunciation of all worldly possessions.

For the next twelve years Mahāvīra led an ascetic existence. As a result of his meditation he finally became a Jina, a victor over his own passions. He became known as *Kevalin* (omniscient), *Arhata* (venerable), and Mahāvīra (Great Hero), and he traveled around northern India, teaching communities of monastics and laity. Mahāvīra added a fifth vow, of poverty, to the original four. Members of the laity, however, were allowed to live a less austere life.

When Mahāvīra knew that the time of his release was approaching, he sat down in a praying position, crossing his legs and clasping his hands. Just as the sun came up, he reached nirvāṇa and then died.

After Mahāvīra's death the sacred texts of Jainism were at first preserved in oral form but then were written down in about 300 B.C. At the same time the Jain monks began to quarrel, finally splitting into the Śvetāmbaras (white-clothed) and the Digambaras (air-clothed), who took a vow of nudity. The Digambaras were antifeminist and rejected the theories that the nineteenth Tīrthaṅkara had been a woman and that Mahāvīra had married. Women were condemned as the world's greatest temptation and the cause of all sinful acts. The Digambaras also believed that since women could not practice nudity, the only way they could attain release was by being born again as men and becoming monks. (In modern times the Digambaras have had to renounce public nudity.)

About A.D. 80 the split between the Śvetāmbaras and the Digambaras became final and exists to the present day. The Digambaras's center is in Mysore in the Deccan region of southern India. Śvetāmbaras are found mainly in the cities of western India. Both sects have their own sacred books and commentaries in Sanskrit or Prakrit, the dialect of Magadha.

Over the centuries, the fortunes of the Jains have risen and fallen. The Jains list—probably inaccurately—Chandragupta, the founder of the Maurya dynasty, Aśoka, and other prominent rulers as their adherents. It is known that an important Jain commentator, Hemaċandra (1088–1172), converted the prince of Gujarat in western India, who turned this region into a Jain state. In periods of prosperity, the Jains built many temples and shrines. During the twelfth century, however, a resurgence of Hinduism led to their persecution, and beginning in the thirteenth century, the Muslim conquest of India was followed by persecutions of all religions other than Islam.

Although Buddhism almost disappeared from India, Jainism survived, owing to the close ties between the Jain monks and the laity. There even was a revival of Jainism under the tolerant Mughul emperor Akbar, whom the Jains regarded as a supporter. More recently there have been reform movements and the formation of new sects. Jainism has continued because of the economic power of its followers and the conservatism of its teaching.

Jain Cosmology

Jains see the universe as eternal and uncreated and reject the concept of a supreme being or creative spirit. The Jain universe has three realms. The lower realm has seven levels containing 8.4 million hells where human beings are punished for their transgressions for varying lengths of time; people guilty of unpardonable crimes are kept in a bottomless abyss from which no escape is possible.

The middle world is the realm of human life, and above it lies the celestial vault, the heavenly realm where the gods live. But this heavenly realm is not the ultimate goal; rather, the goal is to achieve mokṣa, or nirvāṇa.

The middle world is made up of both nonliving matter (*ajīva*) and an infinite number of life monads (*jīvas*). The jīvas are what people's souls consist of and what animate them. They are mingled with particles of their karma, as water is with milk. Karmic matter (ajīva), in turn, adds colors (*leysas*) to people's life monads. There are six colors: black, dark blue, dove gray, flaming red, yellow or rose, and white. Black is the worst of the leysas, indicating cruel creatures that kill or harm other beings. Dark blue creatures are greedy and sensual. Dove gray indicates those who are angry and thoughtless, and fiery red is the color of honest, generous souls. Yellow is the color of souls who are totally dispassionate and impartial.

Actions in people's present and previous existences—even good actions—produce particles of karma that weigh them down and bind them to an endless cycle of existence. Jains believe that by following the path traced by the makers of the river crossing—the path of meditation, austerity, asceticism and, above all, the principle of ahiṁsā—a person's soul can ascend the flight of fourteen steps and free itself from its karma. Then the soul rises up to the top of the universe where it remains forever, motionless and free of suffering.

Jain Ethics

In principle Jains are forbidden to have any occupation that involves the destruction of living beings. They may not eat meat or even eggs. Even farming is taboo, since operations like tilling the soil and weeding the crops may harm living creatures. Nonetheless, many Jains have become successful merchants and scholars.

Each Jain monastic community is governed by an *acarya,* or superior, who decides disciplinary and doctrinal matters. The monks move around the countryside except during the rainy season. At that time, because the wet soil is swarming with small creatures, the monks take refuge in a fixed place and, along with members of the laity, receive religious instruction. Their days and nights are divided into periods for requesting alms, eating, studying, meditating, teaching, mortifying the body, and confessing faults. Many Jain sects have communities of nuns who follow many of the same practices. Monastics are easily identified by their shaved heads.

Members of the laity are encouraged to take twelve vows, but first they must profess their faith in the religion of the Tīrthaṅkaras. In addition, they must renounce all doubt and desire to belong to another religion, accept the reality of karma, and resolve not to praise hypocrites or to associate with them. At this point, a layperson can make the twelve vows, of which the first five are similar to the monastic vows: (1) never intentionally take life or destroy a jīva; (2) never lie or exaggerate; (3) never steal; (4) never be unfaithful to one's spouse or think unchaste thoughts; (5) limit oneself in the accumulation of wealth and give away all extra possessions, for example, contribute to the maintenance of temples or animal hospitals; (6) limit chances of committing transgressions, for example, impose limits on travel; (7) limit the number of personal possessions; (8) guard against unnecessary evils; (9) observe periods of sinless meditation; (10) observe special periods of limitation; (11) spend some time living as a monastic; and (12) give alms to a monastic community.

The Jain path to liberation passes through five stages of knowledge: *Mati* (right perception), *Śruta* (clear knowledge based on scripture), *Avadhi* (supernatural knowledge), *Manaḥparyāya* (clear knowledge of the thought of others), and finally *Kevala* (omniscience, the highest form of knowledge, which was attained by the makers of the river crossing). Those who attain Kevala are said to have become *Siddhas* (perfect ones), and their jīvas (souls) have flown up to the top of the universe where they will remain forever free of karma. The completion of the Jain path may require numerous existences.

When they feel death approaching, Jains are supposed to take a vow of nonattachment and dispose

The Way of a Jain Mendicant

Two passages from Jain texts tell of the sufferings and patience a Jain medicant must endure on the way to nirvāṇa.* The following extract from the *Akaranga Sūtra* describes an incident in the life of Mahāvīra, the last of the Tīrthaṅkaras. The "pathless country" through which Mahāvīra traveled has tentatively been identified as western Bengal.

Always well guarded, he [Mahāvīra] bore the pains (caused by) grass, cold, fire, flies, and gnats; manifold pains.

He travelled in the pathless country of the La*dh*as, in Vaggabhumi and Subbhabhumi; he used there miserable beds and miserable seats.

In La*dh*a (happened) to him many dangers. Many natives attacked him. Even in the faithful part of the rough country the dogs bit him, ran at him.

Few people kept off the attacking, biting dogs. Striking the monk, they cried "*Kh*u*kkh*u," and made the dogs bite him.

Such were the inhabitants. Many other mendicants, eating rough food in Va*gg*abhumi, and carrying about a strong pole or a stalk (to keep off the dogs), lived there.

Even thus armed they were bitten by the dogs, torn by the dogs. It is difficult to travel in La*dh*a.

Ceasing to use the stick (i.e. cruelty) against living beings, abandoning the care of the body, the houseless (Mahāvīra), the Venerable One, endures the thorns of the villages (i.e. the abusive language of the peasants), (being) perfectly enlightened.

As an elephant at the head of the battle, so was Mahāvīra there victorious. Sometimes he did not reach a village there in La*dh*a.

When he who is free from desires approached the village, the inhabitants met him on the outside, and attacked him, saying, "Get away from here."

He was struck with a stick, the fist, a lance, hit with a fruit, a clod, a potsherd. Beating him again and again, many cried.

When he once (sat) without moving his body, they cut his flesh, tore his hair under pains, or covered him with dust.

Throwing him up, they let him fall, or disturbed him in his religious postures; abandoning the care of his body, the Venerable One humbled himself and bore pain, free from desire.

As a hero at the head of the battle is surrounded on all sides, so was there Mahāvīra. Bearing all hardships, the Venerable One, undisturbed, proceeded (on the road to Nirvā*ṇa).*

This is the rule which has often been followed. . . .

The following passage† from the same scripture gives some indication of the minute regulations that Jain monks and nuns observed as they went about begging for alms. Their constant preoccupation was to observe ahiṁsā and avoid doing violence to any living creatures.

A monk or a nun, entering the abode of a householder for the sake of alms, should after examining their alms-bowl, taking out any living beings, and wiping off the dust, circumspectly enter or leave the householder's abode.

The Kevalin says: This is the reason: Living beings, seeds or dust might fall into his bowl. Hence it has been said to the mendicant, &c., that he should after examining his alms-bowl, taking out any living beings, circumspectly enter or leave the householder's abode.

On such an occasion the householder might perhaps, going in the house, fill the alms-bowl with cold water and, returning, offer it him; (the mendicant) should not accept such an alms-bowl either in the householder's hand or his vessel; for it is impure and unacceptable.

Perhaps he has, inadvertently, accepted it; then he should empty it again in (the householder's) water-pot; or (on his objecting to it) he should put down the bowl and the water somewhere, or empty it in some wet place.

A monk or a nun should not wipe or rub a wet or moist alms-bowl. But when they perceive that on their alms-bowl the water has dried up and the moisture is gone, then they may circumspectly wipe or rub it.

A monk or a nun wanting to enter the abode of a householder, should enter or leave it, for the sake of alms, with their bowl; also on going to the out-of-door place for religious practices or study; or on wandering from village to village.

If a strong and widely spread rain pours down, they should take the same care of their alms-bowl as is prescribed for clothes. . . .

This is the whole duty. . . .
Thus I say.

*From Hermann Jacobi, trans., *Gaina Sutras* (New York: Scribner's, 1901), pp. 84–85, vol. 10, *The Sacred Books of the East*, ed. F. Max Müller.

†Ibid., pp. 169–70.

of their earthly goods. They are even encouraged to stop eating, for in this context starving oneself to death is morally acceptable.

Rites and Statues

Jainism, unlike Buddhism, has no cult of relics. All over India, however, Jains have erected temples and sanctuaries, some of which are magnificent. Jain books and temples are frequently adorned with the Jain symbol, a swastika surmounted by three dots and a half moon.

The arms of the swastika symbolize the four stages of birth: those born in hell; those born as insects, plants, or animals; those born as humans; and those born as spirits of gods or demons. The dots stand for the three jewels of Jainism: right faith, right knowledge, and right conduct. The half moon symbolizes mokṣa, or liberation.

In Jain ceremonies, a rosary of 108 beads and votive tablets bearing sacred figures and formulas are used. Indeed, since the ninth century Jain ceremonies similar to the Christian sacraments have marked important events of life from conception and birth to death.

In the Digambara temples the statues of Jain saints are nude and have downcast eyes to indicate spiritual concentration. In the Śvetāmbara temples the images are shown in a seated position with crossed legs. Their statues wear loincloths and have glass eyes. In the Digambara temples the ceremonies can be conducted only by a Jain, but the Śvetāmbaras allow non-Jains to officiate at their rites. Offerings of sweetmeats, flowers, and fruits are made, incense is burned, and lighted lamps are waved before the images.

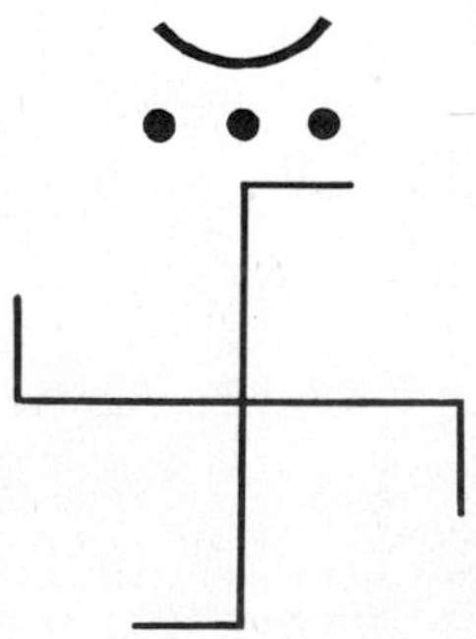

One of the most memorable Jain images is the statue of the Jain saint Gommata near Mysore. Standing fifty-six and a half feet high and measuring thirteen feet around the hips, the figure was carved in about A.D. 983 out of one enormous piece of stone. Every twenty-five years the faithful are permitted to anoint the statue with ghee (melted butter).

Gommata is depicted as he once stood for a year, according to legend, while vines crept up his body. His "air-clad" nudity reflects the mystical serenity of a savior who has divested himself of every earthly bond. In its simplicity the statue sums up the aloofness and austerity of the Jain tradition.[3]

THE WAY OF THE DISCIPLES

The Sikhs are members of one of India's youngest religions. Their name is derived from the Sanskrit *śisya* and the Pali *sikkha,* which both mean "disciple." Founded in northern India in the fifteenth century A.D. by Guru Nanak, Sikhism has today about 9 million adherents, of which about 85 percent live in the Indian state of Punjab. There also are large groups in Delhi, the state of Haryana, and other parts of India. In addition, Sikh communities can be found in Malaysia, Singapore, East Africa, England, Canada, and the United States.[4]

All Sikhs regard themselves as disciples of the ten gurus, a line of religious teachers that began with Guru Nanak (1469–1539) and ended with Guru Gobind Singh, who died in 1708. The Sikh holy book is the *Adi Granth* (Original Book), which is kept in the main Sikh shrine, the Golden Temple of Amritsar.

Rejecting or downplaying external aspects of religious expression, Sikhs aim to achieve the experience of God in their souls. Their primary emphasis is not on prophecy or ritual, but on the consciousness of God in themselves. Sikhs do not

Ornate Jain temple (left) in Calcutta, India. Jain saint Gommata (above) dominates the throng of worshipers that surround this statue carved from a single piece of stone. *Government of India Tourist Office; Religious News Service Photo.*

seek an escape from the world, but rather spiritual insight during earthly life.

Basically Sikhism is an offshoot of Hinduism, although it also owes important insights to Islam, particularly to the Sūfīs (Muslim mystics). For the Sikhs, God is the one and the true, a strictly monotheistic concept derived from the awe Muslims feel for Allah. The religion of the Sikhs is a new way of life with its own distinctive character. Originally advocating tolerance and love between Hindus and Muslims, the Sikhs, after being persecuted, were forced to become militant. Since the time of Guru Gobind Singh, they have identified God with power. Disciples of the gurus are urged to be courageous and to overcome or avoid lust, anger. greed, and egotism. During the British domination of India this ethos, plus the superb physical condition of many young Sikhs, attracted the favorable attention of British officials. As a result, Sikhs became highly respected soldiers and policemen in Burma, Hong Kong, and other parts of the British Empire. These same qualities of manly resolution and loyalty continue today to serve the Sikhs well in the republic of India.

The Sant Background and the Poet Kabir

Sikhism began in the Punjab region of northwestern India. In Nanak's time, the Punjab was much larger than the present Indian state of the same name and included the foothills of the Himalayan and Afghan mountains as well as five rivers—the Jhelum, Chenab, Ravi, Sutlej, and Beas—which

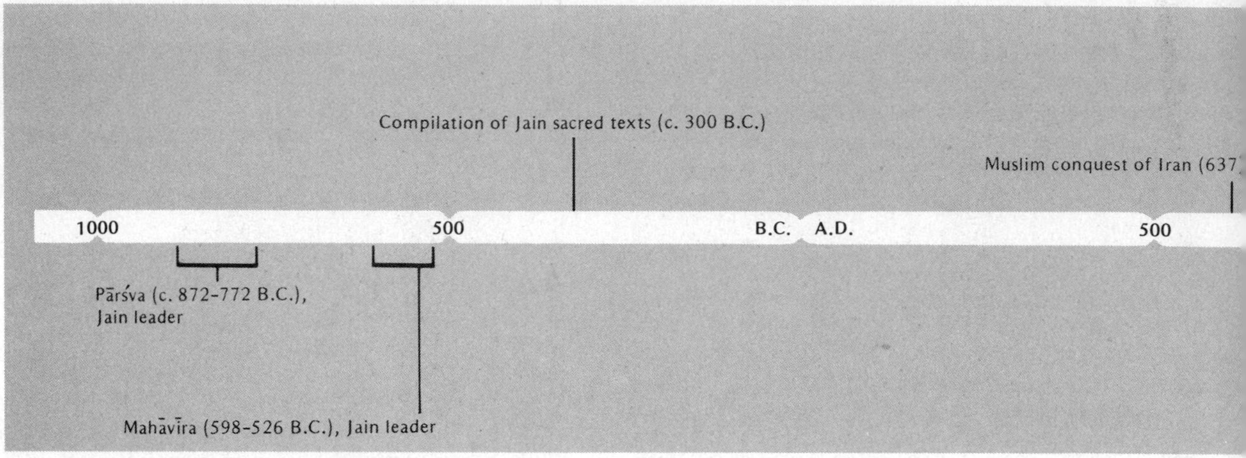

flow into the Indus River. Now a rich farming area, it was then well forested.

The religious and cultural background of Nanak's teaching can be traced to the Sant tradition. The Sants were a devotional group within Hinduism's bhakti movement whose followers worshiped the god Viṣṇu. The Sant tradition began in the Tamil country of southern India and was brought to the north by Ramaniya (around A.D. 1450). The Sants affirmed that God (whom they identified with Viṣṇu) was the only reality in life; everything else was just *māyā* (illusion). Under the direction of a guru, they sought to approach God by means of meditating, repeating God's name, and singing hymns. They rejected the caste system and the religious monopoly of the brāhmaṇs.

Most Sants came from the lower castes of Hinduism. They did not use Sanskrit, the sacred language of the brāhmaṇs, but addressed God in a dialect spoken in the Delhi area. They developed neither scriptures nor rites. Their emphasis was on unity as opposed to duality, and they taught that human beings would continue to encounter suffering on the path toward salvation, that is, unity with God. Unlike the Vedānta tradition of Hinduism, the Sants did not identify God with the world; rather, to them he was manifest in creation, especially through his immanence (the quality of indwelling) in the human soul.

The Sant viewpoint was influenced by the teaching of the Naths, another Hindu group whose members were not in accord with the brāhmaṇs. The Nath founder was a semi-legendary figure named Gorakhnath, who is reported to have lived in the Punjab in the twelfth century. The Naths believed it was possible to obtain release from the cycle of karma and rebirth through asceticism and yoga. Nanak, the founder of Sikhism, was from a Nath family.

Kabir (1440–1518), whose name means in Arabic "the Great," was an important Sant leader. According to legend, he grew up in the area of Banāras and belonged to the *jullaha* caste of weavers. His family were Naths who had converted to Islam. Thus Kabir, who became a poet and a mystic, owed much of his thought and language to both his Nath background and the Ṣūfī mystics.

As a Sant teacher, Kabir rejected the authority of the Hindu Vedas and Upanishads and that of the Qur'ān. He was convinced that all human beings were brothers and sisters before the mystery of the divine and that religion without love was empty and powerless. The path to salvation required the invocation of God's name: "Utter the name of God: He extinguishes birth and death. . . . I utter his Name, and whatever I see reminds me of Him; whatever I do becomes his worship."[5]

Kabir accepted the Hindu belief in karma and rebirth through the transmigration of souls; yet he proclaimed that release was possible through the

TIME LINE

JAINISM AND SIKHISM

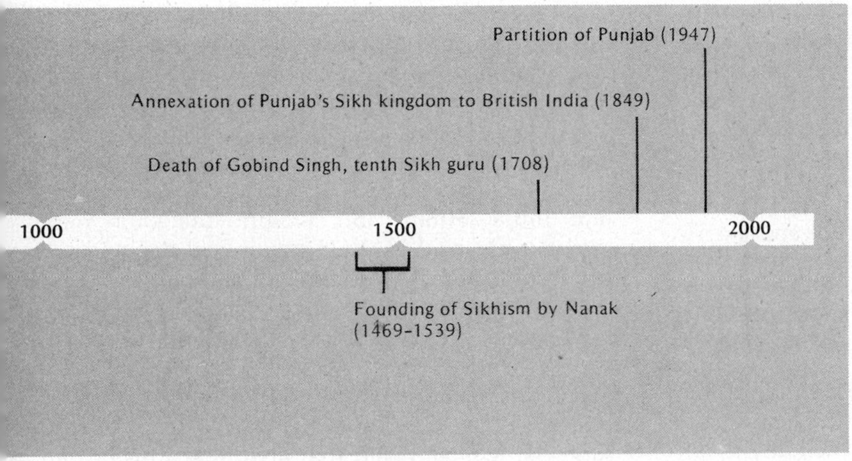

love of God, the true guru, who discharged the arrow of his word into the world. The man or woman slain by this word would find true life in a mystical union with God the ineffable.

Nanak's Career

Nanak, the founder of Sikhism, was born to a warrior caste family in Taluandi, a village on the Rai River about thirty miles from Lahore. His father was a revenue collector for the village's Muslim overseer, and Nanak received a Hindu upbringing. Few details are known about Nanak's life, and Sikh authorities consider his writings in the Adi Granth the only authentic source of information about him. However, popular piety in the *Janam-Sakhis* (Birth Evidences), a noncanonical Sikh writing, has supplied many legends about his life. According to one account, Nanak at the age of seven months could already assume the yogi position. He is said to have rejected the Hindu thread ceremony when he was ten. Later he decided not to study accounting, the profession his father had intended for him. Instead, he took instruction in Hindu lore from a village pandit (Hindu teacher) and also attended a Muslim school, where he acquired a knowledge of Islamic teaching and some instruction in Arabic and Persian.

Much of northern India in Nanak's youth was under the Delhi sultanate, a Muslim kingdom established in the late twelfth century. There, two social systems lived side by side. The Hindus had a tolerant religion but a closed social system based on caste. The Muslims had a more open social system but a dogmatic religion. Nanak adjusted well to life under the Muslim overlords. When his older sister Nanaki married the steward of Daulat Khan, an important Muslim official in a nearby town, Nanak also found service there as an accountant in Daulat Khan's household. The future guru was, according to legend, sixteen years old at the time.

Three years later he married and eventually became the father of two sons. During this time he befriended Mardana, a Muslim servant and musician in Daulat Khan's home. Soon Nanak gathered about him a group of followers who bathed together in a river before dawn every day and met in his home in the evening to sing religious songs he had composed. Mardana accompanied the group on the rebec, a stringed instrument.

When Nanak was thirty years old, he received a divine call. One day he failed to return from his morning bath in the river. His friends, finding his clothes on the bank of the river, dragged the waters in a vain attempt to find his body. Three days later Nanak reappeared. At first he gave no explanation for his absence but made only the following cryptic statement: "There is neither Hindu nor Mussulman [Muslim] so whose path should I choose? I shall follow God's path. God is neither Hindu nor Mussulman and the path which I follow is God."[6] Later Nanak told them that in his vision he had been carried up to God's presence. After receiving a cup of nectar, God gave him the following message:

> I am with thee. I have given thee happiness, and I shall make happy all who take thy name. Go thou and repeat my Name; cause others to repeat it. Abide unspoiled by the world. Practice charity, perform ablutions, worship and meditate. My name is God, the primal Brahma. Thou are the Holy Guru.[7]

Inspired by his vision, Nanak expressed his faith in the following statement that begins the *Japji,* a part of the Adi Granth prayed silently each day by all Sikhs:

> There is but one God whose name is True, the Creator, devoid of fear and enmity, immortal, unborn, self-existent, great and bountiful. The True One was in the beginning, the True One was in the primal age. The True One is, was, O Nanak, and the True One also shall be.[8]

At this point Nanak became a *guru.* (The Sikhs explain this term as meaning one who drives away darkness [*gu*] and preaches enlightenment [*ru*].) Often accompanied by Mardana, Nanak traveled around spreading his religious message and singing hymns. According to legend, he made four journeys, visiting Assam in the east, Sri Lanka in the south, Ladakh and Tibet in the north, and Mecca, Medina, and Baghdad in the west. On one occasion he decided to eat at the home of a poor Hindu carpenter rather than accept the hospitality of a rich Muslim official. When asked the reason for this decision, Nanak squeezed the carpenter's coarse bread in his right hand, and from it came drops of milk. Next he squeezed the rich man's bread in his left hand, and from it came drops of blood. The answer was clear: the poverty of an honest man had merit, but the wealth of a greedy oppressor of the poor was to be despised.

Such accounts in the *Janam-Sakhis* reflect the pious beliefs of Sikhs who lived much later than the founder. Modern scholars do accept that Nanak was a wandering missionary for a while, but most of them doubt that he ever left India. About this time, life in northern India became very unsettled after radical political changes plunged it into a prolonged period of violence and bloodshed. In 1504 Babur (1483–1530), a Muslim conqueror from Central Asia, occupied Afghanistan and shortly thereafter launched a series of military campaigns into India. Hindu and Muslim kingdoms were swept aside, and by 1525 Babur had deposed the sultan of Delhi and laid the foundations of the Mughul Empire.

Nanak, deeply shocked by the cruelty of the invading armies, decided about 1521 to look for a place of refuge and stability. During his travels he is said to have dressed either as a Ṣūfī or a Hindu sannyāsī, which meant that up to that time he had passed through at least three of the stages of a Hindu's life: student, householder, and forest dweller. When he decided to settle down again with his family, Nanak voluntarily returned to the householder stage. In the last years of his life he dressed and conducted himself like any member of the community except in one respect: As a guru, he was entitled to use a special seat, a *gadi,* while teaching his disciples.

The guru and his family established a religious center at Kartarpur, a village built on land donated by a wealthy member of the new faith, and all of whose residents were converts. Nanak continued to make missionary trips to places nearby, and there are records of the debates he conducted with the yogis of other villages. His teaching was in the Sant tradition. Rejecting the magic spells and divine images of popular Hinduism, he urged his followers to meditate, to worship God, and to sing hymns.

At the end of his life Nanak appointed Lehna or Lahina, a member of the warrior caste, as his successor. He did not regard his own sons as suited to guide the community. Calling Lehna to him at a public gathering, the old guru placed before his successor a coconut, the symbol of the universe, and five coins representing air, earth, fire, water, and ether. He then handed over a book of hymns, which represented the message of the new faith, and a woolen string, the symbol of renunciation worn by Ṣūfīs around their hats. Finally Nanak gave Lehna a new name. He was henceforth to be

A turbaned Sikh pilgrim washes his feet before entering the Golden Temple, the most sacred shrine of the Sikhs, in Amritsar, India. The Sikhs' religion has evolved over centuries but its teaching is largely that of Nanak, its founder: religion's ultimate purpose is union with God through indwelling in the human soul.
United Nations.

known as Angad, a pun on *ang* (limb): Lehna would become a "limb" or a "part" of Nanak.

The Founder's Teaching

Although Sikhism has evolved over the centuries, its teaching has remained essentially that of its founder. The Adi Granth states:

> Nanak, without the indwelling Name of God one endures suffering throughout the four ages [of the universe]. What a terrible separation it is to be separated from God and what a blissful union to be united with Him.[9]

As conceived by Nanak, the ultimate purpose of all religion was union with God through his indwelling in the human soul. By receiving divine grace in this way, human beings were freed from the cycle of birth and rebirth and then passed beyond death into a realm of infinite and eternal bliss.

Nanak reinterpreted the Sant tradition and gave it coherence and effective expression. Like Kabir, Nanak believed the climactic union with the formless one could not be expressed. But whereas Kabir's mystical thought was conveyed through pithy sayings, Nanak's teaching offered a clear path to salvation which Sikhs continue to follow today. He compared the way God's salvation was revealed to the experience of persons blinded by their own perversity. Awakened from this condition of stubbornness, they could begin to understand the word of God in the surrounding world. They could hear the voice of God speaking mystically in their souls. By meditating on the divine name, human beings were cleansed of impurities and enabled to ascend higher and higher until they achieved union with the eternal one.

The similarities between the Sikh and Ṣūfī perspectives are obvious. Both find God's revelation in creation, and both speak of the Deity in terms of light and emphasize his unity. Like the Ṣūfīs, Nanak used the figure of a veil that concealed the truth from human perception. Both Sikhs and Ṣūfīs reject worldly wealth and hold that suffering in the world arises as a result of humanity's separation from God. And both describe the ascent of human beings to God as an experience leading through a number of intermediate stages that culminates in the ultimate union.

Despite all these shared ideas, however, Nanak rejected Ṣūfism along with other forms of Islam. In a direct contradiction of Islamic teaching, he accepted the notions of karma and the transmigration of the soul. In short, there is little support for the argument that Nanak sought to reconcile Hindu and Muslim beliefs: He viewed both faiths as wrong in principle. The Adi Granth states categorically, "Neither the Veda nor the Kateb [Qur'ān] knows the mystery."[10] Quite obviously, the founder of Sikhism wished to move toward a new spiritual insight for all humanity.

THE CONCEPT OF GOD

Beside God there is no other—this is the essence of Nanak's approach to the supreme Being. Sikhism is monotheistic, but not in the same way as Judaism. Sikhism does not identify God and the world, as Hindu monism did in its concept of the Brahman. Nanak taught that God's essence could be known only through a personal experience of mystical union, not through the working out of history. God is beyond all human categories, yet is in them as well. Nanak used the names of other deities as conventional figures to speak of God. "God is Hari, Ram, and Gopal, and He is also Allah, Khuda, and Sahib."[11] Despite his many manifestations, God alone exists; there is no other like him. In his primal aspect he is devoid of all attributes, absolute and unconditioned.

For countless ages there was undivided darkness, no heaven, no earth, just *hukam*, the infinite order of God. God endowed himself with attributes that have brought him within the range of human understanding. He is eternal, omniscient, and omnipotent. Yet Nanak did not teach that God had become incarnate, in the same way as Christians speak of Jesus as God-man. Such a concept, in the Sikh perspective, would involve God with death, the supreme enemy, as well as with an unstable world.

THE PROBLEM OF EVIL

The Adi Granth underscores the sinfulness of unsanctified humanity. Human beings in this condition are compared to headless persons, wanderers, and vagrants. Their dominant impulse is said to be *haumai*, which is best translated as "self-centeredness." Persons of haumai are ruled by evil passions. Self-willed and impure, they fail to discern the divine order. In Nanak's view the nature of human beings depended on the affiliations they made. Their nature could be transformed as their focus was lifted from the world to the divine name.

Nanak used the word *māyā* to describe the world. In Sikhism, however, this term does not have the significance of illusion that it does in Vedānta Hinduism. In Nanak's view the world was unreal only to the extent that it was mistaken for something it was not. For Sikhs, "delusion" would be a better definition. To them, creation can be a revelation of God or a snare. Māyā, a mistaken interpretation of nature and the purpose of the world, basically means untruth and separation from God. The world is described as *anjan*, that is, a black salve for the eyes, which in northern India is a traditional symbol of darkness and untruth. Nanak saw the world as real but perishable, whose possessions could not accompany human beings beyond death.

SALVATION

Nanak believed that God himself was responsible for the union between God and humanity that was the climax of the process of salvation. The participation of human beings in this process was dependent on God's prior activity and divine grace. Truth and contentment did not result from what human beings did or said, but from obedience to God.

Nanak's notion of the guru as the communicator of divine truth also was adopted by his successors. He saw the guru as a ladder human beings climbed to reach God or a ship that carried human beings to the realm of God. Identified with the only true reality, God, the guru was vested with the authority to speak God's word.

Nanak did not define the word of God; he viewed it as a function of the deity, rather than an ineffable experience. Only by hearing it could human beings achieve salvation. Sacrifice, charitable gifts for the purpose of acquiring merit, austerities, and religious rites led only to the continuation of human suffering and bondage.

Visitors approach the Golden Temple at Amritsar (left). Unlike Hindu shrines, it is open on all sides. A view (above) of the temple compound.
United Nations.

The Role of the Gurus

From the death of Guru Nanak in 1539 until the death of Guru Gobind Singh in 1708, the teaching of the founder was continued and fostered by his nine successors. During this period of 269 years Sikhism developed from a small community into an important religious and political organization, and the gurus were recognized as leaders of the Sikh community.

Amar Das (ruled 1552–1574), the third guru, had a well dug at Goindwal on the Beas River. Even though Nanak had stated that the only true shrine for his followers was in their hearts, Amar Das believed that changing circumstances required new initiatives, and so the well at Goindwal with its eighty-four steps became a place of pilgrimage and a focus of special rites and festivals.

The fourth guru, Ram Das (ruled 1574–1581), enjoyed the favor of Akbar (ruled 1556–1605), the ruler of the Mughul Empire. With the emperor's permission a village was set up near a pool of water once dear to Nanak. This village became the holy city of the Sikhs, Amritsar, which means "pool of nectar."

CONFLICTS WITH THE MUGHUL EMPIRE

Under Arjan (ruled 1581–1606), the fifth guru, the Sikh community constructed large water reservoirs, began to build the Golden Temple of Amritsar, and enlarged the small pool into an artificial lake. The temple had four doors, an indication that, unlike Hindu shrines, it was open on all sides and that members of the four principal castes had equal status as disciples. Guru Arjan also gathered the hymns of the first four gurus and put them into the Adi Granth, which was enshrined in the Golden Temple.

Arjan composed the hymn of peace, which is sung at Sikh funerals:

I do not keep the Hindu fast or the Muslim Ramadan. I serve him alone who is my refuge. I serve the One Master who is also Allah. I will not worship with the Hindu, nor like the Muslim go to Mecca. I shall serve him and no other.[12]

When Jahangir (ruled 1605–1627) succeeded to the Mughul throne, the tolerance of Akbar's reign toward the Sikhs turned to hostility. The emperor summoned Arjan to his court and demanded the deletion from the Adi Granth of all passages opposing Islamic and Hindu orthodoxy. When Arjan refused, Jahangir had him tortured and executed. Arjan's successor, Hargobind (ruled 1606–1644), obeyed his father's last command to "sit fully armed on his throne and maintain an army to the best of his ability."[13] He moved the center of Sikh power from the plains into the hills.

GURU GOBIND SINGH AND THE KHALSA

The Sikh struggle against the Mughul Empire continued. The ninth guru, Tegh Bahadur (ruled 1666–1675), was executed by Aurangzeb (ruled 1658–1707). The tenth guru, Gobind Singh (1675–1708), who was known as "the lion," reunited the Sikhs in a fellowship of suffering and triumphant devotion.

In 1699 he founded the *khalsa* (community of the pure) and called a gathering of Sikh warriors. Reminding them of the dangers of their situation, the guru called for five volunteers to die for the Sikh cause, claiming that God demanded a blood sacrifice. One by one, the leader led five warriors into his tent and emerged four times with a bloody sword. After the fifth man had gone into the tent, Gobind brought out all his warriors alive. A goat had been substituted for the sacrifice of the five men.

Gobind Singh then administered to the five heroes the rite of *pahul,* a kind of initiation by the sword into a new kind of brotherhood of soldier-saints. He gave them nectar to drink, and each man received a two-edged dagger, was henceforth to be known as *singh* (lion), and was identified by special symbols, the five Ks. He was not to cut the hair of his head or beard (*kesh*), and he was to carry a comb (*kangha*) and wear a steel bracelet (*kara*), a sword (*kirpan*), and short pants (*kacch*). The uncut hair of the head was to be kept in a topknot under a turban. Women could join the khalsa, too. They were to receive a single-edged dagger and to have the title of *kaur* (princess). Thereafter, members of all castes were welcome into the Sikh community.

When Guru Gobind Singh opened the Sikh religion to members of all the Hindu castes, many from the lower castes eagerly embraced the faith. The guru commanded his followers to discard the sacred thread and to avoid all temples and shrines except those established by the Sikhs. When all four of his sons were assassinated, he proclaimed that the line of the gurus would come to an end with himself. In the future there would be only the khalsa, the community of Sikhs, and their holy book, the Adi Granth. To this day Sikhs bow only to their book of scripture. They are faithful to the command of the last guru: "He who wishes to behold the Guru, let him search the Granth."[14]

Though the khalsa is open to men and women of all castes, its members form an elite within the Sikh community. They are admitted only after an initiation ceremony at which they pledge themselves to an austere code of conduct. They are to bathe at dawn each morning and then to spend some time in meditation. They are to avoid liquor, tobacco, and narcotics. They pledge loyalty to the teaching of the gurus and the Adi Granth and swear to join the crusade for righteousness in the world. During the initiation ceremony each candidate comes before the assembly and says: *"Waheguru ji ka Khalsa, sri Waheguru ji ki fateh"* (The khalsa is of God, the victory is to God).[15] He or she is given nectar to drink, which is then sprinkled on the hair and eyes.

Sikhism in the Modern Era

After the death of the last guru, the Sikhs became increasingly rebellious. One of their leaders, Banda

Singh (1670–1716), was captured with seven hundred followers and executed at Delhi. Members of the khalsa took refuge in the hill country, coming out at opportune times to challenge Mughul power. In 1799 the Sikhs captured Lahore and made it the capital of the Sikh kingdom of Ranjit Singh (1780–1839). This kingdom dominated the Punjab and other areas of northwest India. Many *gudwaras* (Sikh shrines) were built at this time, and the Golden Temple at Amritsar was restored to its former splendor. Ranjit Singh's administration also granted religious freedom to Hindus and Muslims.

During the nineteenth century, the Sikhs fought valiantly against the British invaders. When the khalsa was finally crushed in 1849, the Sikh realm was annexed to British India. Because of the fairness of the British administration, however, the Sikhs remained loyal to the British during the Great Mutiny of 1857 and became welcome recruits in the British army. Later the whole Punjab prospered when the British built a system of canals there.

When independence came to the subcontinent in 1947, the Sikhs were bitterly disappointed at Britain's decision to partition the Punjab. West Punjab was given to Pakistan and East Punjab to India. Sikhs and Hindus subsequently joined in a bloody war against the Muslims in Pakistan that resulted in over a million deaths. Eventually two and a half million Sikhs were forced to migrate to East Punjab. Many places sacred to Sikhs, such as the birthplace of Nanak, were left in Pakistan. The Sikh demand for a separate state has continued into the late twentieth century. Sikh fundamentalists turned to violence and occupied the Golden Temple at Amritsar. Not only was there bloodshed when it was stormed in 1984 by national troops on orders from the Prime Minister of India, Indira Gandhi. In reprisal, she was assassinated by one of her body guards, a Sikh. Gandhi was followed in office by her son, Rajiv, as communal violence flared. Sikhs were menaced and attacked throughout the land. Government efforts to pacify the situation were blocked by longstanding resentments and hatred between followers of the different religions. Moderate Sikh leaders were assassinated by fellow Sikhs. Unrest in the Punjab, where the majority of Sikhs still live, became a threat to secular democracy in India.

Sikh Customs

Sikhs are expected to follow the *Rehat Maryada* (Guide to the Sikh Way of Life), a document drawn up at a meeting of leading Sikh authorities and associations held at Amritsar in 1931.[16] A Sikh is defined as anyone who believes in one God, the ten gurus and their teaching, and the Adi Granth. There is no priesthood. Every Sikh is supposed to strive to serve the community of the faithful, lead a life of prayer and meditation, and recite or read a prescribed number of hymns each day.

VISITS TO GUDWARAS

Sikhs are supposed to visit the local gudwara often. The gudwaras vary greatly in size and appearance; some gudwaras are magnificent temples in the elaborate Mughul style; others are simple buildings. All must have a copy of the Adi Granth inside, and all must fly the *nishan sahib*, the yellow flag of Sikhism.

Each congregation meets in the name of the guru; in fact, gudwara means "home of the guru." The main room of the center is the one in which the Adi Granth is displayed on cushions, usually beneath a canopy. The congregation may assemble in the morning or evening; there is no set time or day for services. Men and women remove their shoes before entering the presence of the Adi Granth and cover their heads out of respect. Any man or woman can read from the holy book. Offerings are made and hymns are sung. Worshipers do not turn their backs on the Adi Granth as they leave but walk backward out of the room. At some festivals the Adi Granth is taken in a procession around the town, accompanied by musicians and singers, and on some occasions it is read aloud to the population.

A Sikh preaches to an attentive standing audience in the Golden Temple at Amritsar. There is no set time of day for Sikh services.
United Nations.

COMMUNITY LIFE

The congregation of each gudwara elects its own officers and votes on all important matters. Women can be present at meetings, but they do not usually participate in the discussions. Over the years the Sikhs have had many differences of opinion, and one of the schismatic groups, the Namdharis, believes that the line of the gurus did not die out with Gobind Singh. In recent years some Sikhs have adopted secular habits, though any man who discards the turban and cuts his hair is considered an apostate. Readmission to the community is allowed only after a period of penance.

Although Sikhism has been opposed to the caste system since the time of Nanak, caste distinctions still exist among believers, at least to some degree. The largest Sikh caste today is that of the jats (farmers). Next come the skilled workers, followed by members of the upper classes.

Sikhs differ also on the matter of eating meat. Some eat beef, and others eat all meat except beef. Still others are vegetarians who do not eat meat, fish, or eggs. At community meals (*langars*), no meat is served.

CEREMONIES

Births are joyous occasions for the Sikhs. As soon as the mother has recovered, the entire family visits the gudwara to offer thanks. Babies' names are chosen with great care.

Sikhs have always opposed the Hindu custom of child marriages. Since Sikhs regard marriage as a binding contract, adultery is a serious breach of faith. Divorce is discouraged. Widows may remarry. Most marriages are between members of the same social group or caste. Sikhs are monogamous, and in accord with the teaching of their founder, they show respect to women.

Funerals usually are held on the day after death. Although burials at sea or in the earth are allowed, the accepted method of disposing of the dead is cremation. The body is washed by members of the family, who see that the five Ks are worn. Then a procession of family members and mourners accompanies the body to a pyre, and afterwards the ashes may be thrown into a river.

All Sikhs celebrate the birthdays of Nanak and Gobind Singh as well as the anniversary of the fifth guru's martyrdom. Other festivals take place throughout the year. At some of these rites the entire Adi Granth is read, which may take forty-eight hours to complete. The Sikh holy book is the dominant theme of Sikh worship, since it represents the living presence of the ten gurus and the word of God.

Notes

1 Heinrich Zimmer, *Philosophies of India,* Bollingen Series 26 (Chicago: University of Chicago Press, 1969), p. 182. Originally published by Princeton University Press, Princeton, N.J., 1951. The discussion of Jainism in this chapter is based largely on Zimmer's work and on Carlo della Casa, "Jainism," in *Historia Religionum: Handbook for the History of Religion,* 2 vols., ed. C. Jouco Bleeker and Geo Widengren (Leiden, Netherlands: E. J. Brill, 1971), 2:346–371.

2 Ninian Smart, *The Long Search* (Boston: Little, Brown, 1977), p. 219.

3 Zimmer, *Philosophies of India,* p. 214.

4 This account is based on K. S. Khushwant, *Encyclopaedia Britannica,* 15th ed., s.v. "Sikhism," vol. 16, pp. 743–747; and W. Owen Cole and Piara Singh Sambhi, *The Sikhs: Their Religious Beliefs and Practices* (London: Routledge & Kegan Paul, 1978).

5 John Clark Archer, *Faiths Men Live By* (New York: Ronald Press, 1934), p. 314.

6 Cole and Sambhi, *The Sikhs,* p. 9.

7 Archer, *Faiths Men Live By,* p. 315.

8 Adi Granth, p. 1.

9 Tukhāri Chhant 2 (4), Adi Granth, p. 1110. Adi Granth, p. 1. Cited in W. H. McLeod, *Gūru Nānak and the Sikh Religion* (Oxford: Clarendon Press, 1968), p. 148.

10 Mārū Solahā 2 (6), Ādi Granth, p. 1021. Quoted in McLeod, p. 161.

11 Rāmakali Ast 1 (7), Ādi Granth, p. 903. Quoted in McLeod, p. 167.

12 Ādi Granth, p. 1137. Quoted in Cole and Sambhi, *The Sikhs,* p. 27.

13 Cole and Sambhi, *The Sikhs,* p. 29.

14 Archer, *Faiths Men Live By,* p. 320.

15 Cole and Sambhi, *The Sikhs,* p. 14.

16 Ibid., pp. 168–178.

Bibliography

The Concept of Religion and the Religions of Asia

SECONDARY SOURCES

Baird, Robert D. *Category Formation and the History of Religion.* "Religion and Reason, 1, Method and Theory in the Study and Interpretation of Religion." The Hague, Netherlands: Mouton, 1971. An important study that defines religion as ultimate human concern.

Berger, Peter L. *The Sacred Canopy: Elements of a Sociological Theory of Religion.* Garden City, N.Y.: Doubleday, 1967. Religion as the overarching value structure of societies, as discussed by a leading American sociologist of religion.

Blasi, Anthony J., and Andrew J. Weigert. "Towards a Sociology of Religion: An Interpretative Sociology Approach," *Sociological Analysis,* 37 (1976), 189–204. Levels of social analysis for the study of religion.

Bowker, John W. *The Sense of God: Sociological, Anthropological, and Psychological Approaches to the Origin of the Sense of God.* Oxford, England: Clarendon Press, 1973. Multidisciplinary approach to religion viewed as a route-finding activity.

Comstock, W. Richard. "A Behavioral Approach to the Sacred: Category Formation in Religious Studies," *Journal of the American Academy of Religion,* 49 (1981), 625–643. Defends the "sacred" as a central concept in the interpretation of religion, especially when understood as a rule for behavior in religious traditions.

Durkheim, Emile. *The Elementary Forms of the Religious Life.* Translated by Joseph Ward Swain. New York: Free Press, 1965. Originally published in France, 1912; English translation, 1915. Older but still basic work by one of the founders of the sociology of religion.

Eck, Diana L. *Darsan: Seeing the Divine Image in India.* Chambersburg, Pa.: Anima Books, 1981. Simply and beautifully expressed introduction to Hindu symbolism.

Eliade, Mircea. *Yoga: Immortality and Freedom.* 2nd ed. Translated by Willard R. Trask. Bollingen Series LVI. Princeton: Princeton University Press, 1970. Definitive history of Hindu yoga. Stresses the importance of sacrifice in Hindu tradition and interprets Hindu yoga as a process of rebirth or transformation.

Eliade, Mircea. *Rites and Symbols of Initiation: The Mysteries of Birth and Rebirth.* Translated by Willard R. Trask. New York: Harper & Row, Pub., 1965. Rites of passage from one life stage to another and from ordinary social roles to special religious roles in many cultures interpreted as symbolic transformation by an influential historian of religions.

Geertz, Clifford. "Religion as a Cultural System." In *Anthropological Approaches to the Study of Religion,* edited by M. Banton. A.S.A. Monographs, no. 3. London: Tavistock, 1963. Definition of religion as a cultural system of symbols, by a leading cultural anthropologist.

Larson, Gerald James. "Prolegomenon to a Theory of Religion." *Journal of the American Academy of Religion,* 46 (1978), 443–463. Religion defined by stressing its analogical affinity to language.

Little, David, and Sumner B. Twiss. *Comparative Religious Ethics.* San Francisco: Harper & Row,

1978. Suggests a universal structure of religions as a basis for comparing religious prescriptions for right behavior.

Luckmann, Thomas. *The Invisible Religion: The Problem of Religion in Modern Society.* New York: Macmillan, 1967. New forms of religion in industrialized society.

Otto, Rudolf. *The Idea of the Holy.* 2nd ed. Translated by John W. Harvey. London: Oxford University Press, 1950. Published in Germany, 1917; first English-language edition, 1923. Landmark cross-cultural study of the sacred from the standpoint of religious experience.

Slater, Peter. *The Dynamics of Religion: Meaning and Change in Religious Traditions.* New York: Harper & Row, Pub., 1978. Study of continuity and change in religious history as an interplay of faith and tradition.

Smart, Ninian. *The Phenomenon of Religion.* New York: Herder and Herder, 1973. ———. *The Science of Religion and the Sociology of Knowledge: Some Methodological Questions.* Princeton, N.J.: Princeton University Press, 1973. Two important examinations of methodological problems in the study of religion.

Smith, Wilfred Cantwell. *The Meaning and End of Religion.* New York: Macmillan, 1962. Influential criticism of the concepts of "religions" and "isms" as abstractions. Emphasis is on individual faith in relation to cumulative religious traditions.

Spiro, Melford E. "Religion: Problems of Definition and Explanation." In *Anthropological Approaches to the Study of Religion,* edited by M. Banton, A.S.A. Monographs, no. 3. London: Tavistock, 1963. Anthropological discussion of fundamental issues in the study of religion. Religion is defined as belief in supernatural beings.

Streng, Frederick J. "Studying Religion: Possibilities and Limitations of Different Definitions." *Journal of the American Academy of Religion,* 40 (1972), 219–237. ———. *Understanding Religious Life.* 2nd ed. Encino, Calif.: Dickenson, 1976. Religion emphasized as the ultimate transformation, as seen from the perspective of the history of religion.

Thompson, Laurence G. *Chinese Religion: An Introduction.* 3rd ed. Belmont, California: Wadsworth, 1979. An excellent introduction to the continuous themes within Chinese religious history utilizing the impressive approach of C.K. Yang, *Religion in Chinese Society* (Berkeley, California: University of California Press, 1961).

Tillich, Paul J. *Systematic Theology.* Vol. 1. Chicago: University of Chicago Press, 1963. Major work of a great twentieth-century Christian theologian who made the conception of religion as "ultimate concern" popular.

Turner, Victor W. *The Ritual Process: Structure and Anti-Structure.* Symbol, Myth, and Ritual Series. Ithaca, N.Y.: Cornell University Press, 1969. Important study of the structure of ritual processes and of the liminal phase of rituals.

Van Gennep, Arnold. *The Rites of Passage.* Translated by Monika B. Vizedom and Gabrielle L. Caffee. Chicago: University of Chicago Press, 1976. Originally published in 1909 and still a very useful study of the rites of passage.

Waghorne, Joanne Punzo, and Norman Cutler. *Gods of Flesh, Gods of Stone: The Embodiment of Divinity in India.* Chambersburg, Pa.: Anima Press, 1984. A highly readable and engaging account of mediations between sacred realities and human being in Hindu tradition through images, *gurus,* and possession.

Whitehead, Alfred North. *Religion in the Making.* Living Age Books. New York: Meridian Books, 1960. Originally published in 1926, a short, readable interpretation of religion by a major twentieth-century philosopher who treated religion as the liminal activity the individual does with his or her own solitariness.

Yinger, J. Milton. *The Scientific Study of Religion.* New York: Macmillan, 1970. An excellent sociology of religion that defines religion as ultimate concern, but also relates this model to concrete sociological data.

PART ONE: HINDUISM

PRIMARY SOURCES

Bolle, Kees, trans. *The Bhagavadgita.* Berkeley, Calif.: University of California Press, 1979. A clear literary translation suitable for undergraduates.

Bühler, Georg, trans. *The Laws of Manu.* Mystic, Conn.: Lawrence Verry, Inc., 1965. Originally published in 1866.

Dimmitt, Cornelia, and J. A. B. Van Buitenen, trans. *Classical Hindu Mythology: A Reader in the Sanskrit Puranas.* Philadelphia, Pa.: Temple University Press, 1978.

Dimock, Edward, trans. *In Praise of Krishna: Songs from the Bengali.* Chicago: University of Chicago Press, 1967.

Embree, Ainslee T., ed. *The Hindu Tradition.* Westminster, Md.: Random House, 1972. Selections from Hindu writings of all periods. Originally published in 1966.

Griffith, Ralph T. H., trans. *The Hymns of the Rigveda.* Rev. ed. Livingston, N.J.: Orient Book Distributors, 1976. Originally published 1920–1936.

Hume, Robert E., trans. *The Thirteen Principal Upanishads.* Rev. ed. 1931. New York: Oxford University Press, 1971.

Tulsi Das. *Ramayana of Tulsi Das.* Livingston, N.J.: Orient Book Distributors, 1978. A revision of the 1877 translation by Frederick S. Growse.

Goldman, Robert P., trans. with others. *The Rāmāyana of Vālmīki,* vols. I and II (Princeton: Princeton University Press, 1984ff.). A continuing publication, in English version, of the critical edition.

SECONDARY SOURCES

Adams, Charles J., ed. *Reader's Guide to the Great Religions,* 2nd rev. ed. New York: Free Press, 1977, pp. 106–155, "Hinduism." Annotated bibliography.

Carpenter, James Estlin. *Theism in Medieval India.* Columbia, Mo.: South Asia Books, 1977. Originally published in 1921.

Deussen, Paul. *Philosophy of the Upanishads.* New York: Dover Pubs., 1966. Originally published in 1906.

Dowson, John. *A Classical Dictionary of Hindu Mythology.* Mystic, Conn.: Lawrence Verry, Inc., 1973. Originally published in 1879.

Eliade, M. *Yoga: Immortality and Freedom.* Princeton, N.J.: Princeton University Press, 1970. Originally published in 1958.

Farquhar, John Nicol. *An Outline of the Religious Literature of India.* Delhi: Motilal Banarasidass, 1967. Originally published in 1920.

Gonda, Jan. *Visnuism and Sivaism.* New York: International Publications Service, 1976. Originally published in 1970.

Hiriyanna, M. *Essentials of Indian Philosophy.* Edison, N.J.: Allen and Unwin, 1978. Originally published in 1949.

Hopkins, Thomas. *The Hindu Religious Tradition.* Encino, Calif.: Dickenson Publishing Co., 1971. A historical survey of the development of Hinduism.

Keith, Arthur Berriedale. *The Religion and Philosophy of the Veda and Upanishads.* 2 vols. Livingston, N.J.: Orient Book Distributors, 1976. Originally published. in 1925.

Kumarappa, Bharatan. *The Hindu Conception of Deity as Culminating in Ramanuja.* Atlantic Highlands, N.J.: Humanities Press, 1979. Originally published in 1934.

Lingat, Robert. *The Classical Law of India.* Berkeley, Calif.: University of California Press, 1973. Originally published in 1967.

Mitchell, George. *Hindu Temple.* New York: Harper & Row, 1978.

Pandey, Raj Bali. *Hindu Samskaras.* Livingston, N.J.: Orient Book Distributors, 1976. On the Hindu domestic rituals and their history. Originally published in 1949.

Sarma, D. S. *Renaissance of Hinduism.* Varanasi: Banāras Hindu Univeristy Press, 1944. On the leaders and movements in modern Hinduism.

Sivaraman, K. *Saivism in Philosophical Perspective.* Livingston, N.J.: Orient Book Distributors, 1973.

Stevenson, Margaret. *Rites of the Twice-born.* New York: International Publications Service, 1971. Originally published in 1920.

Stutley, Margaret and James. *Harper's Dictionary of Hinduism.* New York: Harper & Row, 1977.

Wheeler, Sir Mortimer. *The Indus Civilization.* 3rd ed. New York: Cambridge University Press, 1968.

Whitehead, Henry. *Village Gods of South India.* New York: Garland Publishing Co., 1980. Originally published in 1921.

Zaehner, Richard C. *Hinduism.* New York: Oxford University Press, 1962. An introduction of Hinduism stressing selected periods and traditions.

Zimmer, Heinrich. *Myths and Symbols in Indian Art and Civilization.* Princeton: Princeton University Press, 1971. Originally published in 1946.

PART TWO: BUDDHISM

PRIMARY SOURCES

Beyer, Stephan, trans. *The Buddhist Experience: Sources and Interpretations.* Encino, Calif.: Dickinson, 1974. An anthology of texts from a wide variety of Buddhist traditions.

Cowell, E. B.; F. Max Müller; and Takakusa Junjirō, trans. *Buddhist Mahayana Texts.* New York: Dover, 1969. Originally published as vol. 49 of the *Sacred Books of the East.* A collection that contains the three basic texts (sūtras) of the Buddhist Pure Land traditions.

Davids, T. W. Rhys, trans. *Buddhist Sutras.* New York: Dover, 1969. Originally published as vol. 11 of the *Sacred Books of the East.* An old but still useful collection drawn from the *Sutta Pitaka* of the Pali canon. If only one text or set of texts can be read, this collection would be an appropriate choice.

Evan-Wentz, W. Y., trans. *Tibet's Great Yogi Milarepa.* 2nd ed. London: Oxford University Press, 1951. A fascinating hagiography that relates the life of a Tibetan yogi famed for his magic powers and his attainment as a living Buddha.

Freemantle, Francesca, and Chogyam Trungpa, trans. *The Tibetan Book of the Dead.* Berkeley, Calif.: Shambala Press, 1975. A distinctive interpretation of the supposed transition from the moment of dying to the point of enlightenment or rebirth.

Hurwitz, Leon, trans. *Sutra of the Lotus Blossom of the Fine Dharma.* New York: Columbia University Press, 1976. A rich and highly imaginative Mahāyāna text important to East Asian Buddhism, particularly the Tian Tai (Tendai) schools of China and Japan and the Nichiren school and its offshoots in modern Japan.

Matics, Marion, trans. *Santideva's Entering the Path of Enlightenment.* New York: Macmillan, 1970. An influential devotional poem that represents the Indian Madhyamika tradition founded by Nagarjuna.

Reynolds, Frank E., and Mani B. Reynolds, trans. *Three Worlds According to King Ruang.* Berkeley Buddhist Research Series, no. 4. Berkeley, Calif.: Lancaster and Miller, 1981. A Thai Buddhist treatise on cosmology and ethics that presents an important Theravāda perspective in which the philosophical and more popular aspects of the tradition are joined.

Yampolsky, Philip, B., trans. *The Platform Sūtra of the Sixth Patriarch.* New York: Columbia University Press, 1967. A basic text of Chan Buddhism that purports to recount the life and a famous sermon of the Chinese master Hui-neng (638–713).

SECONDARY SOURCES

Bloom, Alfred. *Shinran's Gospel of Pure Grace.* AAS Monograph no. 20. Tucson: University of Arizona Press, 1965. An account of the life and teachings of the founder of Japan's Jōdo Shinshū (True Pure Land) sect.

Ch'en, Kenneth. *The Chinese Transformation of Buddhism.* Princeton, N.J.: Princeton University Press, 1973. A wide-ranging examination of China's adaptation of Buddhism, by one of the leading scholars in the field.

Conze, Edward. *Buddhist Thought in India.* London: George Allen & Unwin, 1962. A concise survey of early Buddhist doctrine and its development in the various Buddhist schools of India.

Cook, Francis. *The Jewel Net of Indra.* University Park, Pa.: Pennsylvania State University Press, 1978. An introduction to the highly sophisticated philosophy of China's Hua-yan school.

Dutt, Sukumar. *Buddhist Monks and Monasteries of India.* London: Humanities Press, 1962. This book remains the best English-language survey of Indian Buddhism up to the Pala period.

Foucher, Alfred. *The Life of the Buddha According to the Ancient Texts and Monuments of India.* Translated and abridged by Simone Boas. Middletown, Conn.: Wesleyan University Press, 1963. A fine account of the legend of the Buddha as depicted in

Indian art at the beginning of the Christian Era. If only one additional secondary source can be read, this book would be an appropriate choice.

Kim, Hee-Jin. *Dogen Kigen: Mystical Realist.* AAS Monograph no. 29. Tucson: University of Arizona Press, 1975. A study of the life and teaching of the founder of the Sōtō Sect of Japanese Zen Buddhism.

Reynolds, Frank E.; Gananath Obeyesekere; and Bardwell Smith; *Two Wheels of Dharma.* AAR Monograph no. 3. Missoula, Mont.: American Academy of Religion, 1972. A collection of essays dealing with early Buddhism and the development of the Theravāda tradition in Sri Lanka.

PART THREE: CHINA, JAPAN, AND INDIA

China

PRIMARY SOURCES

Waley, Arthur, trans. *The Analects of Confucius.* New York: Random House, 1938. Extensive introduction and notes emphasizing the historical context of Confucius's thought.

Waley, Arthur, trans. *The Way and Its Power.* New York: Grove Press, 1958. Important for its explanatory materials and its emphasis on the mystical elements of Lao-zi's thought.

Watson, Burton, trans. *Chuang-tzu: Basic Writings.* New York: Columbia University Press, 1964. Best-balanced modern translation of this difficult work.

The I Ching or Book of Changes. Translated into German by Richard Wilhelm and into English by Cary F. Baynes. Princeton, N.J.: Princeton University Press, 1967. Extensive introduction and notes. The best attempt so far to render this enigmatic text intelligible to the modern reader.

Wing-tsit Chan, trans. and comp. *A Source Book in Chinese Philosophy.* Princeton, N.J.: Princeton University Press, 1963. A large selection of documents with short but useful introductions. If only one text can be read, it should be this one, but it needs to be balanced with sociological and anthropological materials.

SECONDARY SOURCES

Blofeld, John. *Beyond the Gods: Buddhist and Taoist Mysticism.* New York: Dutton, 1974. Engaging account of Buddhist and Taoist piety by an informed traveler in China in the 1930s.

Bredon, Juliet, and Igor Mitrophanow. *The Moon Year.* Shanghai: Kelly & Walsh, 1927. An encyclopedia of folk religion based on the yearly festival calendar.

Chang, Garma C. C. *The Practice of Zen.* New York: Harper & Row, Pub., 1959. Despite its title, an insightful and sober account of Chan Buddhism. Invaluable for its translations of autobiographies of monks and other religious virtuosi.

Creel, H. G. *The Birth of China.* New York: Ungar, 1937. Popular account of life and attitudes in the Shang and Western Zhou periods. Draws heavily on archaeology.

de Bary, William Theodore, ed. *The Unfolding of Neo-Confucianism.* New York: Columbia University Press, 1975. A collection of scholarly articles emphasizing the religious dimension of Neo-Confucianism. A good balance to the purely philosophical approach.

Fingarette, Herbert. *Confucius—The Secular as Sacred.* New York: Harper & Row, Pub., 1972. Sensitive and very readable interpretation of Confucius as a social and religious reformer with insights still useful for modern people.

Levenson, Joseph R. *Confucian China and Its Modern Fate.* Berkeley and Los Angeles: University of California Press, 1958. Sociological study of interaction of Confucian elite with political and cultural forces in Chinese history. Extensive discussion of the Confucian attempts and failure to meet the challenge of modernity.

Lifton, Robert Jay. *Revolutionary Immortality: Mao Tse-tung and the Chinese Cultural Revolution.* New York: Random House, 1968. Very readable interpretation of the Cultural Revolution from a psychological viewpoint.

MacInnis, Donald E., comp. *Religious Policy and Practices in Communist China.* New York: Macmillan, 1972. Collection of documents translated from Chinese and eyewitness accounts of religious life in China under Mao.

Overmeyer, Daniel L. *Folk Buddhist Religion.* Cambridge, Mass.: Harvard University Press, 1976. Valuable study of secret societies in Chinese history.

Saso, Michael R. *Taoism and the Rite of Cosmic Renewal.* Pullman: Washington State University Press, 1972. An anthropological account based on extensive fieldwork of contemporary folk Taoism as practiced in Taiwan. A needed corrective to the tendency to view Taoism as a purely philosophical and individual phenomenon.

Taylor, Rodney Leon. *The Cultivation of Sagehood as a Religious Goal in Neo-Confucianism: A Study of Selected Writings of Kao P'an-lung.* Missoula, Mont.: Scholars Press, 1978. Translations of writings showing Neo-Confucian meditation and other religious practices and attitudes.

Wright, Arthur F. *Buddhism in Chinese History.* New York: Atheneum, 1965. A short popular account of Chinese Buddhism. Especially valuable in evaluating the impact of Buddhism on Neo-Confucianism and later Chinese culture.

Yang, C. K. *Religion in Chinese Society.* Berkeley and Los Angeles: University of California Press, 1967. A historical study of traditional Chinese religious values and their social functions. A good one-volume companion to the Wing-tsit Chan collection.

Japan

PRIMARY SOURCES

Aston, W. G., trans. *Nihongi. Chronicles of Japan from the Earliest Times to* A.D. *697.* Originally published in 1896; reissued in London: George Allen & Unwin, 1956. A continuous narrative constructed out of much of the same mythological material as in the *Kojiki* but with many variant tales and historical asides toward the end.

Phillipi, Donald L., trans. *Kojiki.* Tokyo: Tokyo University Press, 1968. Because of its extensive explanatory notes, the best introduction to Shinto mythology. Troublesome in that its system of transliteration of Japanese names and terms is not standard but attempts to recover the archaic forms.

———., trans. *Norito. A New Translation of the Ancient Japanese Ritual Prayers.* Tokyo: Institute for Japanese Culture and Classics, Kokugakuin University, 1959. If only one primary source can be read, it should be this collection of ritual texts, which contains much mythological material.

Tsunoda, Ryusaka; William Theodore de Bary; and Donald Keene, comps. *Sources of Japanese Tradition.* 2 vols. New York: Columbia University Press, 1958. Contains many useful documents (in vol. 2) relating to the Shinto revival in the Tokugawa period and the imperial restoration and ultranationalism of the modern period.

SECONDARY SOURCES

Aston, W. G. *Shinto: The Way of the Gods.* London: Longmans, Green & Co., 1905. Old but still unsurpassed study of ritual and ethics based primarily on literary evidence.

Blacker, Carmen. *The Catalpa Bow: A Study of Shamanistic Practices in Japan.* London: George Allen & Unwin, 1975. A cogent attempt to reconstruct the form and meaning of ancient shamanism through the study of more recent practices, folklore, and literary and archaeological sources.

Buchanan, Daniel C. "Inari, Its Origin, Development, and Nature," in *Transactions of the Asiatic Society of Japan,* 2nd series, no. 12 (1935), 1–191. Dated but valuable study of this important Shinto cult.

Earhart, H. Byron. *A Religious Study of the Mount Haguro Sect of Shugendo: An Example of Japanese Mountain Religion.* Tokyo: Sophia University Press, 1970. A detailed account of one of the survivors of the ancient *yamabushi* cults.

Herbert, Jean. *Shinto: At the Fountain-Head of Japan.* London: George Allen & Unwin, 1967. A wealth of information valuable mainly as an encyclopedia of Shinto. Marred by an apologetic and sometimes theological stance that tries to defend Shinto from "Westernized scholarship."

Hori, Ichirō. *Folk Religion in Japan: Continuity and Change.* Edited by Joseph M. Kitagawa and Alan L. Miller. Chicago: University of Chicago Press, 1968. Essays by a leading Japanese scholar showing the enduring power of folk religion and its usefulness in understanding such phenomena as shamanism, the new religions, mountain religion, and Shinto-Buddhist amalgamation.

Kitagawa, Joseph M. *Religion in Japanese History.* New York: Columbia University Press, 1966. The most complete history of all the Japanese religious groups showing their development and interactions. Especially valuable for the modern period.

McFarland, H. Neill. *The Rush Hour of the Gods: A Study of the New Religious Movements in Japan.* New York: Macmillan, 1967. Despite the title, a valuable and readable introduction to the new religions phenomenon including non-Shinto forms.

Matsumoto, Shigeru. *Motoori Norinaga: 1730–1801.* Cambridge, Mass.: Harvard University Press, 1970. Detailed study of the life and thought of this important "national scholar."

Muraoka, Tsunetsugu. *Studies in Shinto Thought.* Translated by Delmer M. Brown and James T. Araki. Tokyo: Ministry of Education, 1964. Good source for modern trends in Shinto scholarship and theology.

van Straelen, Henry. *The Religion of Divine Wisdom: Japan's Most Powerful Movement.* Kyoto, Japan: Veritas Shōin, 1957. A detailed account of Tenrikyō.

Webb, Herschel. *The Japanese Imperial Institution in the Tokugawa Period.* New York: Columbia University Press, 1968. Important study emphasizing the significance of the emperior's religious dimension for an understanding of his function in modern Japanese history.

Jainism

PRIMARY SOURCES

Ghoshal, Sarat C., ed. *The Sacred Books of the Jainas.* Bibliotheca Jainica, 11 vols. New York: AMS Press, 1917–1940. Reprint of the 1940 edition.

Jacobi, Hermann, trans. *The Gaina Sutras. The Sacred Books of the East,* edited by F. Max Müller, vols. 22 and 45. London: Oxford University Press, 1884. Also available in an American edition. New York: Scribner's, vol. 10, 1901. The basic texts.

SECONDARY SOURCES

Casa, Carlo della, "Jainism." In *Historia Religionum: Handbook for the History of Religion,* edited by C. Jouco Bleeker and Geo Widengren, vol. 2 of 2 vols. Leiden, Netherlands: E. J. Brill, 1971. An authoritative presentation by a professor at the University of Turin.

Jain, Muni Uttam Kamal. *Jaina Sects and Schools.* Delhi, India: Concept Publishing Company, 1975. A useful, up-to-date account.

Jaini, Padmanabh S. *The Jaina Path of Purification.* Berkeley and Los Angeles: University of California Press, 1979. An excellent introduction that focuses on both the practice of the religion and its history.

Mehta, Mohan Lal. *Outlines of Jaina Philosophy: The Essentials of Jaina Ontology, Epistemology and Ethics.* Bangalore, India: Jain Mission Society, 1954. A careful presentation that contrasts Jainism with other religions and philosophies.

Roy, Ashim Kumar. *A History of the Jainas.* New Delhi: Gitanjali Publishing House, 1984. A useful recent study of Jain history which gives major attention to the different parties in the religion.

Schurbring, Walther. *The Doctrine of the Jainas.* Translated by Walter Beurlen. Delhi, India: Motilal Banarsidass, 1962. A scholarly work by a professor at the University of Hamburg.

Stevenson, Mrs. Sinclair. *The Heart of Jainism.* London: Oxford University Press, 1915. A balanced view by a sympathetic Christian observer.

Zimmer, Heinrich. *Philosophies of India.* Bollingen Series 26, edited by Joseph Campbell. Chicago: University of Chicago Press, 1969. The chapters on Jainism are especially valuable. Originally published by Princeton University Press, Princeton, N.J., 1951.

Sikhism

PRIMARY SOURCE

Singh, Trilochan; Bhai Judh Singh; Kapur Singh; Bawa Harkishen Singh; Khushwant Singh, eds. Revised by George S. Fraser. *Selections from the Sacred Writings of the Sikhs*. London: George Allen & Unwin, 1960. A useful collection of the basic documents.

SECONDARY SOURCES

Cole, W. Owen, *The Guru in Sikhism*. London: Darton, Longman & Todd, 1982. A careful, indeed definitive study of the role of the succession of Sikh leader-teachers, well written and clear.

———, and Piara Singh Sambhi. *The Sikhs: Their Religious Beliefs and Practices*. London: Routledge & Kegan Paul, 1978. A useful, highly readable presentation by a lecturer at Leeds Polytechnic and the president of the Leeds Gudwara.

Khushwant, K. S. *A History of the Sikhs*. 2 vols. Princeton, N.J.: Princeton University Press, 1963 and 1966. A major reference work by an authority in the field.

———. "Sikhism." In *Encyclopaedia Britannica*, 15th ed., vol. 16. A brief, well-organized account.

———. *The Sikhs Today*. Columbia, Mo.: South Asia Books, 1976. New edition of an earlier work that offers a sympathetic treatment of the faith by a member who brings a critical insight into his heritage.

McLeod, W. H. *Early Sikh Tradition: A Study of the Janam-Sakhis*. Oxford: Clarendon Press, 1980. An important and skillful study set in the context of the history of religions.

———. *The Evolution of the Sikh Community: Five Essays*. Oxford: Clarendon Press, 1976. A historical study that discusses the tradition's sociological and theological bases.

———. *Gūru Nānak and the Sikh Religion*. Oxford: Clarendon Press, 1968. The best available study.

Index